MW00995568

100 BUILDINGS

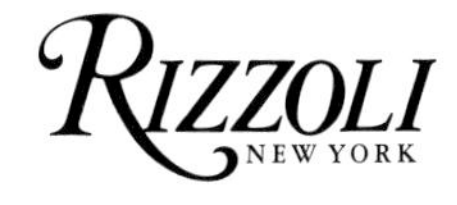

New York · Paris · London · Milan

Project Manager
Eui-Sung Yi

Production Manager
Ryan Doyle

Book Design
Lily Bakhshi

Content Management
Nicole Meyer
Sarah Moseley

Writing
Val Warke
with
Eric Keune
Andrea Simitch

Foreword
Thom Mayne

Research and Production Assistants
Yitao Chen
Stanley Cho
Patrick Geske
Adeline Morin
Cameron Northrop
Beyza Paksoy
John Paul Salcido
Kevin Sherrod
Young Sun
Jane Suthi
Way Tang
Andrea Tzvetkov

First published in the United States of America in 2017 by
RIZZOLI INTERNATIONAL PUBLICATIONS, INC.
300 Park Avenue South, New York, NY 10010
www.rizzoliusa.com

ISBN-13: 978-0-8478-5950-4
Library of Congress Control Number: 2017937552

Photography credits begin on page 262.

Distributed to the U.S. Trade by Random House, New York

Printed and bound in China

2017 2018 2019 2020 / 10 9 8 7 6 5 4 3 2 1

11 · 07 · 17

Mark

CONTENTS

"TO A MORE ENGAGED STUDENT"

Thom +

Foreword
THOM MAYNE

In my most recent decade of teaching architecture, I've noticed a declining awareness of historical precedent among my students. References tend toward the broad and thin, often resulting in a very real missed opportunity to engage in meaningful architectural discourse. Perhaps this is due to the parallel growth and use of digital media, or maybe the explanation lies with some other, more intangible cultural shift. But one instance at a recent thesis jury stands out as particularly illustrative. The project under discussion was a derivative of Kisho Kurokawa's capsule housing in Ginza. The references were obvious to most of the jurors, but surprisingly not to the student. Since she had heard neither of Kurokawa nor of the Capsule Tower, the conversation was necessarily truncated. Had she been aware of the historical precedent, she would have been able to engage in the conversation about its conceptual connection to Metabolism and to place this final project of her educational career within a broader intellectual framework. In subsequent conversations with my colleagues, it became apparent that this was not an unusual phenomenon. There was widespread agreement that students and laypeople alike would benefit from an awareness and appreciation of the most important and influential buildings that have come before and that will continue to inform the development of architecture beyond today.

This book is meant to function as a reference source, as part of a toolkit needed by students and others who are interested in broadening their understanding of the rich and powerful influence of architecture in the twentieth century. I started by asking a broad range of practicing architects to list the 100 buildings of the past century that every architectural student should know. I had anticipated that the diversity of the group queried would produce a wide-ranging list. In fact, there were thousands of projects proposed that were then sorted by frequency. The top 100 are listed in this volume and cross-referenced in a graphic table by the names of the architects who proposed them. The result speaks to the universality of the works in the final list, each of which demonstrated a pivotal moment in architectural development during the past century.

I believe that an inquisitiveness and comprehension of these twentieth century works is invaluable. The period is notable for its broad-ranging experimentation and its enormous social, cultural, and political ambition. An awareness of these forerunners—of their influences on the profession, of their effects on the public, of the chances taken and the successes realized—will amplify and invigorate our future creative output.

SPECIAL THANK YOU.

Over the course of my journey as an architect, I have found the great built works of the early twentieth century and the contemporary works of my youth to be instrumental in forming, energizing, questioning, challenging, and inspiring my practice. To synthesize this project and to unify its resources could not have been possible without the dedication of many people.

First, I must thank Eui-Sung Yi. As the director of The Now Institute and a principal at Morphosis, I am indebted to him as my partner in teaching, thinking, and navigating the estuary between academia, theory, and practice. A dedicated teacher and a critical leader, Eui-Sung has a commitment to compiling, examining, and teaching the seminal 100 buildings illustrated in this volume that cannot be understated. We began this project five years ago, after a decade of teaching and working together. His persistence, and his belief in the power of architecture to transform, was the key in guiding this book to its completion.

The final production of this book would not have been possible without my team at Morphosis: managing principal Brandon Welling, whose calm industriousness keeps us in focus; Nicole Meyer and Sarah Moseley for relentless writing, rewriting, and editing; and of course the design talents of Lily Bakhshi.

The core of the book was developed through the dedication of my team at The Now Institute: Ryan Doyle, whose coordination and persistence brought the project alive; Kevin Sherrod, John Paul Salcido, Beyza Paksoy, Yitao Chen, and Way Tang, who each provided essential research and production support.

The book's validity and relevance rests with the architects who graciously and generously recorded their lists of essential buildings. Architecture is indebted to each of you. This project curated works of incredible differentiation, linking together great values of intelligence, innovation, and continued inquisition.

I must also mention my dear friend Val Warke, who graciously volunteered his time and words to ensure the integrity of the effort. And finally, my wife, Blythe, who is a most necessary guiding light and essential grounding in my life.

–Thom Mayne

Additional thanks to

Ana Tostões, Docomomo International
Hubert-Jan Henket, Docomomo International
The faculty and students of UCLA Architecture and Urban Design
The faculty and students of the Southern California Institute of Architecture
The faculty and students of the University of Southern California School of Architecture

Shareefa Abdulsalam
Nick Bruni
Lori Choi
Çağdaş Delen
Niloufar Golkarihagh
Ran Israeli
Sara Jafarpour
Barak Kazenelebogen
Grace Ko
Pegah Koulaeian
Deborah Liu
Elisabet Ollé
Rupal Rathi
Sai Rojanapirom
Dunia Abu Shanab
Luyan Shen
Jihun Son
Niketa Sondhi
Devika Tandon
Rizzie Walker
Crystal Wang
Yake Wang
Tessa Watson
Robin Williams
BaoCheng Yang
Halina Zárate

THE NOW INSTITUTE is an urban-planning and research center hosted at UCLA's Architecture and Urban Design Department, with a focus on the investigation and application of urban strategies to complex problems of resilience, culture, sustainability, and mobility. Led by Pritzker Prize–winning architect and distinguished professor Thom Mayne and Director Eui-Sung Yi, The Now Institute has established a new territory that integrates academic and professional pursuits and spans cities across the United States and the world, including Los Angeles, New Orleans, Madrid, Beijing, Port-au-Prince, and Cap-Haïtien.

In its more than ten years of research initiatives, The Now Institute has stimulated discourse on contemporary conditions that developed into actionable solutions in partnership with civic and business leaders, developers, architects, urbanists, cultural producers, students, and the general public. Example projects include sustainable infrastructure strategies for a growing Los Angeles; water, education, and infrastructure solutions in Haiti; urban agriculture responses to food access inequity; and analyses of the geo-cultural issues of man-made islands in Asia.

www.thenowinstitute.org

THE NOW INSTITUTE

DOCOMOMO INTERNATIONAL is a non-profit organization dedicated to the documentation and conservation of buildings, sites and neighbourhoods of the Modern Movement. It aims to:

- Bring the significance of the architecture of the Modern Movement to the attention of the public, authorities, professionals and the educational community.
- Identify and promote the surveying of the works of the Modern Movement.
- Oppose destruction and disfigurement of significant works.
- Attract funding for documentation conservation and (re)use.

In support of these goals, Docomomo International wishes to extend its field of actions to new territories, establish new partnerships with institutions, organizations, and NGOs active in the area of modern architecture, develop and publish the international register, and enlarge the scope of its activities in the realm of research, documentation and education.

www.docomomo.com

do_co,mo.mo_

Note from The Now Institute

The physical realization of a building is an immensely challenging and difficult journey. One cannot simply rely on a strong concept, but must also engage in a heuristic process integrating technical, political, economic, and social constraints. Therefore, each of the 100 buildings included in this book represents a humbling and inspirational accomplishment for architects. Evaluated in the context of their time, these projects demand our absolute respect.

The raison d'être of the book is to establish a decisive list of great architecture by asking accomplished architects who build to list the 100 built projects essential to a young architect's education. The projects listed needed to have been constructed between 1900 and 2000, a demonstration of modern architecture's capacity to invent and adapt in response to the dynamic evolution of society in the twentieth century. These lists were cross-referenced with one another to establish the 100 projects that most frequently appeared.

The size and format of the book was chosen to encourage portability and to allow consistency of imagery. A necessary consideration in documentation was that the scale of the projects range significantly, from single-family residences to large commercial projects. The typical documentation for each project includes one horizontally oriented drawing (site plan, floor plan), one vertically oriented drawing (section, elevation), and one three-dimensional view (axonometric, massing diagram). The drawing scales between projects are not consistent with one another. Rather, the drawings are scaled to maximize available space on the page, and scale bars are provided for reference. One photograph of each project is included. Documentation is based on data from as many resources as possible. Whenever possible, the architect or the architect's own monograph was referenced. If a monograph was not available, the drawings were compiled and verified from at least three sources to minimize potential errors. Due to the size of the drawings, many tertiary details have been omitted, as an emphasis was placed on communication of concept, structure, space, and organizational parti.

It is acknowledged that the resulting 100 built works included here are in no way a definitive or scientifically developed list. In many cases, architects submitted far more than 100 projects, and many architects were hard-pressed to reduce their list to a mere 100. For this reason and to promote further investigation, the list provided from each architect has been included in the back section of the book. Each architect's submission lists their top 100 selections chronologically, and many were adamant that these lists not be considered a ranking of the projects in their mind. The exception to this is the submittal of Zaha Hadid, whose unfortunate departure from us prevented her from paring down her list. In this instance, we have preserved her full original list. The References section at the end of the book has been compiled to document invaluable resources throughout our research, and to assist with further investigation of each project.

Finally, it should be noted that this endeavor developed organically and informally through conversation among respected colleagues. The resulting contributors developed in a similar manner. Many of the architects were solicited by us for input, while others made submittals to us solely based on word of mouth. Many solicited by us were not able to respond, and we were not able to solicit many that we would have liked. To this end, we hope the book is viewed as a snapshot in time, representing the relative diversity accessible to us through this process.

Eui-Sung Yi
Director

100 buildings

01 Villa Savoye
02 Chapelle Notre-Dame du Haut
03 German Pavilion (Barcelona Pavilion)
04 Centre Pompidou
05 S.C. Johnson & Son Headquarters
06 Farnsworth House
07 Salk Institute
08 La Maison de Verre
09 Couvent Sainte-Marie de La Tourette
10 TWA Flight Center
11 Berliner Philharmonie
12 Guggenheim Museum Bilbao
13 Edgar J. Kaufmann House (Fallingwater)
14 The Woodland Cemetery
15 Seagram Building
16 Solomon R. Guggenheim Museum
17 The Eames House (Case Study House No. 8)
18 Leicester University Engineering Building
19 Casa del Fascio
20 L'Unité d'Habitation
21 Habitat '67
22 Kimbell Art Museum
23 Schröderhuis
24 Nakagin Capsule Tower
25 Postsparkasse
26 Casa Malaparte
27 Sydney Opera House
28 Rudolph Hall (Yale Art and Architecture Building)
29 Phillips Exeter Academy Library
30 AEG Turbine Factory
31 Frederick C. Robie House
32 Schindler House
33 National Congress, Brazil
34 Bauhaus Dessau
35 Hongkong and Shanghai Bank Headquarters
36 Glasgow School of Art
37 Villa Mairea
38 The Assembly, Chandigarh
39 Stockholm Public Library
40 National Olympic Gymnasium
41 Sendai Mediatheque
42 Einstein Tower
43 Lever House
44 Diamond Ranch High School
45 Glass House
46 Ford Foundation Headquarters
47 Olympic Stadium, Munich
48 Gehry House
49 Igualada Cemetery
50 Crown Hall
51 Vanna Venturi House
52 Lovell Health House
53 Tugendhat House
54 Baker House
55 Barragán House and Studio
56 The Beinecke Rare Book & Manuscript Library
57 Museu de Arte de São Paulo
58 Brion Family Tomb
59 National Assembly Building, Bangladesh
60 Neue Staatsgalerie
61 National Museum of Roman Art
62 Maison à Bordeaux
63 Casa Milà
64 Säynätsalo Town Hall
65 Lloyd's of London
66 Institut du Monde Arabe
67 Parc de la Villette
68 Jewish Museum Berlin
69 Hillside Terrace Complex I–VI
70 Smith House
71 New National Gallery
72 Castelvecchio Museum
73 Piscinas de Marés
74 Michaelerplatz House (Looshaus)
75 Rusakov Workers' Club
76 Mill Owners' Association Building
77 Stahl House (Case Study House No. 22)
78 The Breuer Building (Whitney Museum of American Art)
79 Rooftop Remodeling Falkestrasse
80 Larkin Company Administration Building
81 Fiat Works
82 Villa Müller
83 Van Nelle Factory
84 Dymaxion House
85 Querini Stampalia Renovation
86 House VI
87 Beurs van Berlage
88 Gamble House
89 Lovell Beach House
90 Turin Exhibition Hall
91 Municipal Orphanage, Amsterdam
92 Carpenter Center for the Visual Arts
93 Free University of Berlin
94 Bagsværd Church
95 SESC Pompéia
96 Centre Le Corbusier (Heidi Weber House)
97 Gallaratese II Apartments
98 Centraal Beheer Building
99 Vitra Fire Station
100 Yokohama International Port Terminal

NORTH AMERICA

CANADA
Habitat '67

MEXICO
Barragán House and Studio

UNITED STATES OF AMERICA
Baker House
Carpenter Center for the Visual Arts
Crown Hall
Diamond Ranch High School
Dymaxion House
Edgar J. Kaufmann House (Fallingwater)
Farnsworth House
Ford Foundation Headquarters
Frederick C. Robie House
Gamble House
Gehry House
Glass House
House VI
S.C. Johnson & Son Headquarters
Kimbell Art Museum
Larkin Company Administration Building
Lever House
Lovell Beach House
Lovell Health House
Phillips Exeter Academy Library
Rudolph Hall
Salk Institute
Schindler House
Seagram Building
Smith House
Solomon R. Guggenheim Museum
Stahl House (Case Study House No.22)
The Beinecke Rare Book & Manuscript Library
The Breuer Building (Whitney Museum of American Art)
The Eames House (Case Study House No.8)
TWA Flight Center
Vanna Venturi House

SOUTH AMERICA

BRAZIL
Museu de Arte de São Paulo
National Congress, Brazil
SESC Pompéia

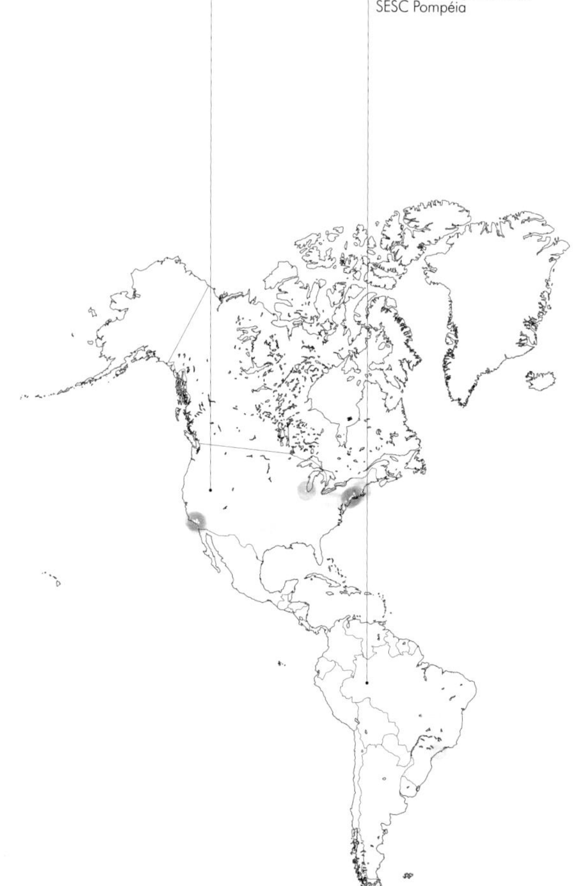

EUROPE

AUSTRIA
Michaelerplatz House (Looshaus)
Postsparkasse
Rooftop Remodeling Falkestrasse

CZECH REPUBLIC
Tugendhat House
Villa Müller

DENMARK
Bagsværd Church

ENGLAND
Leicester University Engineering Building
Lloyd's of London

FINLAND
Säynätsalo Town Hall
Villa Mairea

FRANCE
Centre Pompidou
Chapelle Notre-Dame du Haut
Couvent Sainte-Marie de La Tourette
Institut du Monde Arabe
La Maison de Verre
L'Unité d'Habitation
Maison à Bordeaux
Parc de la Villette
Villa Savoye

GERMANY
AEG Turbine Factory
Bauhaus Dessau
Berliner Philharmonie
Einstein Tower
Free University of Berlin
Jewish Museum Berlin
Neue Staatsgalerie
New National Gallery
Olympic Stadium, Munich
Vitra Fire Station

ITALY
Brion Family Tomb
Casa del Fascio
Casa Malaparte
Castelvecchio Museum
Fiat Works
Gallaratese II Apartments
Querini Stampalia Renovation
Turin Exhibition Hall

THE NETHERLANDS
Beurs van Berlage
Centraal Beheer Building
Municipal Orphanage, Amsterdam
Schröderhuis
Van Nelle Factory

PORTUGAL
Piscina Leça

SCOTLAND
Glasgow School of Art

SPAIN
Casa Milà
German Pavilion (Barcelona Pavilion)
Guggenheim Museum Bilbao
Igualada Cemetery
National Museum of Roman Art

SWEDEN
Stockholm Public Library
The Woodland Cemetery

SWITZERLAND
Centre Le Corbusier

ASIA

BANGLADESH
National Assembly Building, Bangladesh

CHINA
Hongkong and Shanghai Bank Headquarters

INDIA
The Assembly, Chandigarh
Mill Owners' Association Building

JAPAN
Hillside Terrace Complex I–VI
Nakagin Capsule Tower
National Olympic Gymnasium
Sendai Mediatheque
Yokohama International Port Terminal

RUSSIA
Rusakov Workers' Club

AUSTRALIA

AUSTRALIA
Sydney Opera House

10/

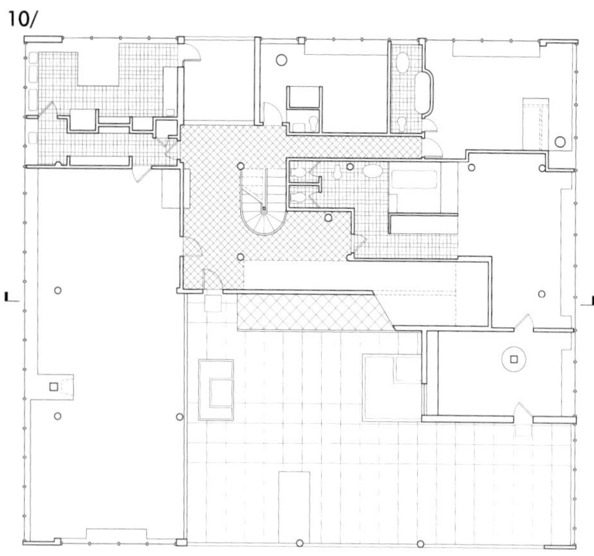

Floor Plan

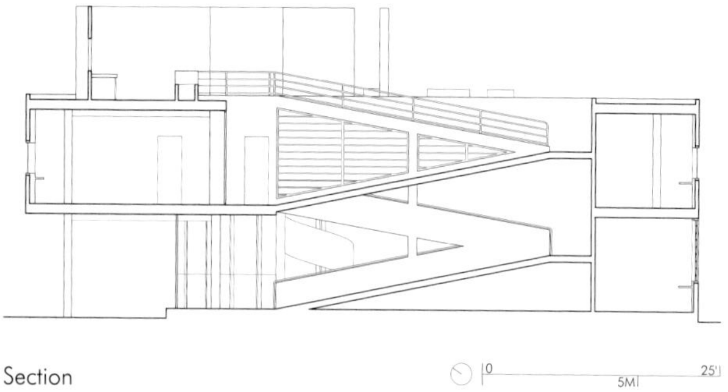

Section

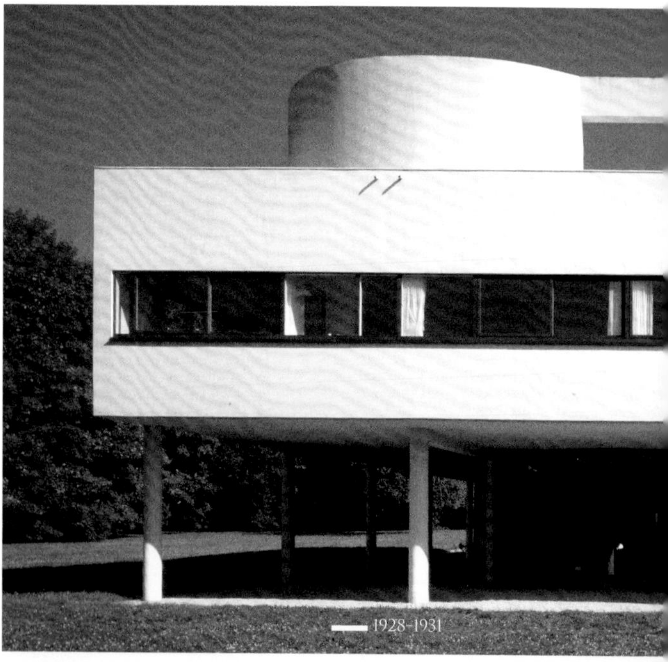

0 5M 25'

1928–1931

48° 55′ 28″N

01

VILLA SAVOYE

LE CORBUSIER and PIERRE JEANNERET
Poissy, France
1928–1931, restored 1963–1997

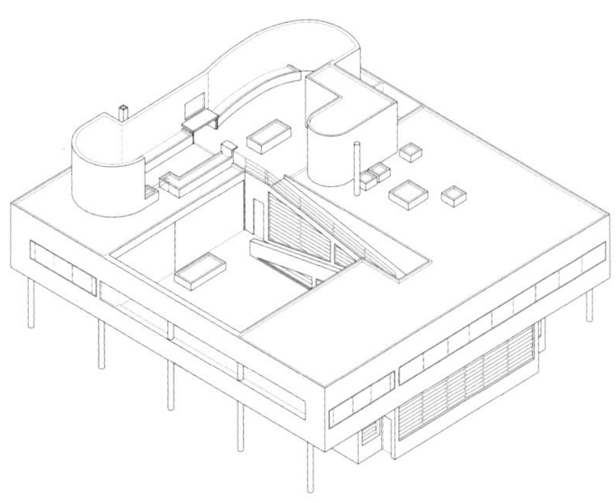

A work that articulates Le Corbusier's five points for a new architecture, Villa Savoye offers supporting pilotis, a free plan, a free facade, horizontal ribbon windows, and a rooftop garden. The project would become known as a manifesto of Purism in architecture, with the sculptural and often polychromic figures of bathrooms, closets, stairs, and walls contrasting with the white geometric simplicity of the overall structure's enclosing rectangular "canvas." Built as a country retreat, this "machine for living" reinterprets the classical villa in concrete and glass, with the ground floor shaped by the turning radius of an automobile and, within, a continuous ramp that erupts through the dominant horizontal planes, experientially uniting ground and sky, a demonstration of Le Corbusier's *promenade architecturale*.

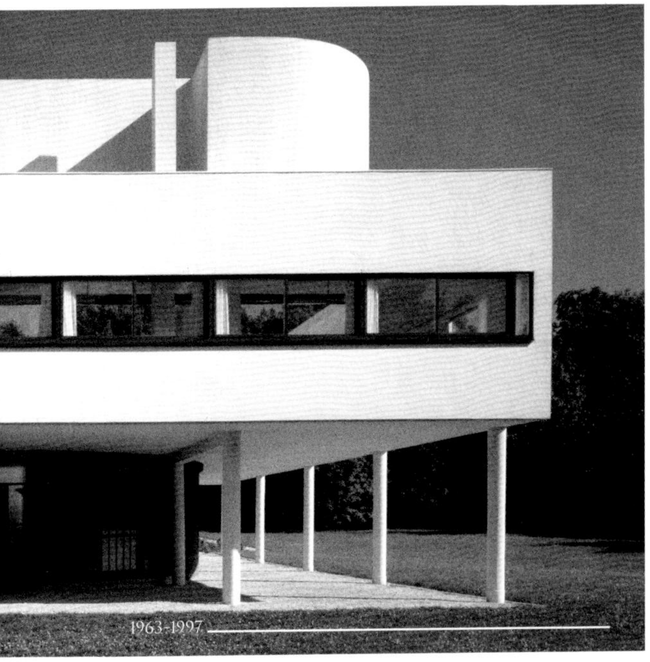

2° 01′ 42″E

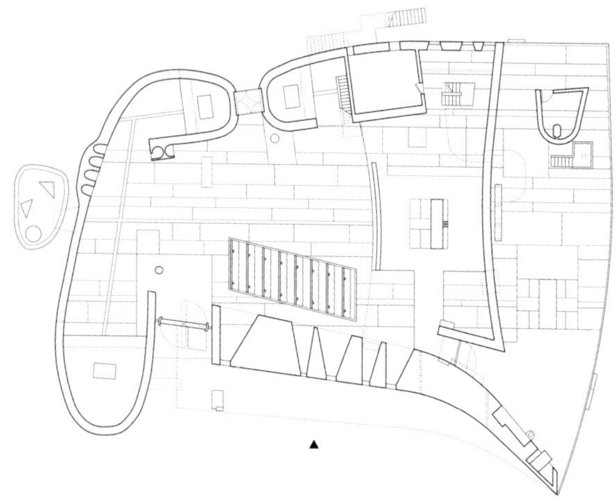

Floor Plan

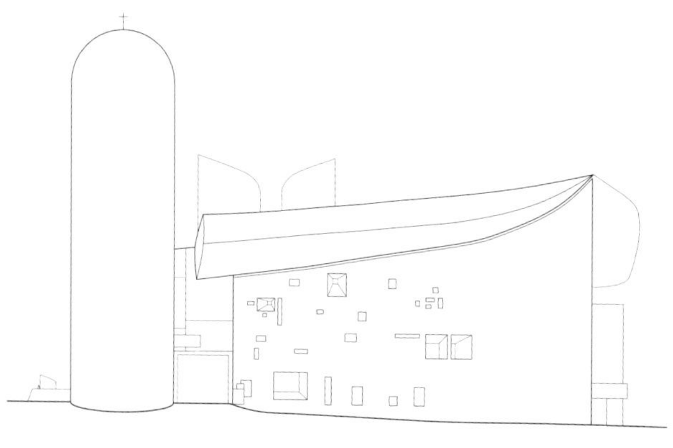

Elevation

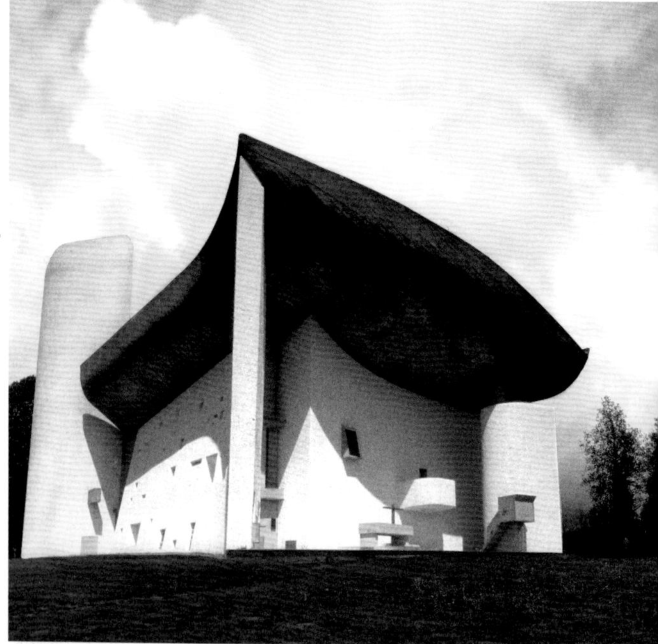

47° 42′ 16″N

02

CHAPELLE NOTRE-DAME DU HAUT

LE CORBUSIER
Ronchamp, France
1950–1955

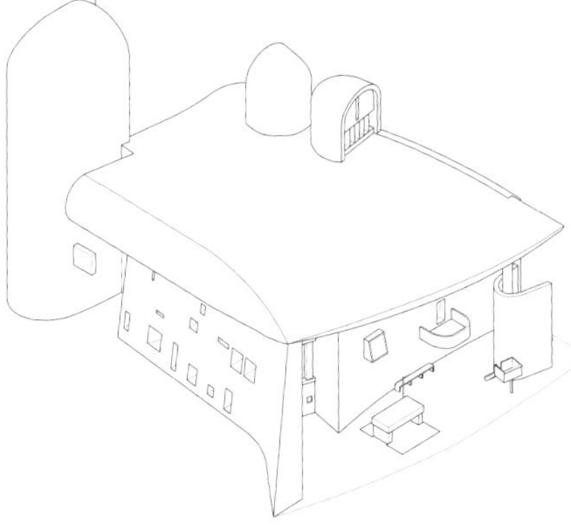

Though condemned at the time as an impressionistic indiscretion, the Pilgrimage Chapel at Ronchamp is one of the most iconic religious works of the twentieth century. The building plays an illusion of density against an astonishing lightness. One approaches uphill against an almost medieval, concave thickened wall—actually a concrete frame containing the rubble of the previous chapel, ruined during World War II—above which a hollowed concrete convexity seems to float. Moving clockwise, this is followed by two convex surfaces punctuated by three light towers. The fourth side, another concavity, provides an acoustic shell and spatial enclosure for the large outdoor altar. In the center of this wall is a square window box containing the historic, hollowed wooden statue of the Madonna, a model for the towers. Inside, the floor follows the natural slope of the ground downward toward the altar.

6° 37′ 15″E

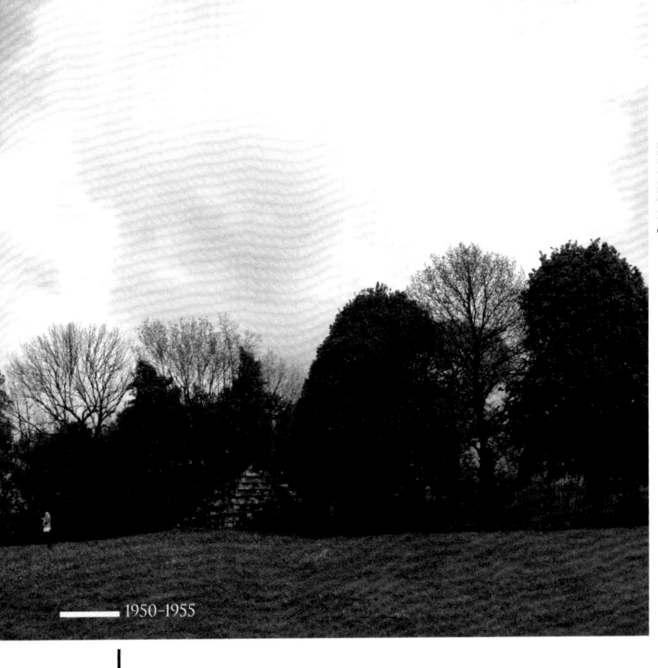

1950–1955

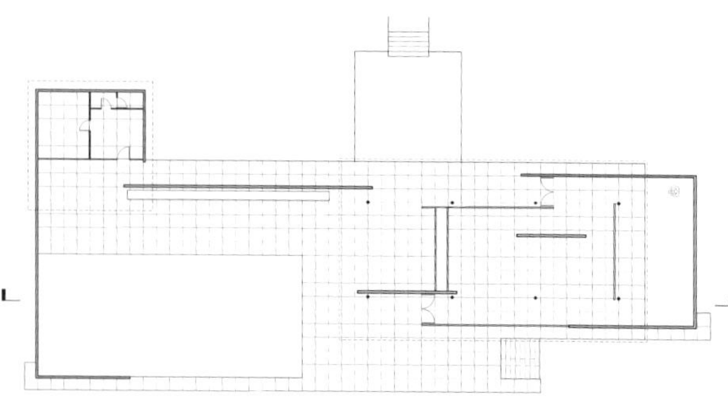

Floor Plan

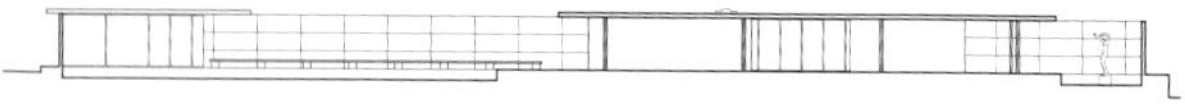

Section

0 10M 50'

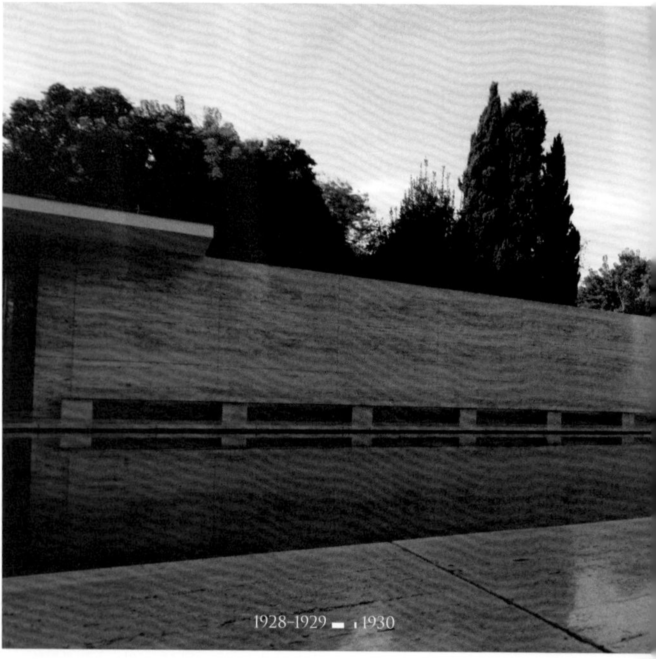

1928–1929 1930

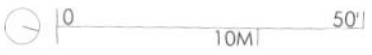

41° 22′ 14″N

03

GERMAN PAVILION
BARCELONA PAVILION

MIES VAN DER ROHE
Barcelona, Spain
1928–1929, destroyed 1930, restored 1986

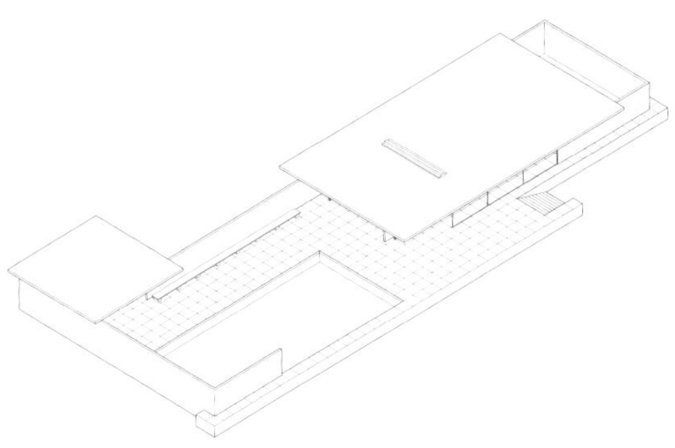

Built as a temporary structure for the International Exhibition of 1929 in Barcelona, the German reception pavilion is one of classical modernism's greatest masterpieces of "appearance." The roof of the main pavilion *appears* to be levitated by eight attenuated chromed cruciform columns. Beneath this roof is an irregular arrangement of marble walls that *appear* to be glass, of glass walls that *appear* to be mirrors, and of a milky glass wall that *appears* to be luminous. The entire structure *appears* to be the result of rational functionalism, and *appears* to represent by association the postwar Weimar Republic as one of prosperity, rational foresight, and exuberant modernity, with a nod to classical integrities. Demolished after the exhibition, the pavilion was rebuilt in 1986.

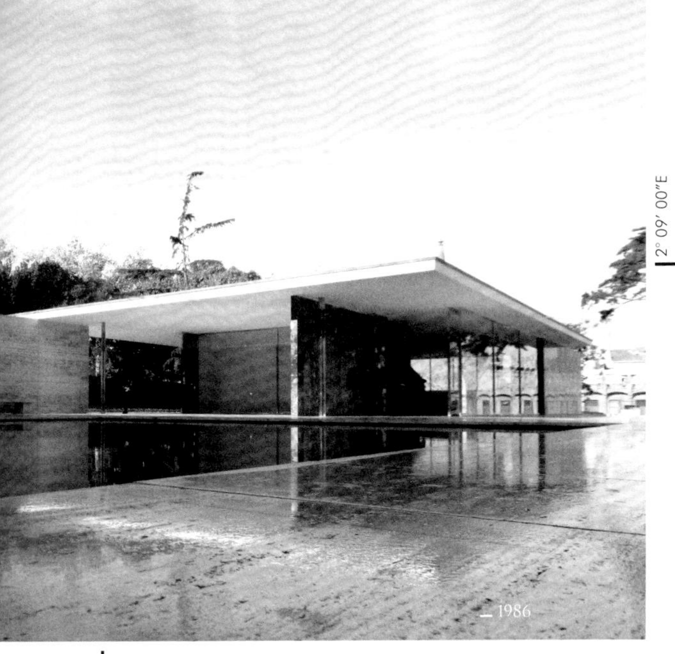

— 1986

2° 09′ 00″E

16/

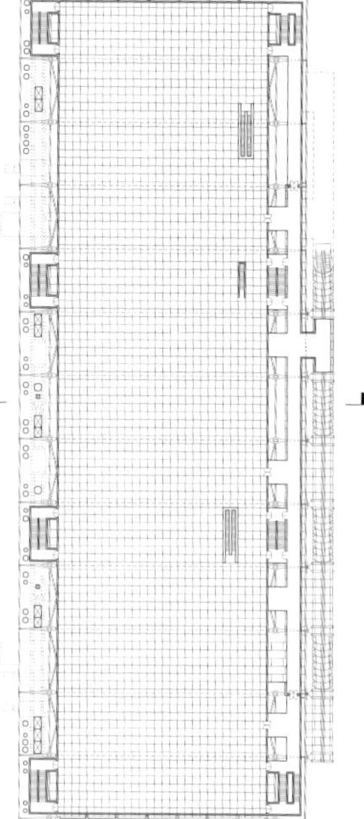

Floor Plan

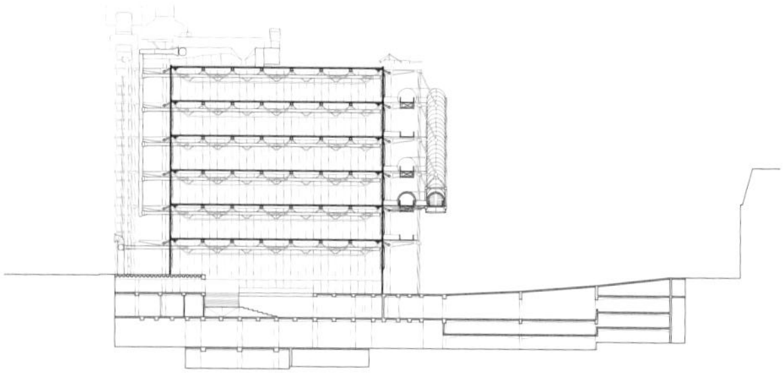

Section

0 20M 100'

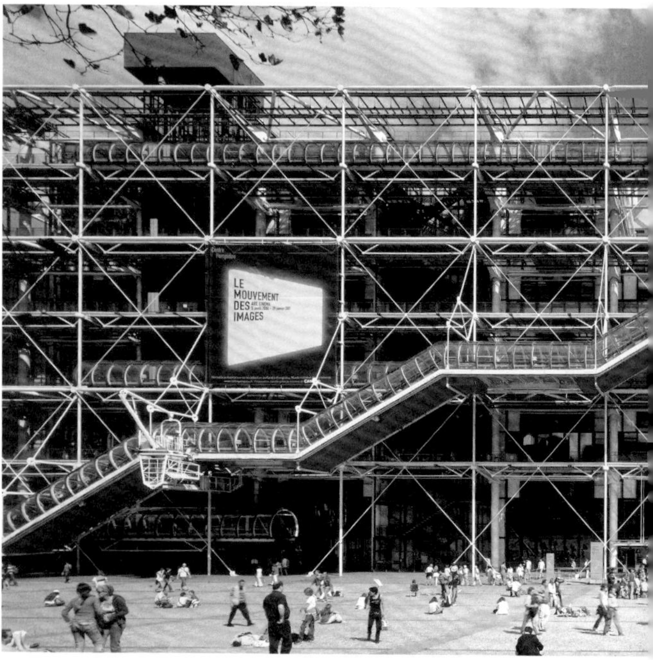

48° 51′ 39″N

04

CENTRE POMPIDOU

RENZO PIANO and RICHARD ROGERS
Paris, France
1971–1977

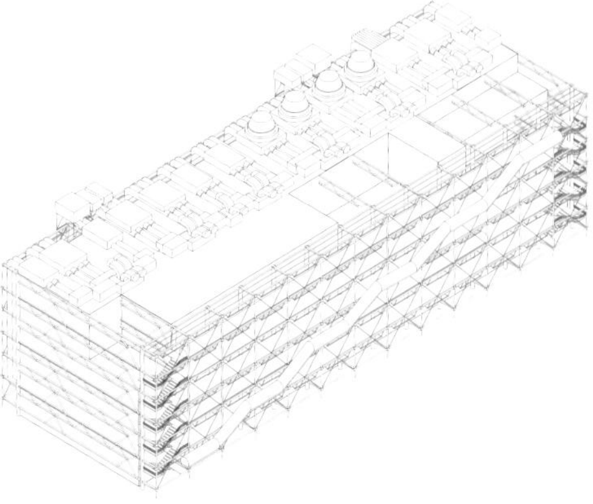

Essentially an inside-out building, the Centre Pompidou reverses the typical relationships of a building's components, with large, flexible free-span spaces hidden behind exposed and brightly colored circulation, structural, and mechanical systems. This configuration elevates functional systems to the level of art, mystifying functionality even while demystifying. The structure permits considerable intermingling of its various programs: art museum, library, cultural center, café, shop, and administrative offices. Visitors ascend above the rooflines of Paris within the glass-enclosed tubes of the escalators (originally conceived to be relocatable based on curatorial demands). An important aspect of the building is the public plaza—sectionally reminiscent of that in Siena—created by consolidating the mass to one half of the site.

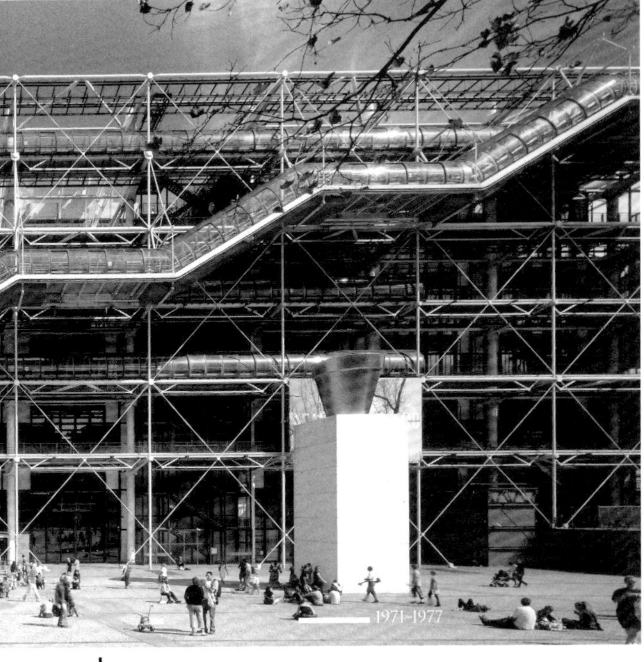
1971–1977

2° 21′ 08″E

42° 43′ 46″N

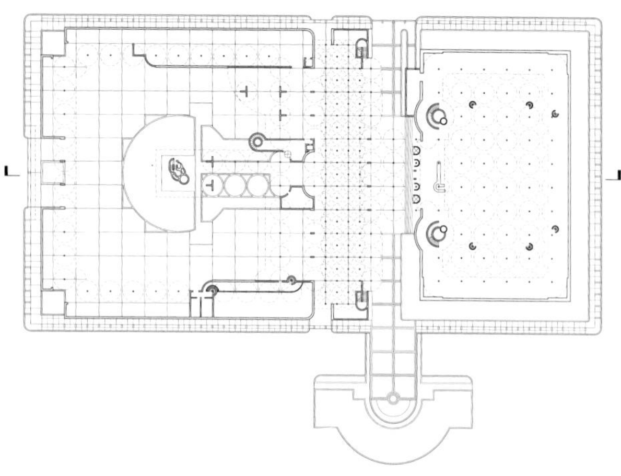

Floor Plan

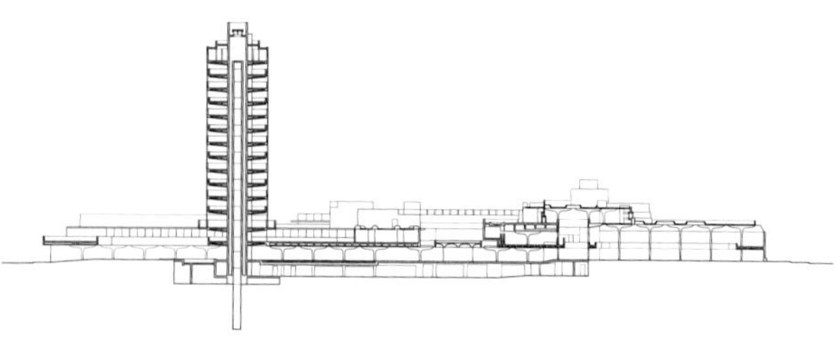

Section

0 100′
20M

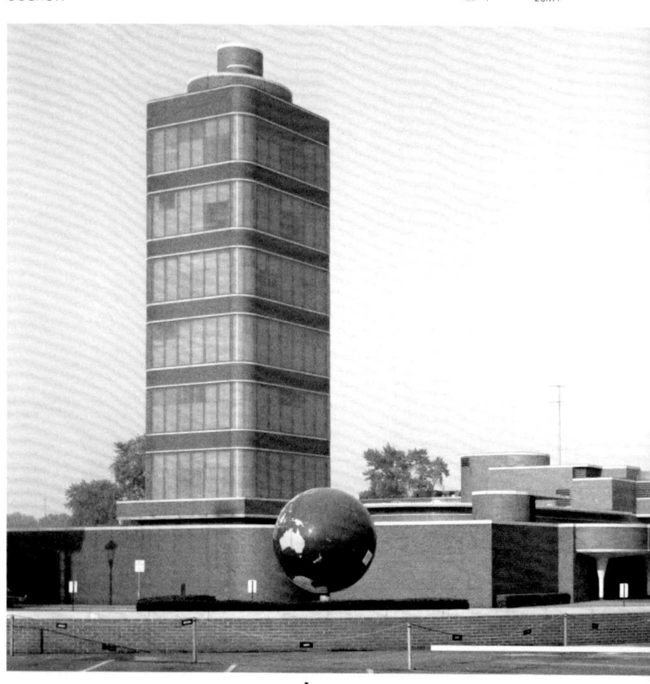

87° 47′ 29″W

05

S.C. JOHNSON & SON HEADQUARTERS

FRANK LLOYD WRIGHT

Racine, Wisconsin, USA

main building: 1936–1939; research tower: 1944–1951

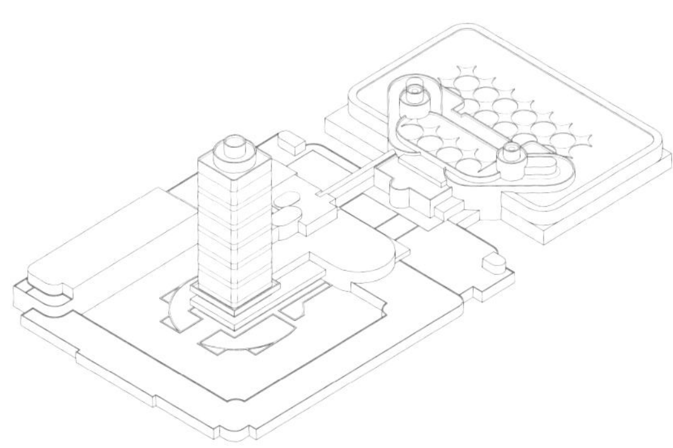

The sprawling exterior of the original S.C. Johnson & Son Headquarters is unified by a sinuous series of horizontal bands of brick and stacked tubes of Pyrex that belie the verticality of the giant dendriform columns of reinforced concrete that populate the large, vertical space of the "great workroom." These columns, less than a foot at their base, flare upward to diameters of eighteen feet at their tops, with more glass tubing filling the gaps between the discs. The Pyrex tubes serve to diffuse light on the interior, with the intention of improving the lighting conditions in the work spaces. Connected to the main building with a bridge, the later research tower alternates circular mezzanine floors with square research floors, all cantilevered from a central concrete core and flaring slightly as they extend upward. While the original structure was seen as being primarily solid on the exterior, the tower is primarily translucent, with massive walls of Pyrex tubing alternating with shorter bands of brick.

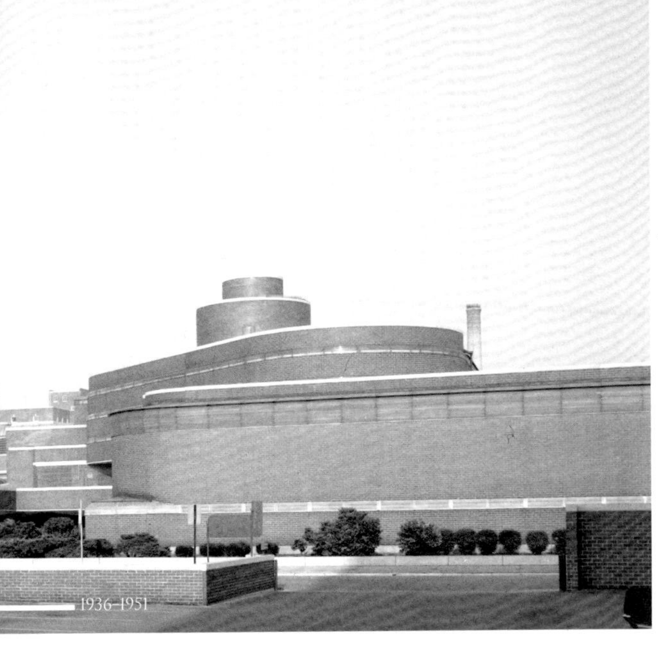

1936–1951

41° 38′ 06″N

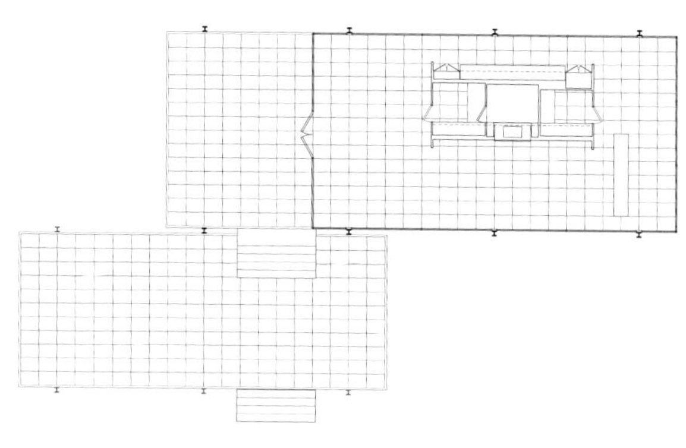

Floor Plan

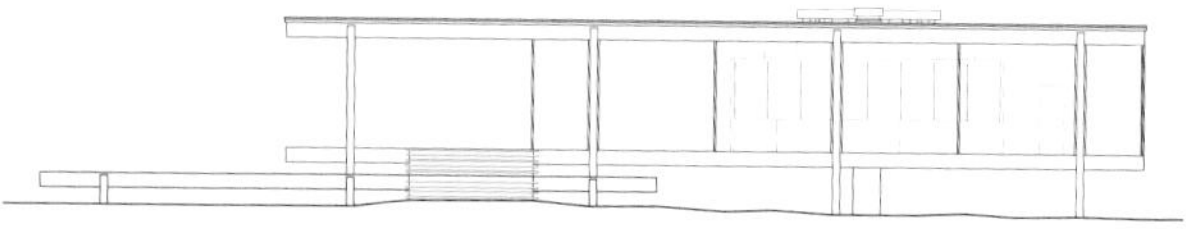

Elevation

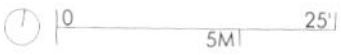

0 25′ 5M

88° 32′ 09″W

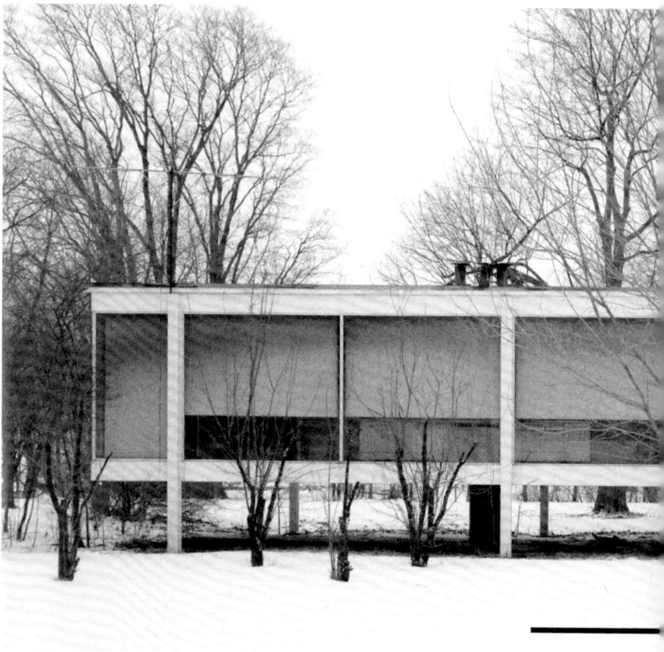

06

FARNSWORTH HOUSE

MIES VAN DER ROHE
Plano, Illinois, USA
1945–1951

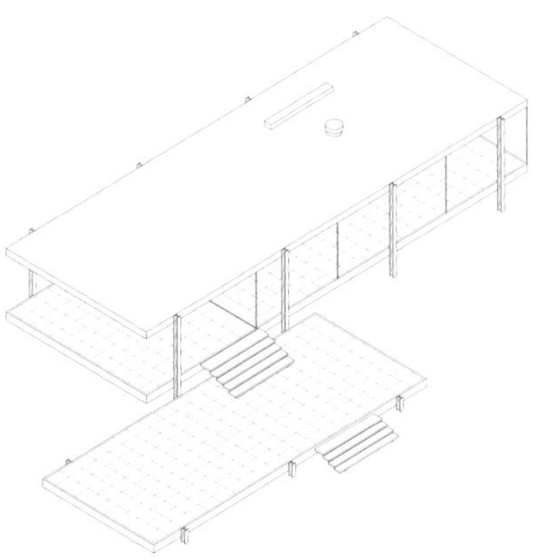

A single-story geometric form that exemplifies the notion of dwelling in its simplest state, this weekend retreat materializes Mies's famous dictate, "Less is more." Conceived as a glass pavilion in a natural setting, the concept uses the surrounding environment as its protective shield from the outside and as its phenomenal enclosure from within. The open, prismatic unity is composed of three horizontal planes (podium, floor, and roof slabs) lifted above the ground by external steel columns, with crystalline glass panels spanning between the structural elements. The interior is divided by only two objects, one containing bathrooms, kitchen, utility space, fireplace, and storage; the other a small bedroom storage unit. Despite its visual modernity, the Farnsworth House can be read as a reinterpretation of a classical ideal: a new translation of plinth, support, and architrave.

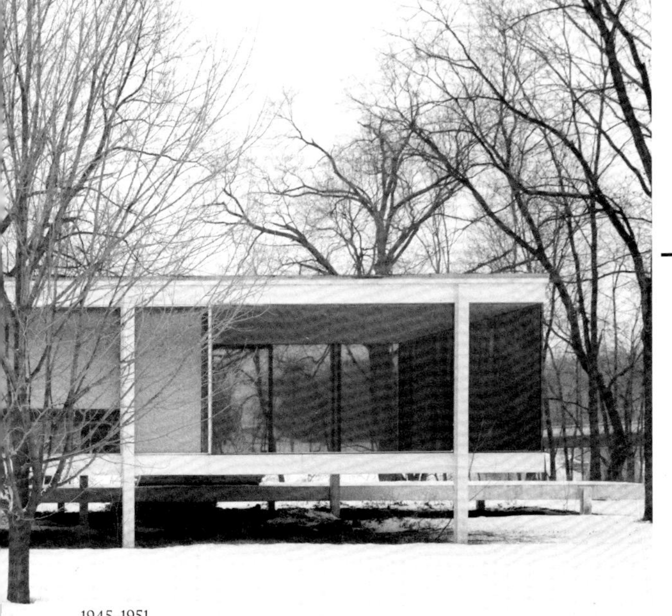

32° 53′ 15″N

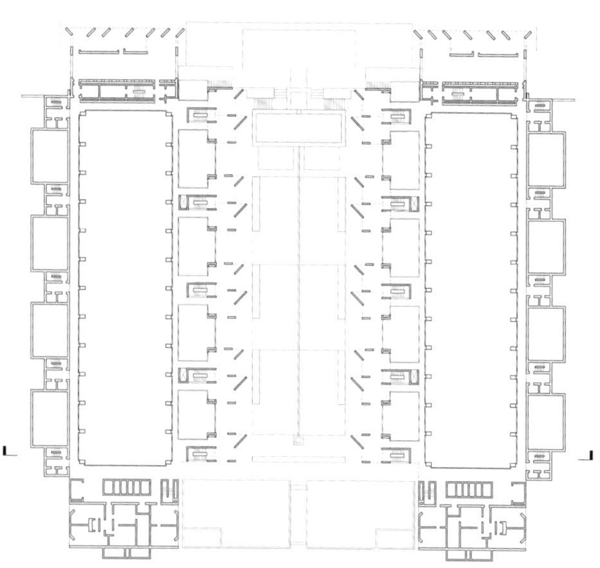

Floor Plan

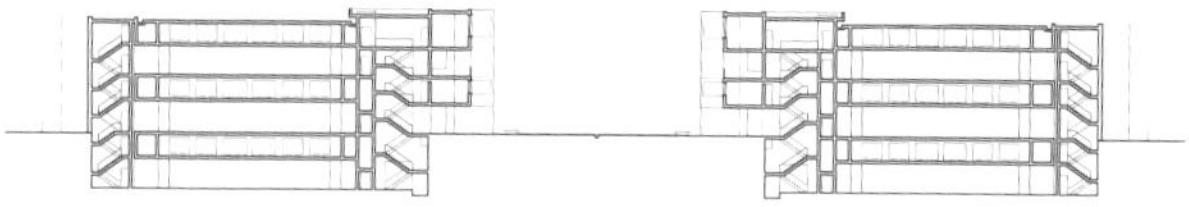

Section

0 20M 100'

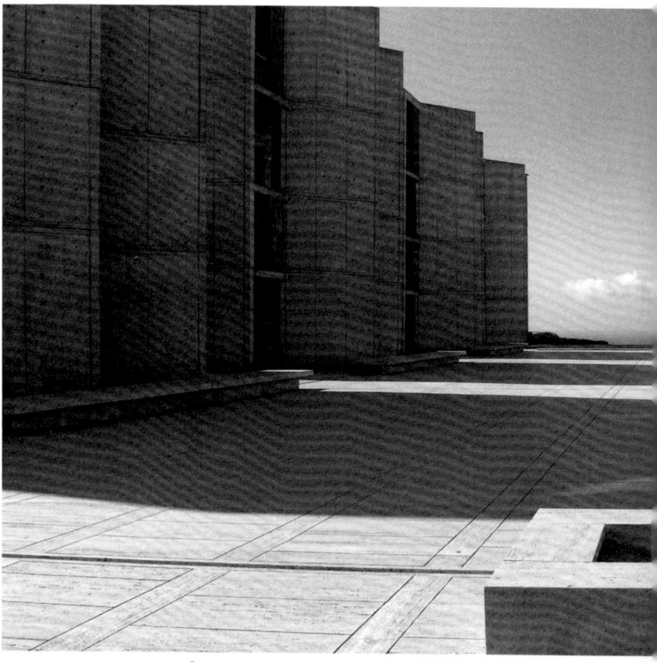

117° 14′ 43″W

07

SALK INSTITUTE

LOUIS KAHN
La Jolla, California, USA
1959–1965

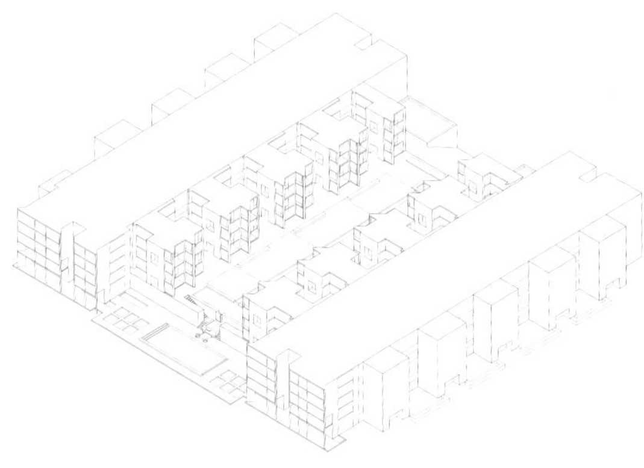

A giant research machine cloaked in a serene homage to the sea, the Salk Institute combines Kahn's "servant" versus "served" programming strategy with his profound poetic sensibilities. Built of a combination of concrete mixed with volcanic ash and teak, the buildings that compose the institute are symmetrically disposed along a Barragán-inspired central travertine courtyard, with a thin trough of water drawing the eye from a point of origin near the entry toward the distant sea and horizon. The concrete faces of the side pavilions lend the space its initial sense of austerity, while the wooden facade elements on the obverse side consistently look toward the sea. Much of the massive program is underground, with natural light brought to the sunken laboratories through a grid of light wells.

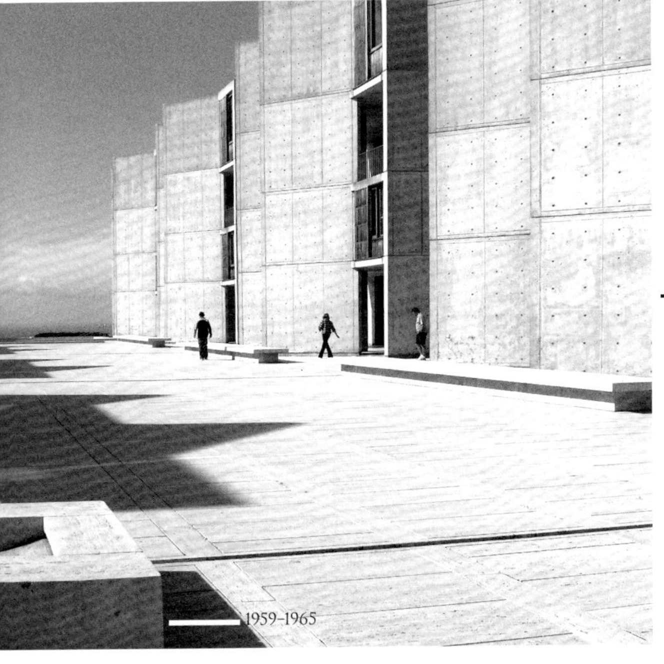

1959–1965

24/

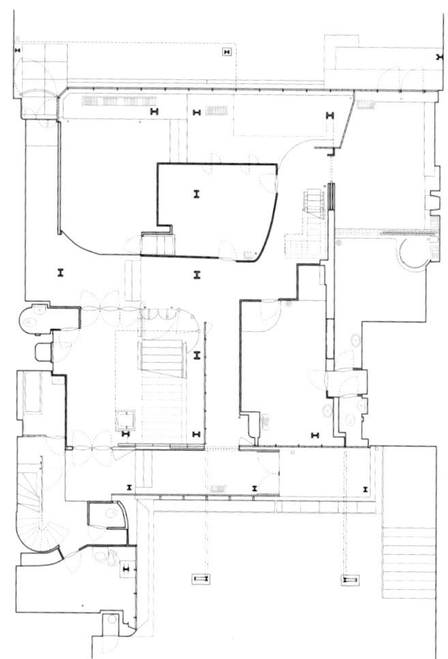

Floor Plan

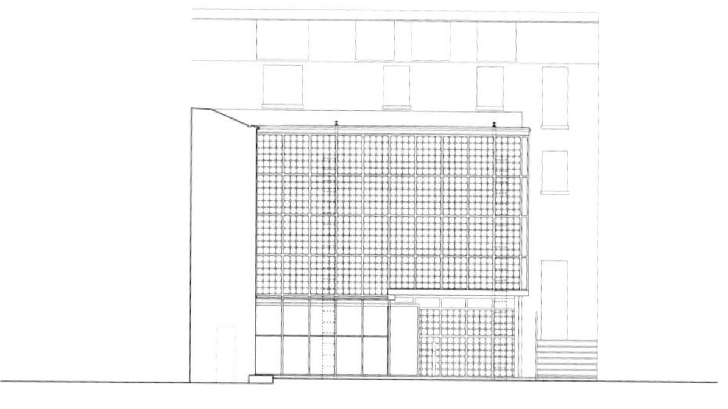

Elevation

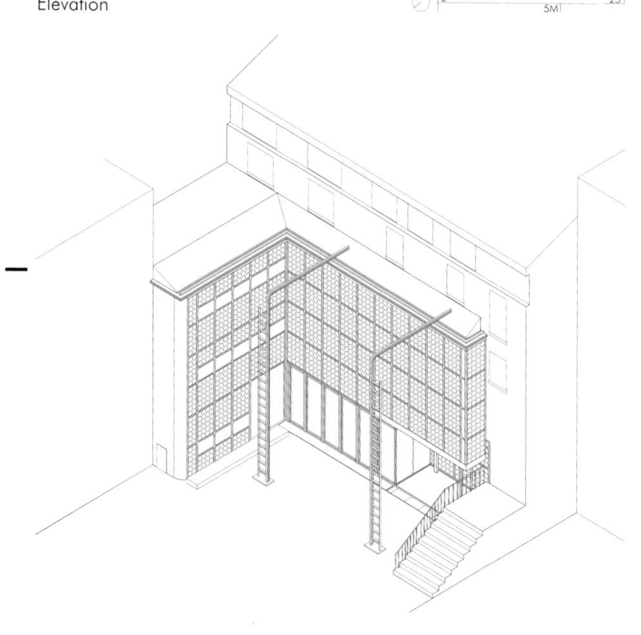

1928–1932

48° 51′ 41″N

08

LA MAISON DE VERRE

PIERRE CHAREAU and BERNARD BIJVOET
Paris, France
1928–1932

Designed by Pierre Chareau, with Bernard Bijvoet, La Maison de Verre ("The House of Glass") is a forerunner of an early and explicitly industrial offshoot of modern architecture. The house maintains a consistent adherence to a palette of industrial materials and fixtures, with traditional Art Deco home decor (also designed by Chareau) set within a luminous semitransparent, multistory facade of glass block, illuminated at night from the exterior. Steel, glass, and glass block are used as the main building materials. Sited both in a courtyard and within a three-story volume located entirely beneath an existing fourth-floor apartment, the house uses variously oriented wide-flange columns and steel construction to create its own "free plan." Mechanical fixtures form a unique set of relationships throughout the house. For example, during the day, a rotating perforated panel hides an extraordinary private staircase from patients of the ground-floor medical suite of the Dr. Jean Dalsace. Spatial separation on the interior is convertible by the use of folding, sliding, and rotating panels and cabinets of glass, sheet, or perforated metal.

2° 19′ 41″E

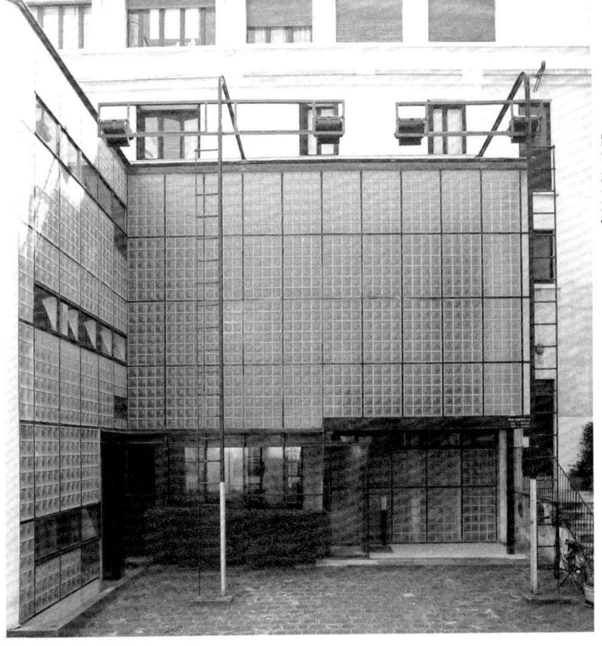

26/

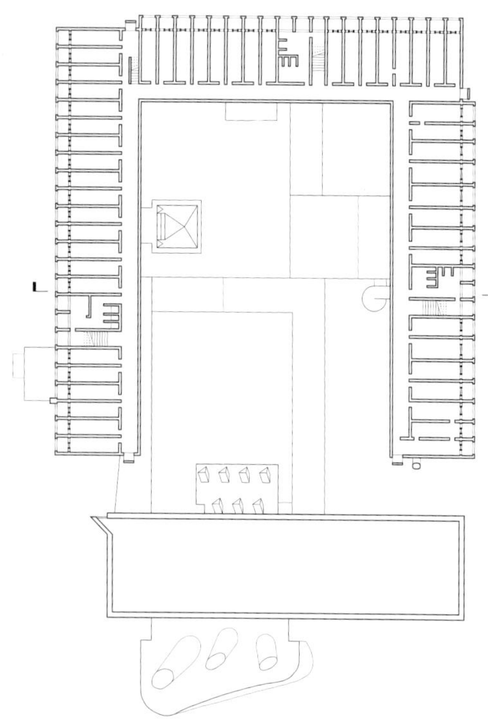

Floor Plan

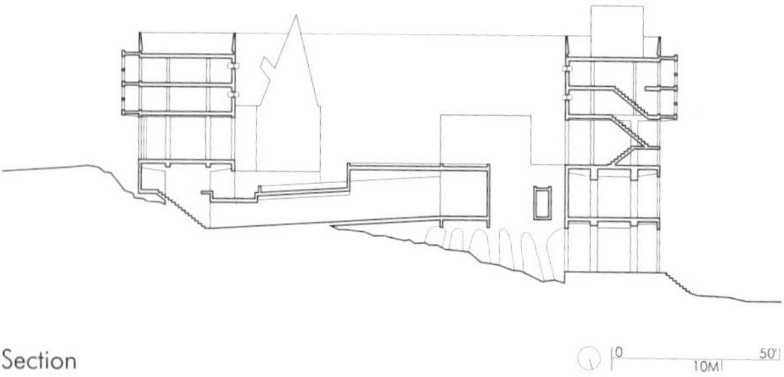

Section

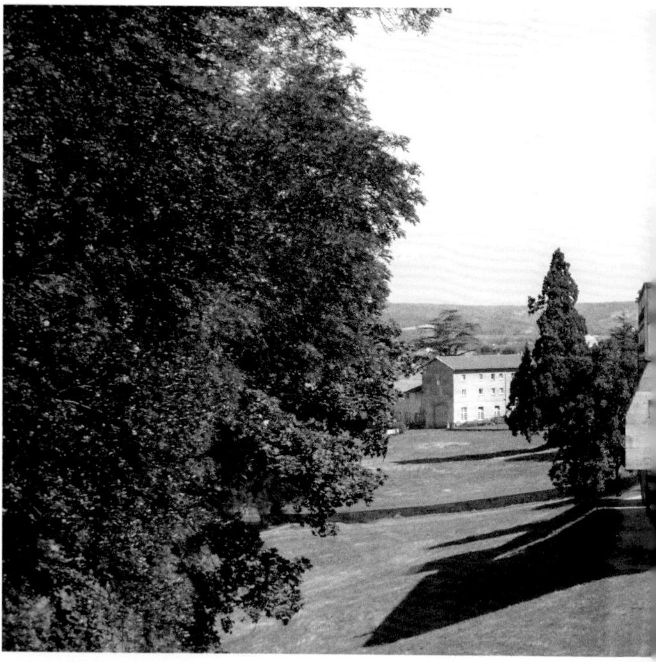

0 10M 50'

45° 49′ 10″N

09

COUVENT SAINTE-MARIE DE LA TOURETTE

LE CORBUSIER
Éveux-sur-l'Arbresle, France
1953–1960, restored 1981

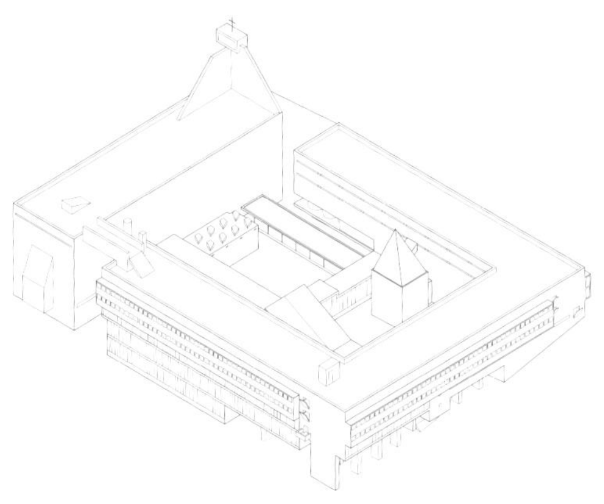

A Dominican monastery outside Lyon integrates Le Corbusier's thoughts about ritual, landscape, light, sound, and movement. The dialectics of plan versus section provide the basis for a series of provocative displacements: while the plan represents an almost prototypical monastery, the sloping ground plane and flat roof motivate considerable sectional invention. One approaches from below along the emphatically blank surface of the main sanctuary. The entry is at the top of the slope, near the centroid of the overall mass. Monastic cells and individual chapels hover in a U-shape above this level, while spaces for gathering, dining, and worship pinwheel downward. Fenestration within echoes the musical notation of collaborator Iannis Xenakis. The Modulor proportioning system is used throughout to achieve a unified expression of elements.

4° 37′ 21″E

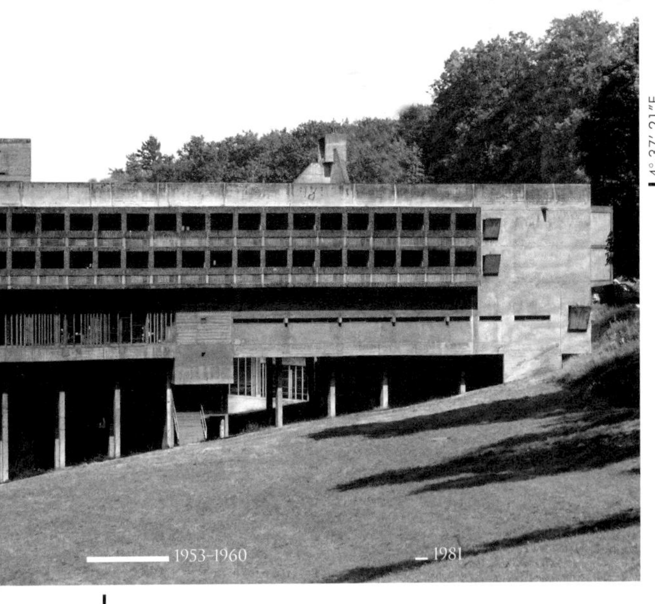

40° 38′ 45″N

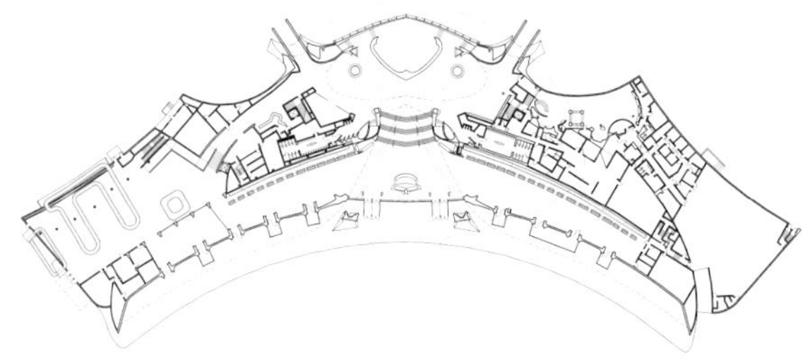

Floor Plan

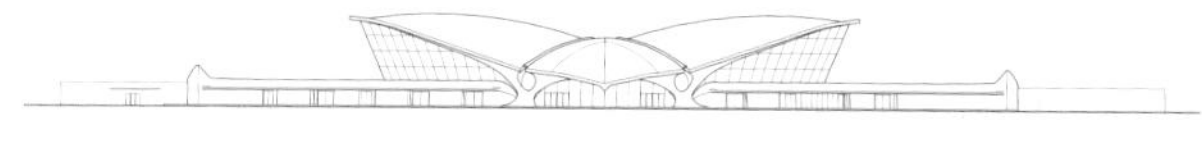

Elevation

0 20M 100'

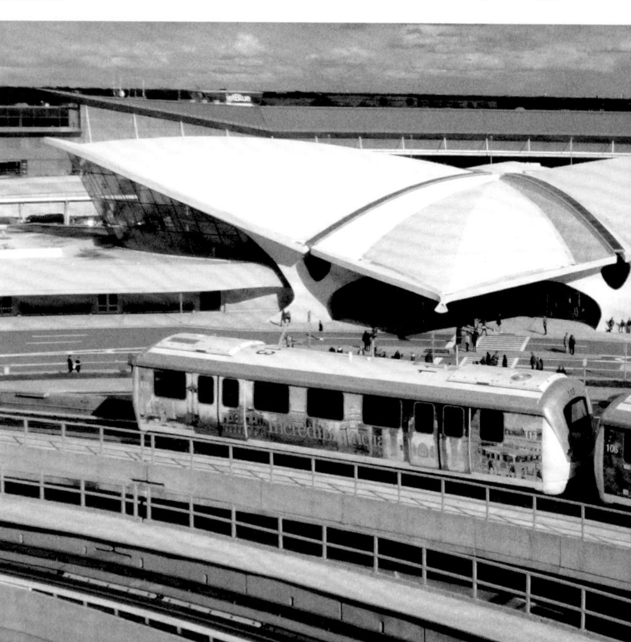

73° 46′ 40″W

10

TWA FLIGHT CENTER

EERO SAARINEN
Queens, New York, USA
1956–1962

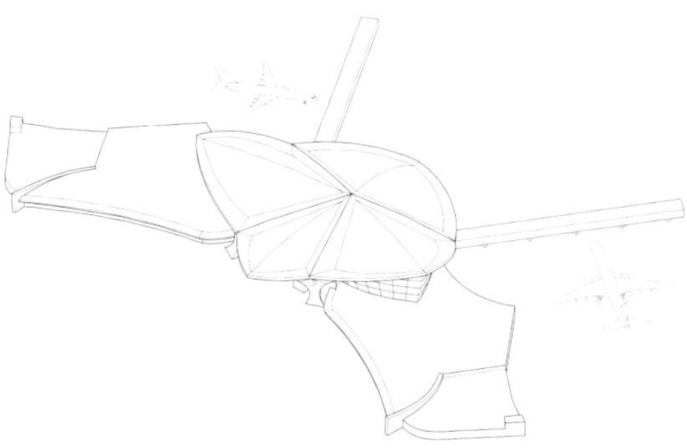

Compared to the Guggenheim Bilbao, Eero Saarinen's TWA terminal is a sculptural form of a different species. Metaphorically suggesting a colossal bird with outstretched wings, perched and ready to ascend, the terminal evokes—visually and experientially—the "spirit of flight" with its continuous, sinuous network of stairs, platforms, and passages. The complex, three-dimensional curvatures of the terminal's main hall are achieved through reinforced, board-formed cast-in-place concrete. A pair of extended satellite terminals are entered through gently arched, tube-like concrete bridge structures, choreographed by the architect to minimize the perception and experience of a long walk to the plane while heightening a sense of arrival. The terminal provides a completely designed environment, in which every detail reiterates and reinforces the aesthetic intentions of Saarinen's conception.

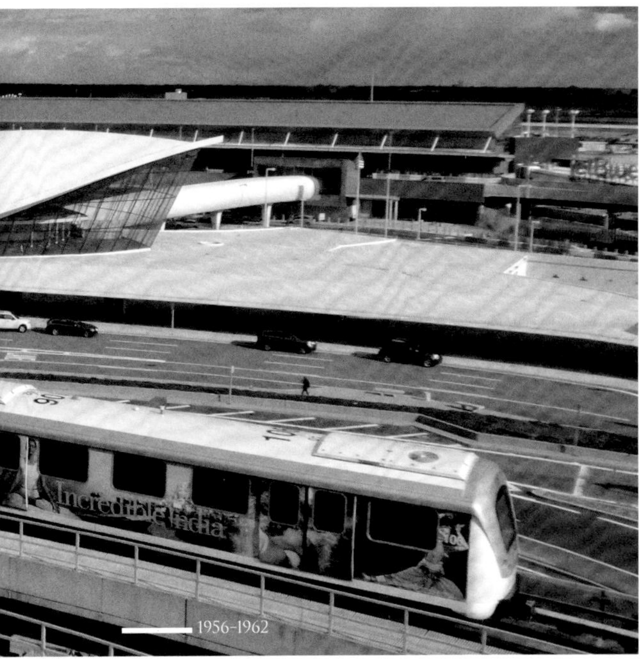

1956–1962

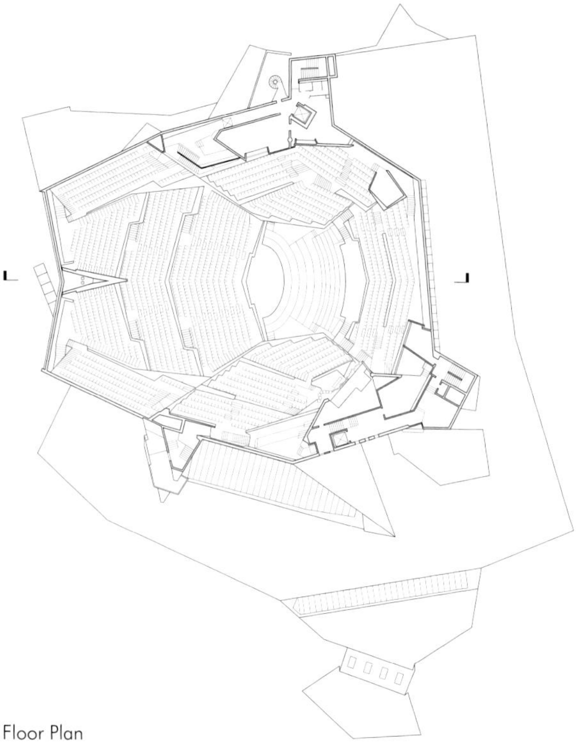

30/

Floor Plan

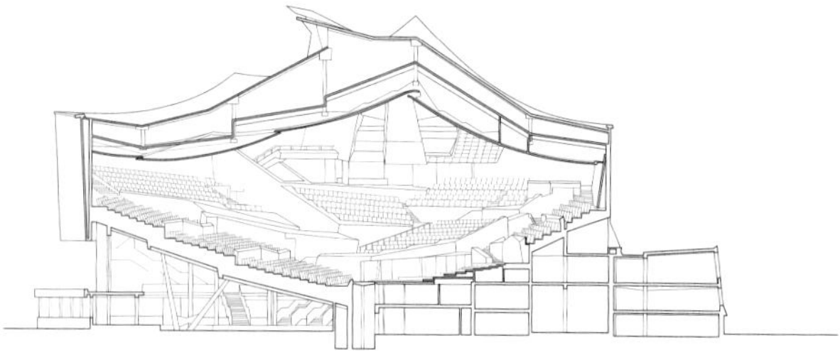

Section

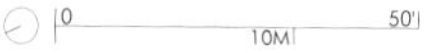

0 10M 50'

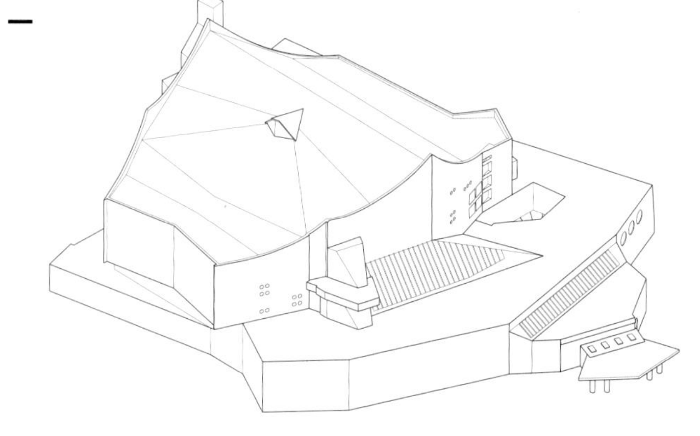

52° 30′ 36″N

11

BERLINER PHILHARMONIE

HANS SCHAROUN
Berlin, Germany
1956–1963

When the architect Scharoun announced his intention of placing music in the center of the building—both figuratively and literally—he developed one of the first examples of what has been called "vineyard seating." With the orchestra located near the center of the principal hall, the audience is distributed around the orchestra in cascading tiers of large loges of seating; the audience always feels close to the performance and gets a sense of being a part of a smaller musical community. The entire space is shaped so as to optimize acoustics, with its tentlike ceiling focusing sound evenly throughout the auditorium. While the exterior appears idiosyncratic, it actually expresses fairly directly the volume of the interior, with the metal-clad central "mountain" of the hall surrounded by the glazed roofs and concrete canopies of the ancillary spaces, a clear expression of Scharoun's concept of an organic architecture.

13° 22′ 11″E

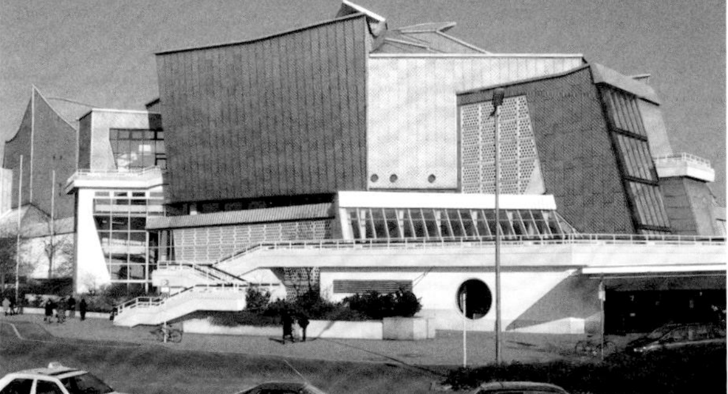
1956–1963

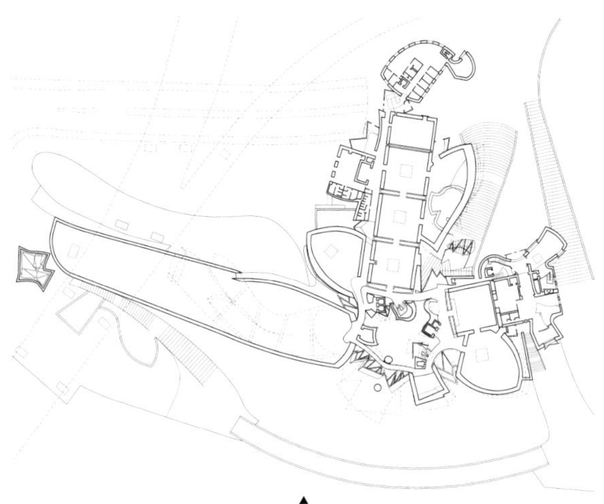

Floor Plan

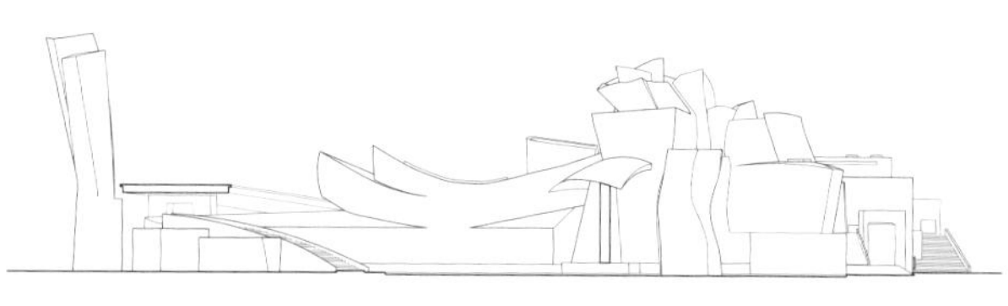

Elevation

0 100'
20M

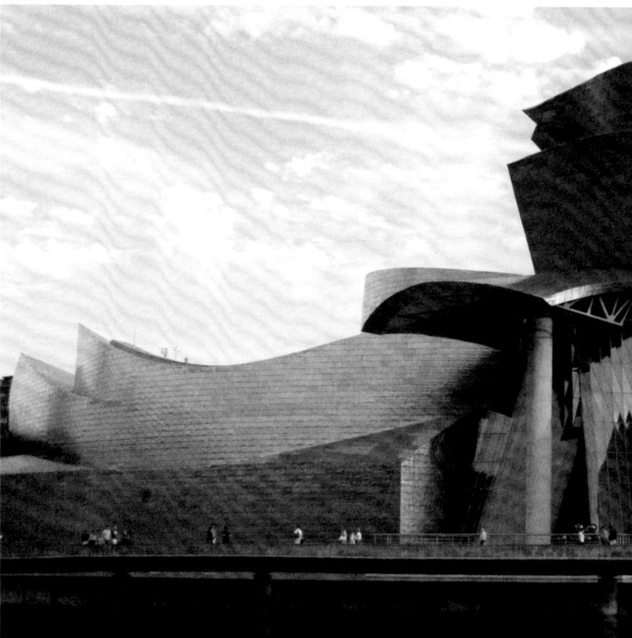

2° 56' 00"W

12

GUGGENHEIM MUSEUM BILBAO

FRANK GEHRY (GEHRY PARTNERS, LLP)
Bilbao, Spain
1991–1997

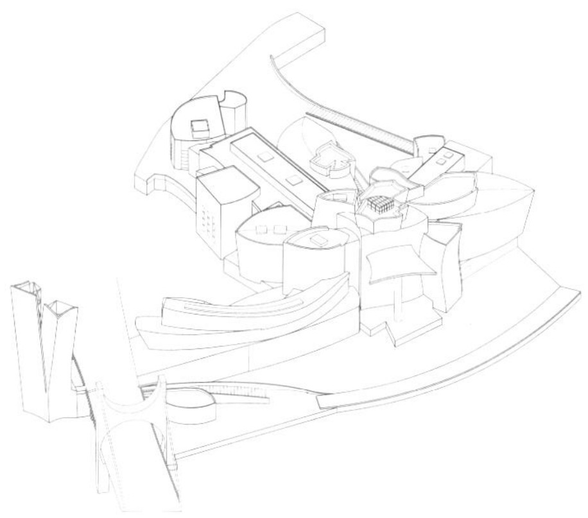

A complex combination of multiple freeform sculpted planes, the Guggenheim Museum in Bilbao introduces a new role of the art museum as a work of art itself in an urban context. Built as part of a redevelopment plan to renew and modernize the industrial urban context within which it is inserted, the building alternately reclines and erupts along the river, slithers beneath a bridge, and presents a tower that unites the upper and lower levels of the city. The remarkable twisting curves were made possible through advances in 3-D design software, in this case CATIA. This technology initiates a period where digital design can be transferred directly from the architect to the fabricator. The popular success of the building and the subsequent social and economic transformations in a once depressed, industrial city reinstated the concept of architecture as a valuable amenity and coined the expression "Bilbao effect."

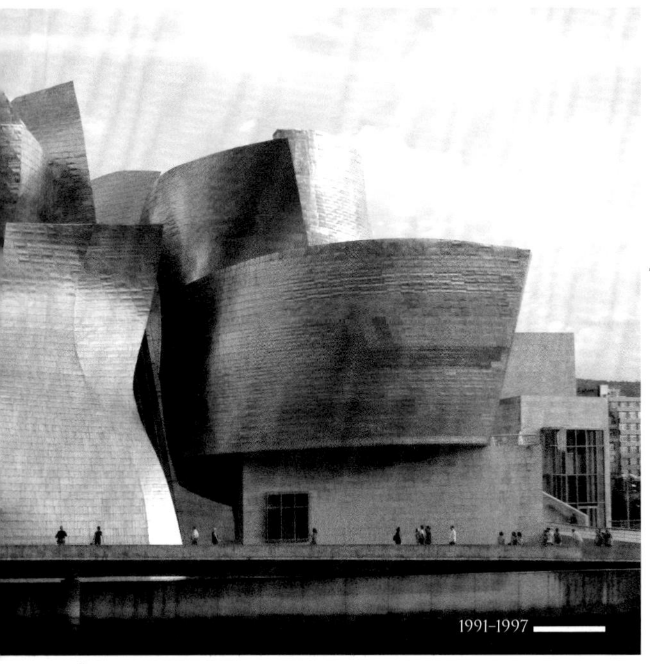

1991–1997

39° 54′ 23″N

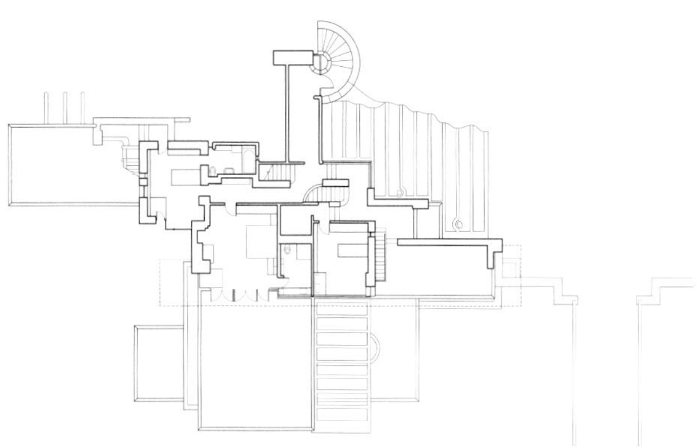

Floor Plan

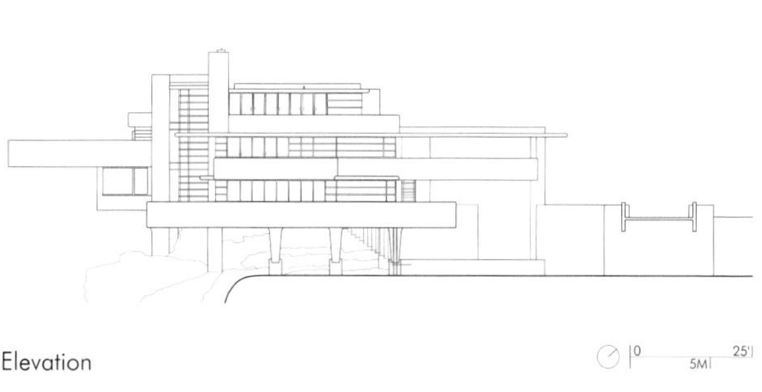

Elevation

79° 28′ 05″W

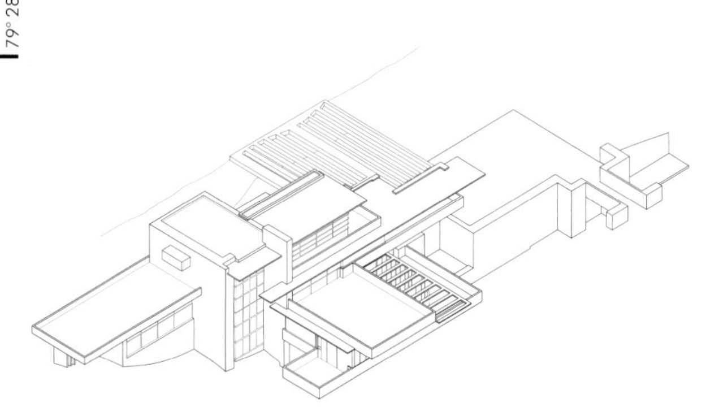

1934–1937

13

EDGAR J. KAUFMANN HOUSE
FALLINGWATER

FRANK LLOYD WRIGHT
Mill Run, Pennsylvania, USA
1934–1937

An essay on cantilevers and acoustics, verticality and—most emphatically—horizontality, this weekend house is the most iconic iteration of Wright's concept of organic architecture. At times firmly grounded, and at other times possessing an apparent expression of antigravity, nature sometimes erupts through the floors and walls of the house, and sometimes the house teases nature by rendering its eponymous waterfall an exclusively sonic event and by sending a stairway down toward—without touching—a rushing stream. Architecture's various elements—steel-sash windows, stone piers, and concrete terraces—are expressed as continuities throughout the house at a variety of scales.

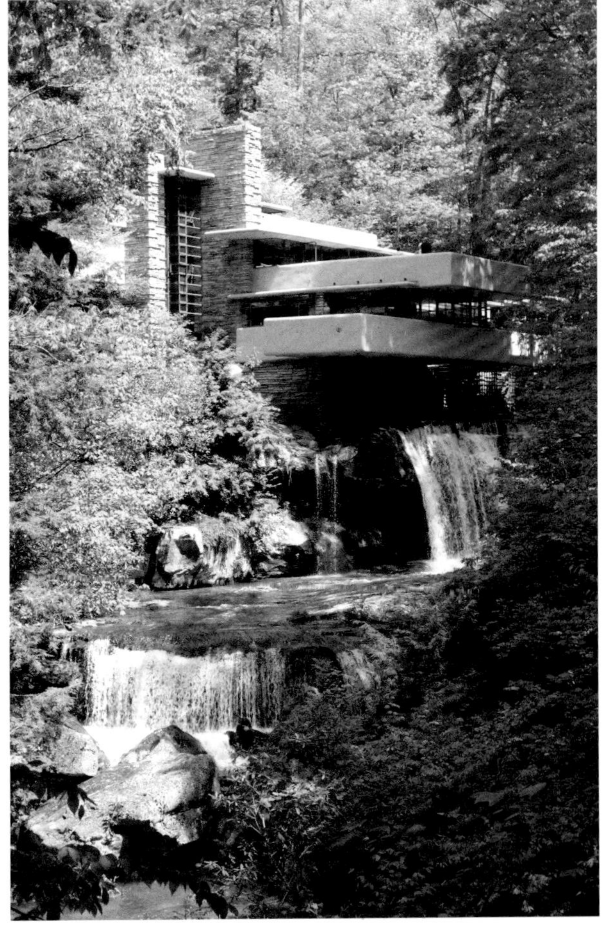

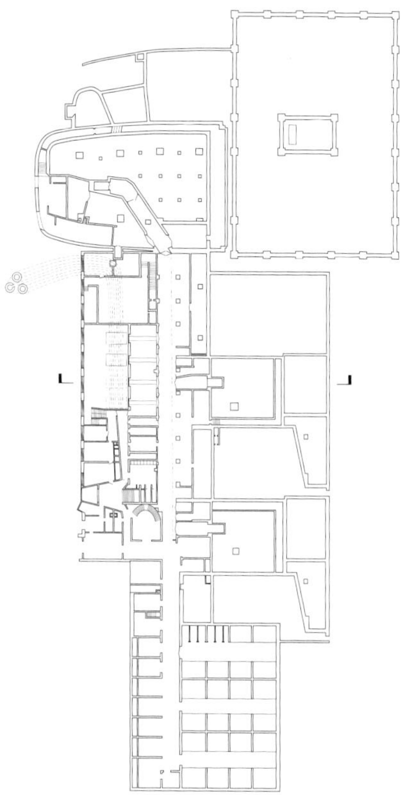

Floor Plan

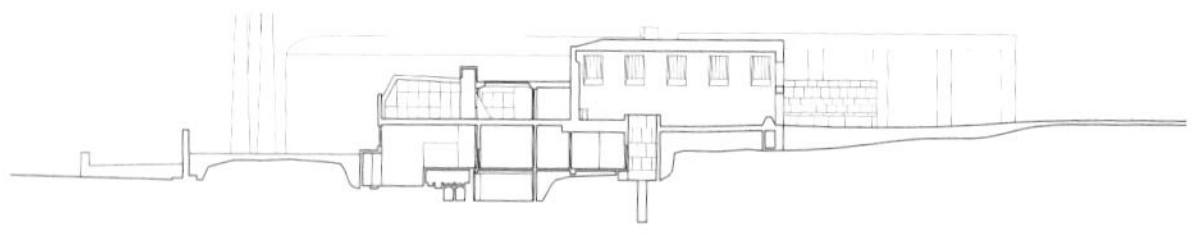

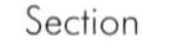

Section

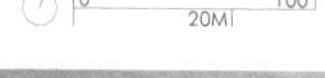

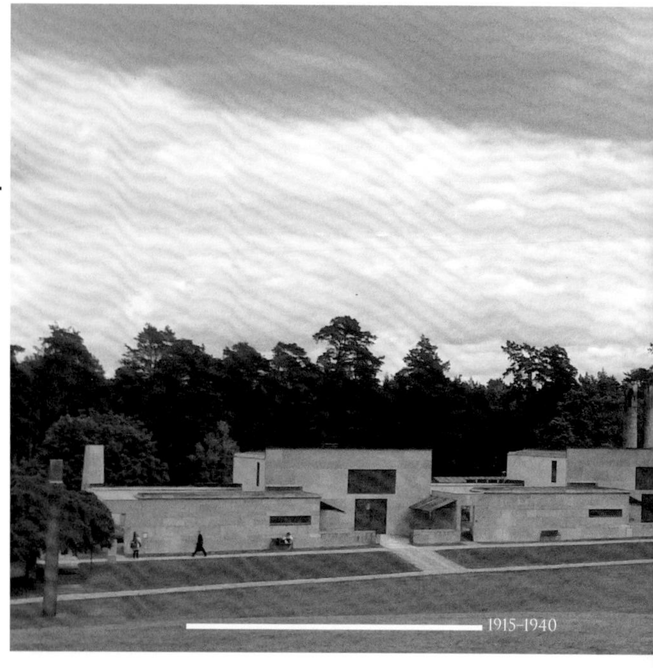

59° 16′ 17″N

14

THE WOODLAND CEMETERY

ERIK GUNNAR ASPLUND and SIGURD LEWERENTZ
Stockholm, Sweden
1915–1940

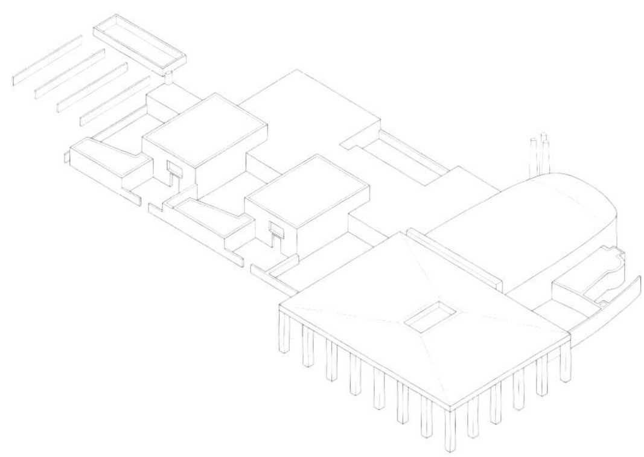

A product of the combined efforts of Erik Gunnar Asplund and Sigurd Lewerentz, the Woodland Cemetery (or Skogskyrkogården) is a winning competition entry from 1915. Fully within the tradition of the Scandinavian "church garden," the project opened a network of paths and a series of landscaped vistas within the natural forested beauty of the site, with a series of chapels, crematoriums, fountains, groves, and auxiliary buildings dispersed throughout, all contributing to a larger narrative of peace, hope, and restfulness. The project represents an important transition between early Nordic classicism and the distinct modernism of Asplund (Lewerentz left the project after his design of the Resurrection Chapel complex). The architects designed everything from the paving patterns to the fixtures, rendering the project a captivating and influential vision for the holistic experience of nature. In 1994, the project was named a UNESCO World Heritage Site.

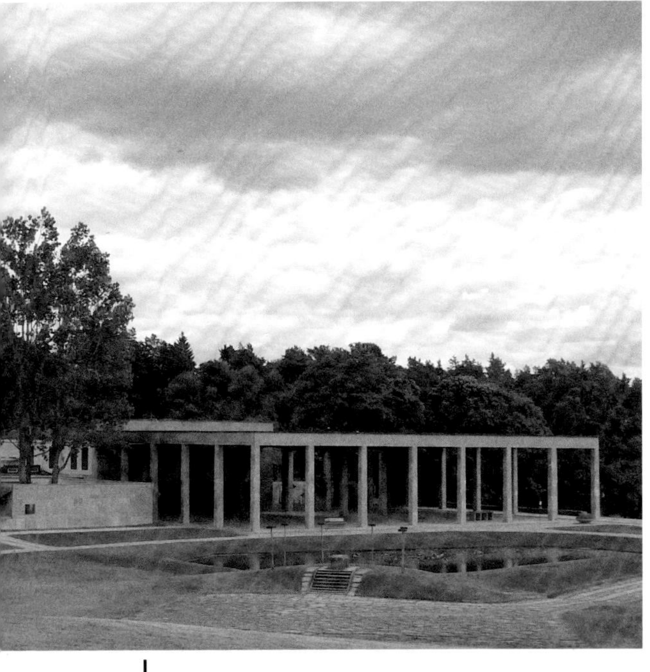

18° 06′ 10″E

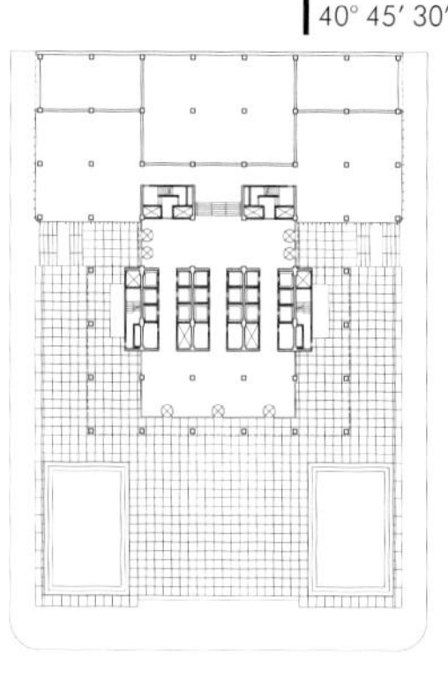

Floor Plan

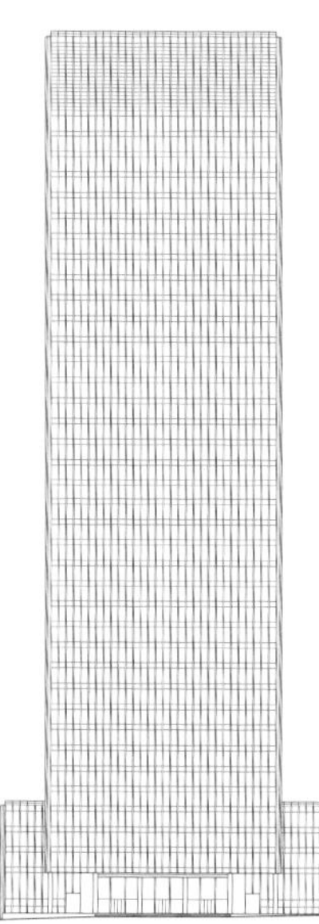

Elevation

0 100′
20M

73° 58′ 20″W

15

SEAGRAM BUILDING

MIES VAN DER ROHE and PHILIP JOHNSON
New York, New York, USA
1954–1958

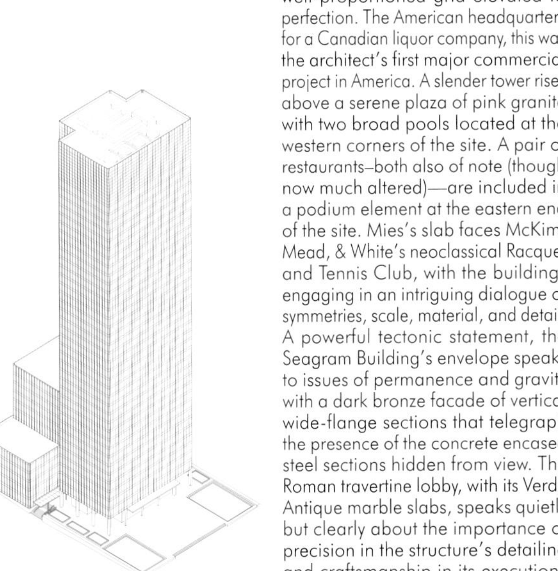

In Mies's Seagram Building, we find the power of the simple, elegant, well-proportioned grid elevated to perfection. The American headquarters for a Canadian liquor company, this was the architect's first major commercial project in America. A slender tower rises above a serene plaza of pink granite with two broad pools located at the western corners of the site. A pair of restaurants–both also of note (though now much altered)—are included in a podium element at the eastern end of the site. Mies's slab faces McKim, Mead, & White's neoclassical Racquet and Tennis Club, with the buildings engaging in an intriguing dialogue of symmetries, scale, material, and detail. A powerful tectonic statement, the Seagram Building's envelope speaks to issues of permanence and gravity with a dark bronze facade of vertical wide-flange sections that telegraph the presence of the concrete encased steel sections hidden from view. The Roman travertine lobby, with its Verde Antique marble slabs, speaks quietly but clearly about the importance of precision in the structure's detailing and craftsmanship in its execution.

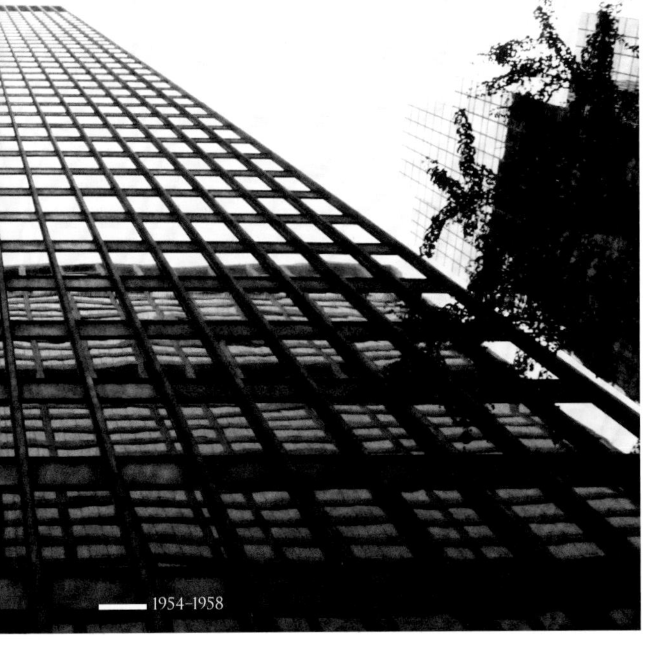

40° 46′ 59″N

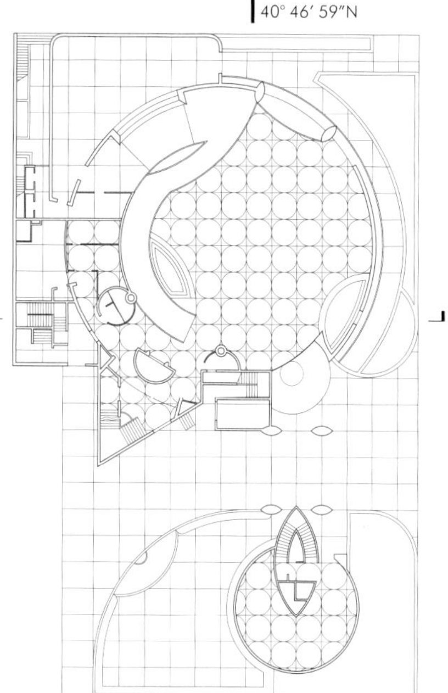

Floor Plan

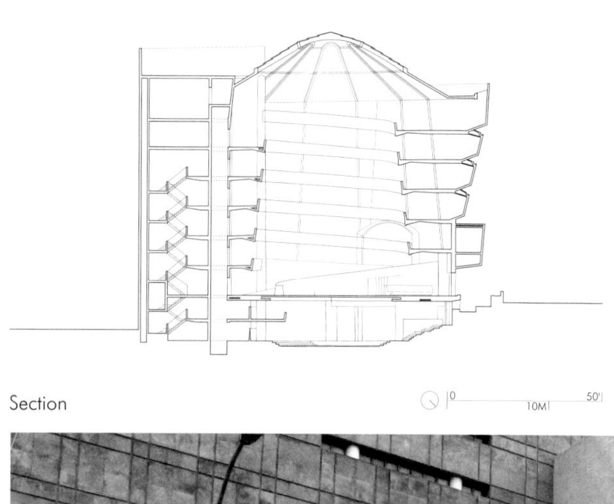

Section

0 10M 50′

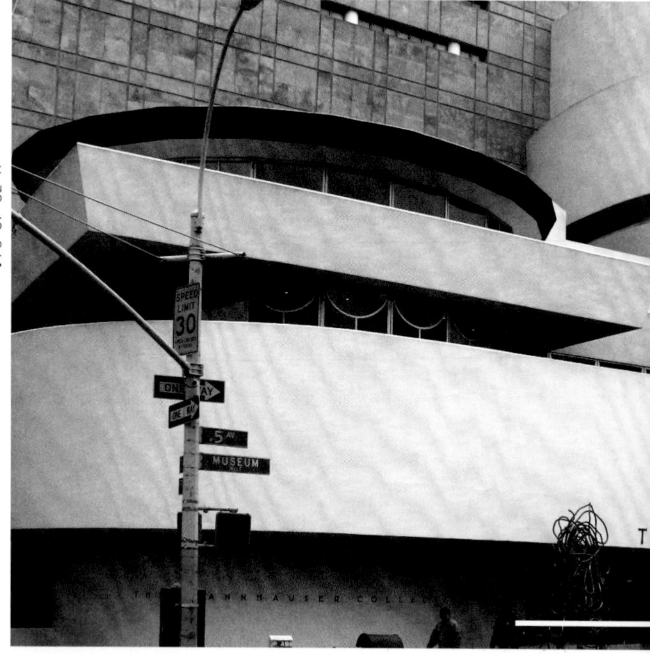

73° 57′ 32″W

16

SOLOMON R. GUGGENHEIM MUSEUM

FRANK LLOYD WRIGHT
New York, New York, USA
1943–1959

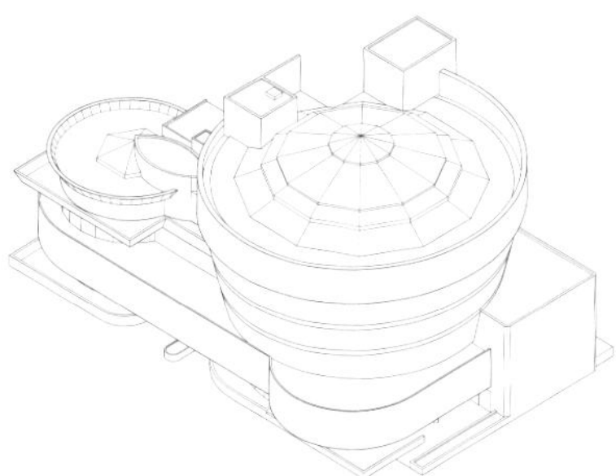

Gutsy, if not egocentric in its dense urban environment, this museum's conical volume rebels against the block structure of New York while seeming to nudge its way into Central Park, vying with the much larger Metropolitan Museum of Art for monumental status. A unification of form, structure, and space, the Guggenheim Museum constitutes an urban version of what Wright called organic architecture. Rich in plasticity, the white, inverted frustum of reinforced concrete emerges from a similarly bulbous plinth. This volume is shaped by the continuous spiral ramp on the interior—a promenade intended to be initiated from the top—that cantilevers from the gallery niches while shaping the figure of the central court topped by a glazed dome. Incisions in the exterior surfaces of the large drum serve to scale the structure while allowing baffled light into the gallery spaces within and registering the nature of the circulatory spiral.

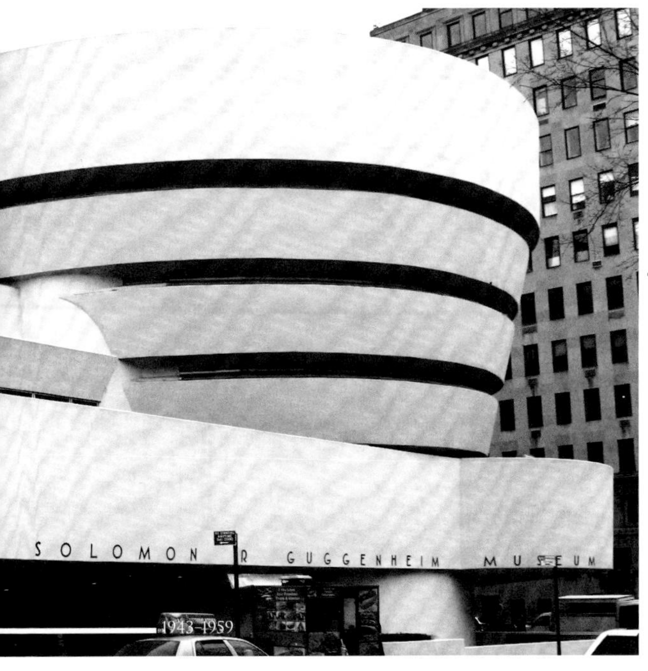

34° 01′ 49″N

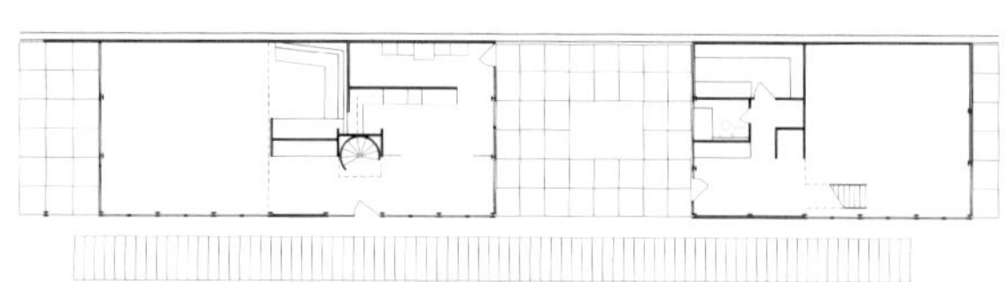

Floor Plan

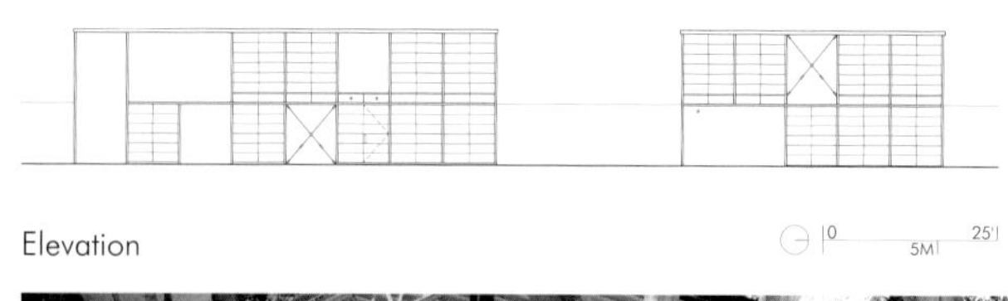

Elevation

0 25′
5M

118° 31′ 10″W

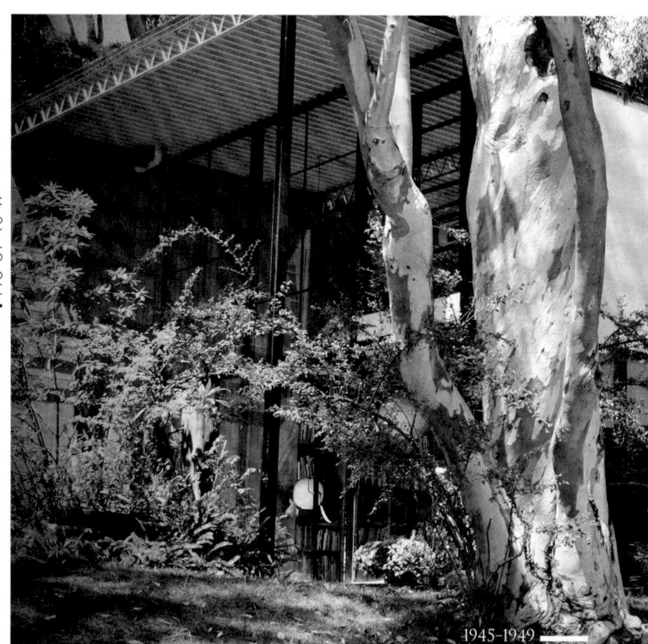

17

THE EAMES HOUSE
CASE STUDY HOUSE No. 8

CHARLES and RAY EAMES
Pacific Palisades, California, USA
1945–1949

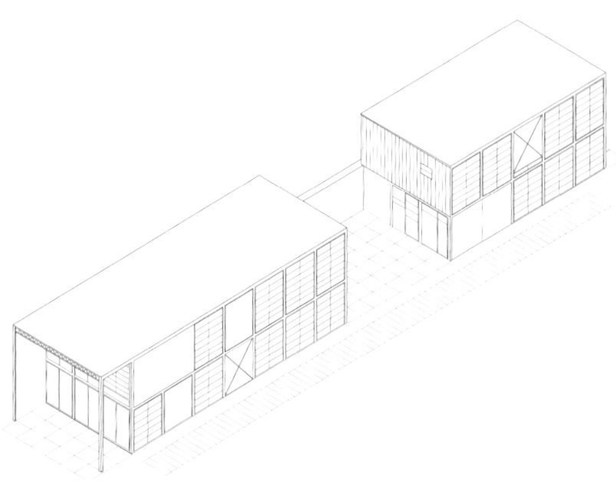

Charles and Ray Eames were the quintessential American designers of the twentieth century, designing virtually everything from toys to textiles, tools to furniture, books, films, and exhibitions. Their Case Study House No. 8, designed to be a prototype residence built of prefabricated materials and with techniques developed during World War II, brings their industrial design skills to architecture. The house is divided into two components—the residence and the studio—that together follow the contours of a steep hillside. A retaining wall against the slope forms one boundary of the compound, with the pavilions comprised of exposed steel–framed structures that demonstrate their modular organization in both plan and section. The pavilions are enveloped by gridded glass doors and windows, interspersed with multicolored opaque panels.

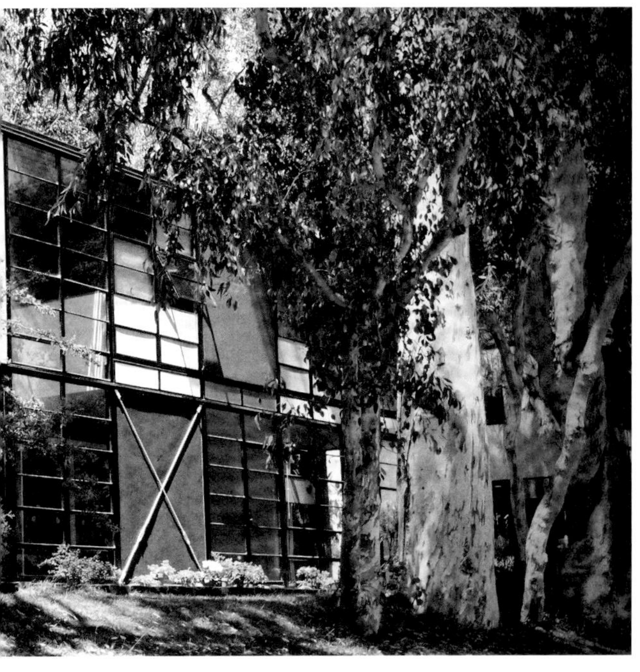

44/

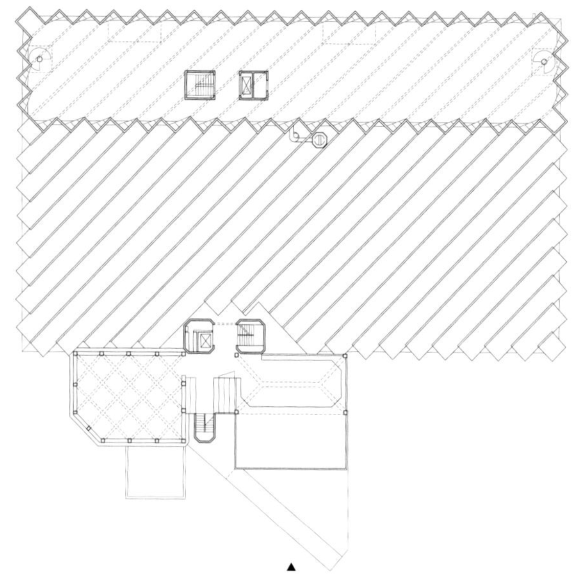

Floor Plan

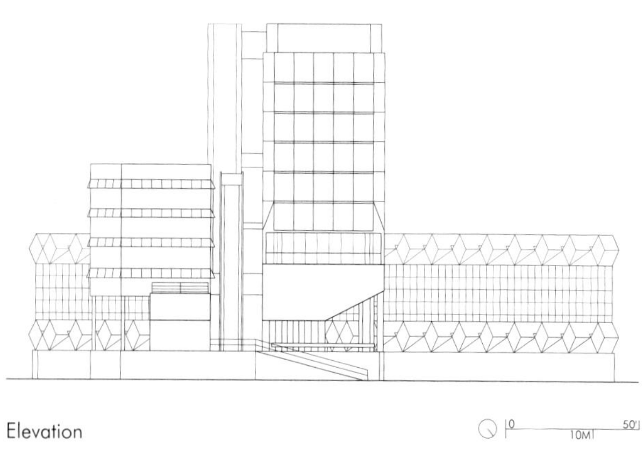

Elevation

1° 07' 25"W

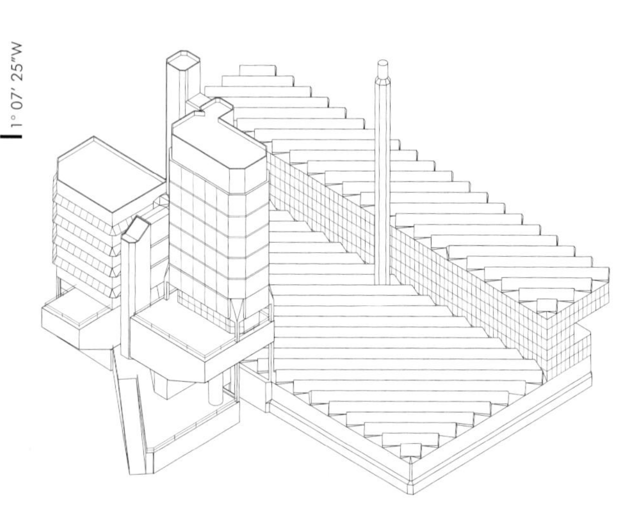

52° 37′ 13″N

18

LEICESTER UNIVERSITY ENGINEERING BUILDING

JAMES STIRLING and JAMES GOWAN
Leicester, England
1959–1963

Alternately petite and monumental in its scale and alternately modern and Gothic in its temperament, Stirling and Gowan's roguish Leicester Engineering Building was intended to present in a more comprehensive version the academic "machine" with which Stirling had experimented since his school days. Though its parts are shaped ostensibly by the functional aspects of its program—45-degree saw-toothed skylights for its open workshop spaces, controlled lighting in columnless laboratories, considerable daylight and views from the office tower, the opaque volumes of the auditoria candidly expressed—the building clearly evokes aspects of Constructivist composition and industrial romanticism. The interstitial circulatory elements, with their highly irregular—almost awkward—glazed prismatic enclosures both isolate and connect these various programmatic elements.

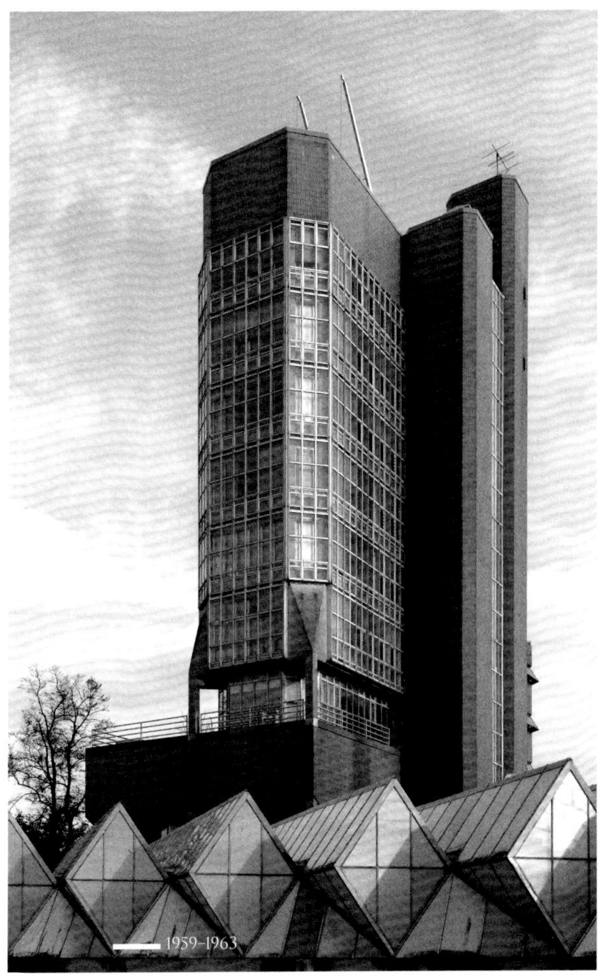
1959–1963

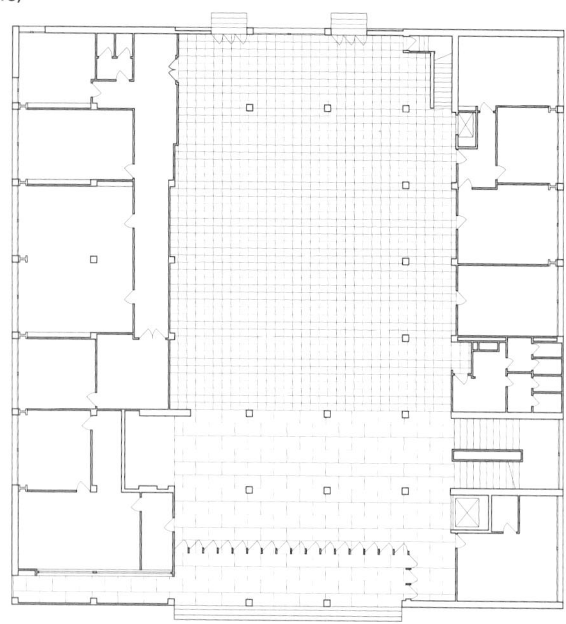

Floor Plan

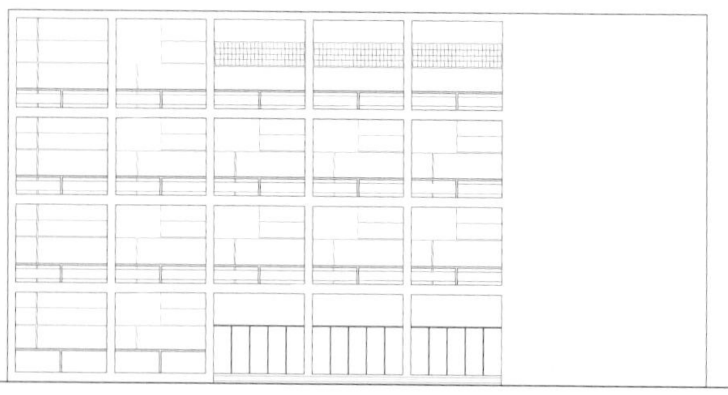

Elevation

0 5M 25'

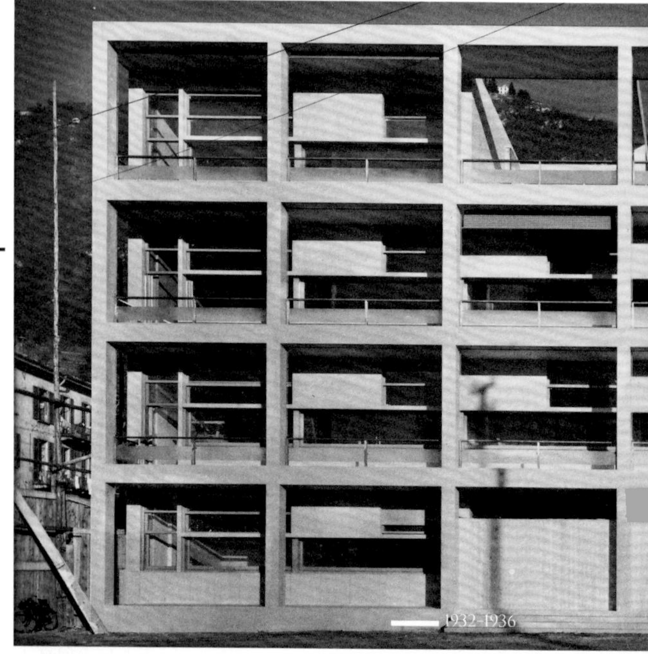

45° 48′ 44″N

19

CASA DEL FASCIO

GIUSEPPE TERRAGNI
Como, Italy
1932–1936

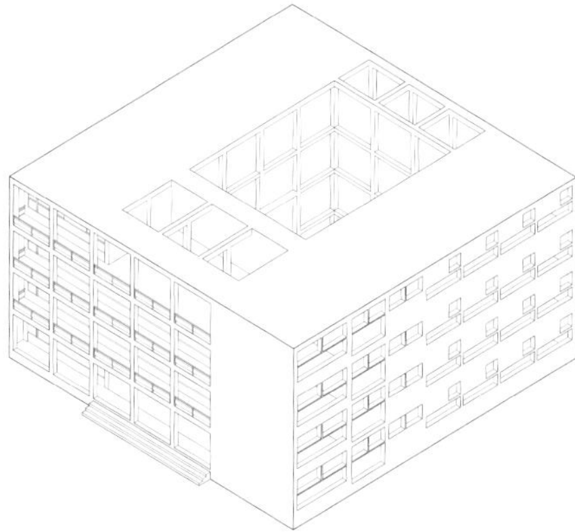

Based on the plan of the Palazzo Farnese in Rome, Giuseppe Terragni's Casa del Fascio (now Casa del Popolo) was a high point of Italian modernism, before the Fascist regime began to turn toward a more overt and affected neoclassicism. The building is articulated as a series of elements—frame, wall, and glass—almost abstract in their reductivism, that constantly transform in meaning as they continuously shift positions in relationship to one other. Each of the block's four facades provides a distinct variation of surface and depth, relating to the various programs and sunscreening necessities. The glass-roofed central "courtyard" is an extension of the piazza, with a series of sixteen glass doors that can be opened simultaneously, originally so that parades could begin within the structure before marching out into the city.

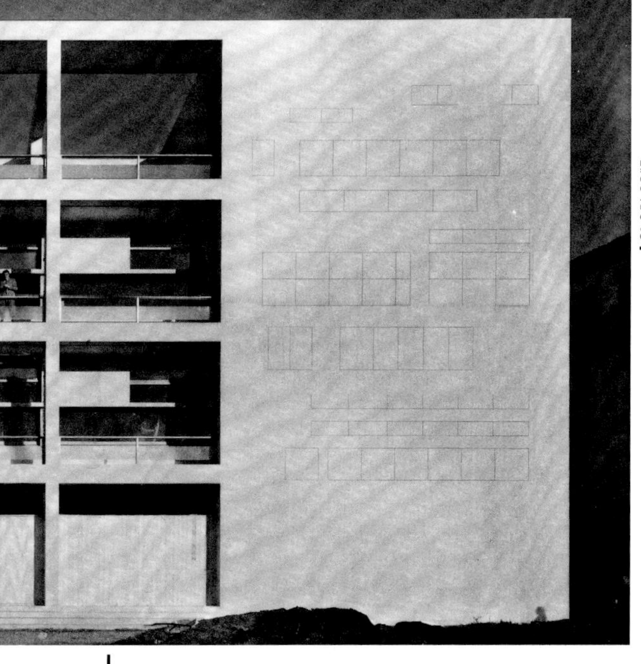

9° 05′ 09″E

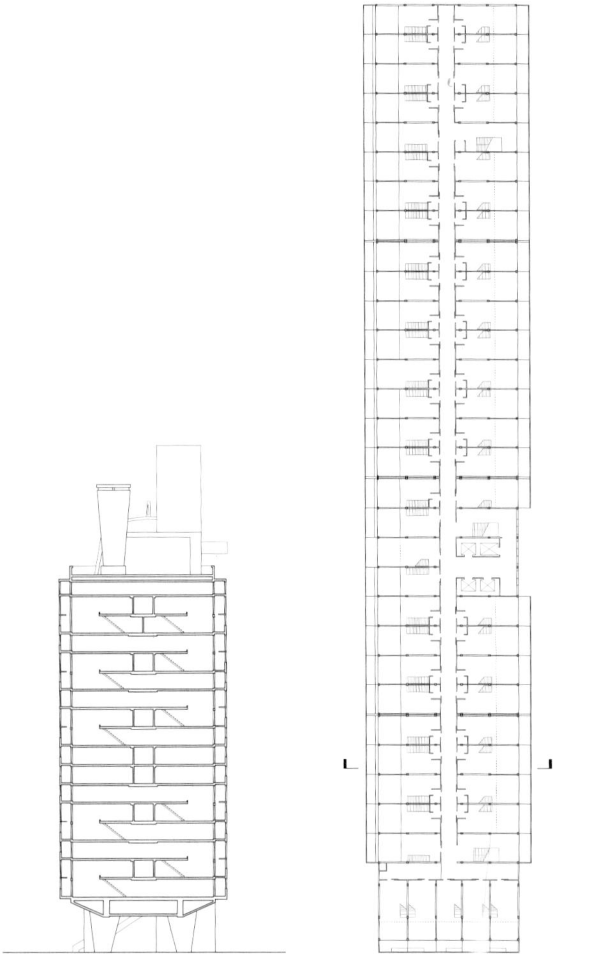

Section and Floor Plan

0 10M 50'

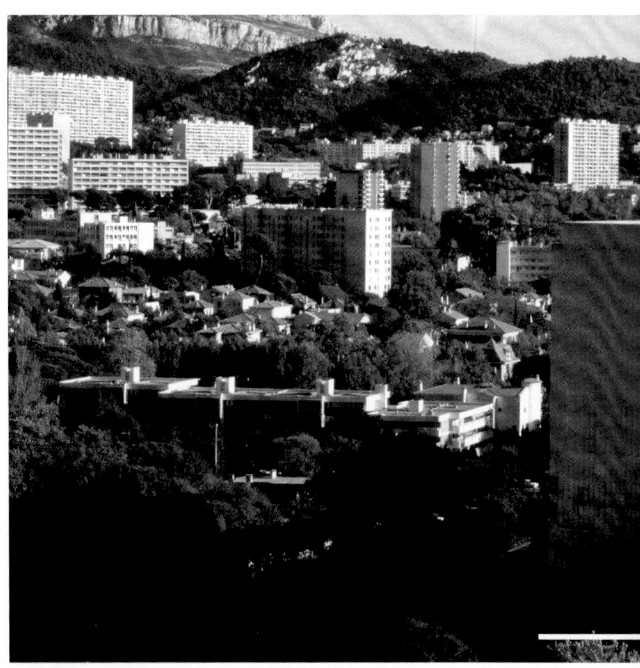

43° 15′ 42″N

20

L'UNITÉ D'HABITATION

LE CORBUSIER
Marseille, France
1945–1952

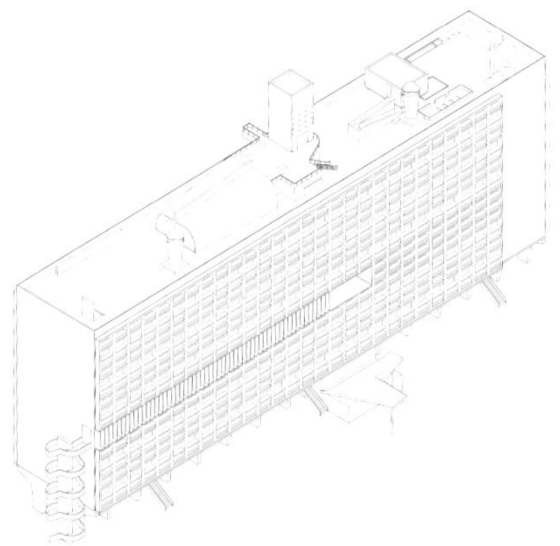

Constructed in five different cities, the Unités represent Le Corbusier's "five points" elevated to the scale of the city. A mixed-use, multifamily cruise ship of a building, the original Unité d'Habitation in Marseille reflects Le Corbusier's vision of communal living within the demands of postwar France. It was the prototypical "tower in the park," allowing the ground plane to flow freely beneath a building that houses up to 1,600 residents, while the roof becomes a small city of its own, with numerous volumes housing shared public spaces. The units designed for this complex—famously illustrated by the photograph of a hand inserting a unit shaped like a piano key into a gridded frame—allowed for cross-ventilation, permitted double-height spaces, created numerous terraces, and required corridors only on every third floor, minimizing circulation while maximizing exposure to breezes and views.

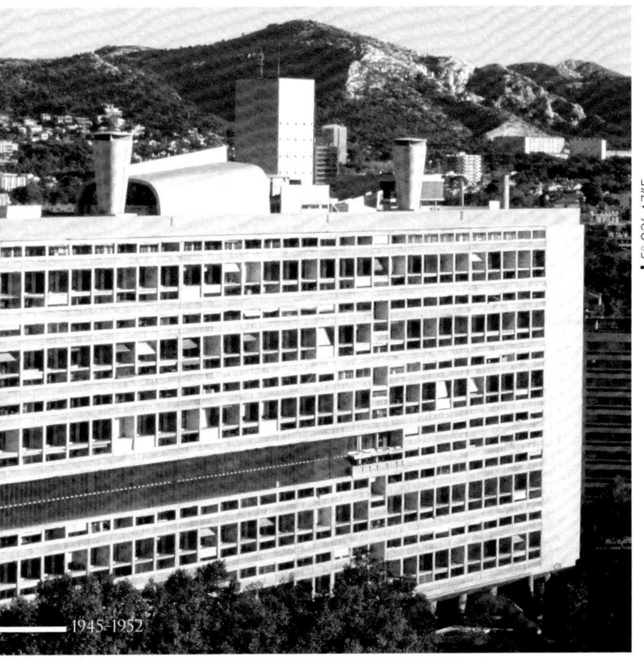

5° 23′ 47″E

1945–1952

45° 29′ 60″N

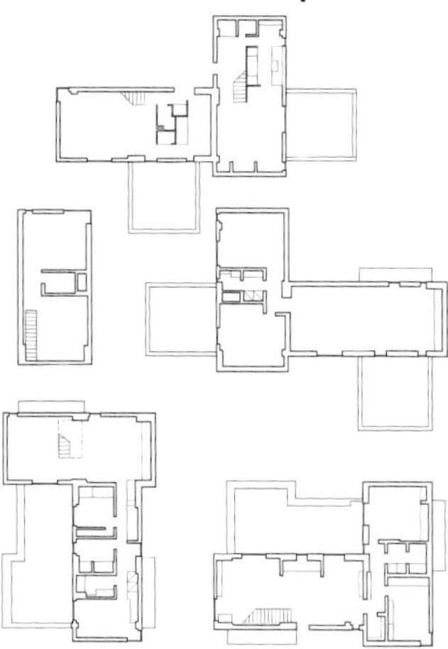

Sample Floor Plan

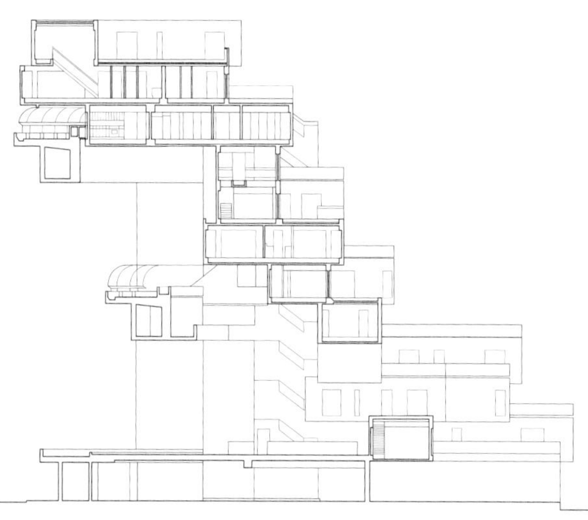

Section

0 25′ 5M

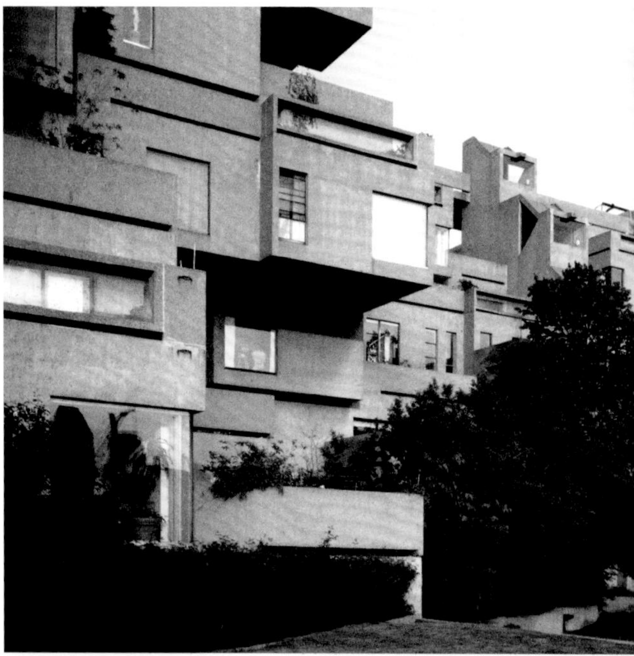

73° 32′ 37″W

21

HABITAT '67

MOSHE SAFDIE
Montréal, Canada
1967

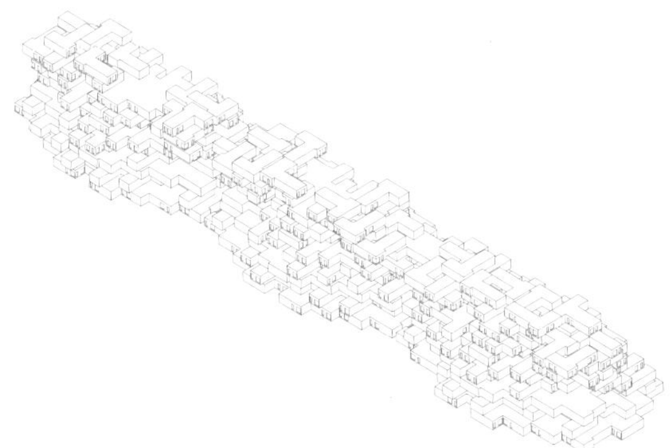

Constructed for the 1967 World Expo in Montréal, Moshe Safdie's Habitat '67 reimagined urban apartment living with a new three-dimensional housing typology intended to be constructed of prefabricated modular units (although the extreme differences in structural loading require the lower modules to be vastly different from the upper ones). Aiming for high density without sacrificing the quality of living in the suburbs, the units are organized within a network of three pyramids, with their vertical cores separated behind. The staggered formations of the "boxes," with varying setbacks and voids, allow for the appearance of an organic, village-like living situation with a rich array of urban gardens. A reaction to housing as efficient machine, Habitat '67 introduces the urban hill town.

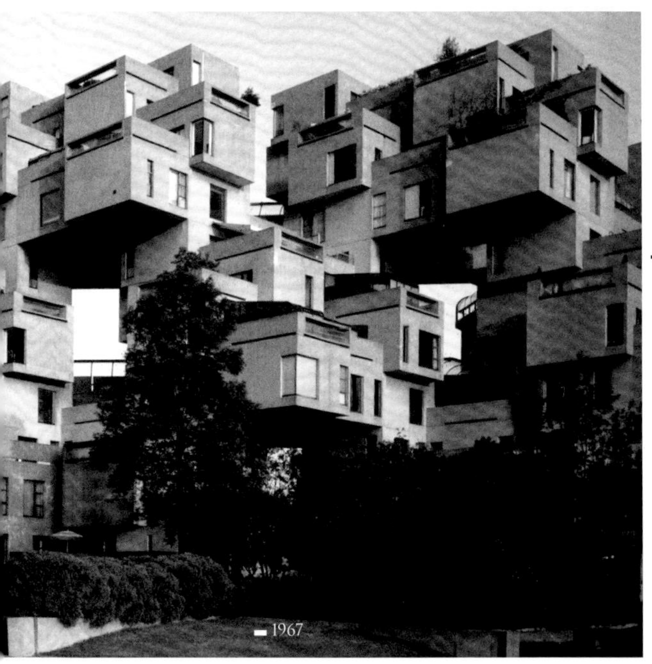

1967

32° 44′ 56″N

Floor Plan

Section

0 10M 50′

97° 21′ 54″W

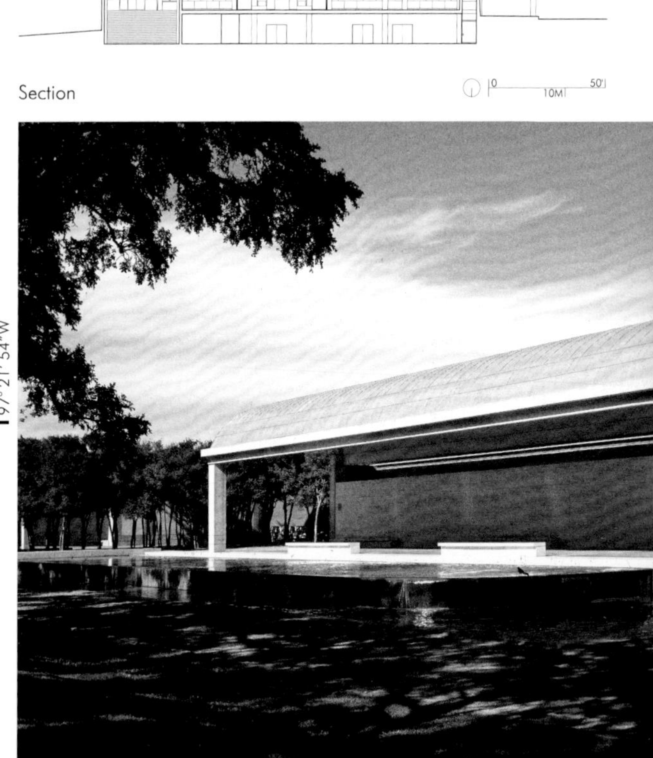

22

KIMBELL ART MUSEUM

LOUIS KAHN
Fort Worth, Texas, USA
1966–1972

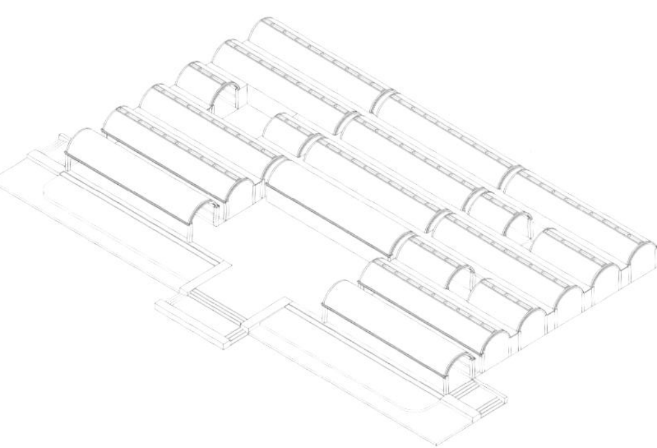

A perfect integration of Kahn's Beaux-Arts training with his contemporary exploration into primal volumes and light, the Kimbell's parti relies on five parallel barrel-vaulted bays (with a sixth set of bays acting as a portico) surfaced with travertine and contextualized by a curated forest. Within this picturesque siting and with a familiar language, rich materiality, and low profile, the Kimbell Museum becomes a quiet and accessible classically-symmetrical cultural monument. However, upon entering, the museum reveals extraordinary instances of spatial complexity, with several staggered courtyards, the capacity for unexpected programming, flexible circulation, and a myriad of daylight apertures, highlighted by the iconic skylight assembly that runs the longitudinal spine of each of the cleft barrel vaults. As it facilitates the curators' preferred use of daylight for exhibition, this highly engineered filtering fixture serves as an emblematic symbol for the museum and provides a contemporary counterpoint to the classic stone-and-concrete structure of the building.

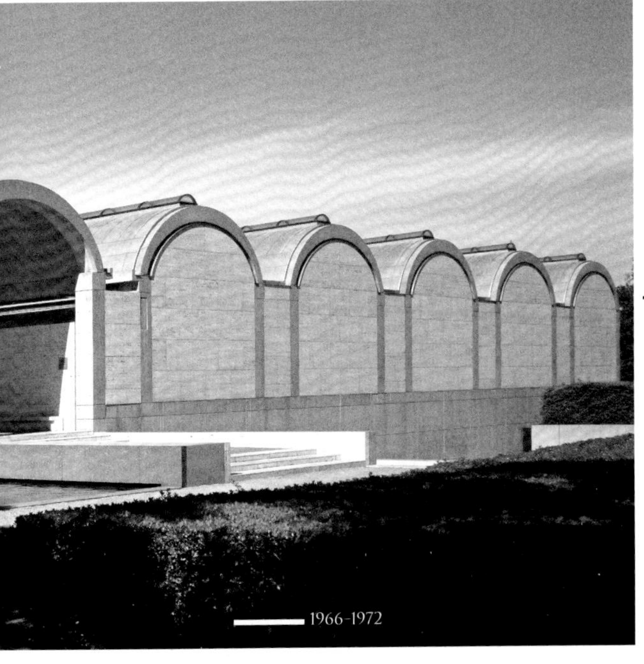

54/

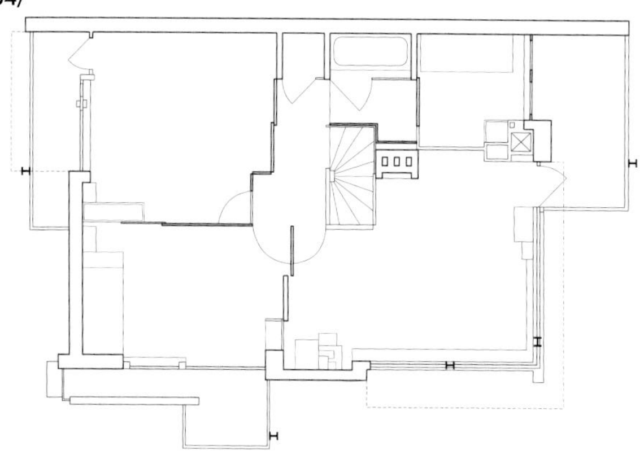

Floor Plan

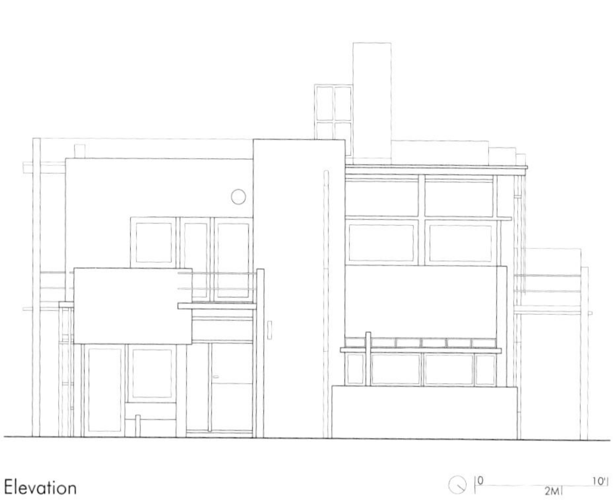

Elevation

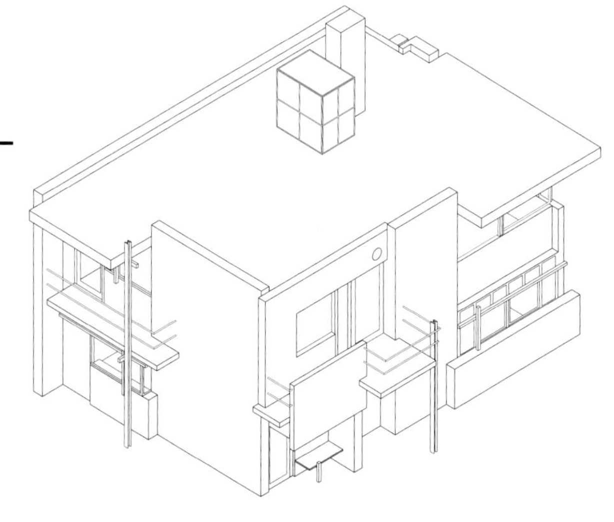

52° 05′ 07″N

23

SCHRÖDERHUIS
RIETVELD SCHRÖDER HOUSE

GERRIT RIETVELD
Utrecht, The Netherlands
1924, restored 1984–1985

A prime exemplar of the De Stijl movement, the Schröderhuis is located at the end of a row of earlier townhouses in Utrecht, and presents a cubic volume that fragments, dematerializes, and reassembles the features of these houses into a complex composition of lines and planes. These reinterpreted elements continuously extend between the interior and exterior, blurring the delineation and leaving little distinction between the two. Obsessive in its rectilinearity, with the windows even opening perpendicular to the facade planes, the house is composed almost exclusively of multi colored planar surfaces in every dimension and scale. Structural steel profiles stand in strong, solid colors detached from the walls. On the interior, rather than the traditional static aggregation of rooms, there is a dynamic, changeable open space, with movable walls on the upper floor allowing for zones of usage while reinforcing the building's continuous flow of space.

5° 08′ 51″E

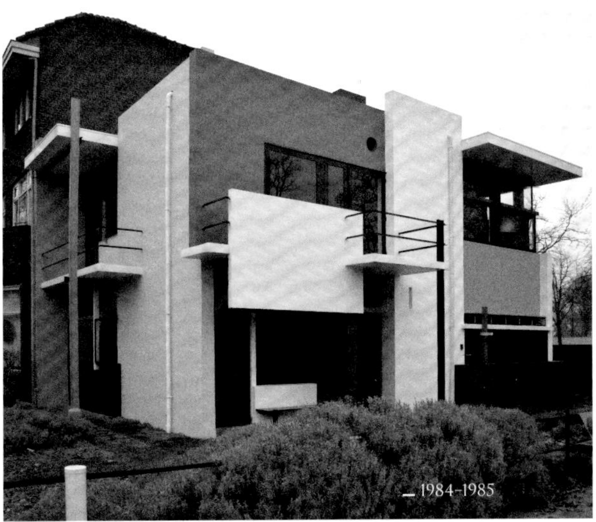
— 1984–1985

56/

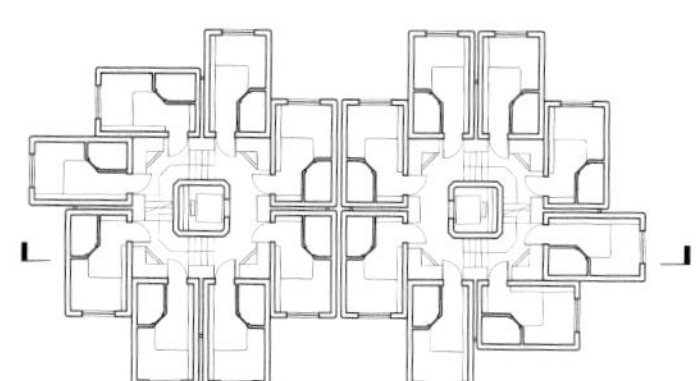

Floor Plan

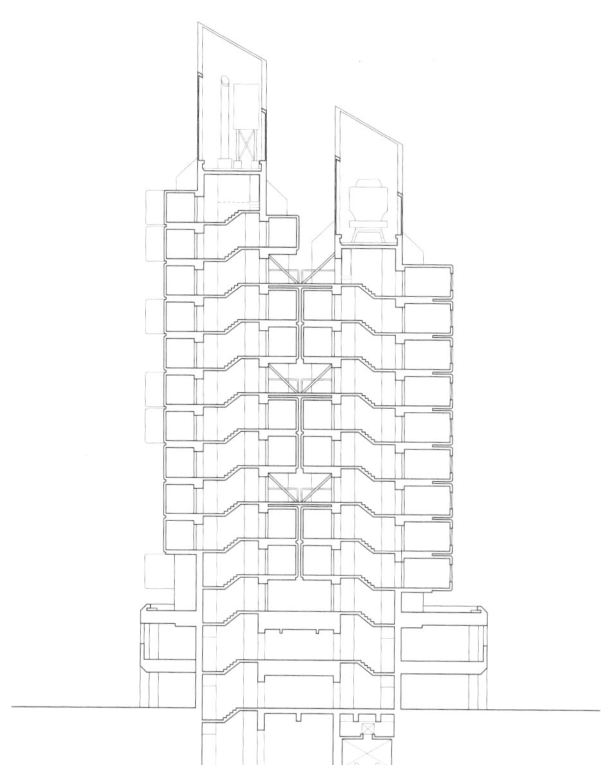

Section

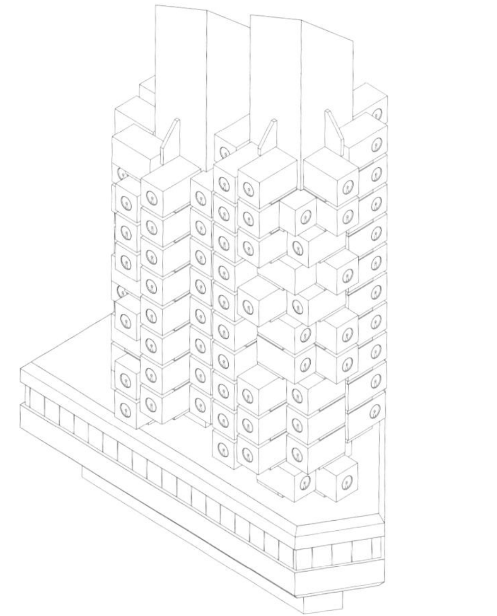

35° 39′ 57″N

24

NAKAGIN CAPSULE TOWER

KISHO KUROKAWA
Tokyo, Japan
1970–1972

A rare remaining example of Japanese Metabolism and a symbol of Japan's postwar cultural revival and optimism, the Nakagin Capsule Tower also represents the construction of one of late modernism's most pervasive fantasies: the fixed armature with prefabricated, pluggable components. A mixed-use residential and office building, it was designed to host traveling executives. Detachable modular-steel capsules are connected to two concrete cores containing stairs and elevators, one fourteen stories tall, the other twelve. Because of the variable stair landing, the 140 capsules are connected to the concrete shafts in multiple levels, providing an image of dynamism. Although the pre assembled interiors of the capsules were designed to accommodate either an office or studio apartment, the capsules could also be combined to host a family. While the initial intention was to replace the capsules with updated ones as they became obsolete, the actual design of the capsules and their attachment systems makes it necessary to remove the capsules only from the top downward.

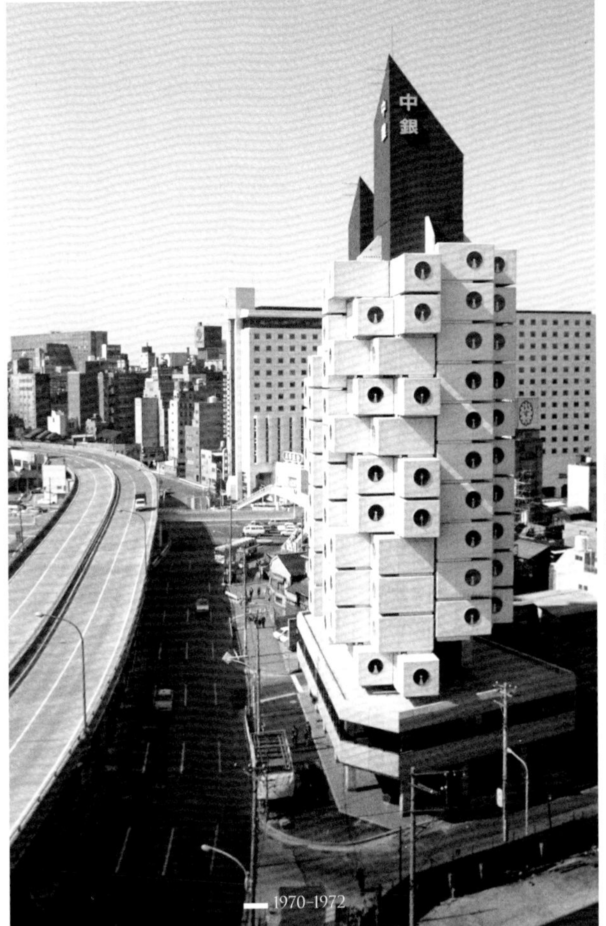

139° 45′ 48″E

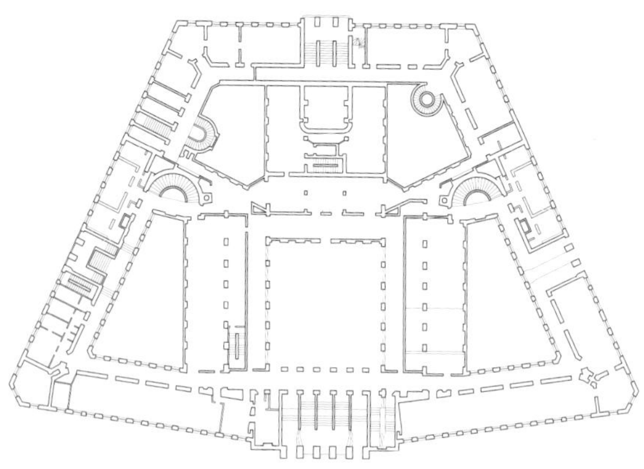

Floor Plan

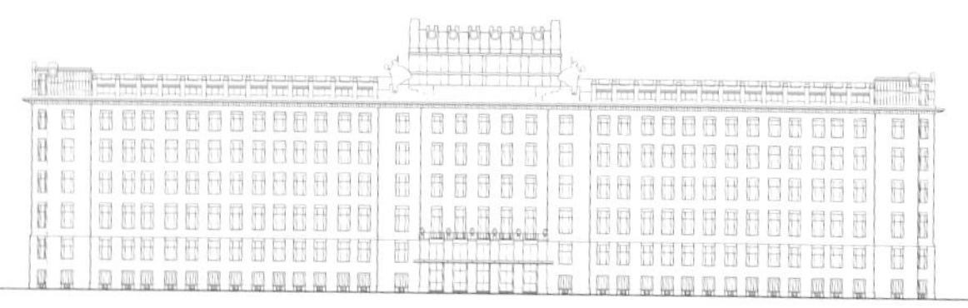

Elevation

0 100'
20M

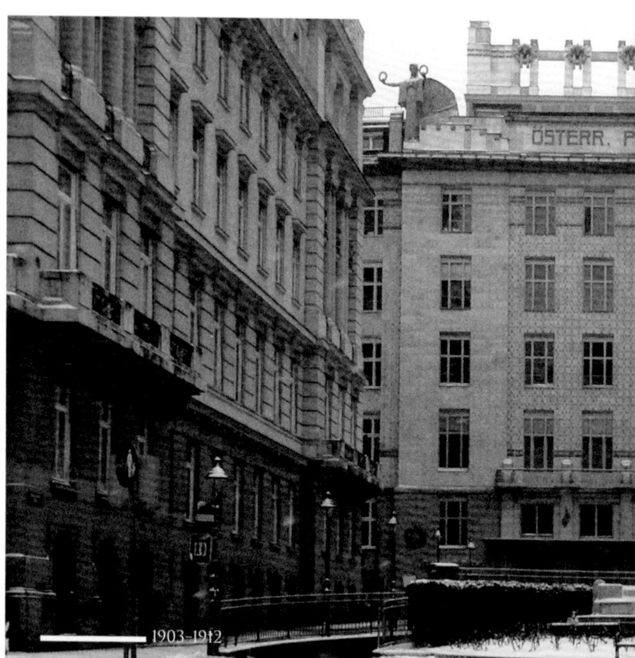

1903–1912

48° 12′ 36″N

25

POST OFFICE SAVINGS BANK

OTTO WAGNER
Vienna, Austria
1903–1912

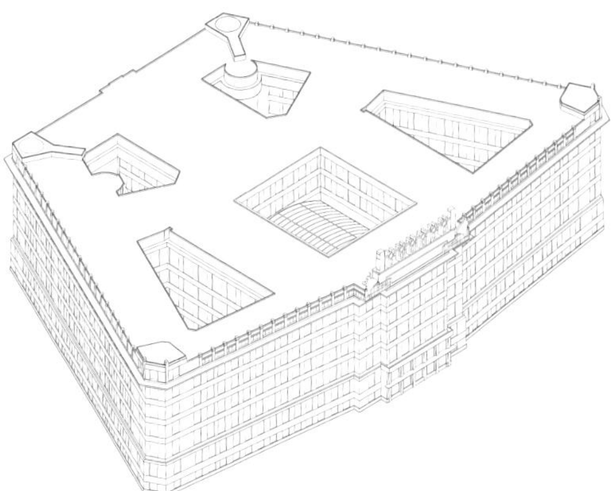

Astonishingly ahead of its time, with "bolted" exterior panels, a glass banking floor, exposed cast-iron columns, a vast glazed atrium (originally to have been hoisted by cables and masts), movable interior office partitions, and an aluminum air-handling system that is exposed and even monumentalized, Wagner's Postsparkasse occupies the cusp between the nineteenth century, with its neoclassicism and Art Nouveau, and twentieth century modernism. Eschewing the false "costuming" of most of Vienna's architecture, Wagner set out to produce a large public institution that was almost completely devoid of gratuitous decoration, with the exception of the wreaths and acroteria (by Othmar Schimkowitz) that were, uncharacteristically, constructed in aluminum. Most of the lighting fixtures and furnishings throughout the structure were also designed by Wagner, with the same starkly elegant aesthetic.

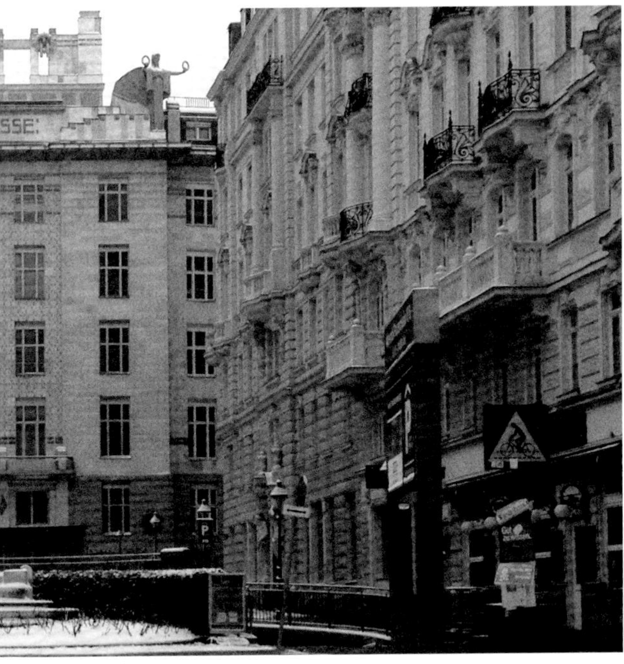

16° 22′ 52″E

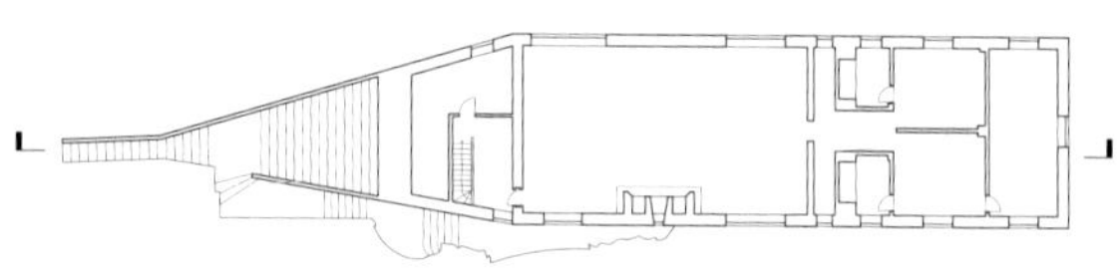

Floor Plan

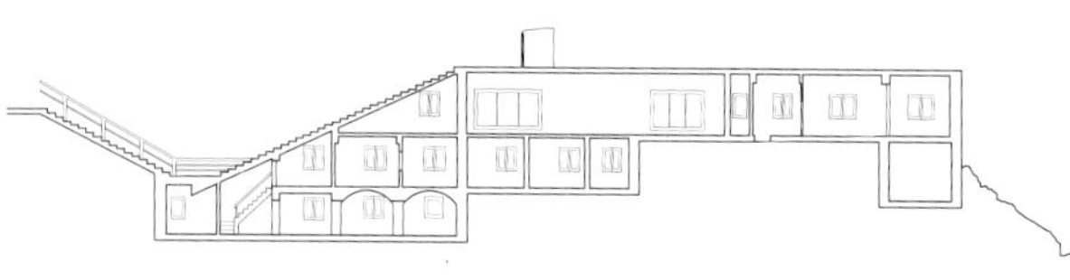

Section

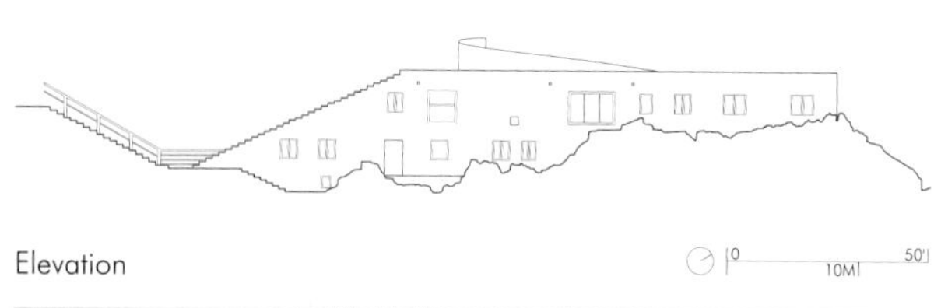

Elevation

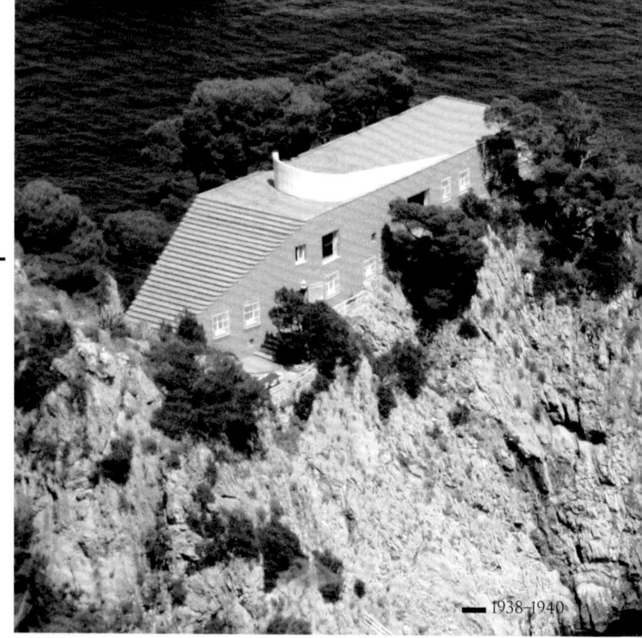

40° 32′ 49″N

26

CASA COME ME
CASA MALAPARTE

CURZIO MALAPARTE
Capri, Italy
1938–1940

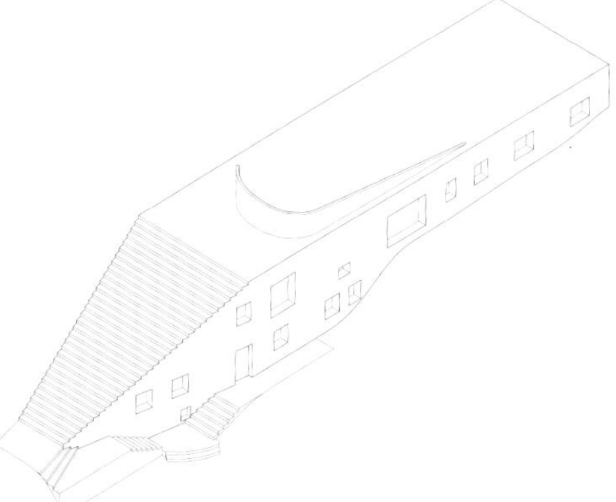

Emerging and merging, crisp and singular, from the rough, rocky cliffs of Capri, overlooking the Tyrrhenian Sea, Casa Malaparte is a house that can be understood concurrently as a stair, a rock, a vertiginous platform, and a refuge. According to Alessia Rositani Suckert, "Though sometimes attributed to architect Adalberto Libera, 'Casa Come Me' is the creation of its owner, Curzio Malaparte, who presented sketches to a draftsman, Umberto Bonetti, envisioning a highly personal, expressive home for himself; literally, a 'house like me'." One can arrive by boat, ascend countless stairs up a huge cliff to find oneself at the base of a monumental, wedge-shaped stair—an autobiographical reference to his exile on the island of Lipari—leading to a large, flat stage that provides only a sail-like screen and an infinite horizon. Beneath and within all of these theatrics is the house itself, with its calculated series of windows opening as framed seascapes from each discrete room.

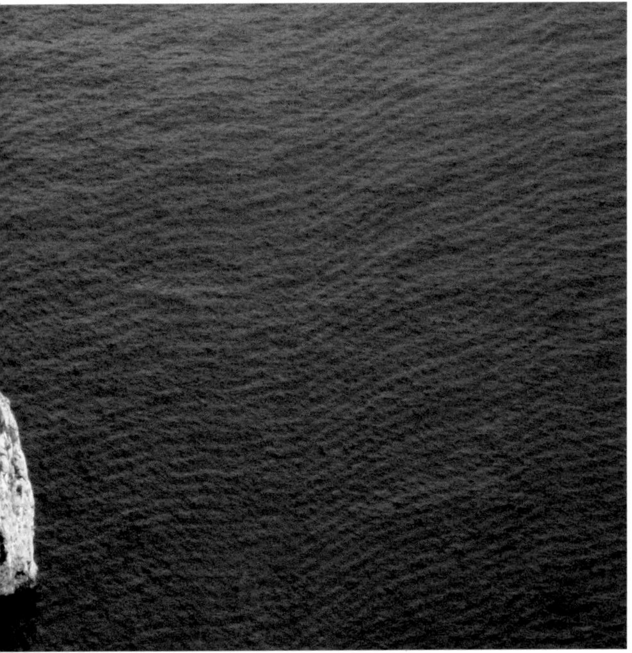

14° 15′ 33″E

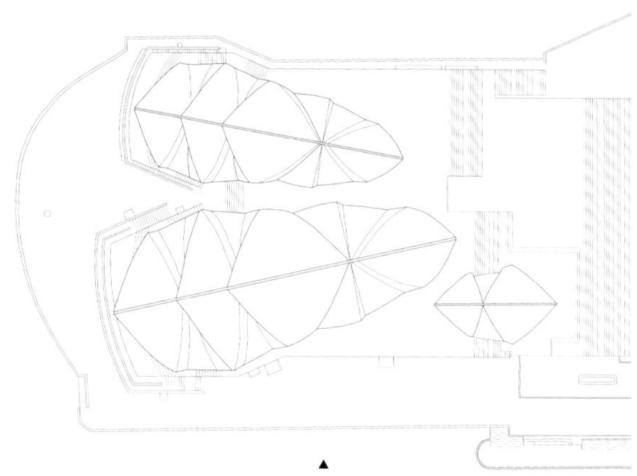

Roof Plan

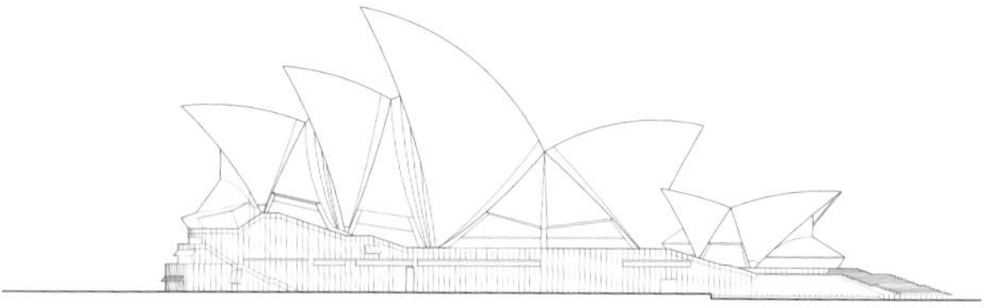

Elevation

0 30M 150'

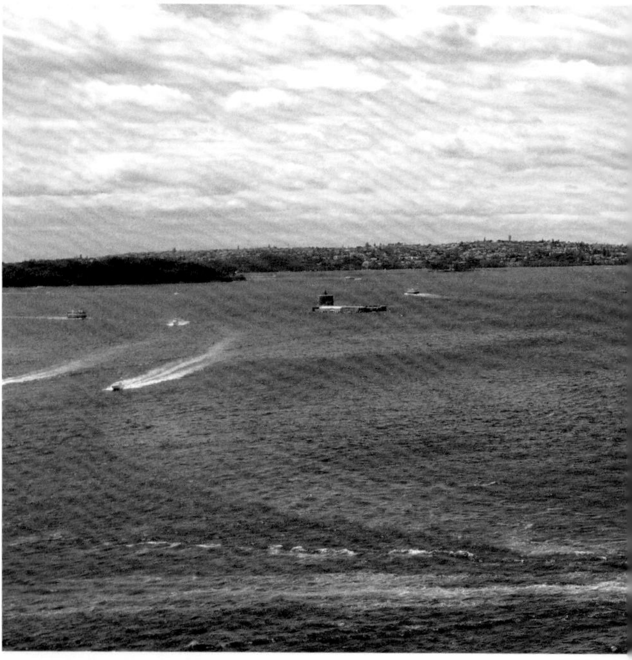

27

SYDNEY OPERA HOUSE

JØRN UTZON
Sydney, Australia
1957–1973

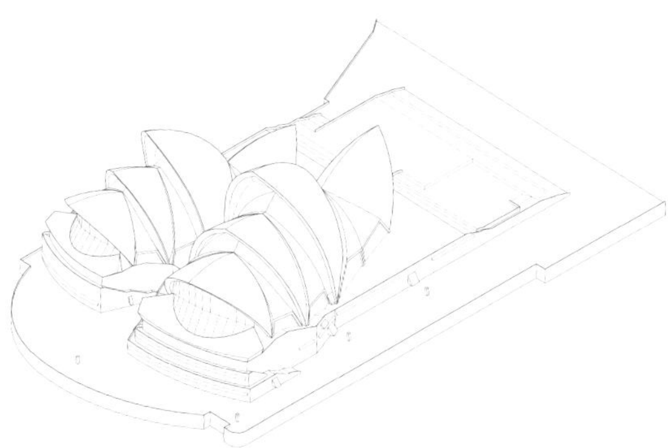

The result of a competition held in 1957, the Sydney Opera House is undoubtedly one of the most iconic buildings of the twentieth century. Located on a peninsula in Sydney Harbor, a graciously stepped plinth leads visitors upward to an array of performance spaces, as well as numerous public spaces overlooking the water. Dominating the plinth are a series of shell-like elements that, despite their apparent freeform qualities, are geometrically derived from sections of a sphere. As developed by Utzon and Ove Arup, this permits the "shells" to be constructed of a series of precast concrete panels attached to precast arches, all cast from the same molds. While Utzon had originally hoped to shape the shells directly in relation to their acoustic properties, this proved too difficult to achieve. Instead, their eventual forms serve to provide ample area for the fly lofts and other mechanical aspects of the various halls.

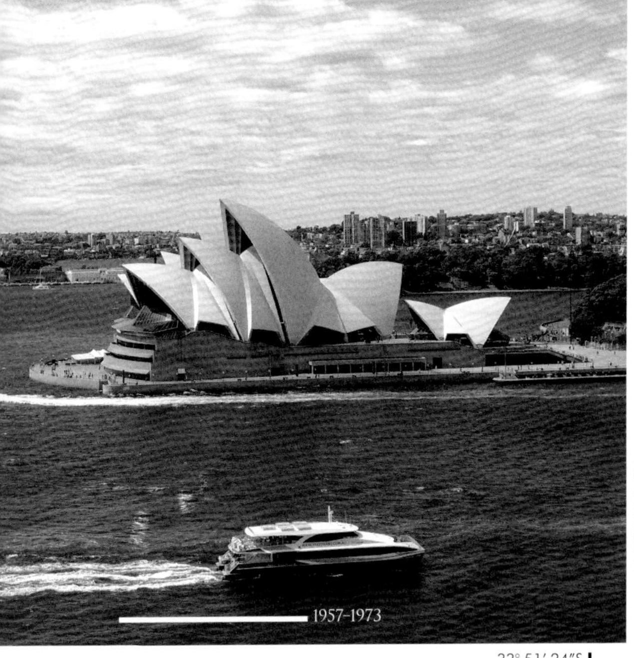

151° 12′ 55″E

33° 51′ 24″S

41° 18′ 32″N

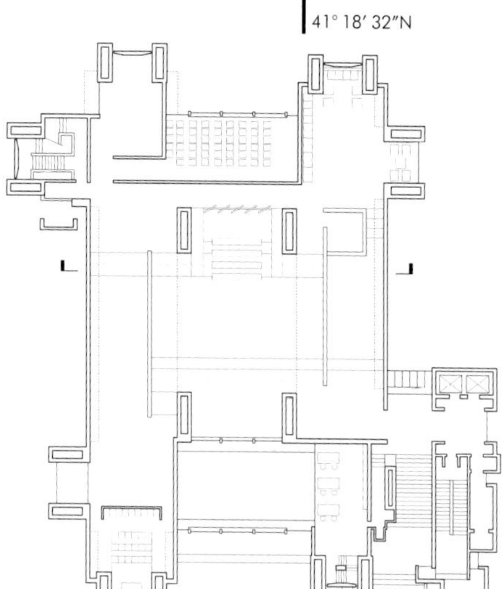

Floor Plan

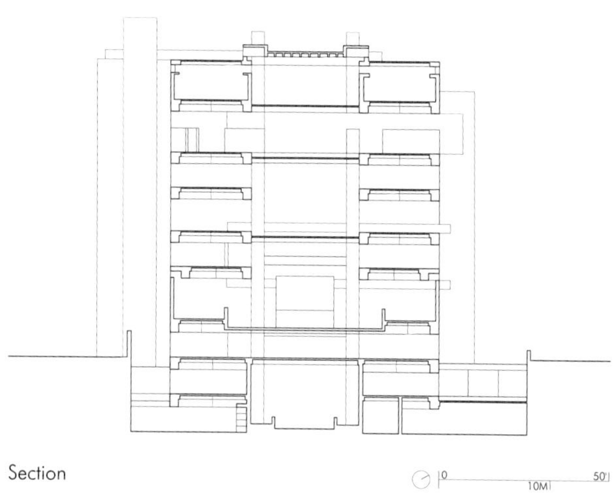

Section

72° 55′ 54″W

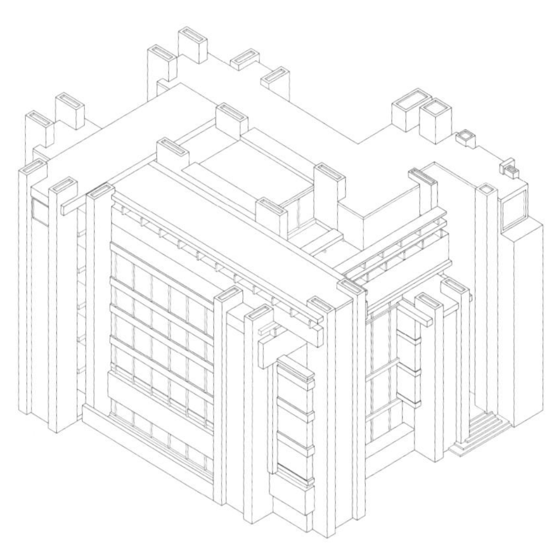

28

RUDOLPH HALL

Yale Art and Architecture Building

PAUL RUDOLPH
New Haven, Connecticut, USA
1958–1964

A baroquely brutalist building, with thirty-seven levels passing through its seven stories and two basement levels, the Yale Art and Architecture Building (now Rudolph Hall) is undoubtedly Paul Rudolph's most intricate—and witty—statement on modernism and its sources. Quite Wrightian in plan, it is distinctly Piranesian in sectional perspective (an important representational technique in Rudolph's design process). Its exterior emphasizes the verticality of its ribbed concrete piers, with thickened horizontal slabs interlocking and intersecting in the interstices. The building is often considered to be a tutorial on the proper resolution of a dense corner site.

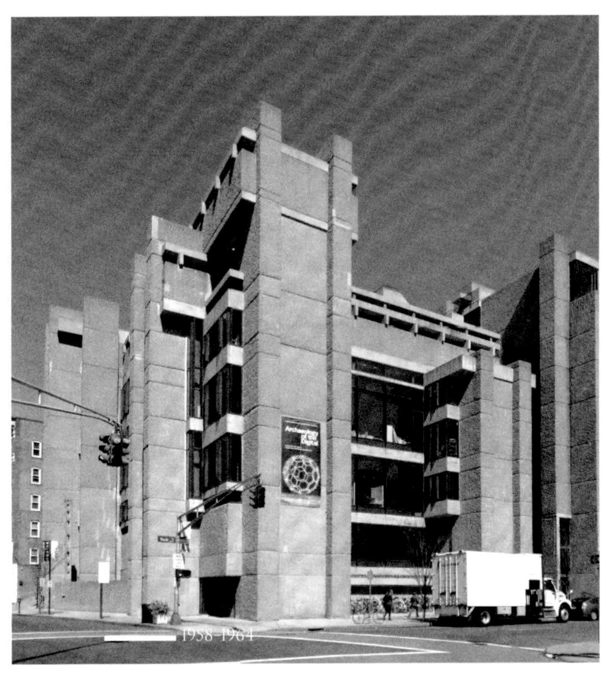

42° 58′ 45″N

Floor Plan

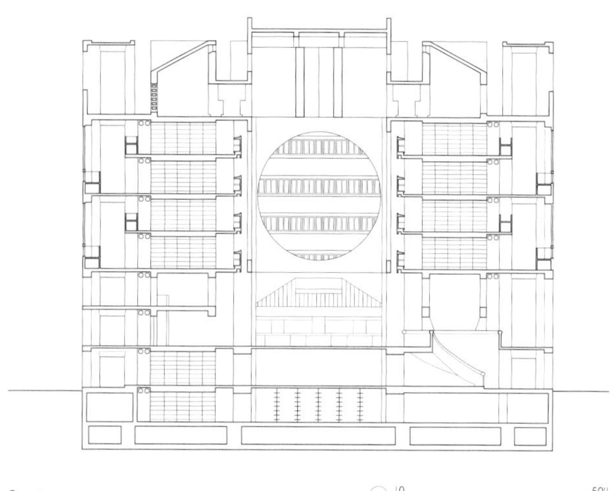

Section

0 10M 50'

70° 56′ 58″W

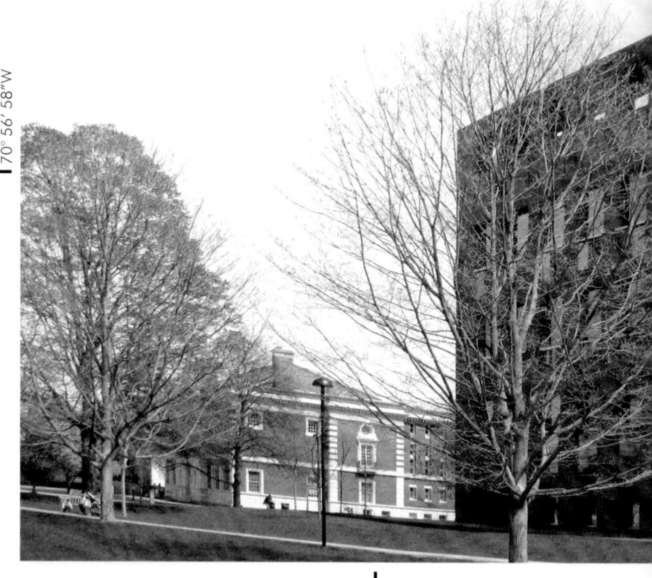

29

PHILLIPS EXETER ACADEMY LIBRARY

LOUIS KAHN
Exeter, New Hampshire, USA
1965–1971

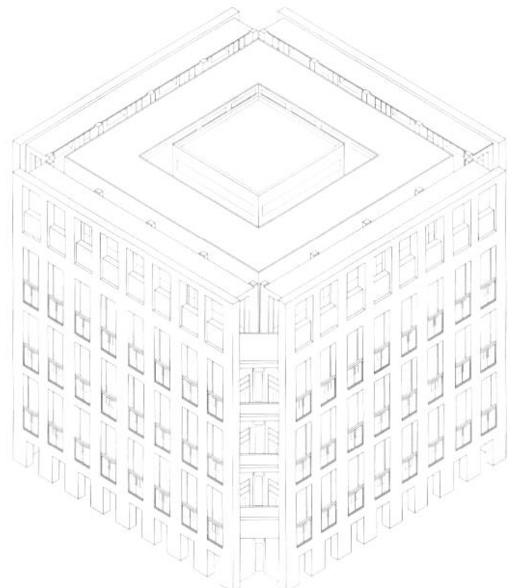

The Exeter Library makes manifest much of Kahn's thinking on the relationship of historical monumentality and modernism, the collective and the individual, and the presence of light and shadow. Book stacks are organized around a four-story interior atrium lit with indirect sunlight and with elevations that are a quartet of immense circular concrete portals, revealing views of the books within. The brick exterior wall is broken down into a grid of smaller-scaled glass-and-teak openings at each floor, with shuttered windows that are integrated within the custom-designed study carrels that line the perimeter. The favored themes of silence and light in this cathedral of a library would go on to be realized in other forms in subsequent projects for art museums in Fort Worth and Yale.

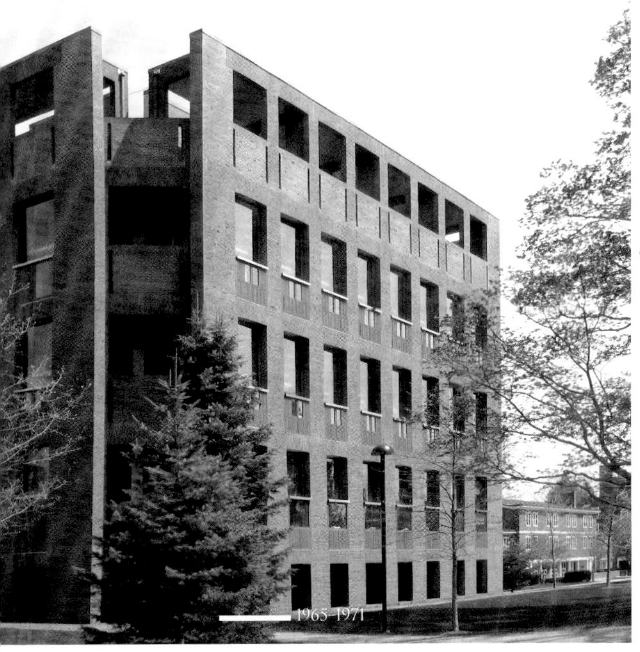

1965–1971

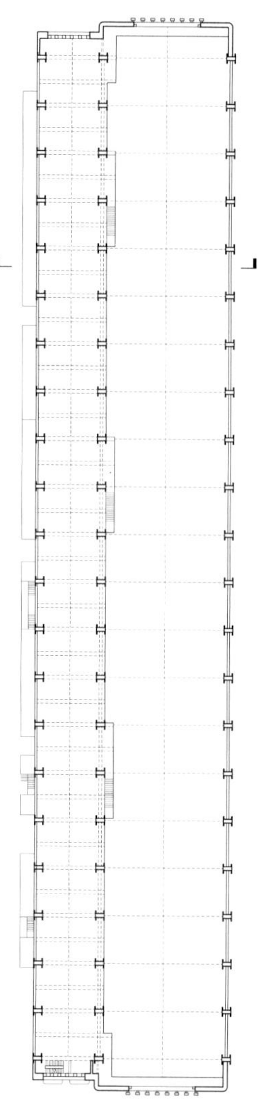

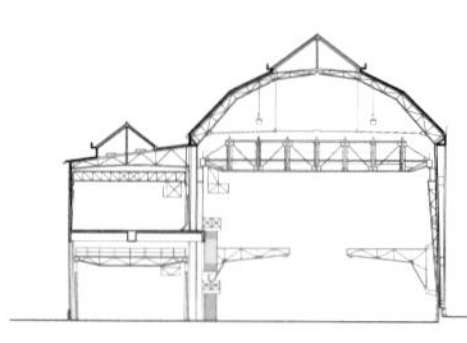

Section and Floor Plan

0 20M 100'

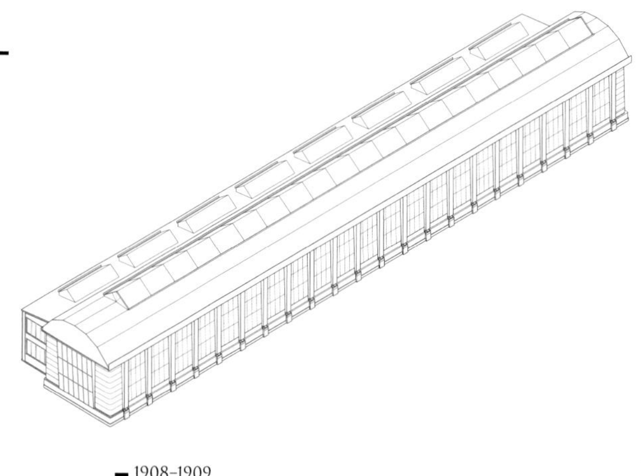

1908–1909

52° 31′ 41″N

30

AEG TURBINE FACTORY

PETER BEHRENS
Berlin, Germany
1908–1909

A progenitor of modern architecture in Berlin, Behrens's turbine hall (engineered by Karl Bernhard) combines a highly reductive two-story block, tapered cast-in-place concrete end walls, and a sequence of segmented, asymmetrical three-hinged steel frames—rather barnlike in contour—with canted glass walls between the exposed steel members, admitting daylight to the building interior. The gentle inclination of the concrete end-wall elements, especially at the corner, stand in stark contrast to the vertical steel columns, exaggerating their thinness while reinforcing the notion that these solid walls are primarily infill and not structural. The steel frames, with their massive exposed hinges above a concrete base, support a continuous steel entablature. The building is a unique expression of the intersection of classical monumentality and factorylike machine modernism, its primary formal expression being that of a tall, elongated basilical space, with a parallel two-storied side aisle: a veritable cathedral of industry at the inception of the twentieth century.

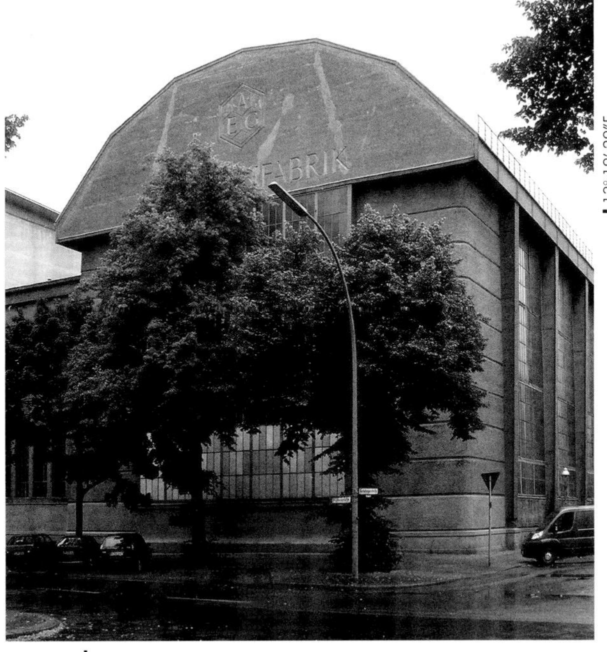

13° 19′ 29″E

41° 47′ 23″N

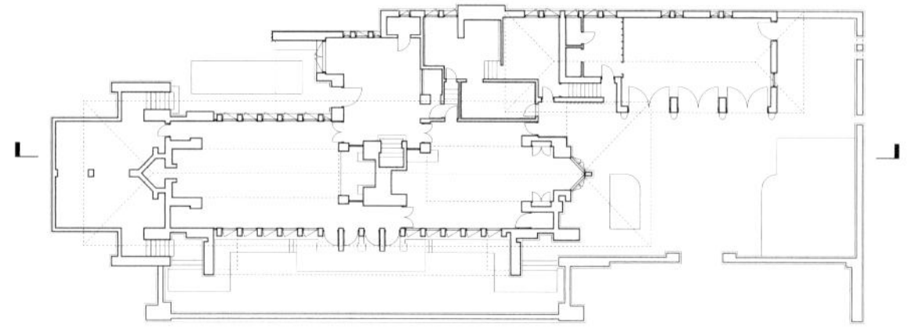

Floor Plan

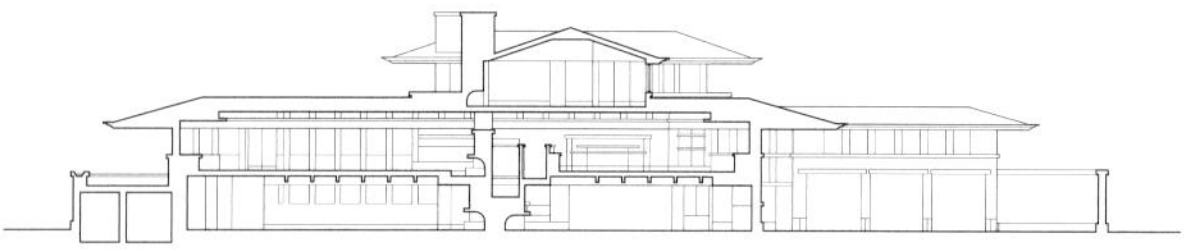

Section

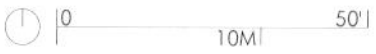

0 10M 50′

87° 35′ 45″W

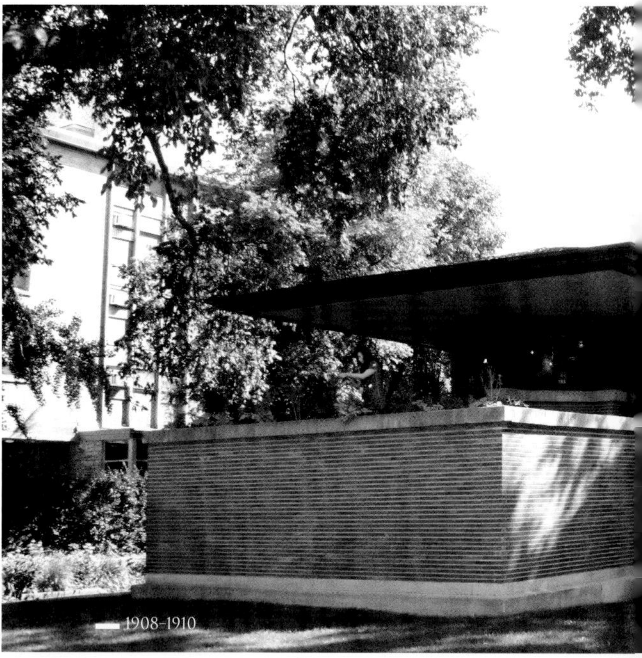

1908–1910

31

FREDERICK C. ROBIE HOUSE

FRANK LLOYD WRIGHT
Chicago, Illinois, USA
1908–1910

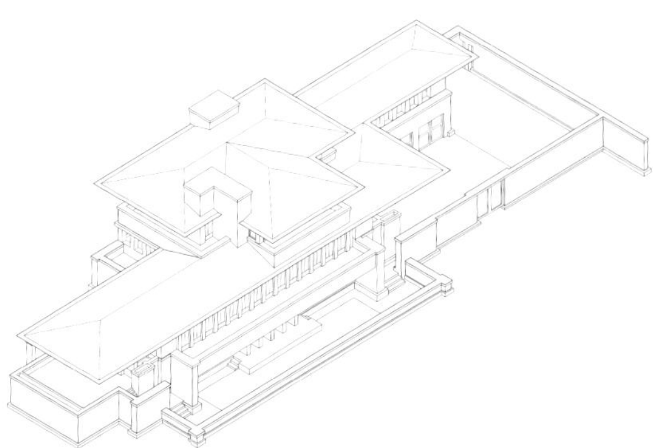

Built for Frederick C. Robie and his family, this is a three-story house with attached garage and motor court. Embodying all of the principles of the Prairie style, the building is perhaps most famous for its overwhelming horizontality of expression—achieved in part by the use of thin Roman bricks along with two unique masonry details: horizontal joints in warm white mortar and vertical joints in dark red mortar matching the bricks. A sloping horizontal strike joint on the mortar casts a pronounced shadow from one course to another. Public rooms—primarily living and dining—are located on a modest plinth looking out to the street; both rooms share visual access to a shared, monumental brick hearth opening to both sides while organizing vertical circulation. Custom stained-glass windows provide a delicate interplay of light and shadow throughout the main space. A billiard room and a children's playroom that open to a walled court serve to separate the house vertically and horizontally from the street.

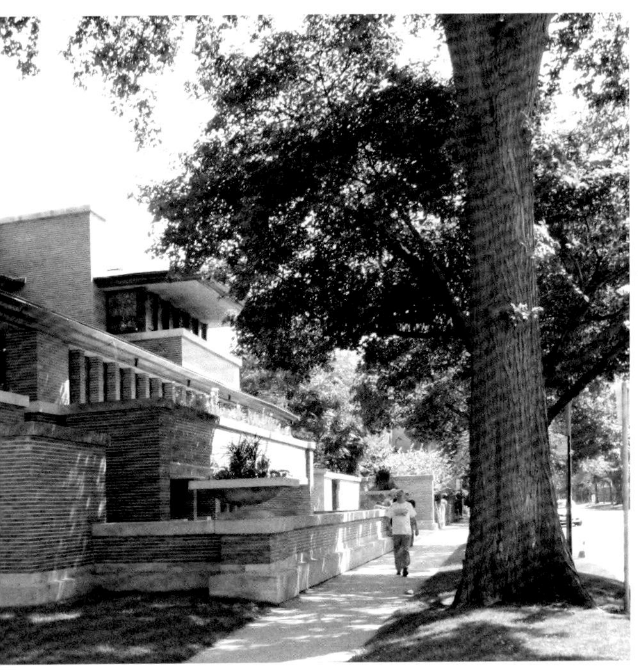

34° 05′ 11″N

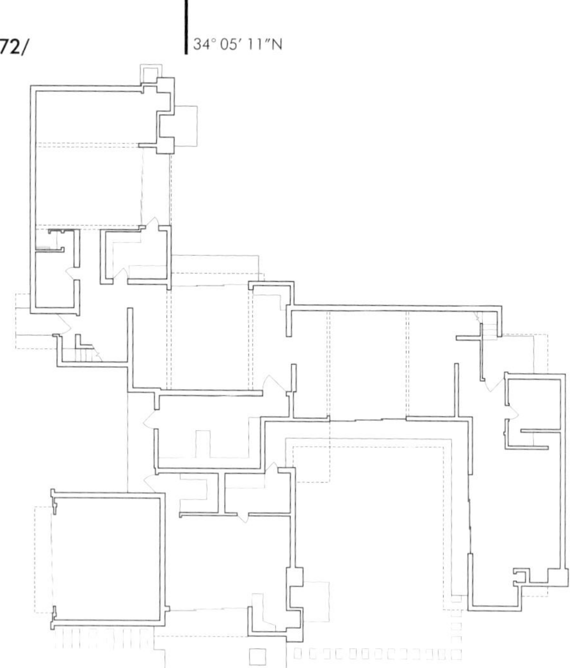

Floor Plan

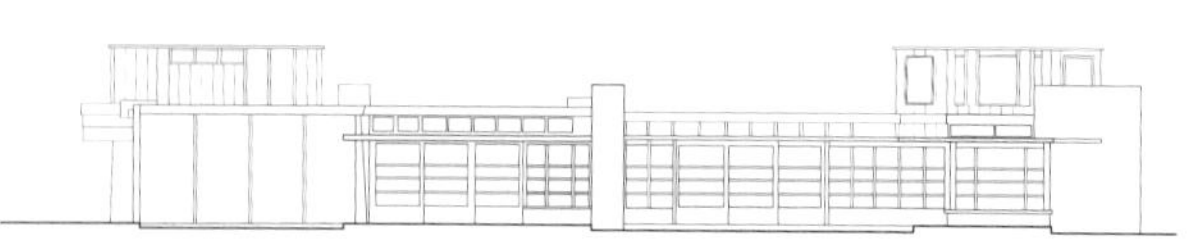

Elevation

118° 22′ 20″W

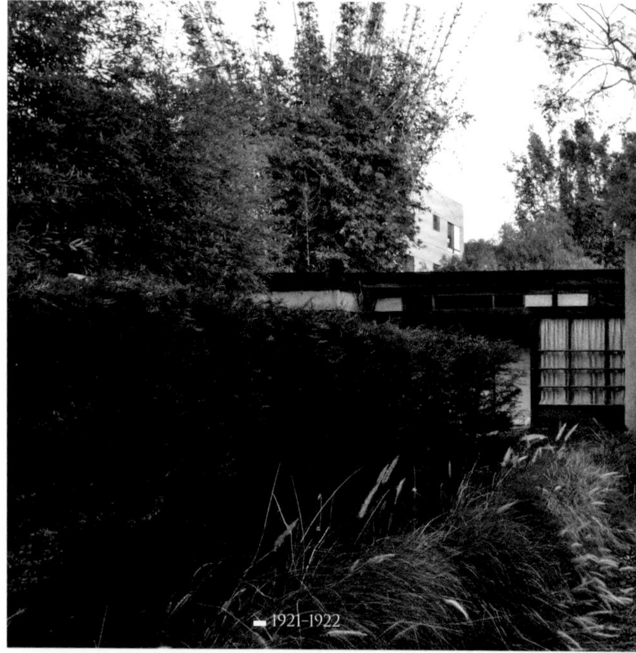

1921–1922

32

SCHINDLER HOUSE

RUDOLF SCHINDLER
West Hollywood, California, USA
1921–1922

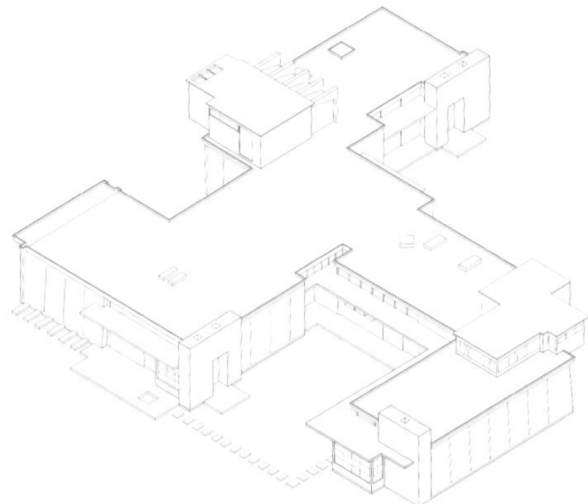

Schindler's design for his house was the birth of Southern California modernism, with complete integration between indoor and outdoor spaces. Rather than locating the house as an object within the suburban lot, Schindler assigned spatial and functional values to the entire site. The result is one of continuous reciprocity between solid and void, enclosure and openness, landscape and building. Courtyards (some with their own exterior fireplaces) and external niches are engulfed within the program as if "rooms" within the house's three-quarter pinwheel, separated only by sliding doors, frames, and canopies, with canted concrete walls bounding the private realms. The house is also experimental in its programmed living spaces, designed for communal living for two couples, with a shared kitchen, private retreats and gardens for each resident, and sleeping porches elevated over the entries.

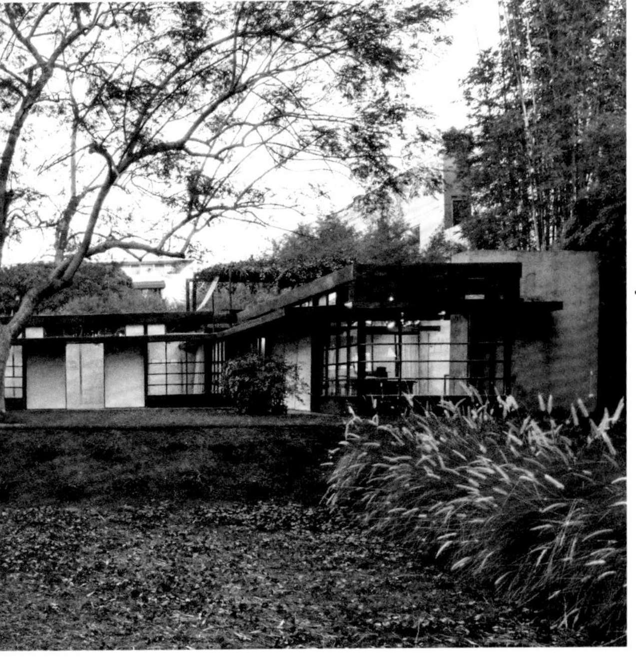

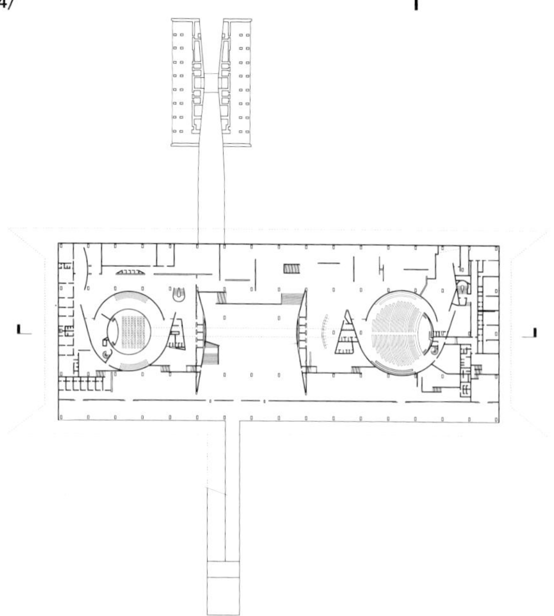

Floor Plan

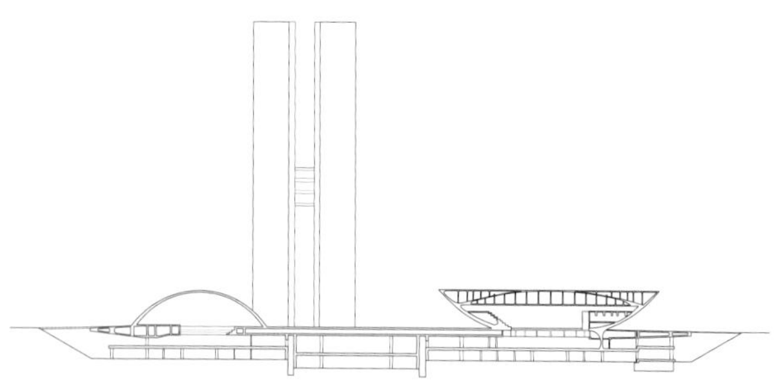

Section

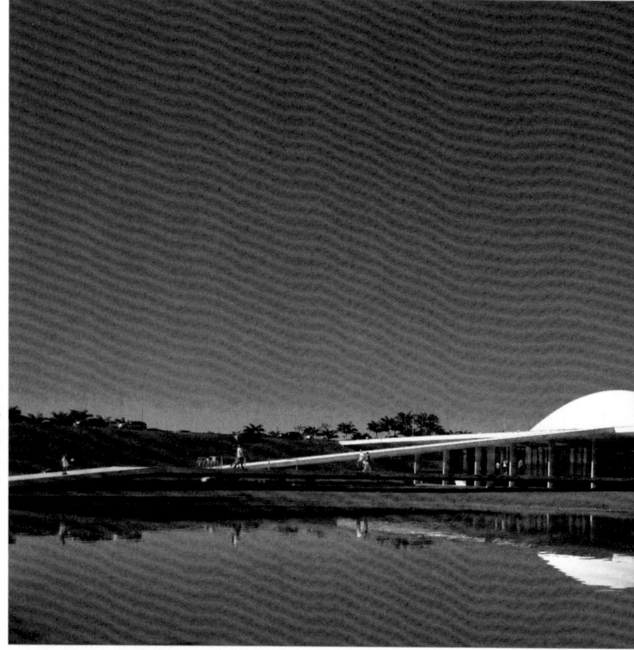

47° 51' 51"W

15° 47' 58"S

33

NATIONAL CONGRESS, BRAZIL

OSCAR NIEMEYER
Brasília, Brazil
1958–1960

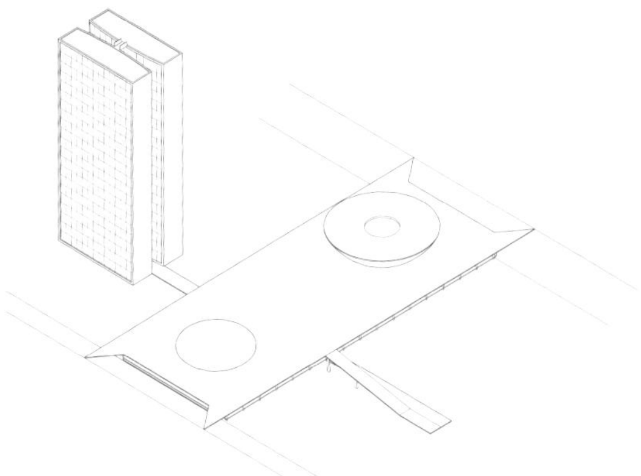

Occupying an end of the vast central axis of Lúcio Costa's airplane-like master plan for the new city of Brasília, Oscar Niemeyer's congress complex uses basic forms to represent Brazil's legislative democracy. Recomposing the elements of Costa's original sketch for the complex, Niemeyer situates two interconnected rectangular stelae (the legislative offices) in a reflecting pool behind a table-like surface upon which rests two truncated spheres, one domed and the other inverted, each holding one of the two houses of the bicameral legislature. The two avenues that form the Monumental Axis slope upward to meet the top of the plinth, providing an elevated horizon that isolates these elements as if components of a giant still life of pure geometries.

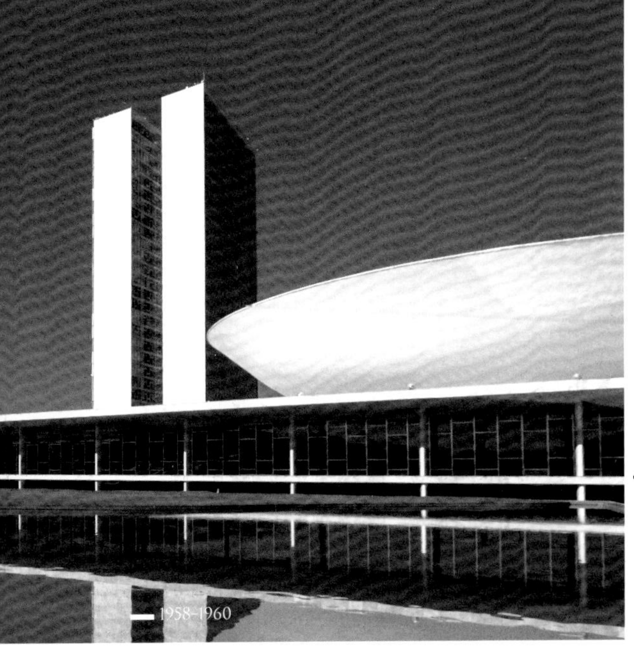

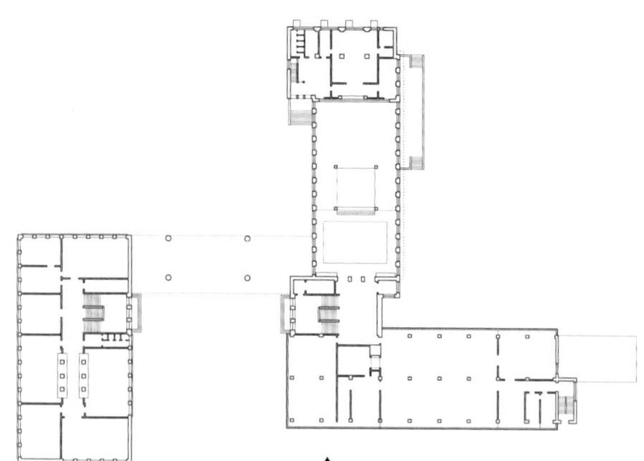

Floor Plan

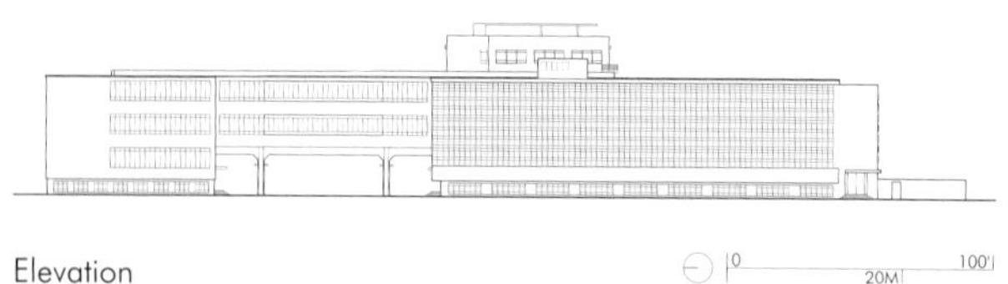

Elevation

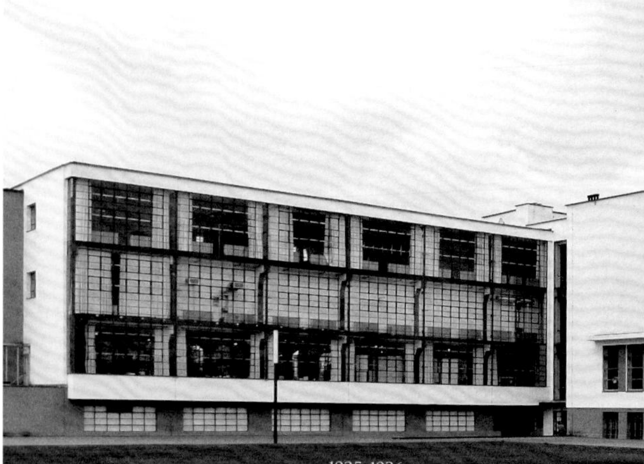

1925–1926

51° 50′ 23″N

34

BAUHAUS DESSAU

WALTER GROPIUS and ADOLF MEYER
Dessau, Germany
1925–1926

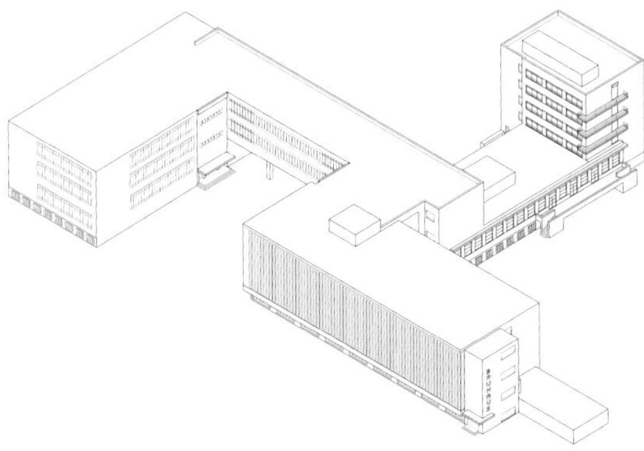

The Bauhaus school represented speculation on a new form of design set to emerge from parallel investigations of fine arts, crafts, and industrial technology (and their tools, materials, and elements), culminating in architecture as a unification of these drives. The Bauhaus building itself represents a great thesis regarding what "modern" would mean, especially in Weimar Germany, where suspicion of the avant-garde—its disruptions and tensions—was perhaps best allayed by positing a formal "style." Its plan represents a clear articulation of its program: a workshop block with its vast industrial glazing is appended to a huge public stair that connects to both the low auditorium/canteen element (that in turn connects to the six-story prefects' studio slab) as well as to the administration bridge to the vocational school. Each component is assigned its own fenestration and structural system, reflective of its ideal usage.

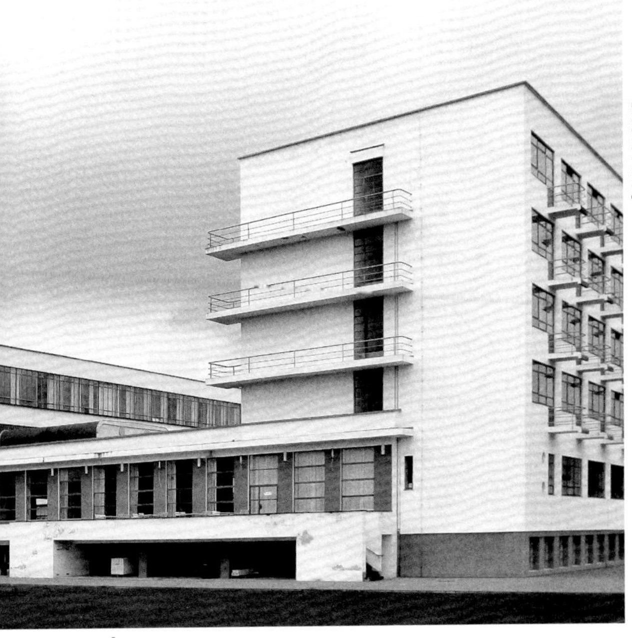

12° 13′ 38″E

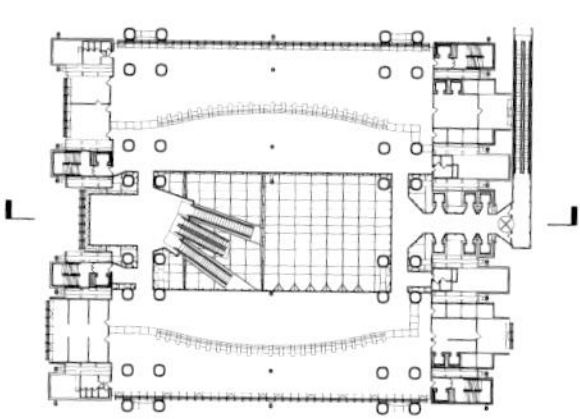

Floor Plan

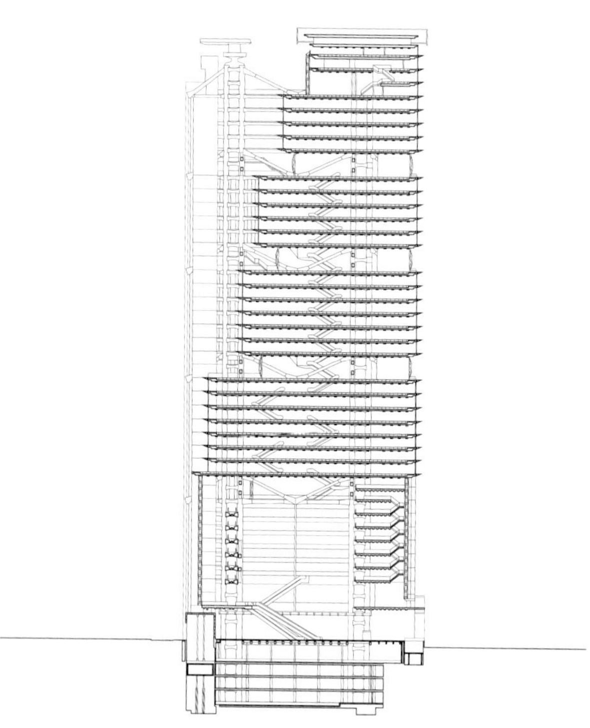

Section

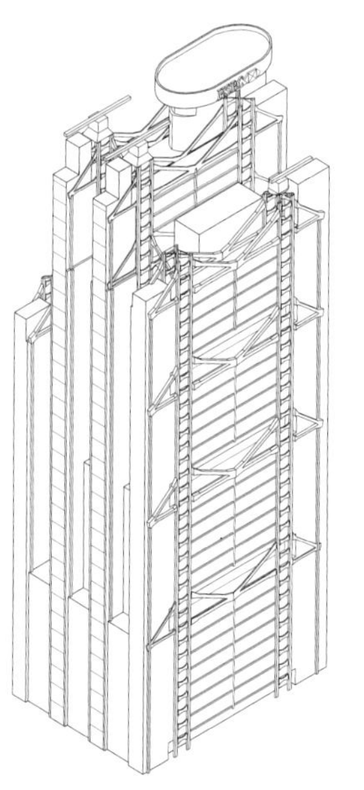

22° 16′ 49″N

35

HONGKONG AND SHANGHAI BANK HEADQUARTERS

NORMAN FOSTER (FOSTER & PARTNERS)
Hong Kong, China
1979–1986

For his first major building outside the U.K. and first tower, Norman Foster was charged with designing "the best bank building in the world." His bank not only redefined the concept of the bank building—from solemn fortress to transparent machine—but also finally achieved the concept of an adaptive, plug-in, prefabricated architecture that had been left largely unfulfilled since the 1960s. Four pairs of tubular masts support five levels of two-story trusses from which intermediate floors are suspended. The resulting three plan bays generate what are in effect three towers, of twenty-nine, thirty-six, and forty-four stories in height. At the base of the building, a public plaza receives natural light from a mirrored "sun scoop" that brings light from the side of the tower through an atrium and down through a bulging glazed ceiling. By providing a wide variety of interior and exterior spaces, an irregular promenade of escalators, and highly adaptable floor areas, the Hongkong and Shanghai Bank Headquarters proved the viability of prefabrication without the liability of monotony.

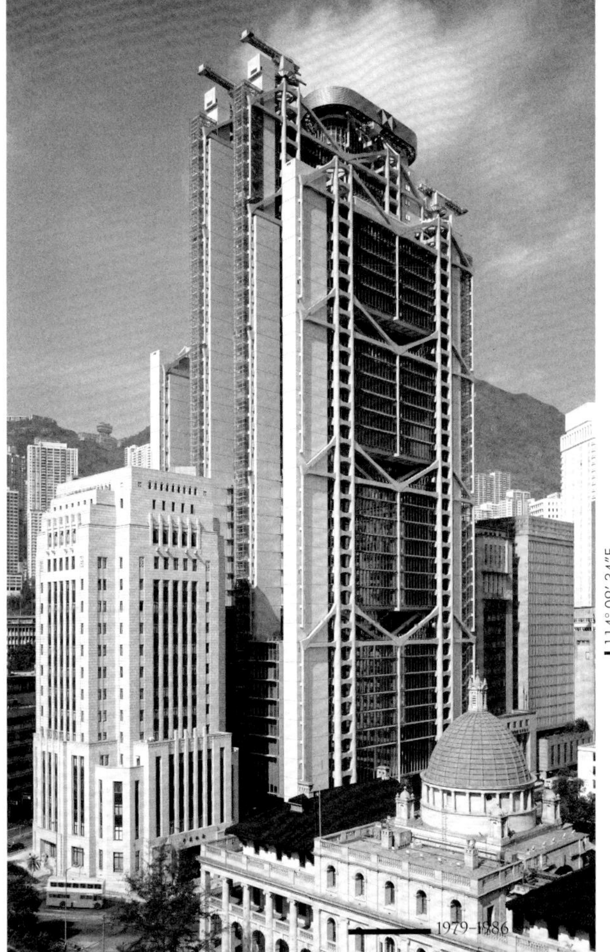

1979–1986

114° 09′ 34″E

80/

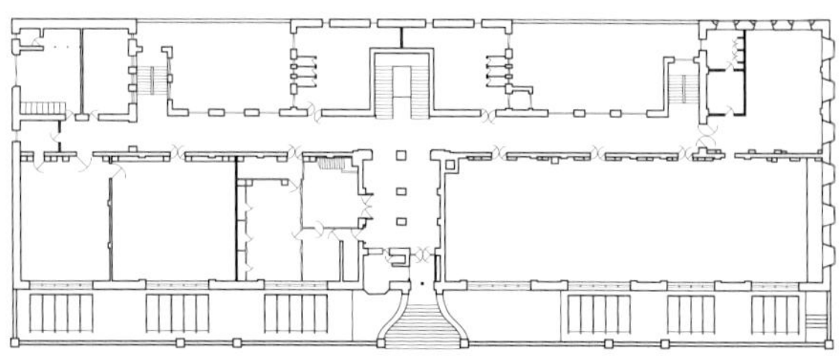

Floor Plan

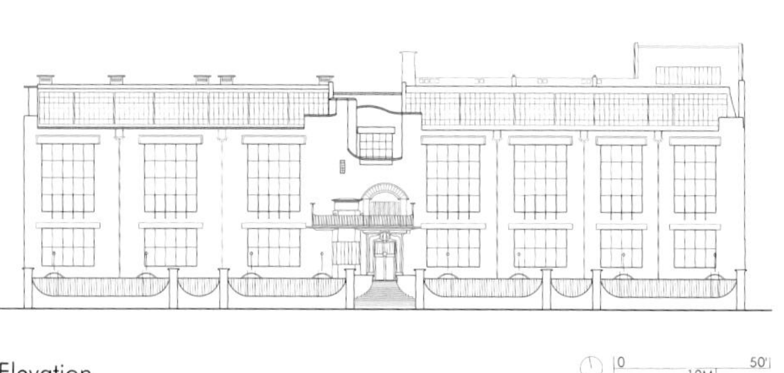

Elevation

4° 15′ 50″W

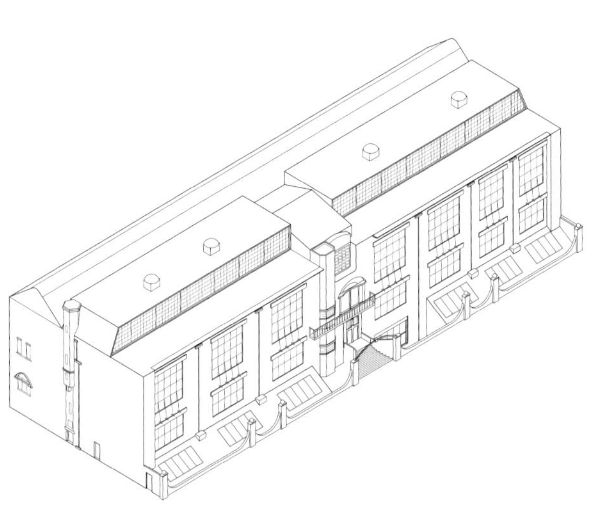

1896–1909

36

GLASGOW SCHOOL OF ART

CHARLES RENNIE MACKINTOSH
Glasgow, Scotland
1896–1909

Often considered one of the first truly "modern" buildings in Europe, the Glasgow School of Art resembled an industrial structure more than it did an academic institution. Built in two phases, the brick and stone masonry structure is remarkable for its large, industrial-type windows that are at times cut into the heavy masonry mass and at other times begin to assume a mass of their own: fluted elements that punctuate the steeply sloping side of the building. An E-shaped plan organizes the spaces, distributing them along a central spine. The bigger studios face the street, achieving an ideal northern orientation, with large glazed openings to light the workspace. While simple in plan, the spaces flow vertically into one another in a complex matrix of gridded wooden elements. With wrought iron used throughout as both a structural and a decorative material—indeed, often blurring the distinction, as with the elaborate window braces and the entry archway—Mackintosh was able to achieve early on the modernist ideal of material simplicity and of function as an integral element of a building's formal disposition. A fire in 2014 caused significant damage to the building; as of 2017, the building was still undergoing restoration.

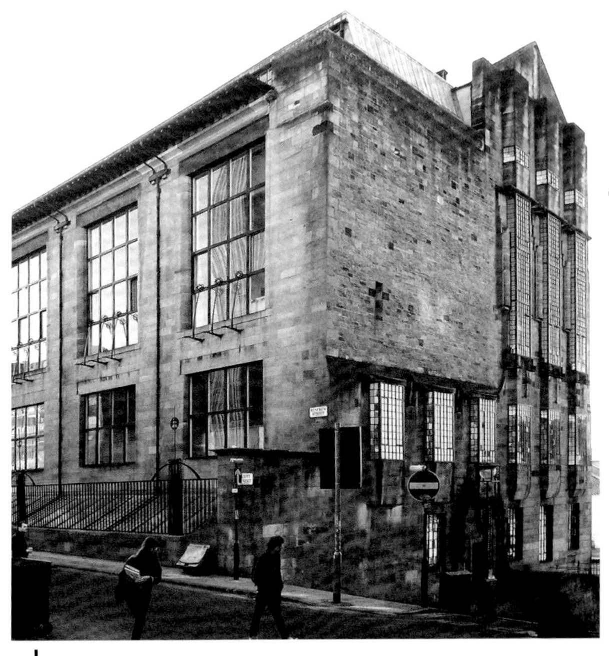

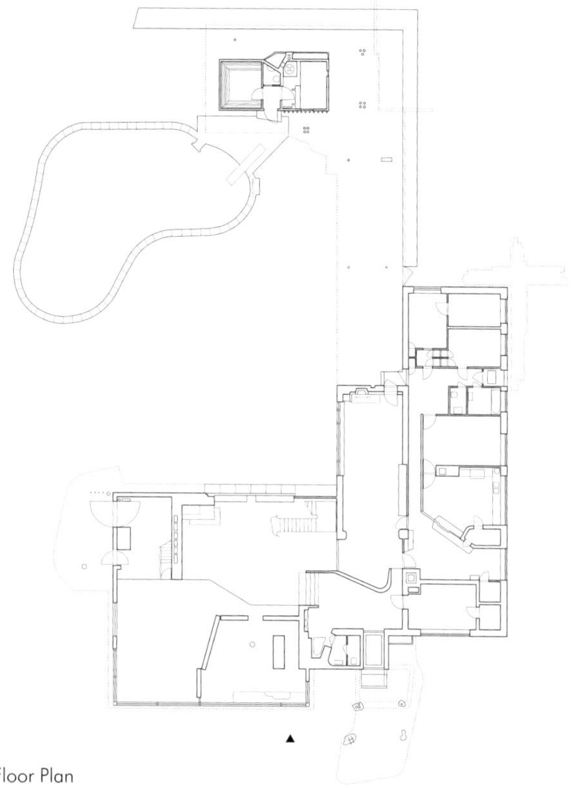

Floor Plan

Elevation

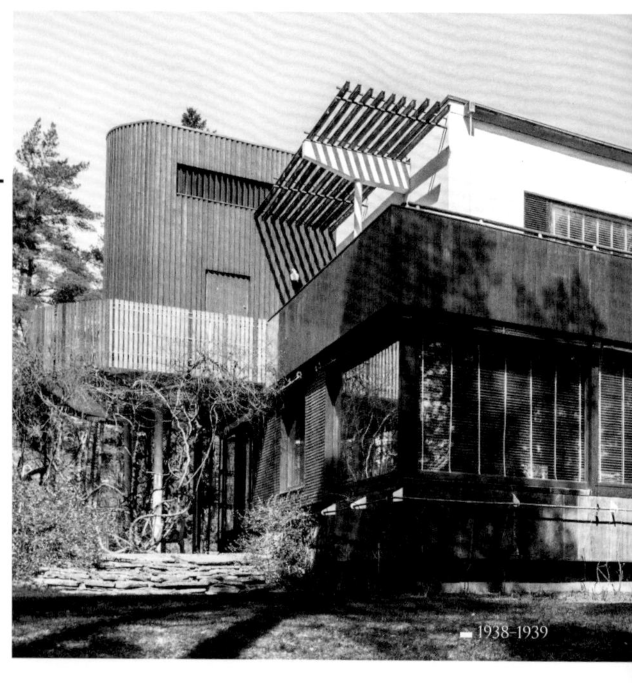

61° 35′ 51″N

37

VILLA MAIREA

ALVAR AALTO
Noormarkku, Finland
1938–1939

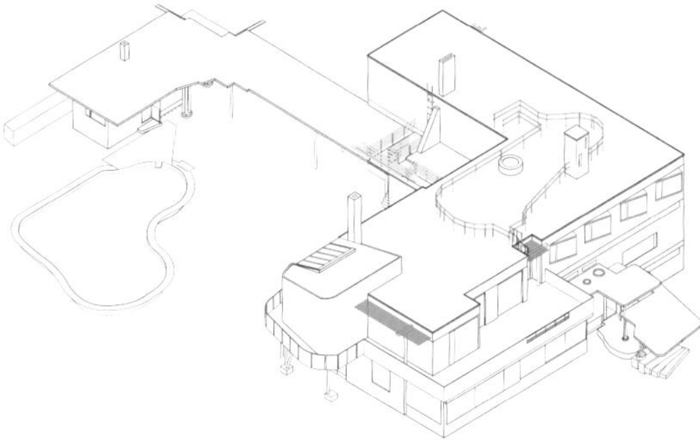

The Villa Mairea represents an accumulative moment in Aalto's work, where the earlier classicism and rustic romanticism have fully merged with functionalism and a reinvigorated sense of being in and of nature; where modern materials and techniques seamlessly intersect with traditional ones; and where curved forms consistently impinge on cubic ones. Since the house was designed for avid collectors of modern art, Aalto hoped that the forms and figures of modern painting would inform and resonate with the house. Located on top of a hill in the midst of a vast pine forest, the trees and the clearing are consistently drawn into the house: structural elements and screens are kept thin and given an irregular cadence, so as to avoid the typical architectural rhythms that the architect has described as "artificial" as well as to reiterate the field of the surrounding pines. The living spaces of the house flow together in one large room that can be subdivided by moving partitions. Some of the external walls are also movable so that the house can more thoroughly merge with nature.

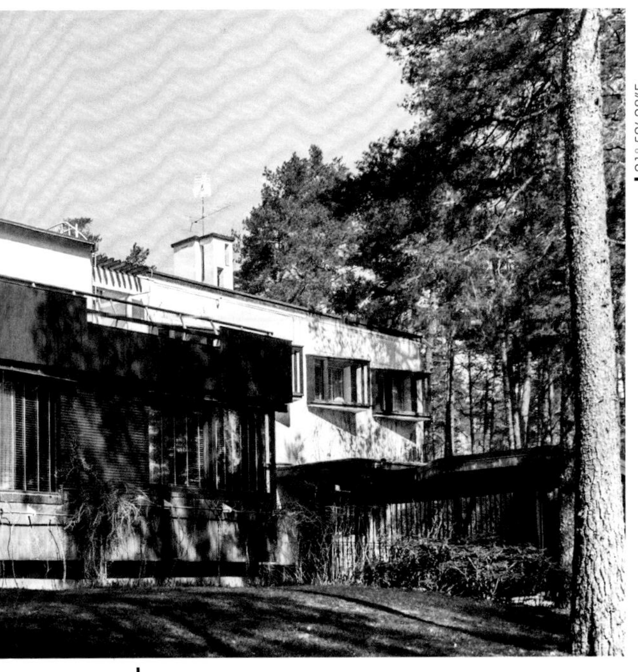

21° 52′ 28″E

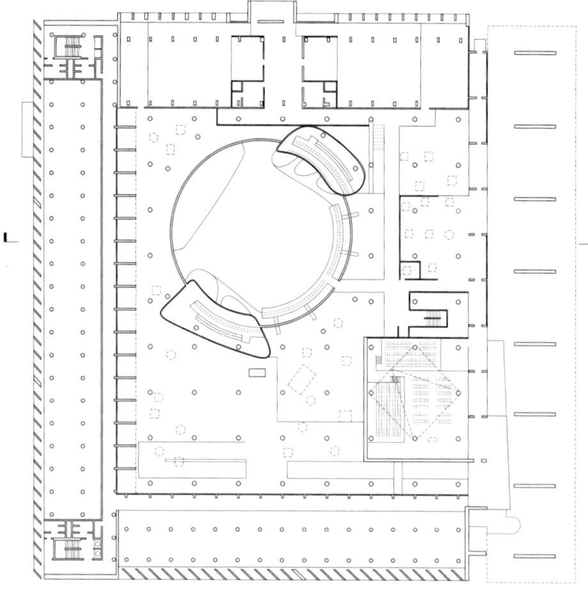

Floor Plan

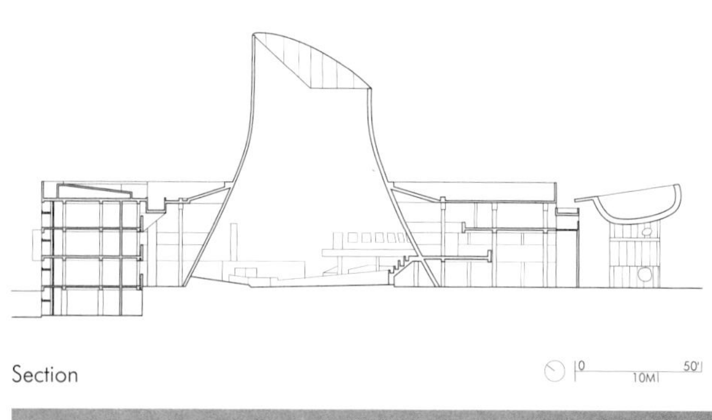

Section

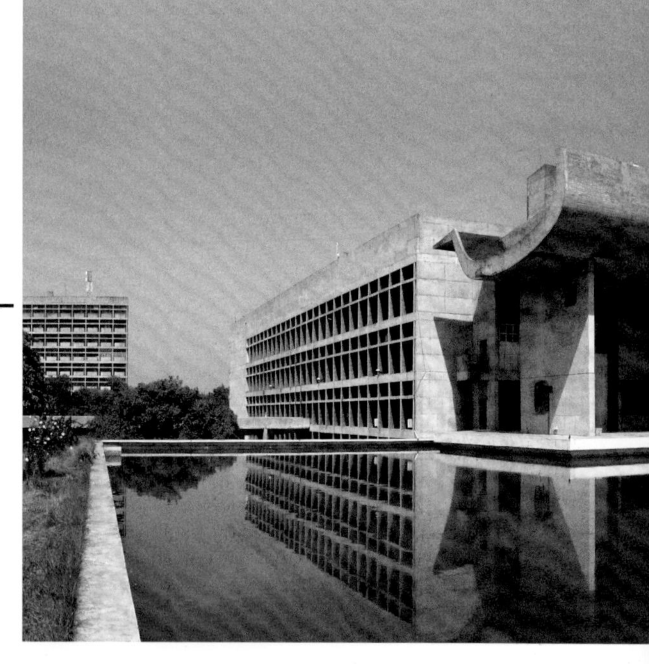

30° 45′ 40″N

38

THE ASSEMBLY, CHANDIGARH

LE CORBUSIER
Chandigarh, India
1951–1964

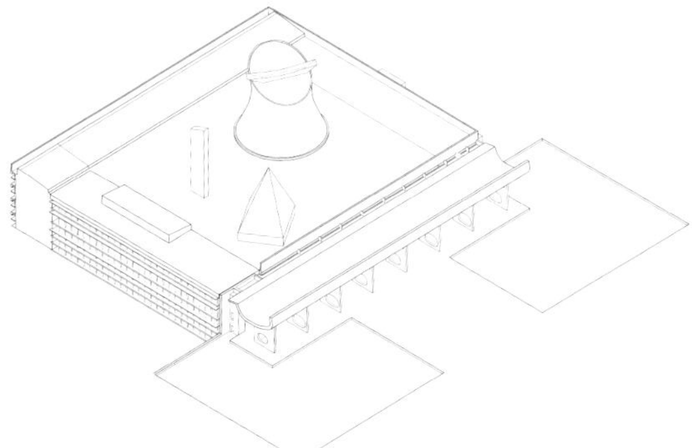

The centerpiece of Le Corbusier's master plan for the capitol complex of the Punjab in northern India, the Assembly hall is composed of a four-story, U-shaped office structure that encloses a three-dimensional composition of sculptural elements. The entry is a broad shaded portico topped with a massive inverted vault that opens upward toward the sky, suggestive of the "open hand" motif that occurs throughout the complex. The main assembly hall is a concrete hyperboloid shell structure contained entirely within the center of the plan, surrounded by a forest of columns and illuminated from above by diffuse natural light. The entire complex is rendered in cast-in-place concrete and accented by a series of multistory murals by the architect—some in the form of enameled metal panels mounted on both sides of immense pivot doors, and others as tapestries that adorn public and ceremonial spaces, depicting aspects of Punjabi culture.

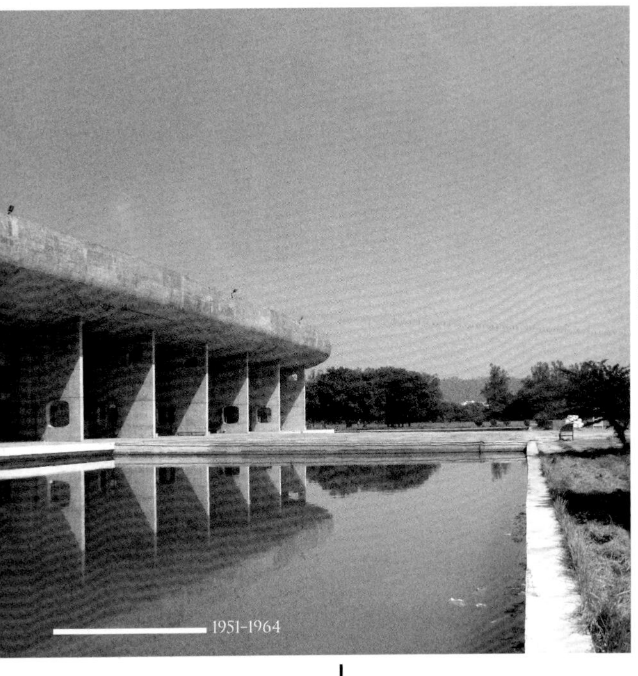

1951–1964

76° 48′ 10″E

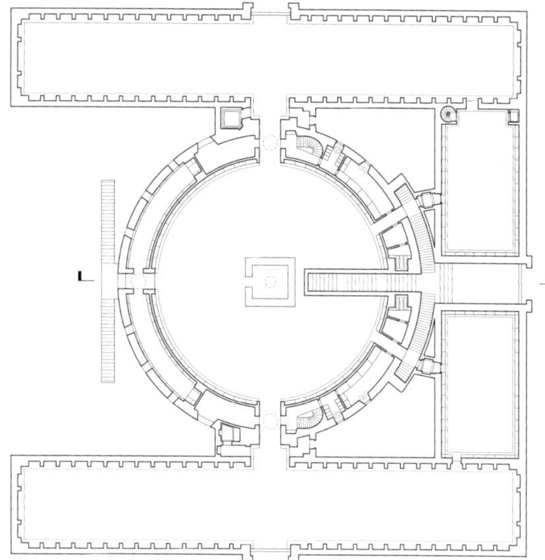

Floor Plan

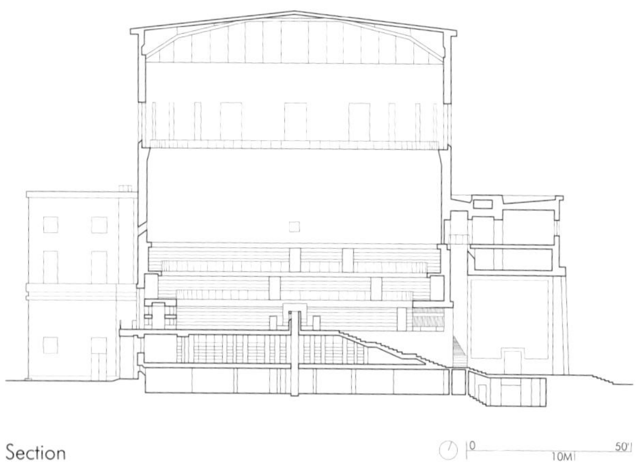

Section

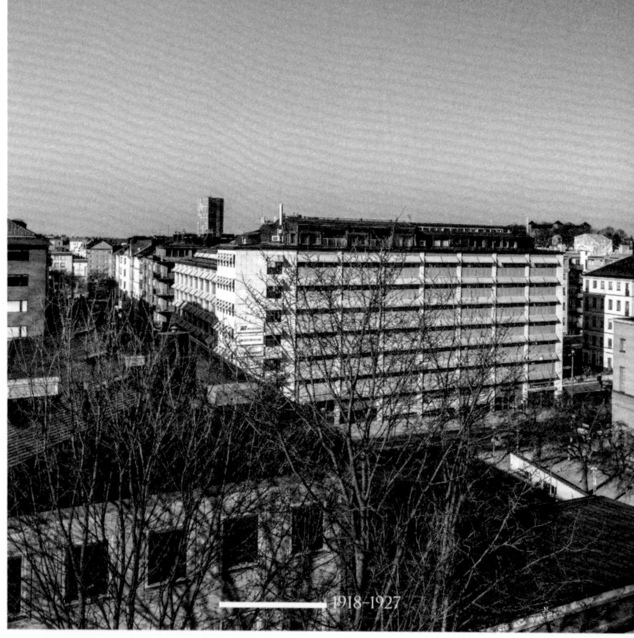

59° 20′ 37″N

39

STOCKHOLM PUBLIC LIBRARY

ERIK GUNNAR ASPLUND
Stockholm, Sweden
1918–1927

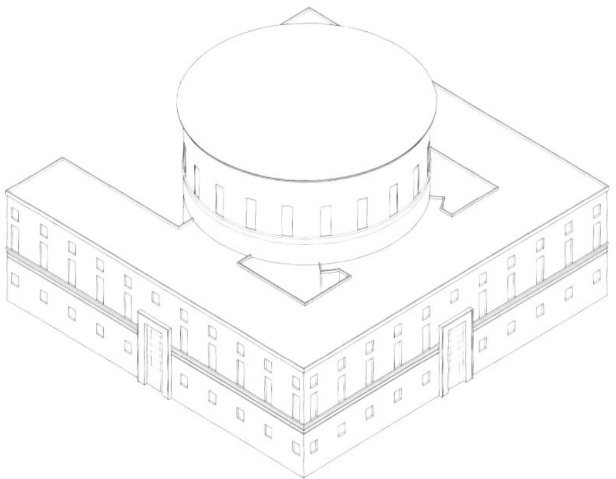

A virtual history of modernism in Scandinavia, Asplund's library began as an exercise in neoclassicism, developed into an exploration of the geometric abstractions of Nordic Classicism, and ultimately was embellished as an exemplar of rational functionalism. Suggestive of Ledoux's Barrière de la Villette, a large ocher cylinder looms above a five-story base that is itself partially elevated on a single-story plinth. Precisely sited to respond to neighboring landmarks, the building is unequally set back from the two boulevards that identify its corner and then rotated four and a half degrees. The setback also establishes a long, cascading main entry that cuts through the base and, once inside, continues upward to the center of the cylindrical space that is in fact twice the height of the drum on the exterior: three tiers of bookshelves in its lower third, and a vast, rugged, celestial space above.

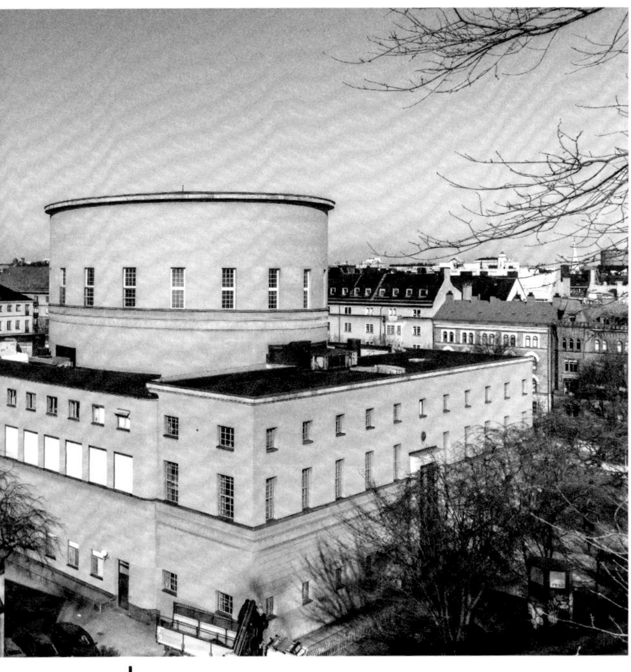

18° 03′ 17″E

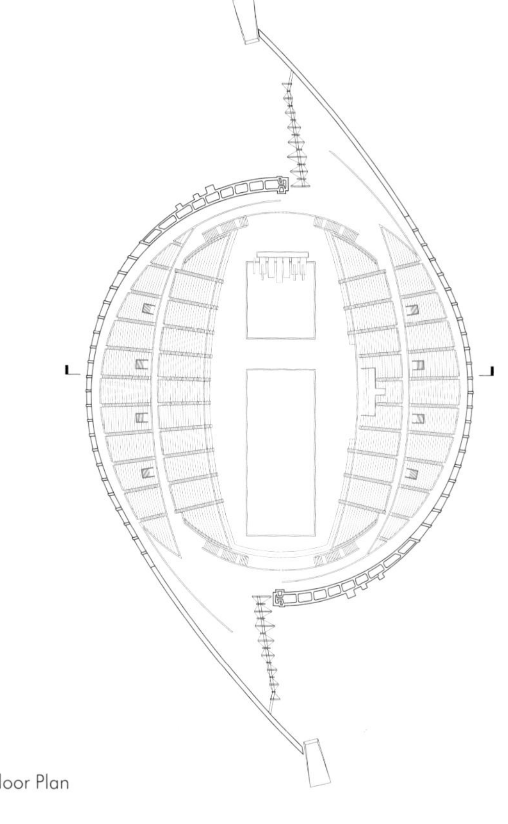

Floor Plan

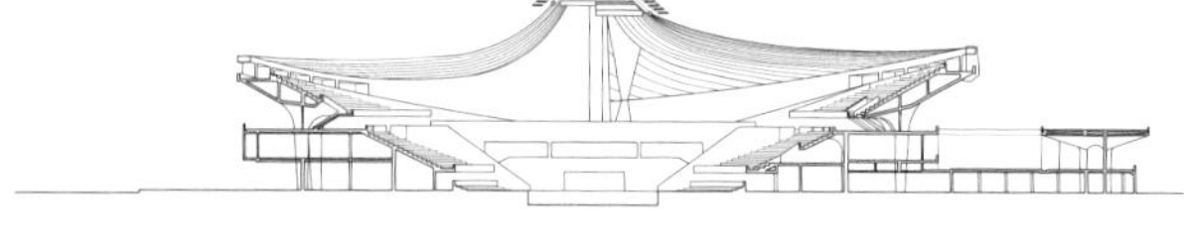

Section

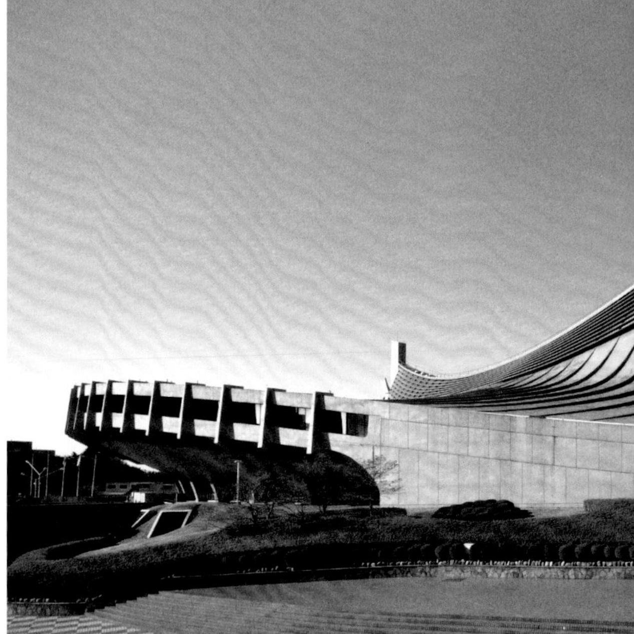

35° 40′ 03″N

40

NATIONAL OLYMPIC GYMNASIUM

KENZO TANGE
Tokyo, Japan
1961–1964

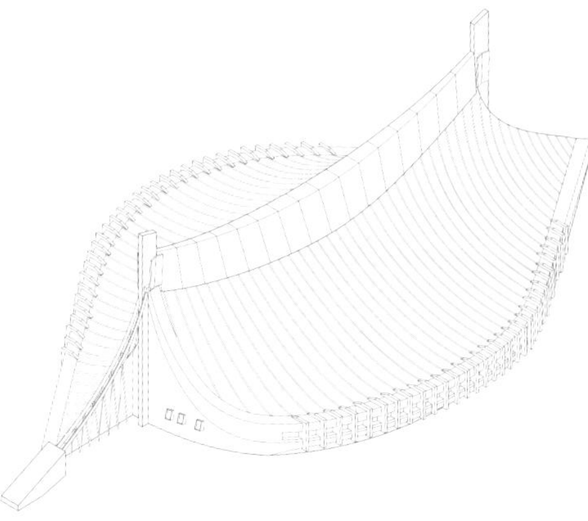

Built for the 1964 Tokyo Olympics, the Yoyogi National Gymnasium exhibited the largest suspended roof of its time. The complex's two buildings are remarkable for their lyrical formal qualities and innovative enmeshing of programs with structures. The larger gymnasium, depicted here, consists of two almost horizontal arches that shape entries and lobbies while containing seating for more than 10,000 visitors. These arches are offset from each other and anchored by two tall concrete masts, between which two 13 inch diameter steel cables span. Cables then connect the central cables with the arches. The project is representative of a distinctly Japanese modernism, suggesting modernism could espouse diverse cultures without necessarily duplicating traditional forms and construction techniques.

139° 42′ 00″E

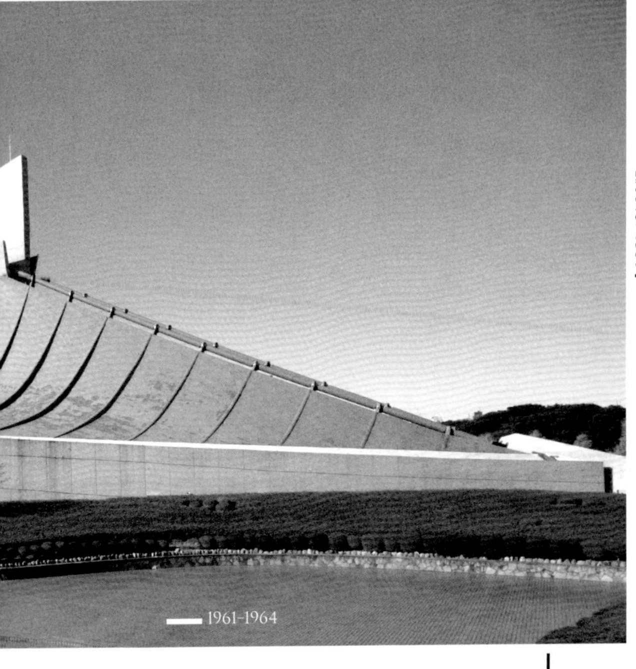

1961-1964

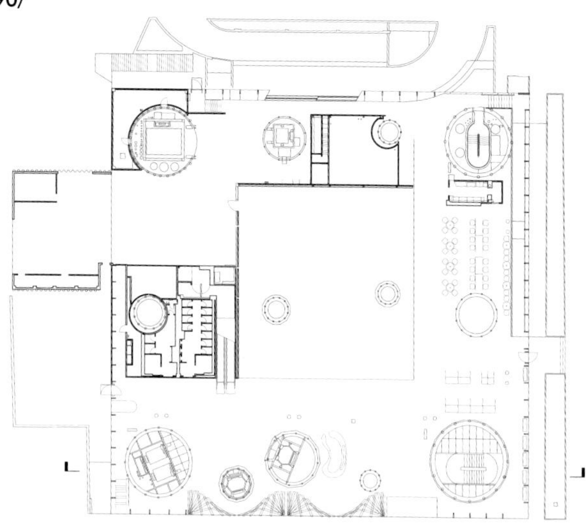

Floor Plan

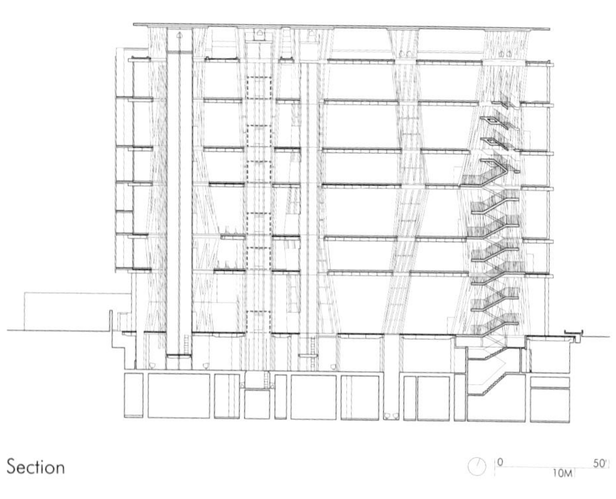

Section

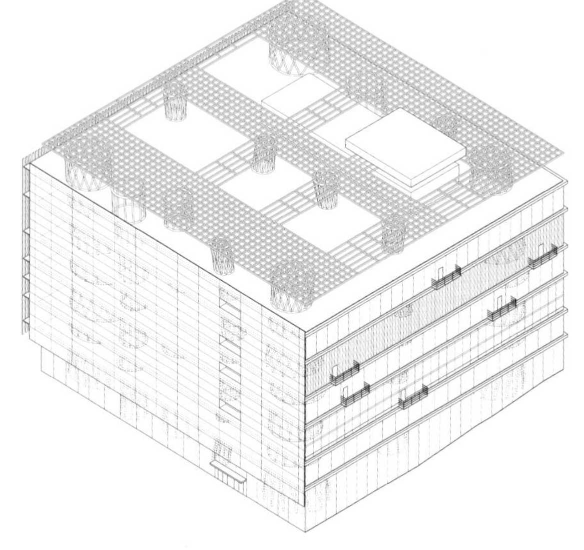

38° 15′ 56″N

41

SENDAI MEDIATHEQUE

TOYO ITO (TOYO ITO & ASSOCIATES, ARCHITECTS)
Sendai, Japan
1995–2000

Designed with the engineer Matsuro Sasaki, Toyo Ito's Sendai Mediatheque uses an innovative structural system to appear paradoxically structureless while maintaining considerable openness and flexibility on each of its six levels. Thirteen large reticular tubes, each composed of a latticelike network of tubular steel elements, appear to twist like tree trunks as they pass through—while supporting—a series of variably spaced steel-paneled floor slabs. Distributed in three rows, these tubes serve as light wells while contributing to the building's structural stability, with some of the smaller ones being primarily structural, others containing elevators or stairs, and the smaller, more twisted "trunks" containing electrical and air-handling systems. On the roof, those tubes in the center of the building's plan are augmented with computer-operated mirrors that bring additional natural light to the depth of the building. The freedom of the plans and variability of the section allows for the building to have distinct elevations on its sides, with maximum transparency and disconnected corners that emphasize the autonomy of the surfaces.

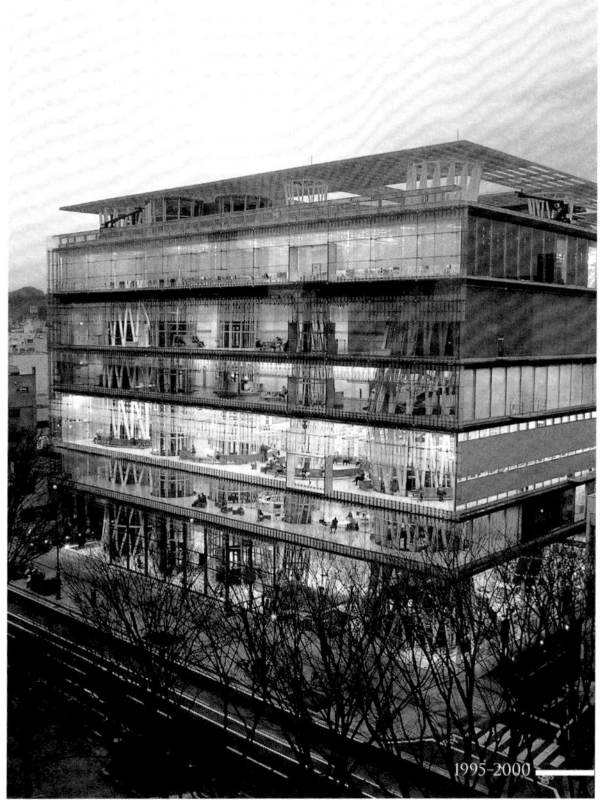
1995–2000

140° 51′ 56″E

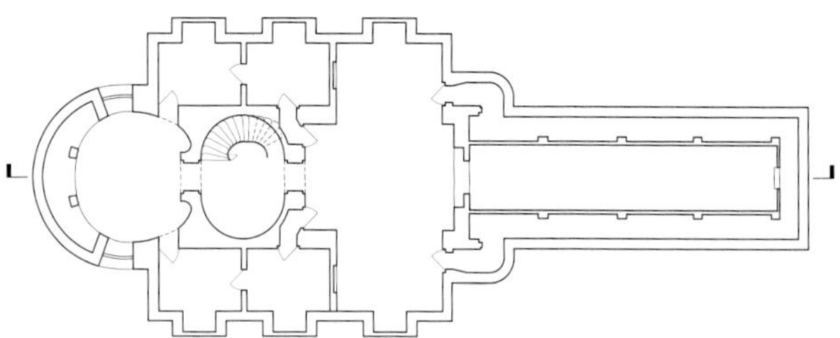

Floor Plan

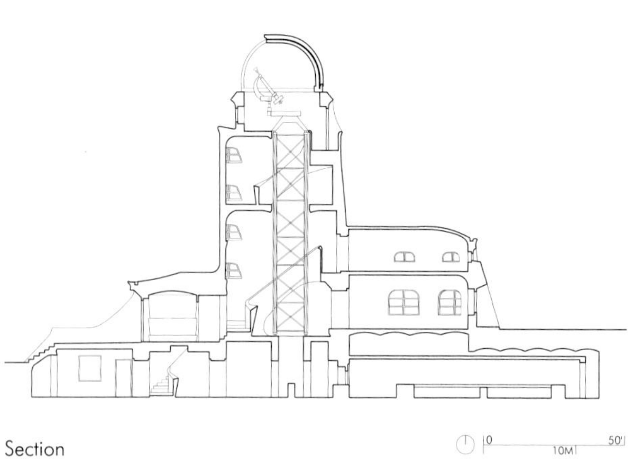

Section

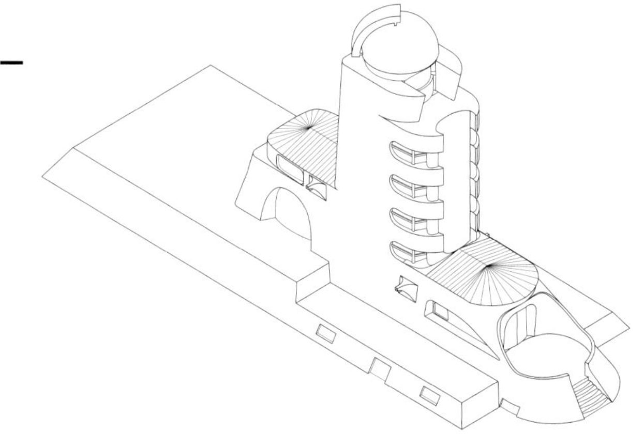

1917–1921

52° 22′ 44″N

42

EINSTEIN TOWER

ERICH MENDELSOHN
Potsdam, Germany
1917–1921

Driven to turn the tiny sketches he produced while in the trenches during World War I into a new kind of architecture, Erich Mendelsohn built the Einstein Tower in Potsdam soon after the war had ended. An early exploration of architecture's capacity for plasticity, the observatory translated the fluidity of these abstract sketches—a bit expressionist, like a Kandinsky, and another bit futurist, like Boccioni—into a singular built form that nevertheless maintained a sense of dynamic reciprocity of solid and void, appropriately dedicated to Albert Einstein. Although conceived in concrete, inadequate construction techniques and material availability caused the structure to eventually be executed in stuccoed brick. The tower remains today an intermediary between the gracefulness of Gaudí's earlier work and the sculptural finesse that would eventually appear in Le Corbusier's Ronchamp.

13° 03′ 50″E

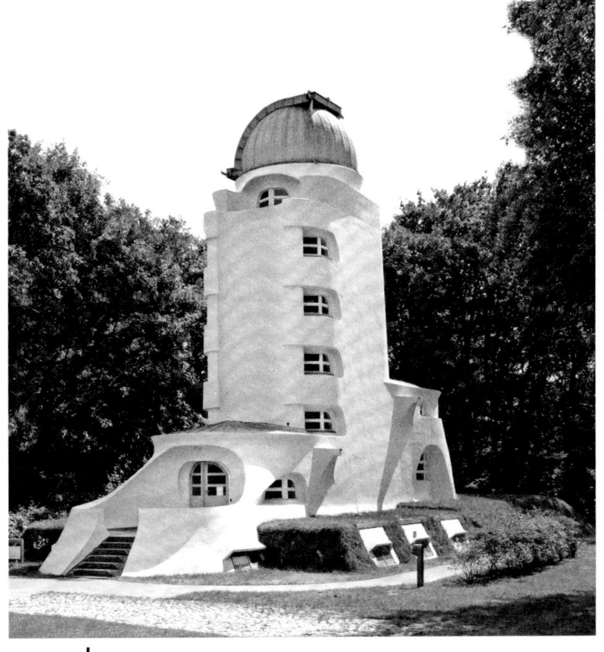

40° 45′ 35″N

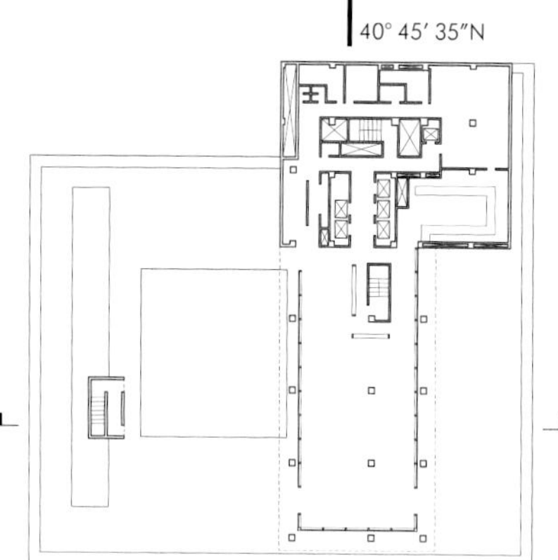

Floor Plan

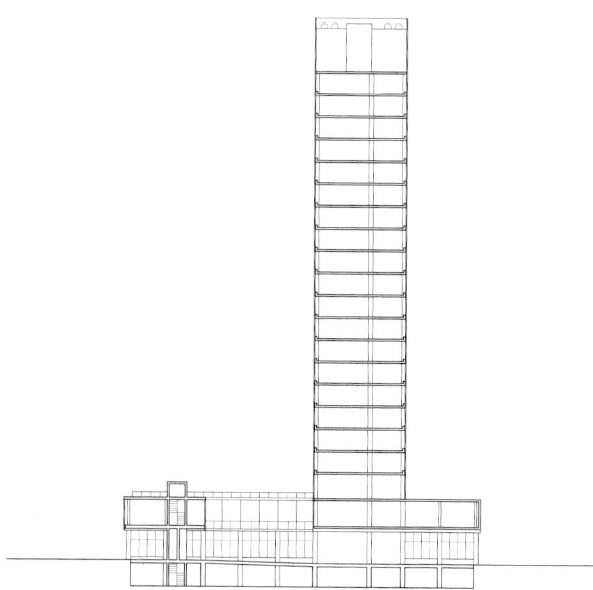

Section

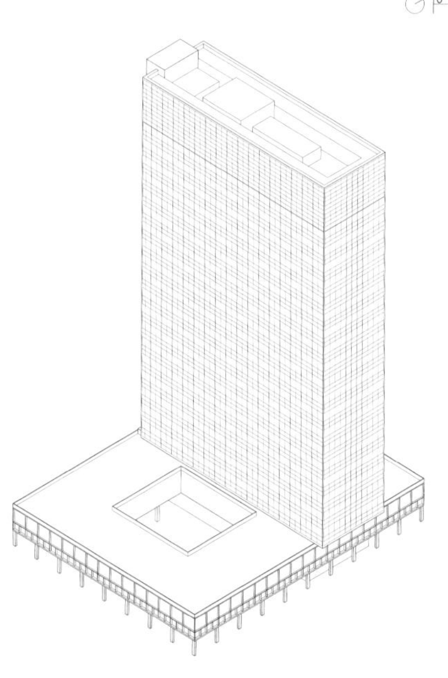

73° 58′ 22″W

43

LEVER HOUSE

GORDON BUNSHAFT and NATALIE DE BLOIS (SOM)
New York, New York, USA
1951–1952

An early example of modern architecture being used in the service of commercial American office space, the Lever House stands one level above the ground on Park Avenue in New York City. Elevating the entire building on pilotis freed up the majority of the ground plane for pedestrians, allowing them to move through the block beneath generous courtyard openings admitting light from above. The majority of the office space is contained within a slender aluminum-and-glass tower element oriented perpendicular to Park Avenue, articulated to conceal the fact that the elevator core is contained within the narrow edge of the building toward the inner block. One of the first curtain-wall constructions in American commercial architecture, the building would prove instrumental in establishing Skidmore, Owings & Merrill's reputation in America in general, and design partner Gordon Bunshaft's legacy in New York in particular. The building was followed soon after by Mies van der Rohe's Seagram Building, located diagonally across the street to the south—an unlikely pair together marking the beginning of modern architecture's domination of the American metropolis.

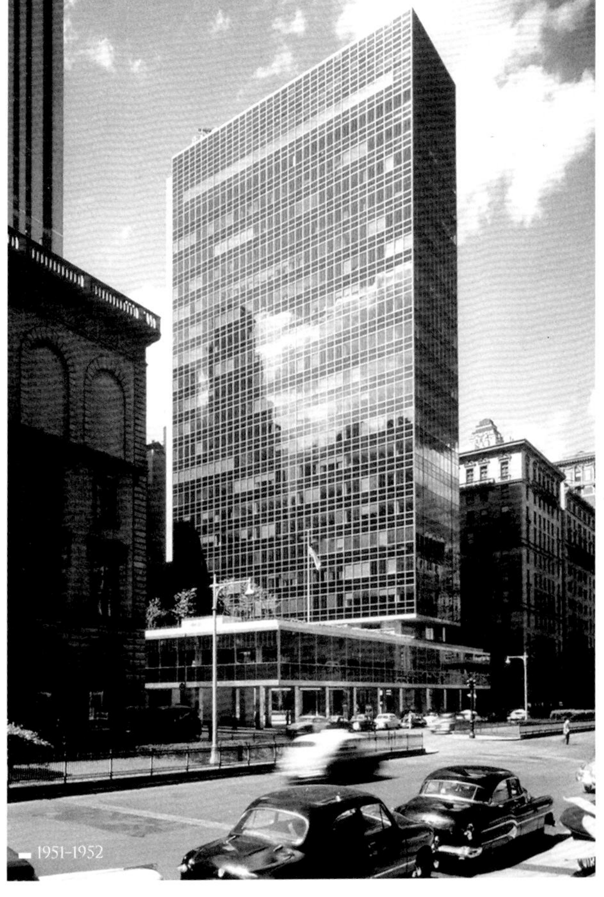

34° 01′ 21″N

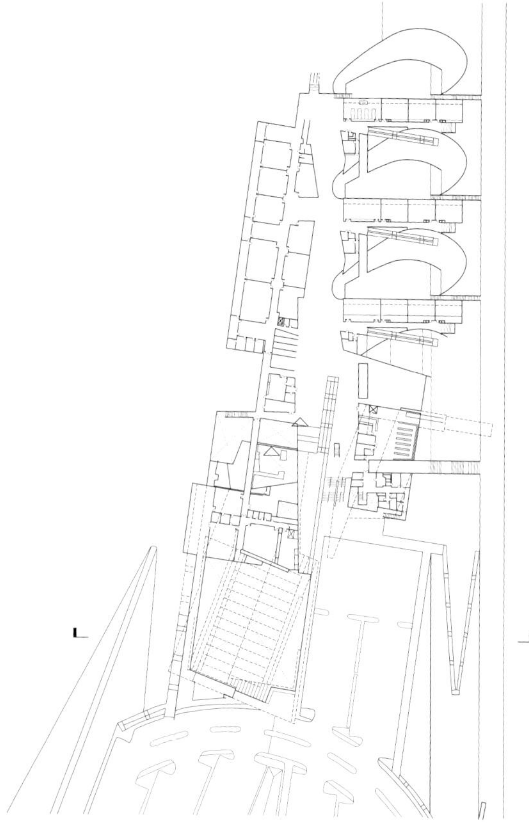

Floor Plan

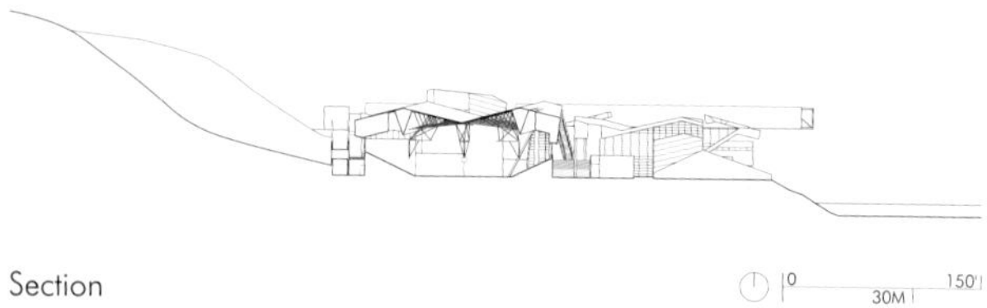

Section

0 150'
30M

117° 46′ 42″W

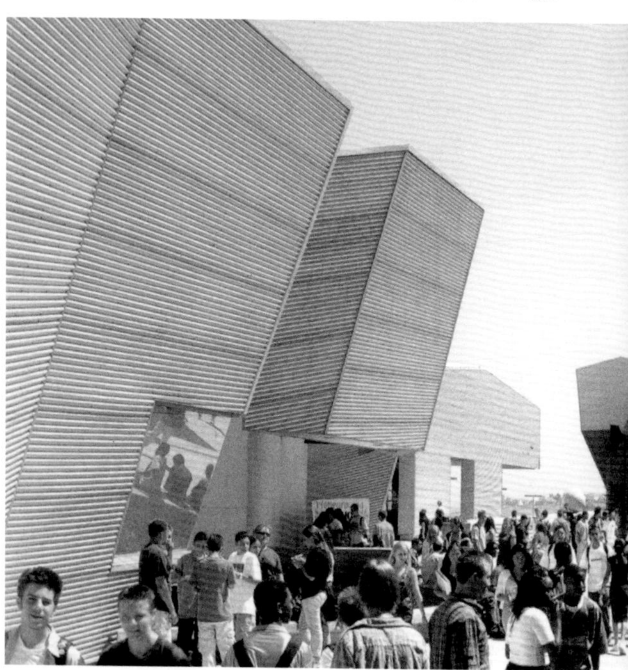

44

DIAMOND RANCH HIGH SCHOOL

MORPHOSIS ARCHITECTS
Pomona, California, USA
1994–1999

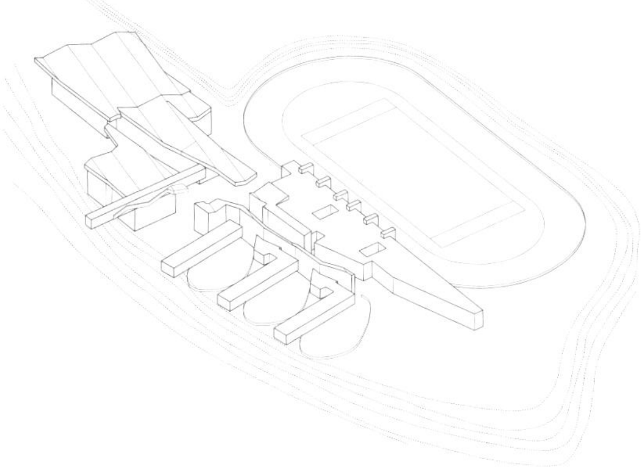

On a large plot of land isolated by highways and a steep hillside, Diamond Ranch High School blurs the distinction between building and landscape, much as the hill towns it seems to evoke. It adopts a topographical approach to a steeply sloping hillside site, embedding selected programs into the hillside. The linear plan is organized along an interior pedestrian street, thereby redefining the traditional typology with two groups of classroom clusters on either side, terminating in a gymnasium and cafeteria volume. A series of linear elements stretch outward toward playing fields situated on the downhill side of the slope. Having been constructed within California's standard public-school funding, Diamond Ranch High School vigorously states that the architecture of schools can be as didactic—and supportive—as the lessons presented within.

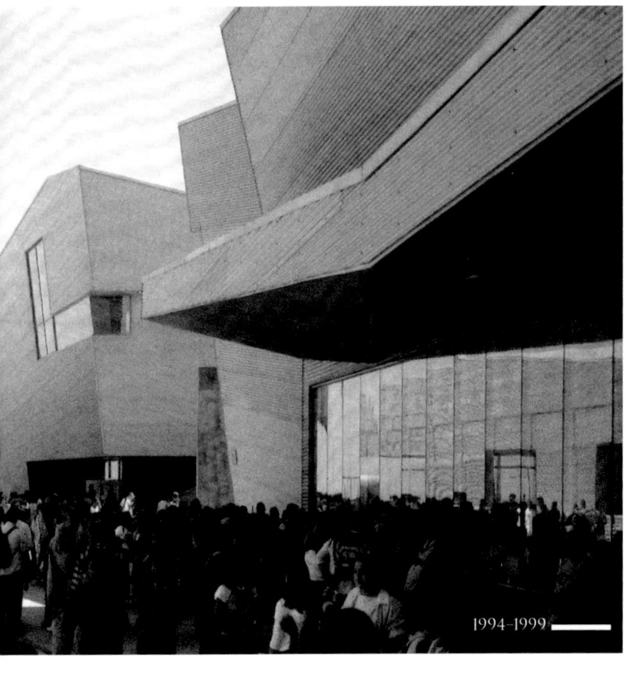

41° 08′ 33″N

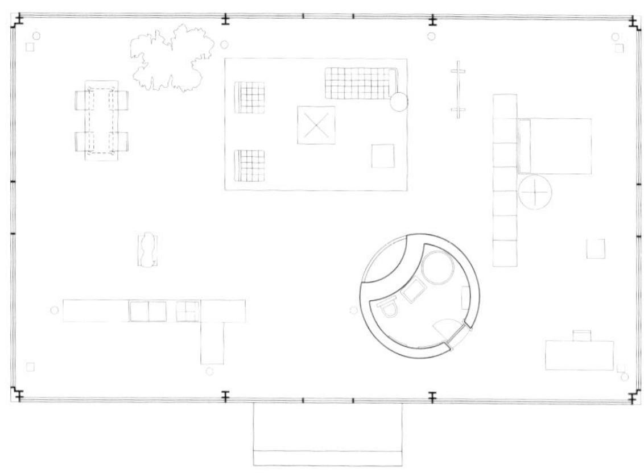

Floor Plan

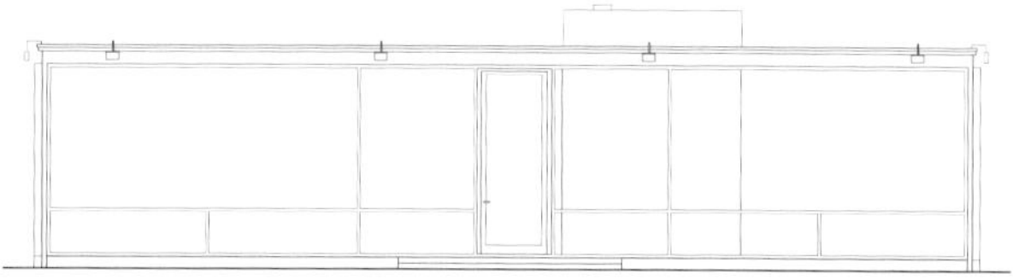

Elevation

0 10′ 2M

73° 31′ 46″W

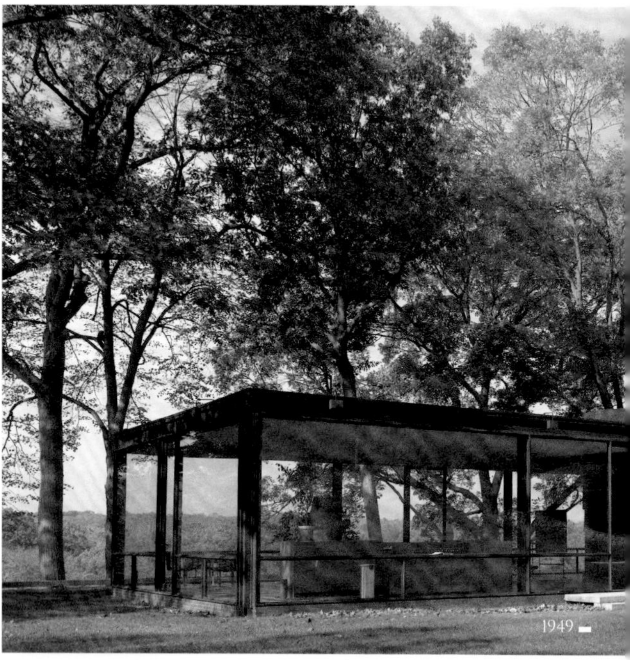

1949

45

GLASS HOUSE

PHILIP JOHNSON
New Canaan, Connecticut, USA
1949

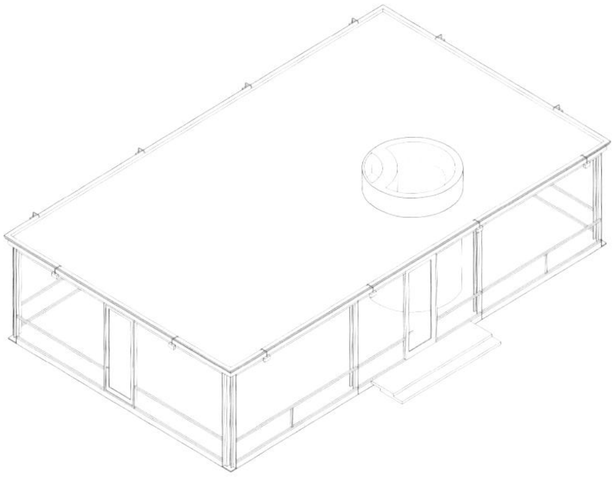

While clearly influenced by Mies's Farnsworth House (a project at the time), to create this exemplar of the minimal house-as-pavilion polemic, Johnson draws the momentum in a distinctly different direction. Firmly grounded rather than floating, internal columns rather than exterior, corners exaggerated rather than absent, a cylindrical core solid rather than a rectilinear box, more reflective than transparent, black rather than white, brick floors rather than travertine—Johnson's Glass House seems to be more of a dialectical object than a facsimile, translating Mies's manifesto into one that is distinctly American. Both depend upon the vastness of their properties to provide privacy for the occupants, but Johnson developed a larger landscape strategy of walls and additional pavilions to support (and compensate for) the austerity of his glass house.

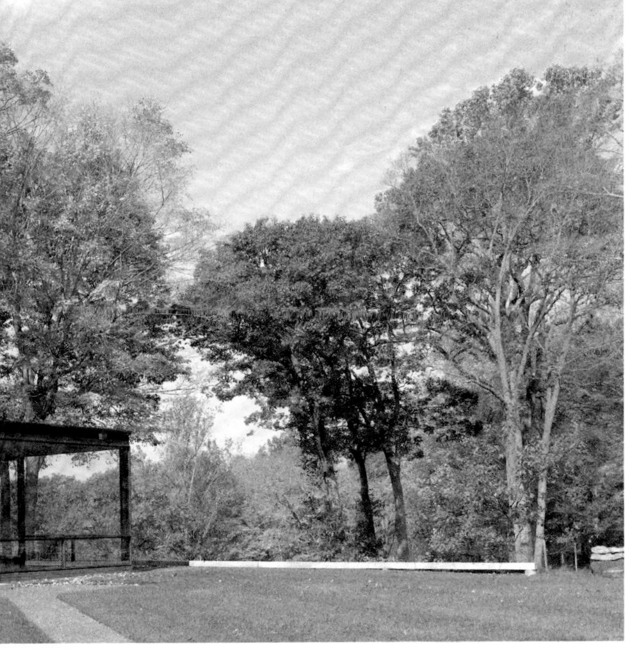

40° 44′ 60″N

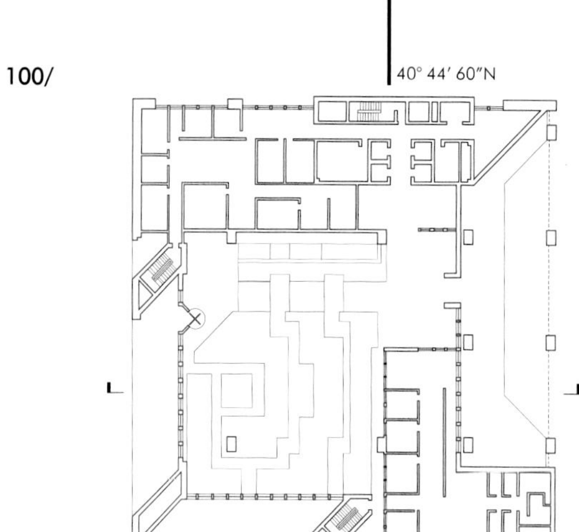

Floor Plan

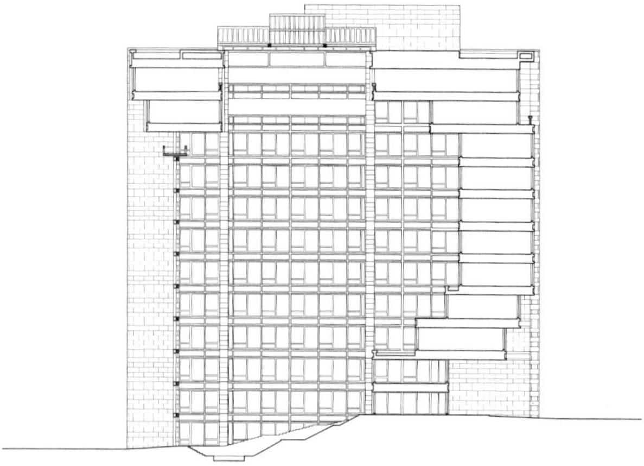

Section

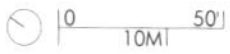

0 50′
10M

73° 58′ 16″W

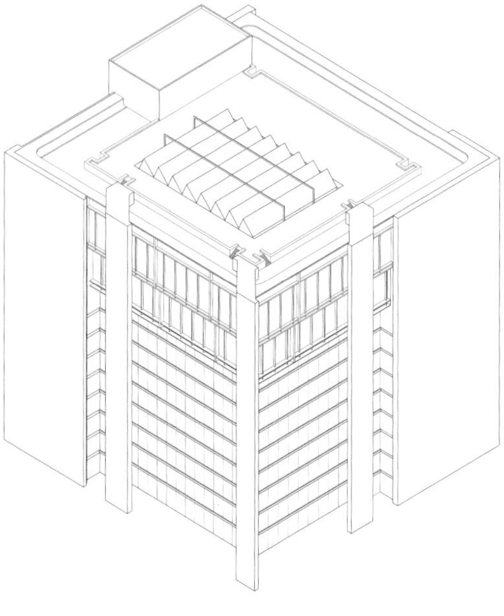

46

FORD FOUNDATION HEADQUARTERS

KEVIN ROCHE, JOHN DINKELOO and ASSOCIATES, LLC

New York, New York, USA

1963–1968

A uniquely conceived office building in midtown Manhattan, the Ford Foundation is organized with its lower nine floors containing L-shaped plans of narrow-span office spaces daylit on two sides, with its upper two floors a square O. Staggered gently in section, the eleven floors containing the main program spaces surround a generously landscaped internal garden court, itself daylit from the south and east, as well as through a skylight built into the spanning trusses on the roof. The primary horizontal building structural elements are expressed as Cor-Ten steel, with the balance of the enclosure in masonry and glass. The building's volume, visible within the glazed atrium, continues the building lines on either side while adjusting for their differing depths. Entry occurs from the north and is sculpted three-dimensionally at its lowest level in part to help negotiate a major grade change across the site, thereby creating a sense of discovery and delight when finally encountering the terraced garden itself.

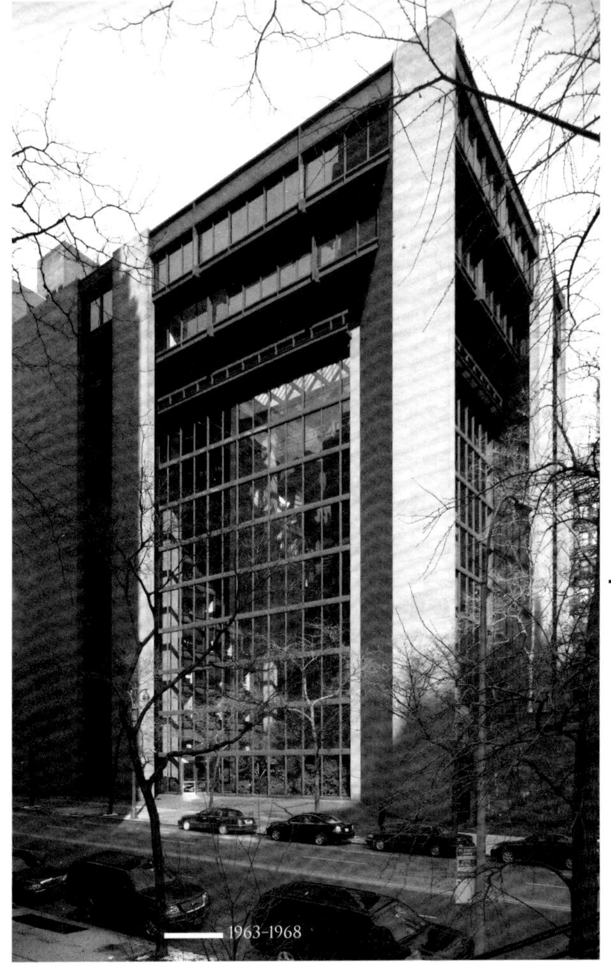

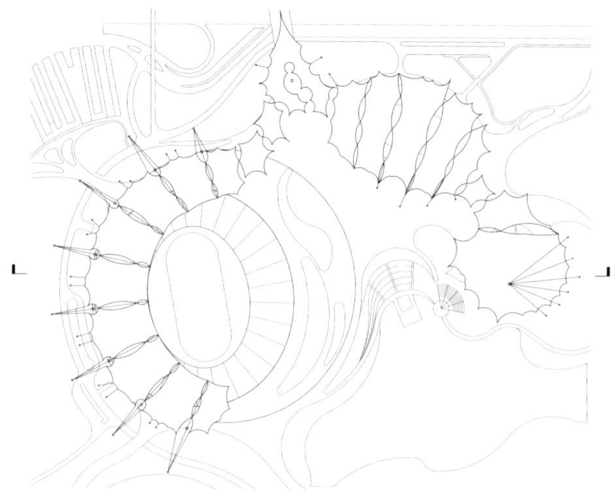

Site Plan

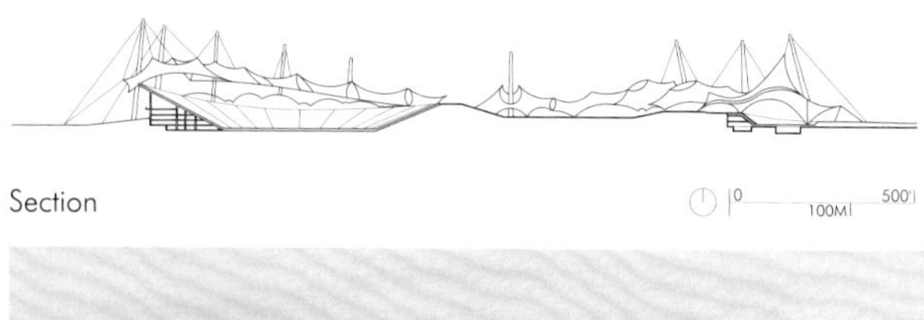

Section

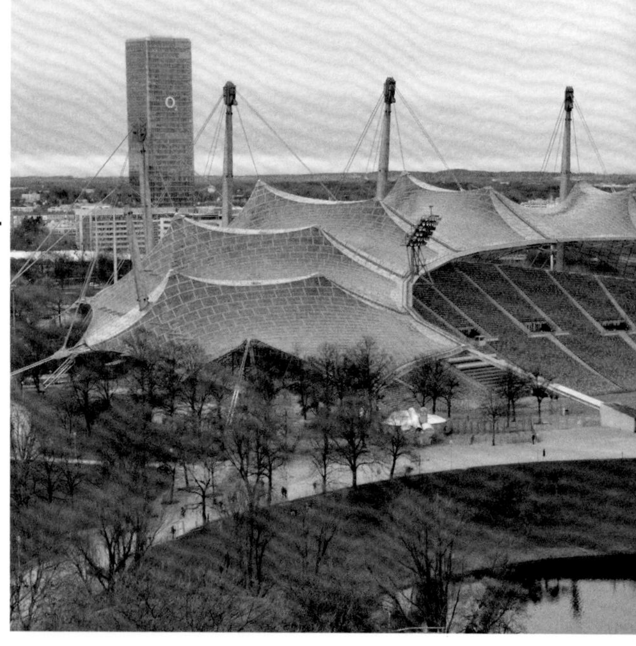

47

OLYMPIC STADIUM, MUNICH

FREI OTTO and GÜNTER BEHNISCH
Munich, Germany
1968–1972

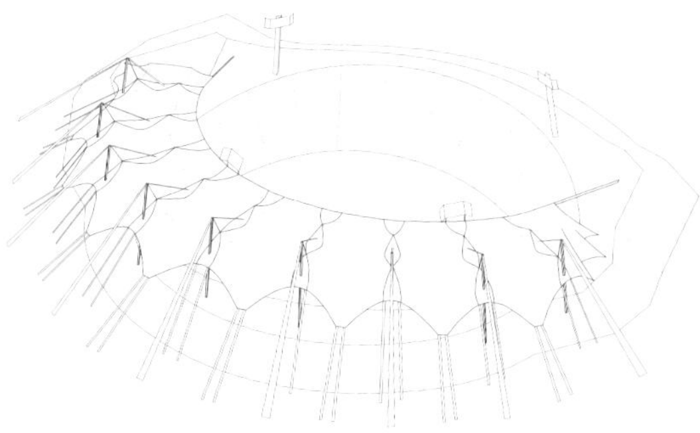

As the 1972 Munich Olympics were the first to be held in Germany after those of 1936, Otto and Behnisch sought to design the Munich Olympic Park of sweeping landscapes with integral grandstands and lightweight canopies flowing throughout, in direct opposition to the ponderous monumentality of the previous games. While the tent is one of the most ancient of architectural constructions, these tensile structures represented the most sophisticated use of materials and design technologies of their time. The structure is composed of a series of tubular steel masts that hold aloft a series of massive steel cables supporting a grid of smaller cables within which either polyester panels coated with PVS or acrylic glass panels are affixed. This structure was fabricated off-site, one of the first constructions to be wholly determined by computer calculations. Beneath this structure, the parklike landscape forms an organic counterpoint to the peaks and crevasses of the roof (metaphorically associated with the nearby Swiss Alps), with the main stadium located in a giant hollow, a bomb crater from World War II.

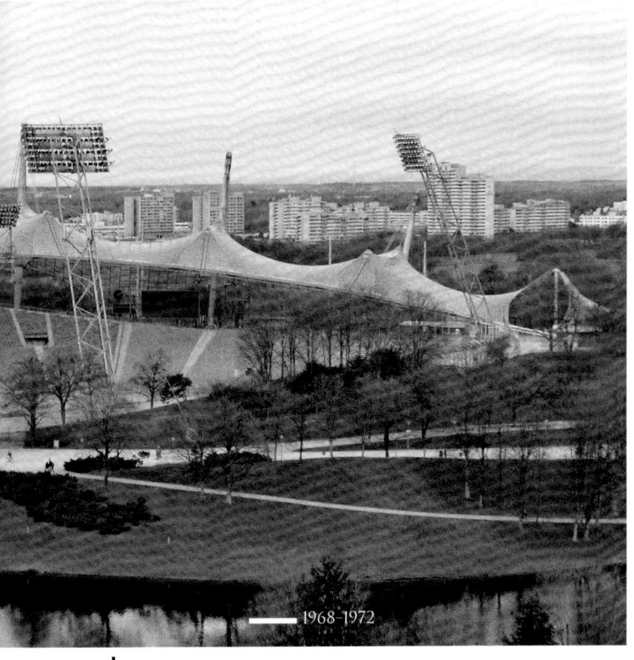

1968–1972

34° 02′ 07″N

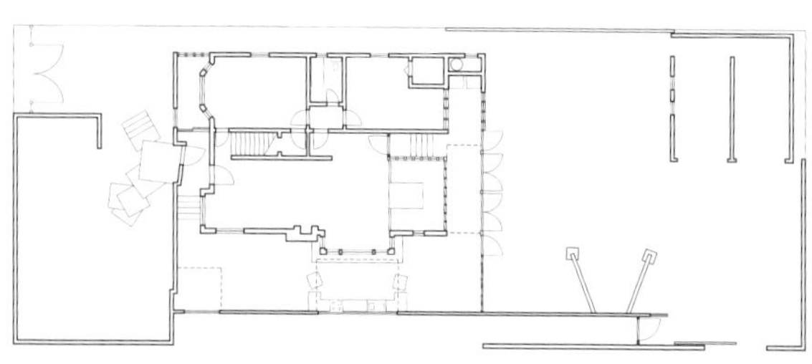

Floor Plan

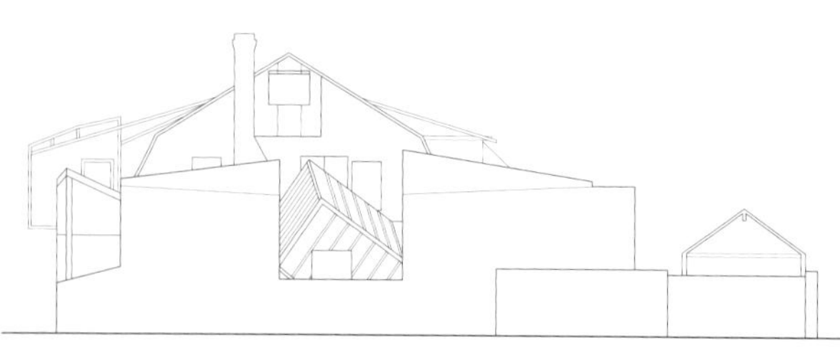

Elevation

0 50′ 10M

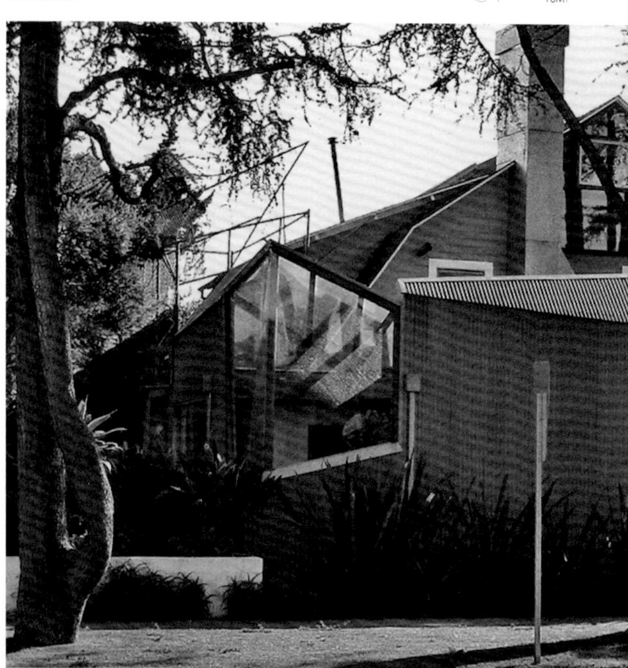

118° 29′ 04″W

48

GEHRY HOUSE

FRANK GEHRY (GEHRY PARTNERS, LLP)
Santa Monica, California, USA
1979

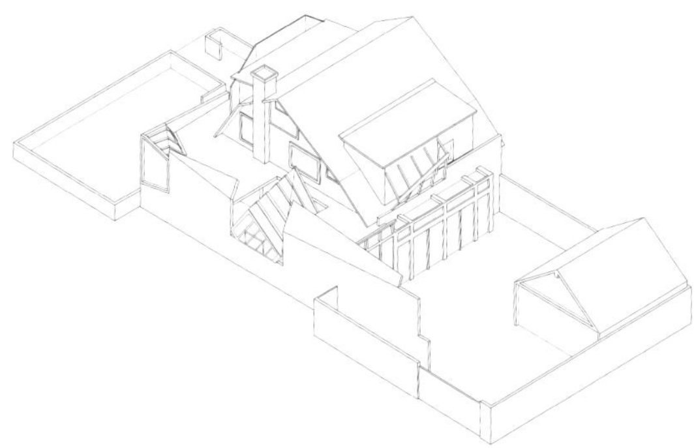

An existing, asbestos-shingled Dutch Colonial bungalow is wrapped on three sides with an amalgamation of planes and volumes of corrugated metal, chain-link fencing, raw plywood, and found windows and doors, all of which appear to have a corrosive effect on the original. The result is a house of multiple reflections and a moiré pattern of screens upon screens, with inside and outside sometimes merged, sometimes displaced. Reminiscent of a Rauschenberg collage—with its disparate materials that are juxtaposed and composed—and of a Duchamp readymade—with its dislocations and redefinitions—the house occupies an intermediary position between architecture and art. Experimental, indefinite, subjective, though also nostalgic (of balloon framing, painted sashes, and articulated moldings), of forms and materials that reveal the industrial in the domestic while domesticating the industrial, the Gehry House places the tidy hierarchies, methodologies, and grand ambitions of twentieth-century architecture into an enlightened disarray.

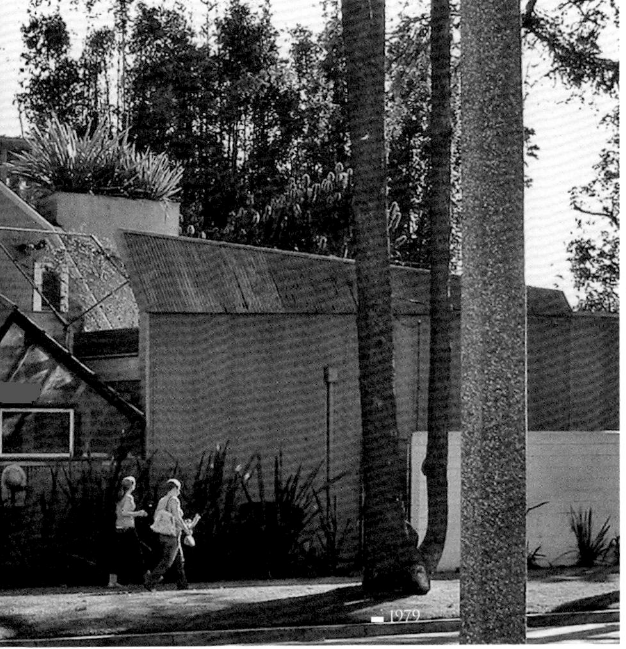

1979

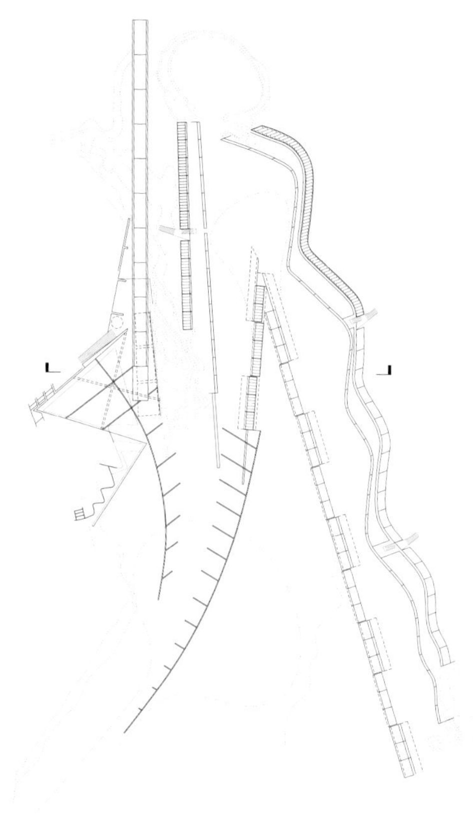

Site Plan

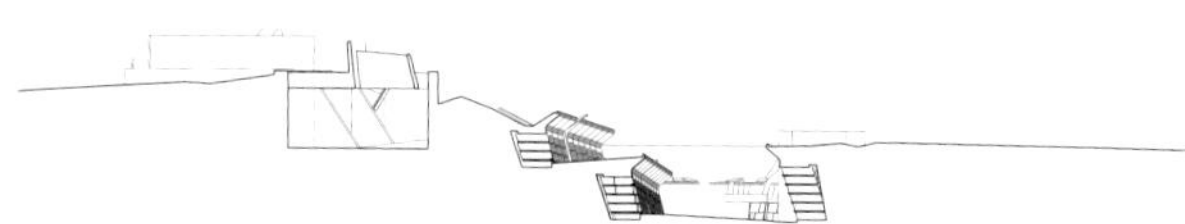

Section

0 20M 100'

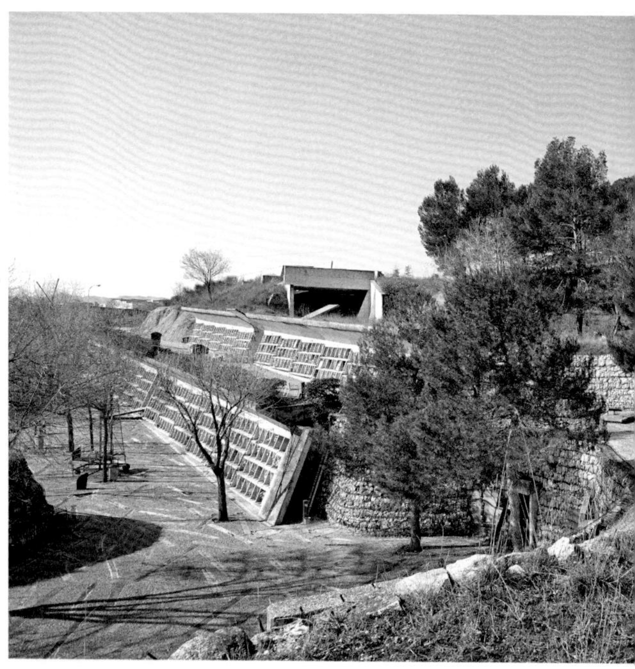

41° 35′ 33″N

49

IGUALADA CEMETERY

ENRIC MIRALLES and CARME PINÓS
Barcelona, Spain
1985–1991

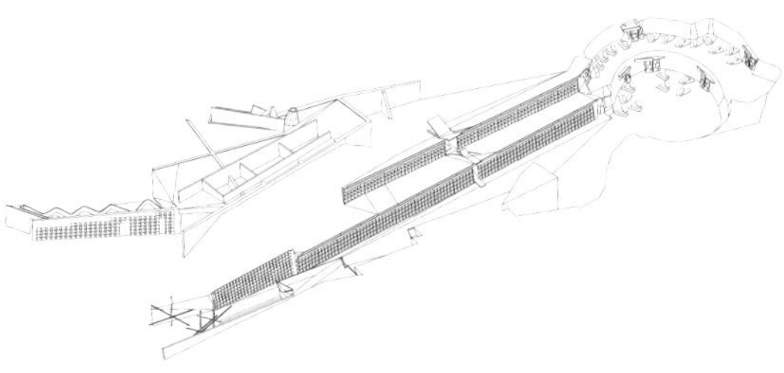

In the tradition of great funerary architecture, the Igualada Cemetery is situated somewhere between metaphor and myth. Built in a very industrial region in which much of the landscape had been quarried, the cemetery burrows into the ground so that visitors become unaware of the context that surrounds them. At the same time, industrial materials—reinforced concrete, often with exposed reinforcing rods, at times the rods by themselves (as if lines drawn in the air), gabion walls with rusting mesh, and rough planking embedded in rougher concrete—are used throughout the construction: a comfort in the familiar. On the one hand, a gash in the earth, on the other hands raised to the sky, the cemetery has a central path populated by a frozen flow of planks leading to a field of tombs that appear to be either just erected or just excavated.

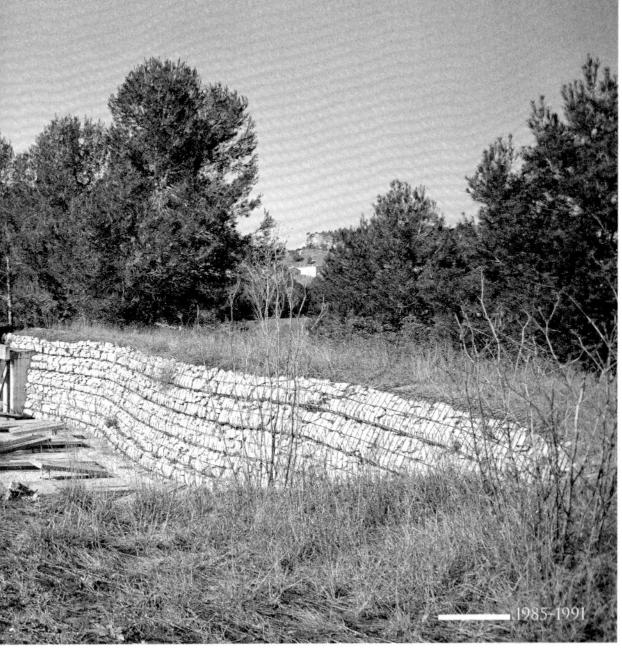

1° 38′ 15″E

41° 49′ 60″N

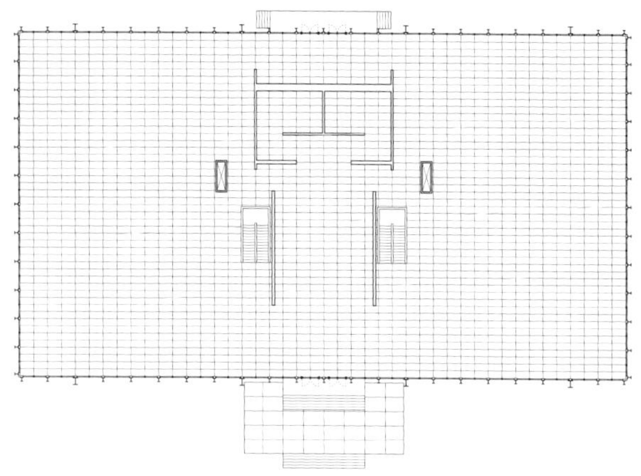

Floor Plan

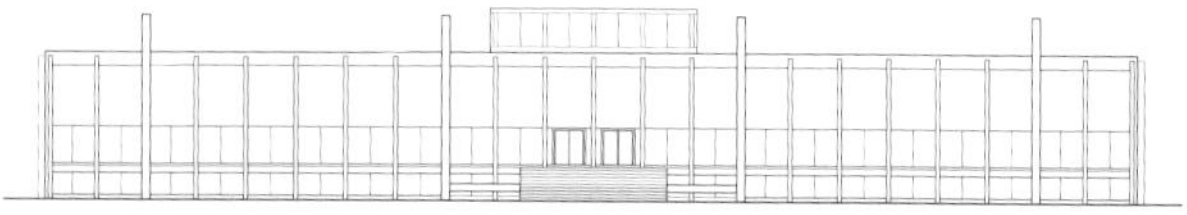

Elevation

0 10M 50′

87° 37′ 38″W

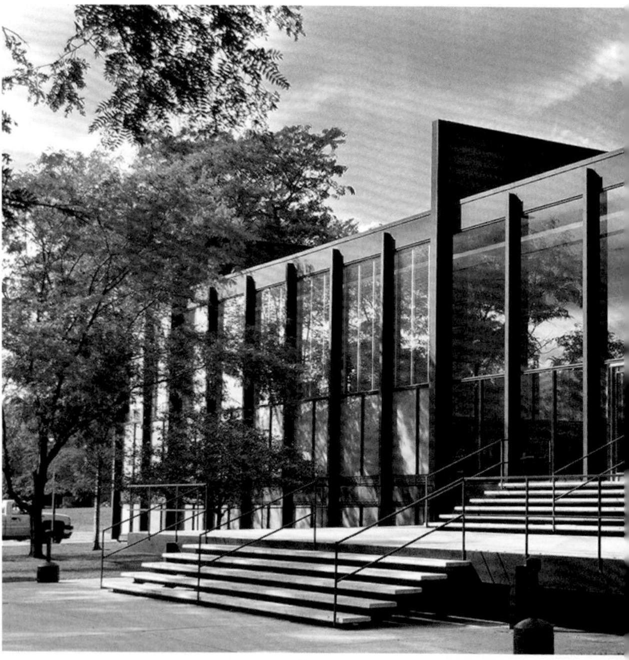

50

CROWN HALL

MIES VAN DER ROHE
Chicago, Illinois, USA
1950–1956

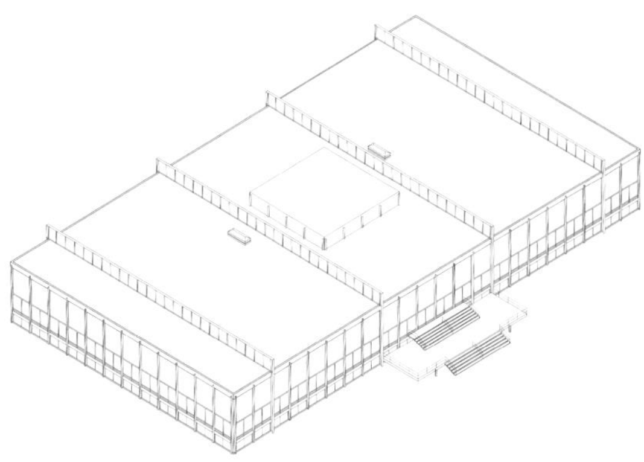

The composition of Crown Hall is characteristic of Mies van der Rohe's work of the 1950s: monumental in expression and programmatically neutral, the building is at first glance a generic glass box, but with distinct attention paid to its detailing and proportions. Its prismatic upper level is elevated, templelike, above the ground plane and onto a plinth. Its roof plane is suspended from a series of deep, long span trusses. Peripherally organized in plan, space is distributed around isolated service cores, essentially symmetrical and arranged according to proportion. The simplicity of this building, designed to be the School of Architecture for the Illinois Institute of Technology in Chicago, translates an idealistic aspiration related to the view of human function: a place with a holistic potential and monumental presence, specific to neither place nor to individual incident.

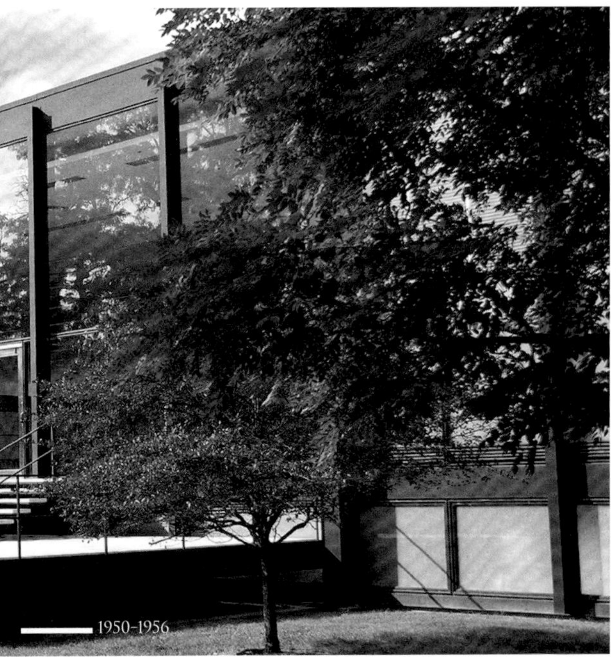

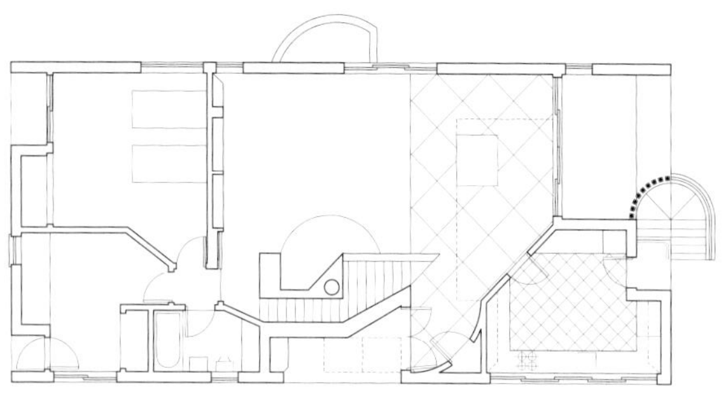

Floor Plan

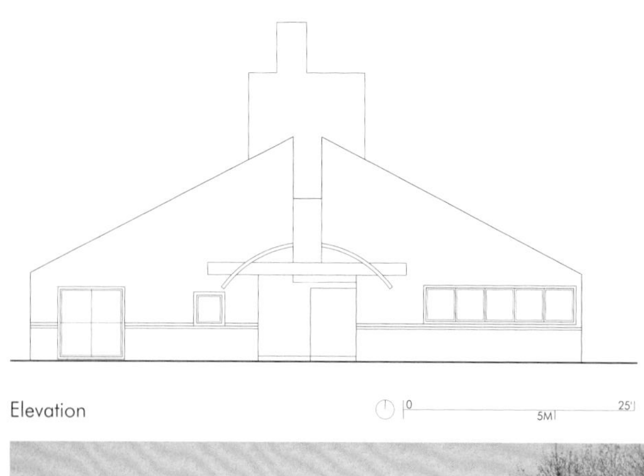

Elevation

0 25′ 5M

75° 12′ 29″W

51

VANNA VENTURI HOUSE

ROBERT VENTURI and DENISE SCOTT BROWN
Chestnut Hill, Pennsylvania, USA
1962–1964

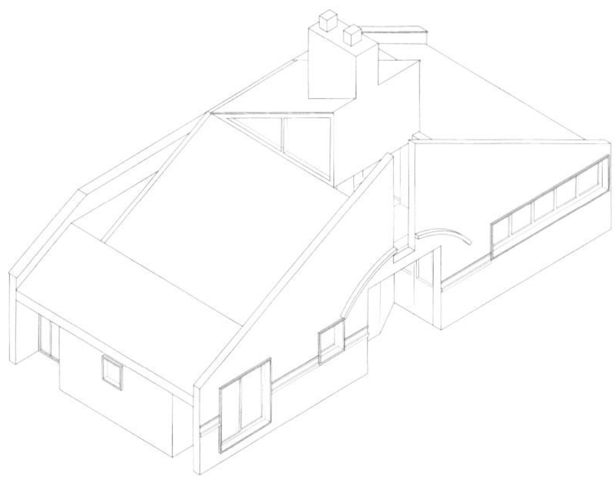

With quotations from the facades of Le Corbusier's Villa at Garches and Moretti's Casa Girasole, combined with plans from Lutyens and McKim, the house Robert Venturi designed for his mother was both an homage and a challenge to modern architecture. Disjunctions and dislocations abound: the fireplace disrupts the stair as they vie for centrality; the volume of the upper floor and the diagonal of the kitchen disrupt a vault attempting to soar over the dining space; a broken arch is inscribed over a beam on the entry facade, which is itself symmetrical in massing but asymmetrical in fenestration; and, in the rear, a large thermal window emerges uncomfortably close to a shed roof. Anxiously remarkable while feigning unremarkability, the house posed a monumental domesticity that seeded the text of Venturi's *Complexity and Contradiction in Architecture* and is considered an initiator of postmodernism.

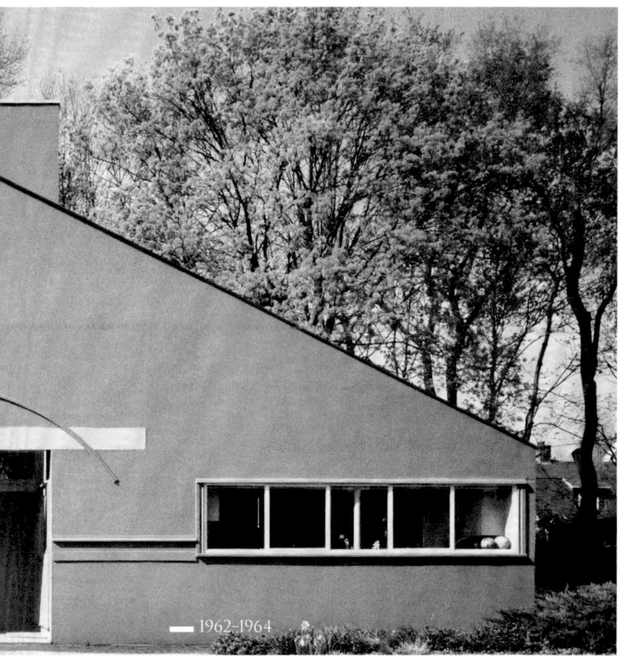

34° 07′ 05″N

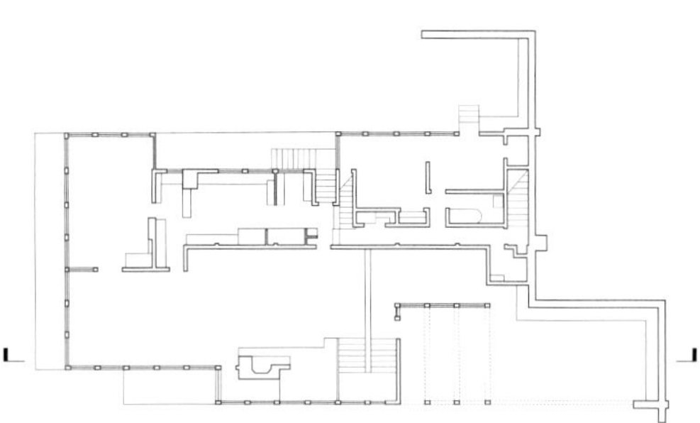

Floor Plan

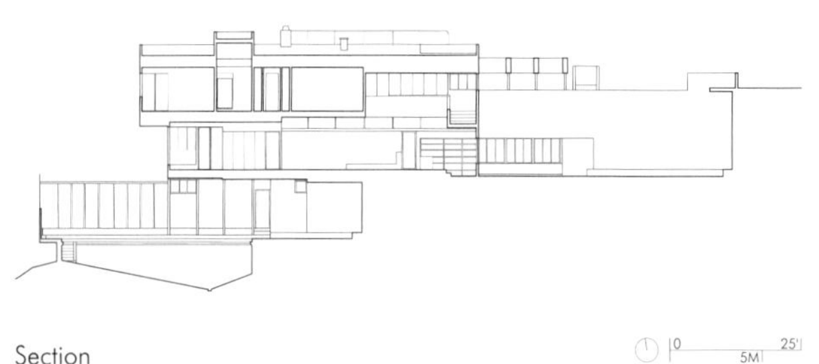

Section

0 25′ 5M

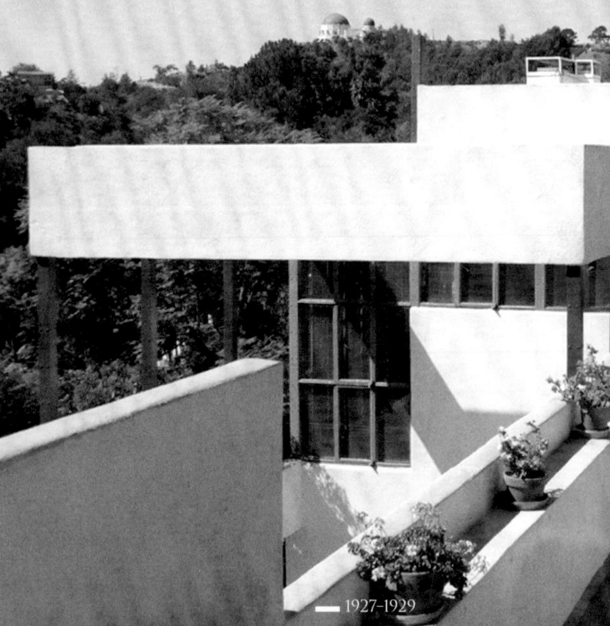

118° 17′ 16″W

1927–1929

52

LOVELL HEALTH HOUSE

RICHARD NEUTRA
Los Angeles, California, USA
1927–1929

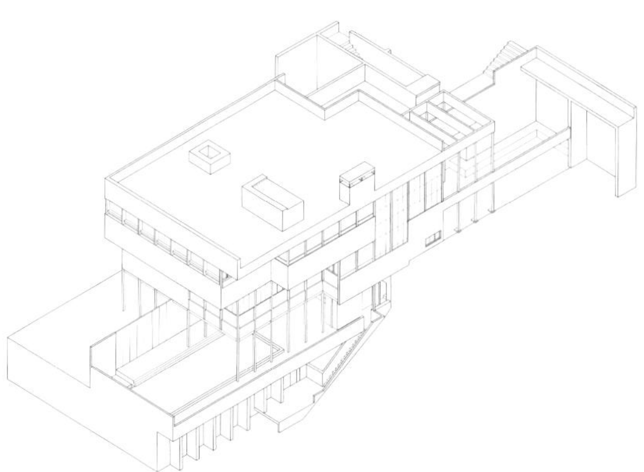

From the first views of its astonishingly thin, steel-frame skeleton (facilitated by steel tension cables anchoring the construction to the hillside), it was obvious that a new type of architecture had arrived in Los Angeles. Publicly sited on a hill overlooking the city, the Lovell Health House represented one of the first uses of steel framing in residential architecture, while also pioneering the use of gunite (now known as shotcrete), sprayed onto insulating panels that were used as formwork. Designed for a naturopath who believed in nude sunbathing, sleeping outside, and ample natural air and sunlight, the "health house," as it came to be called, provided Neutra with the perfect opportunity to explore new construction technologies and materials while designing vast, open interiors that continuously engage the exterior, with suspended balconies, large bands of steel-sashed windows, and distant views of the city.

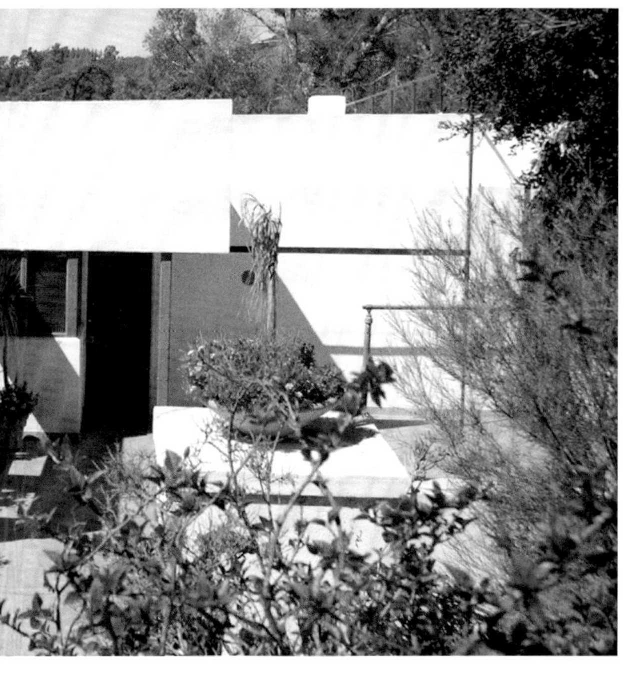

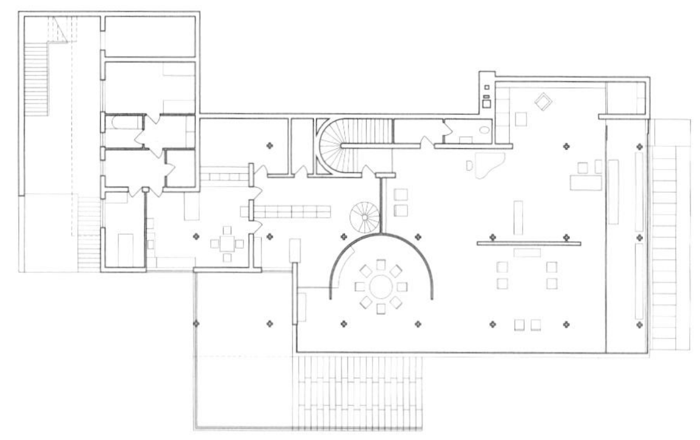

Floor Plan

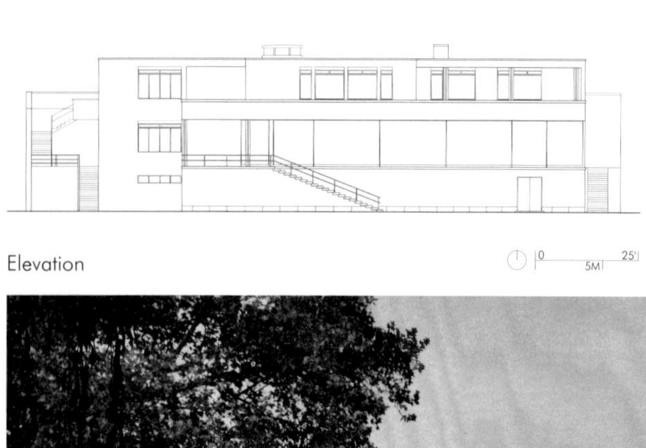

Elevation

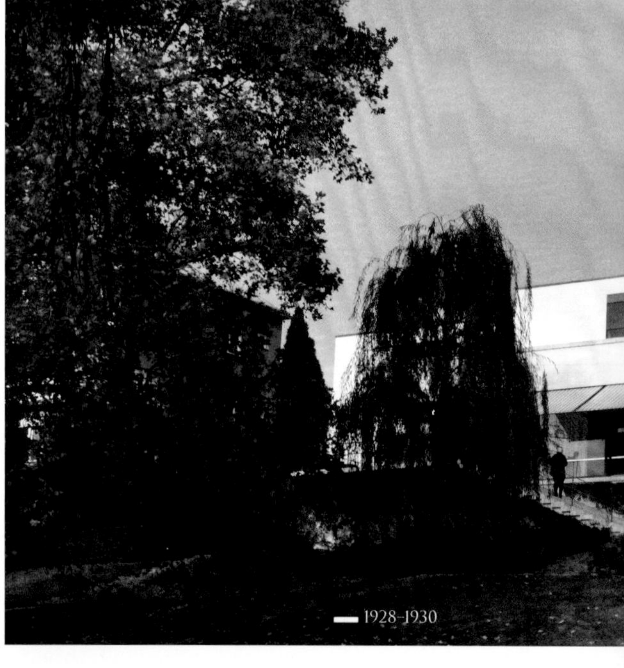

49° 12′ 26″N

53

TUGENDHAT HOUSE

MIES VAN DER ROHE
Brno, Czech Republic
1928–1930

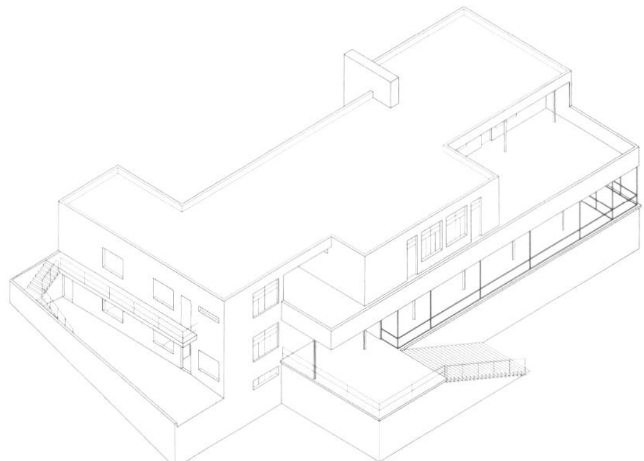

If the German Pavilion at the Barcelona Exposition were to be domesticated—its walls thickened to become bedrooms, its milk-glass volume rounded, its cruciform columns more rounded, and the pieces arrayed over three floors set into a hillside—the Tugendhat House would be the result. One enters the house from the top level to almost immediately descend to a plane of living and social spaces generously bathed in daylight, with enormous floor-to-ceiling window walls on the south and east sides, stretching nearly the full length of the house and offering vistas of Brno below. To express true continuity of space between inside and outside, alternate panels of the glazed elevation retract into the basement, converting the second floor to an outdoor terrace, with the apse-like dining area, clad in Macassar ebony, a private viewing platform to the city.

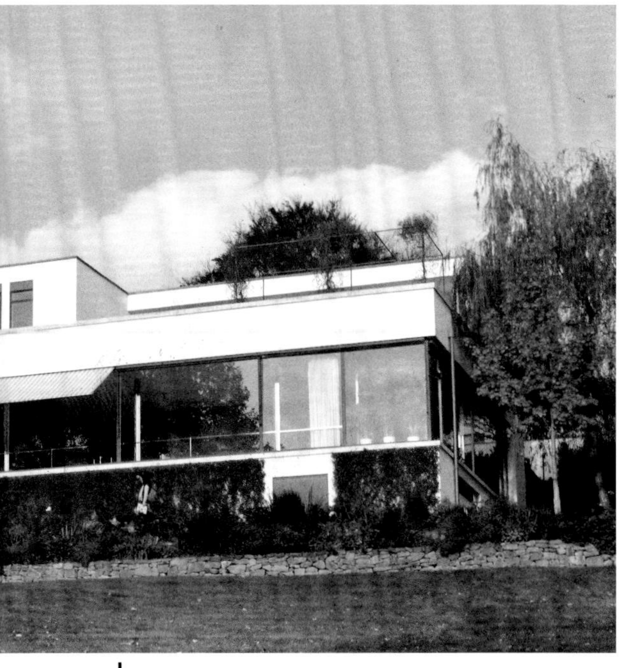

16° 36′ 58″E

42° 21′ 25″N

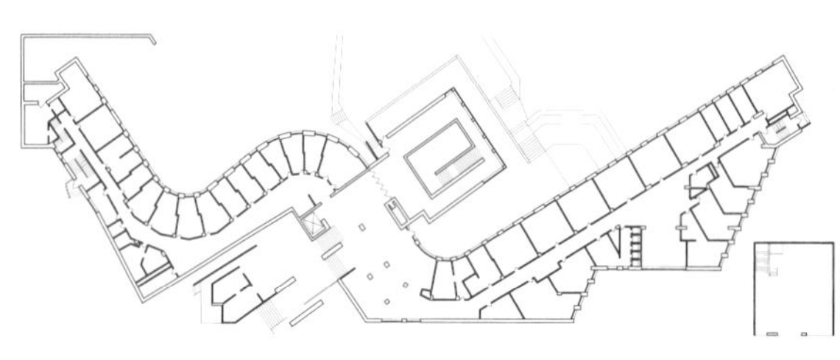

Floor Plan

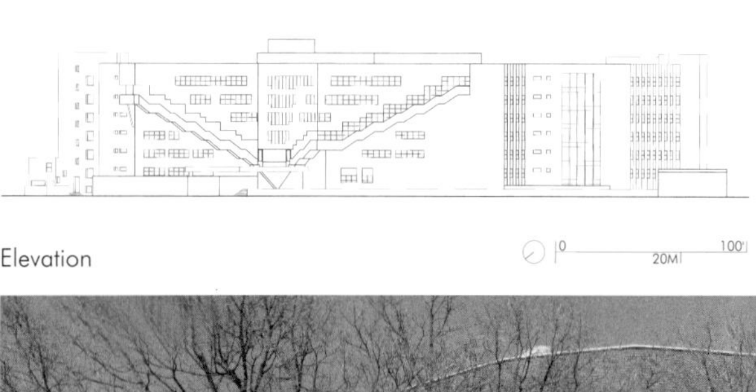

Elevation

71° 05′ 45″W

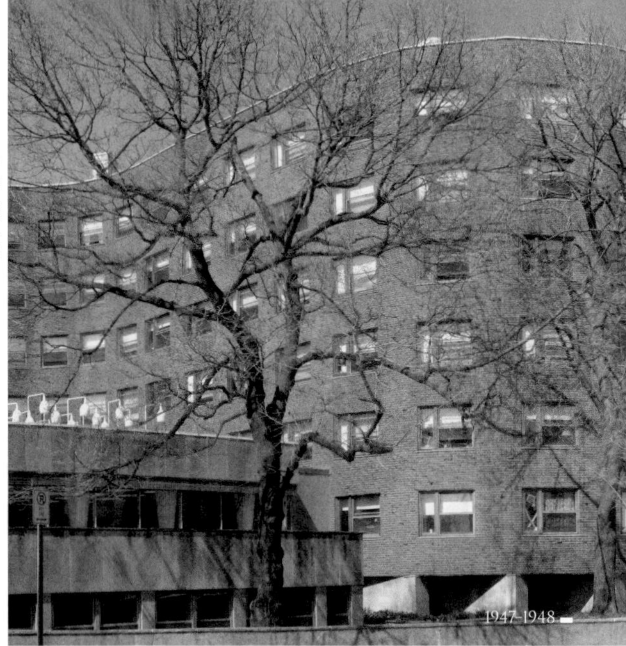

54

BAKER HOUSE

ALVAR AALTO

Massachusetts Institute of Technology, Cambridge, Massachusetts, USA

1947–1948

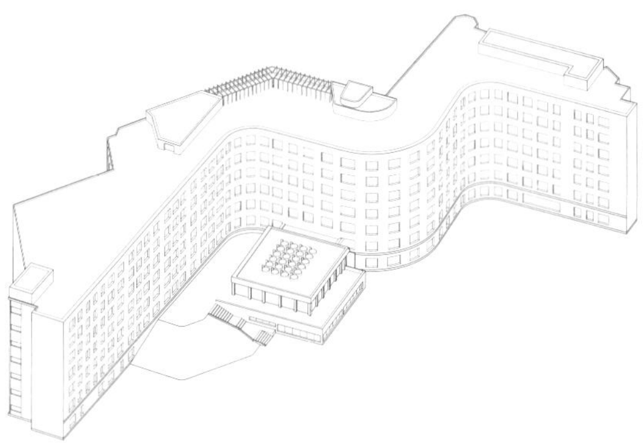

As an architect always concerned about integrating the natural environment with the built environment (and a visiting professor at MIT at the time), Alvar Aalto was well aware of the importance of the Charles River, and of the value of sunlight in a dormitory in Cambridge, Massachusetts. Consequently, the Baker House dormitory places a sinuous brick volume of rooms facing south to the equally sinuous river, with a more urban, jagged volume of glass and concrete facing north, containing cascading stairways and common spaces located off the single-loaded corridor. The curvature of the river volume permits maximum exposure of the rooms to the river while optimizing the lines of sight so as to focus on the river rather than the road in front. Baker House introduced the concept of dormitory as both private refuge and social event.

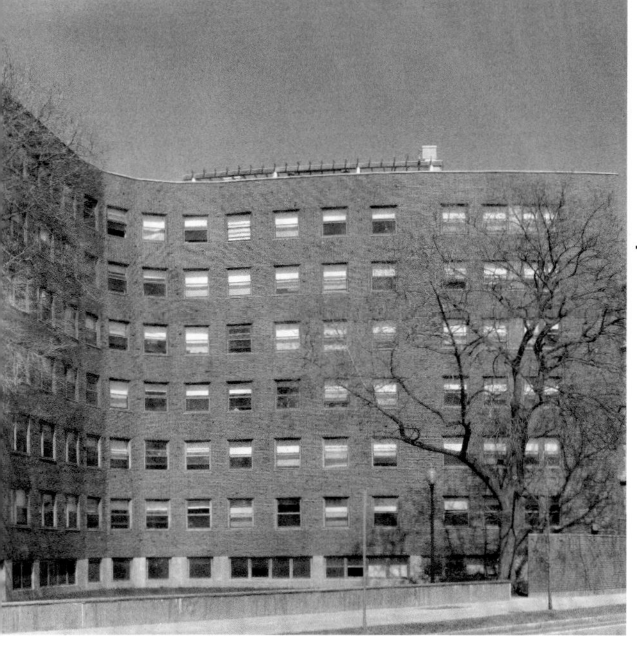

19° 24′ 39″N

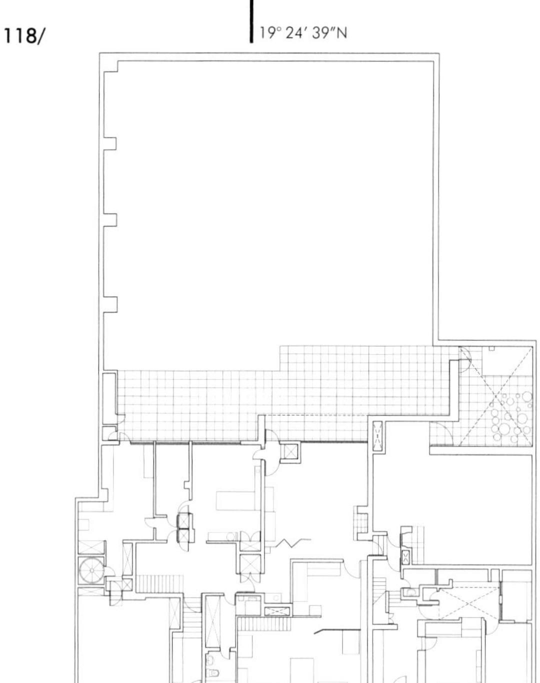

Floor Plan

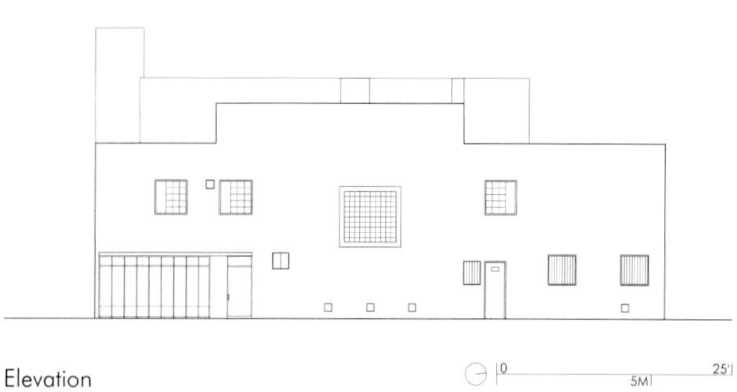

Elevation

99° 11′ 31″W

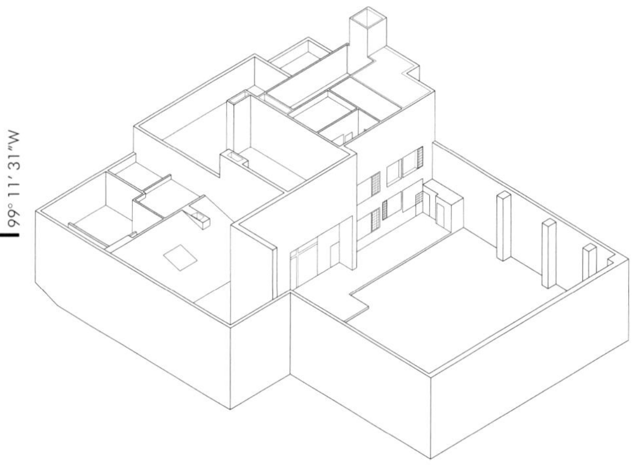

1947–1948

55

BARRAGÁN HOUSE AND STUDIO

LUIS BARRAGÁN
Mexico City, Mexico
1947–1948

Challenging the functionalist doctrines and specious intellectualism of early modernism, Barragán exemplified a new generation of modern, non-European architects inspired and catalyzed by their native cultures and social values. The Barragán House locates these regional initiatives through a sequential spatial unveiling that transforms the house both in plan and in experience. One begins by observing the solid, banal, and homogenized street facade of the house as a physical and conceptual datum: gray, stuccoed, and with apparently random openings, it resembles all of its neighbors. Upon entering through this facade, one is thrust into a series of abstract spaces of deeply saturated colors that dematerialize to reveal hints of a beautiful garden beyond. This choreographed transformation from uncontrolled urbanity, to carefully colored spaces, to a landscaped oasis, and eventually to the rooftop terraces with surfaces as pure as their colors, defines Barragán as an architect who acknowledges and engages in the full spectrum of contemporary environments.

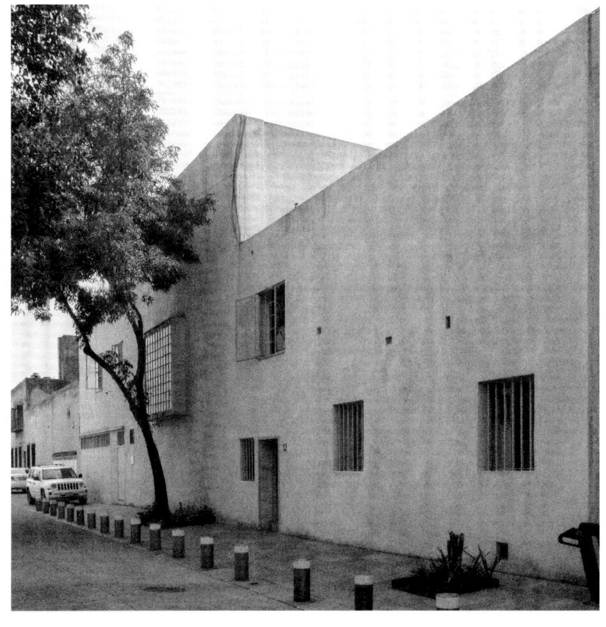

41° 18′ 42″N

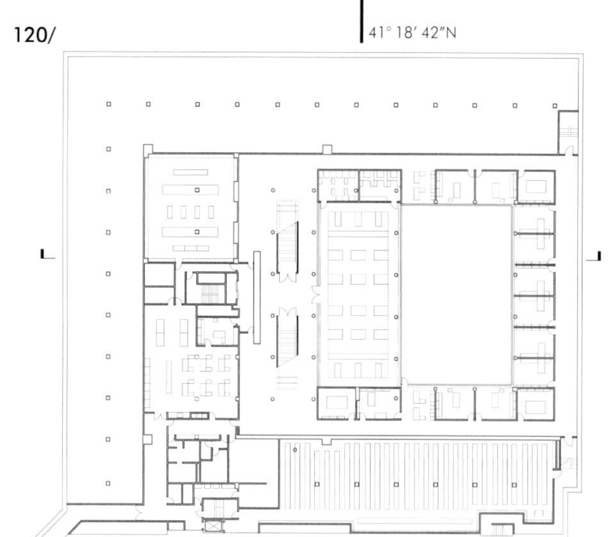

Floor Plan

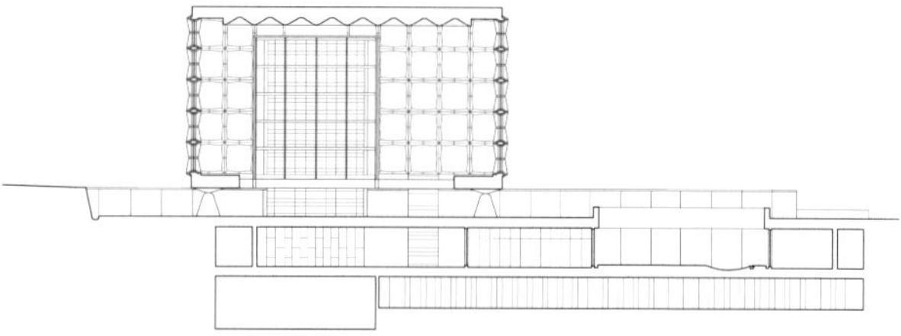

Section

0 10M 50′

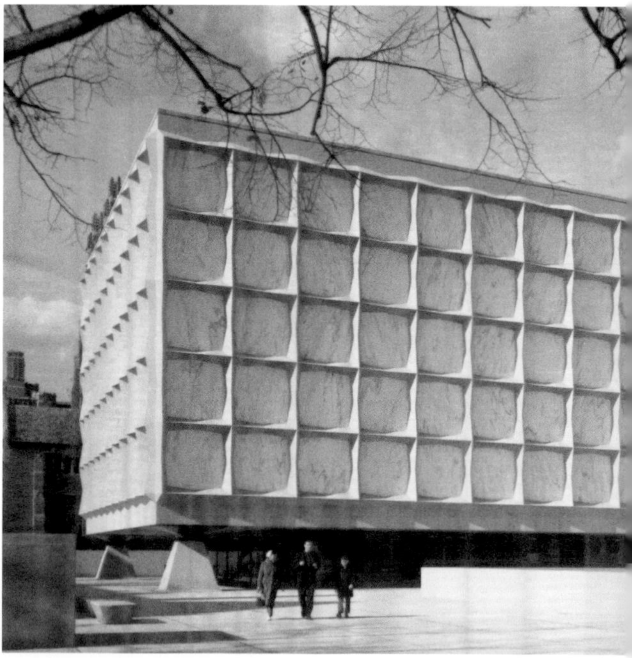

72° 55′ 38″W

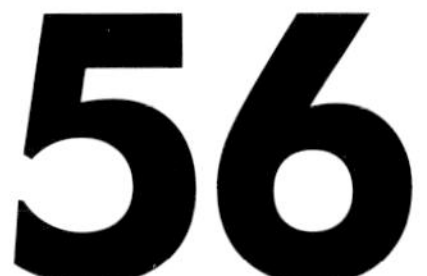

THE BEINECKE RARE BOOK & MANUSCRIPT LIBRARY

GORDON BUNSHAFT (SOM)

Yale University, New Haven, Connecticut, USA

1960–1963

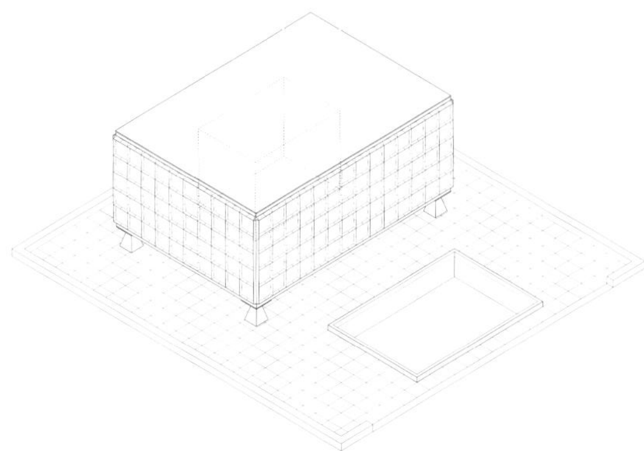

Among Gordon Bunshaft's most poetic and experientially transcendent works, the Beinecke Library at Yale University takes the program of rare book library and turns it into a reverential shrine, cloistered securely within what appears to the viewer to be a solid block of white Vermont marble perched on four massive corner piers. Taking tectonic and material cues from the historic Yale campus, the marble becomes a phenomenally thin membrane through which the soft amber glow of sunlight diffuses during the day, and that glows lantern-like at night, creating what are in effect "stone windows." Standing within the three-story-tall volume is an elegantly detailed bronze-and-glass book tower. An open plaza at grade is cut by a single-level courtyard that brings light into the basement and contains an abstract stone-scape by Isamu Noguchi, using the same marble and allegorically reiterating the building's themes.

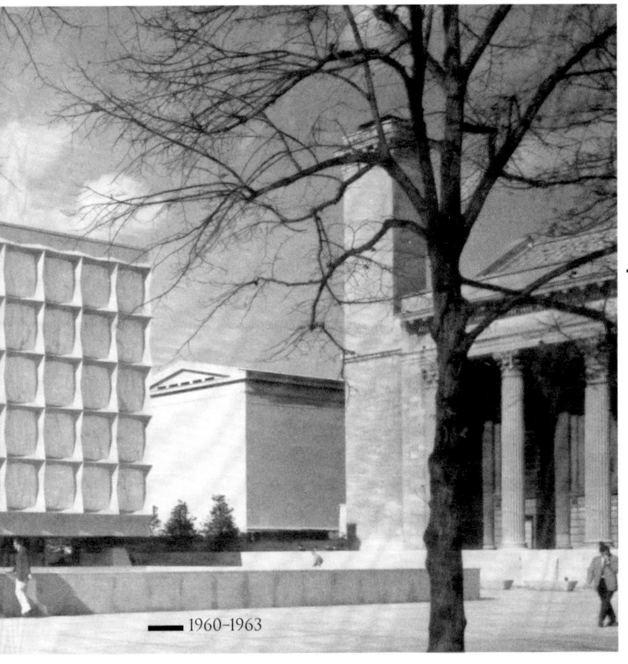

1960–1963

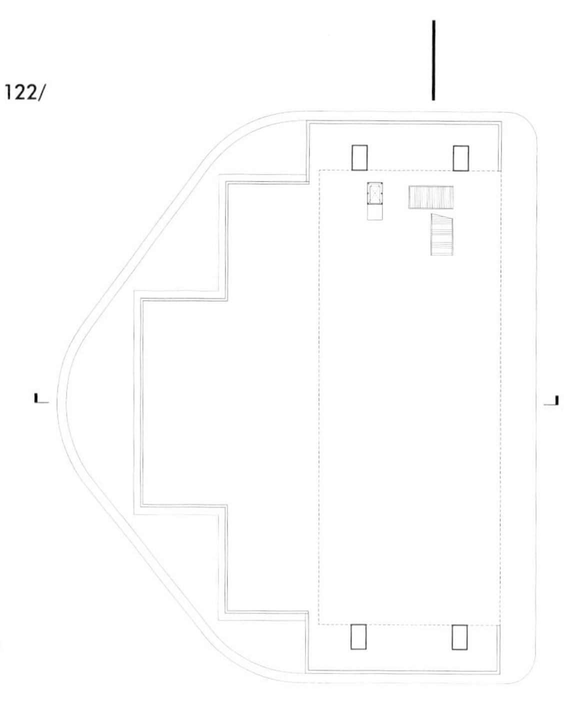

Floor Plan

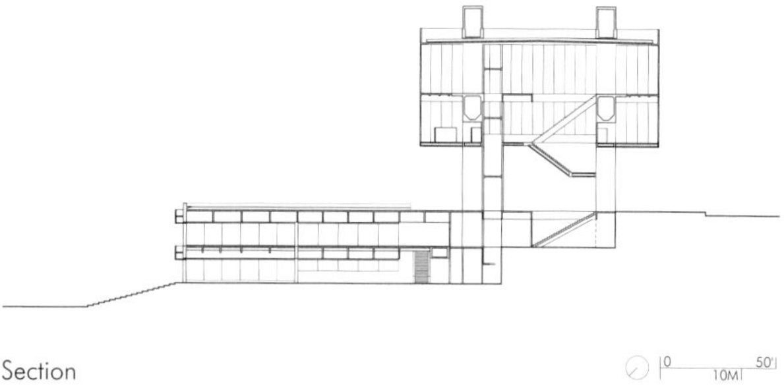

Section

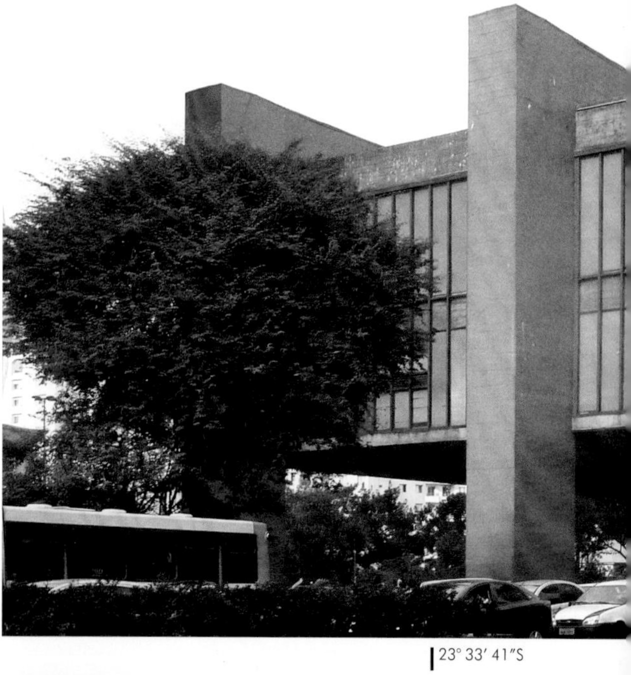

0 50'
10M

46° 39′ 22″W

23° 33′ 41″S

57

MUSEU DE ARTE DE SÃO PAULO

LINA BO BARDI
São Paulo, Brazil
1957–1968

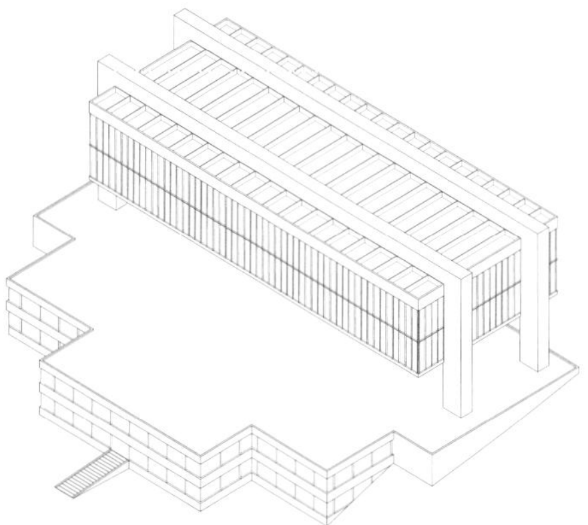

Located along a major avenue, situated above a highway, and forming an edge for Trianon Park, Lina Bo Bardi's MASP is as clever in its urban strategy as it is in its structural resolution. Four large concrete piers each support two beams, one at the roof level and another between the two floors. These beams support a series of crossbeams, with the lower slab suspended from the central crossbeams. The impression is that of a large crystalline box suspended from two concrete frames. This permits the park to continue into a large, uninterrupted public belvedere overlooking the city below. Inside, program is distributed both above and below this terrace. Following Bo Bardi's intent to always reinforce the presence of the public, the galleries above originally featured large spans of glass open to the city on all sides. Additional galleries, a restaurant, a theater, and ancillary spaces are located belowground.

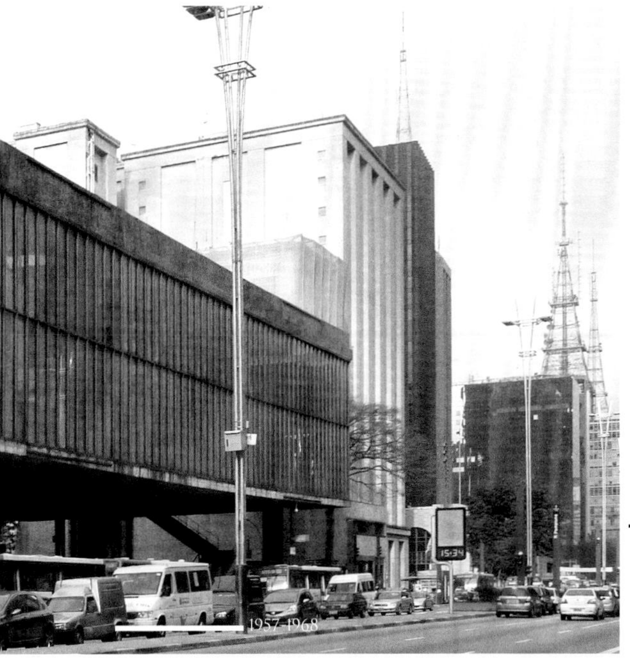

1957–1968

Floor Plan

Section

0 25'
5M

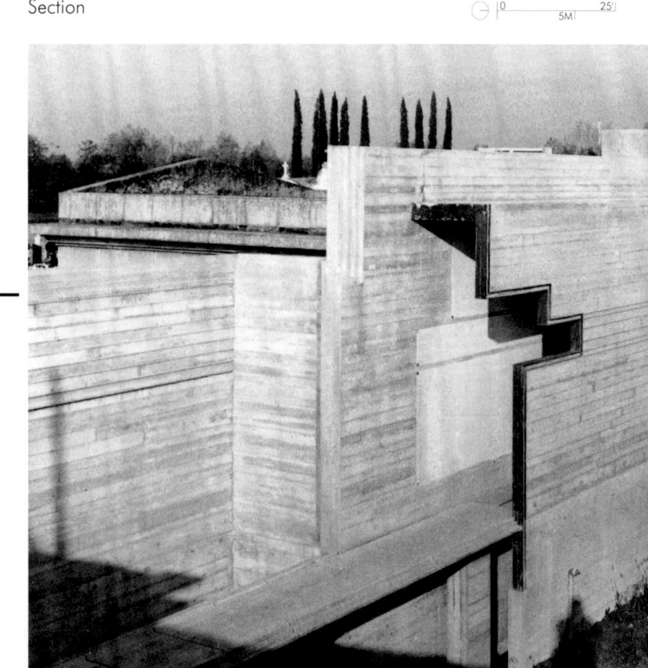

45° 45′ 05″N

58

BRION FAMILY TOMB

CARLO SCARPA
Treviso, Italy
1969–1978

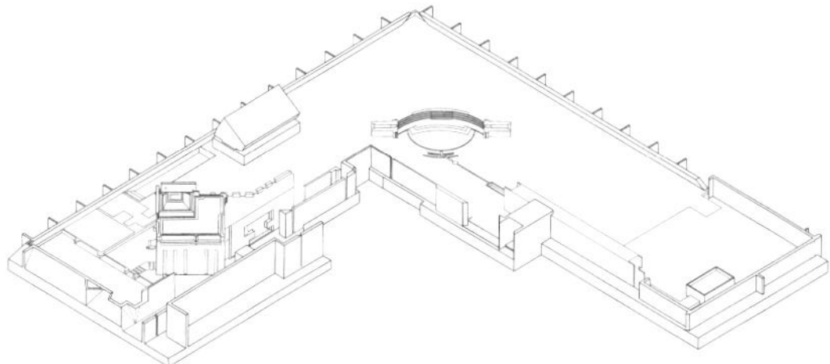

One approaches the private Brion-Vega Cemetery through the modest cemetery of San Vito d'Altivole. In size and massing, its portal is not unlike the other family tombs there. However, once through this portal and faced with the prospect seen through two large interlocking circles—a recurrent theme throughout the Brion-Vega complex—one is aware that this is clearly more than a mEDITAtion on death: it is a fractal world where the whole appears to continuously expand (around a corner, over a wall, across a horizon), and each part seems to fragment into even more parts. The memorial occupies an L-shaped lot that encloses the larger cemetery on two sides. Within, there is a contemplation pavilion in the midst of a pond, a semi-excavated arcosolium containing two sarcophagi and shrouded with a broad arch, an additional family tomb, a chapel, numerous pools, and a utility building/sacristy, all repeating various thematic relationships to earth and sky, water and light. Scarpa provides a wholly poetic experience without specifically reciting poetry, but by saturating the visitor's experience with poetic opportunities.

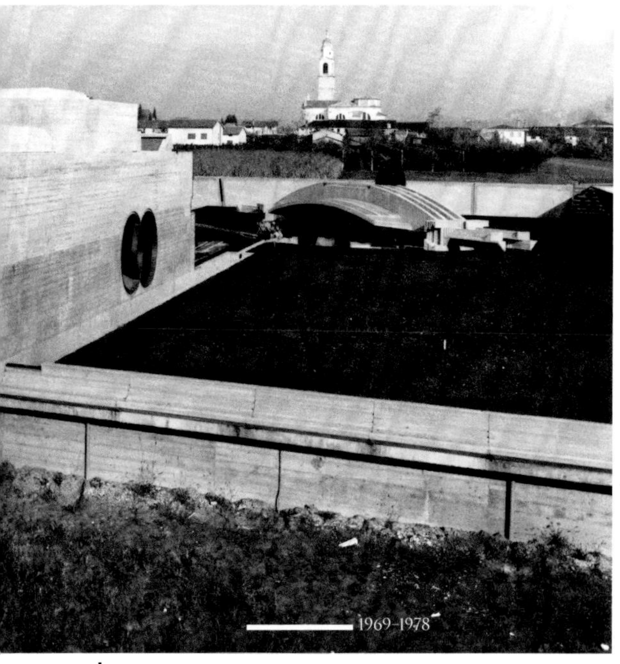

11° 54′ 49″E

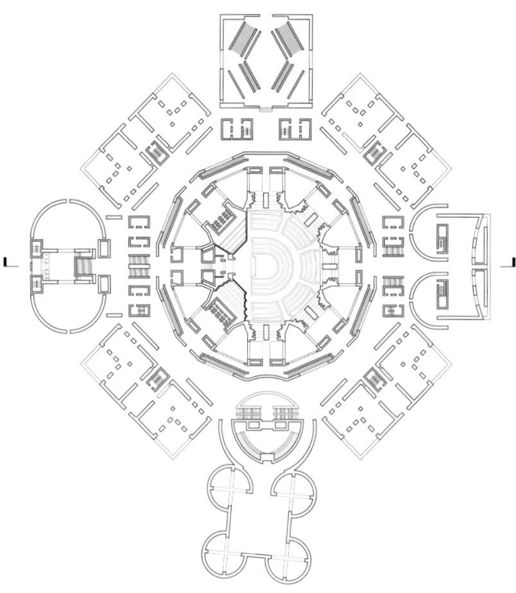

Floor Plan

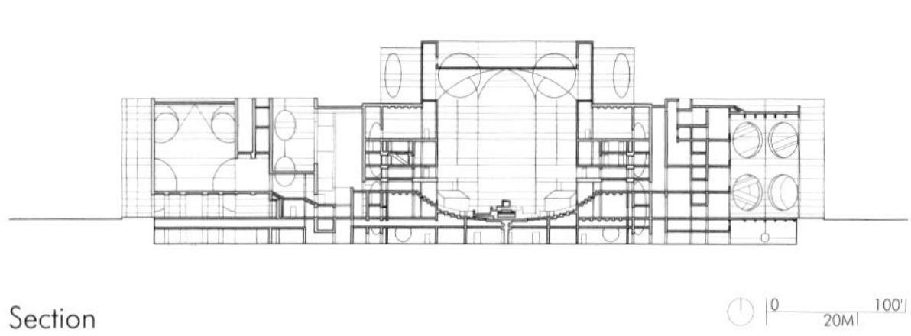

Section

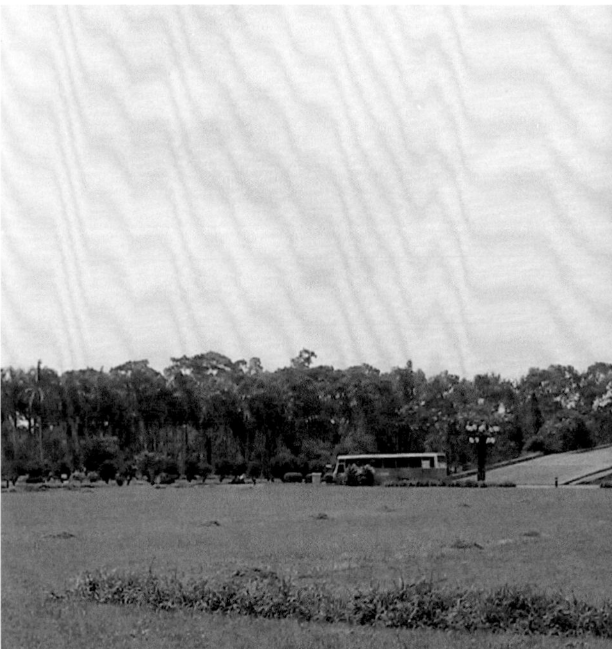

23° 45′ 46″N

59

NATIONAL ASSEMBLY BUILDING, BANGLADESH

LOUIS KAHN
Dhaka, Bangladesh
1962–1983

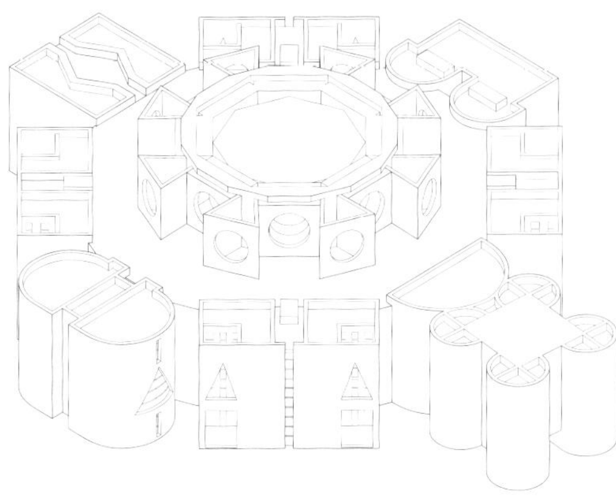

A monumental brick-and-reinforced concrete complex, the National Assembly features pure geometric forms that mark the passing of time and the movement of the sun. Peripheral blocks contain the parliamentary functions and surround the central chamber, which is lit from above by an immense clerestory. The exteriors of the geometric volumes are kept largely mute, with the occasional abstracted opening used to bring cool air in from the surrounding lagoons. Massive, with an indefinite scale, moments of lightness and darkness are its principal delineators of space, with the occasional railing or stair to return it to the realm of human scale. Although columnless, it is essentially composed of huge, occupiable columns. As a virtually new city, it joins that of Luytens's New Delhi, Niemeyer's Brasília, and Le Corbusier's Chandigarh as one of the principal visions of the modern capital in the twentieth century.

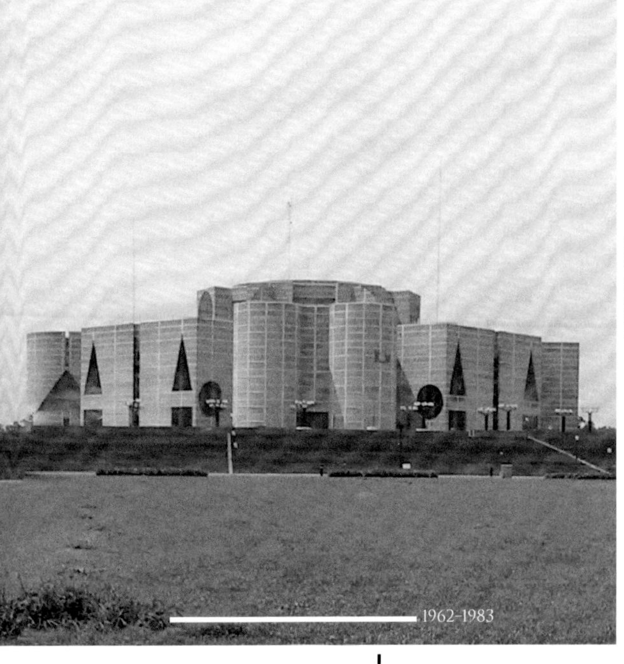
1962–1983

90° 22′ 42″E

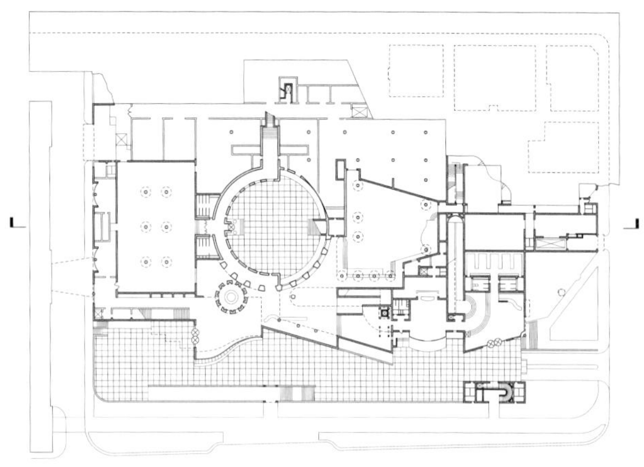

Floor Plan

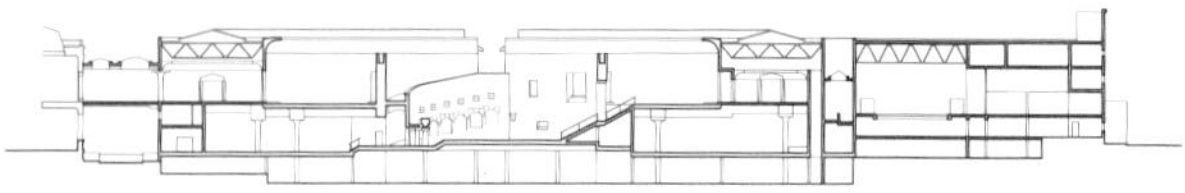

Section

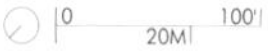

0 20M 100'

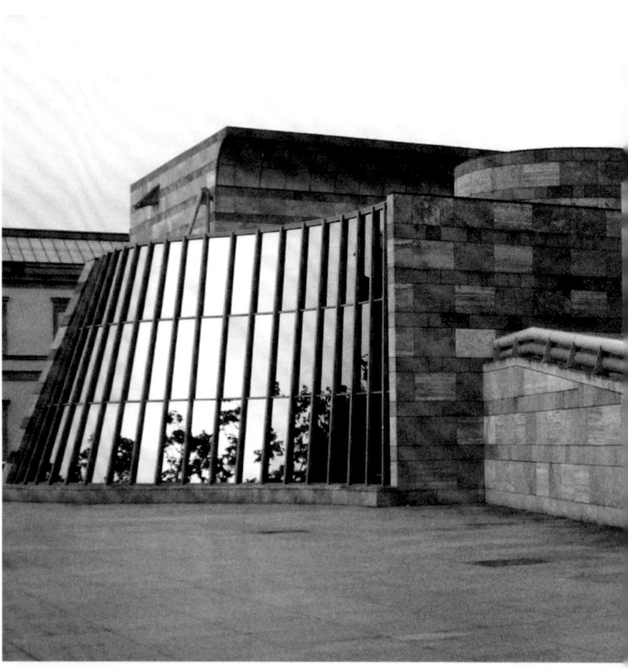

48° 46′ 48″N

60

NEUE STAATSGALERIE

JAMES STIRLING, MICHAEL WILFORD and ASSOCIATES
Stuttgart, Germany
1977–1983

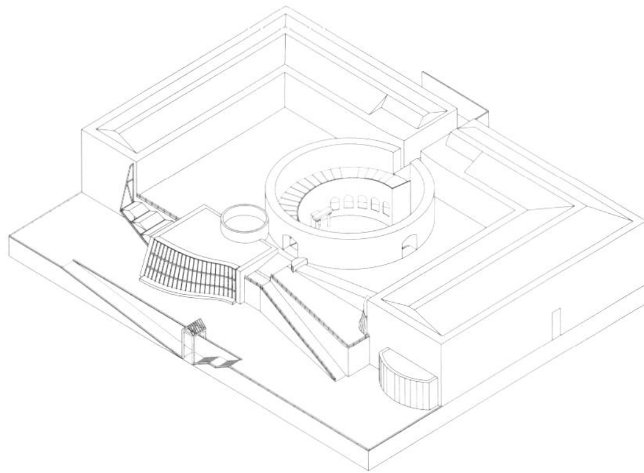

Stirling's 1977 competition-winning design blurs the boundaries between museum and the public realm through a closely interwoven series of plazas and courtyards on a sloping urban site. The building adopts organizational aspects of the historic museum building to which it is linked: most notably a symmetrical plan filled with top-lit galleries arranged as an enfilade. The new building surrounds a circular court, open to the sky, around the perimeter of which the public circulation route traverses. The scale of the compositional elements at the main entry breaks down the formal hierarchy of the plan, eroding the building expression to invite visitors into the interior. The building remains an exemplar of many of Colin Rowe's ideas outlined in the book *Collage City*, in which modern architecture mediates history, urbanism, context, sequence, and the territory between representation and abstraction.

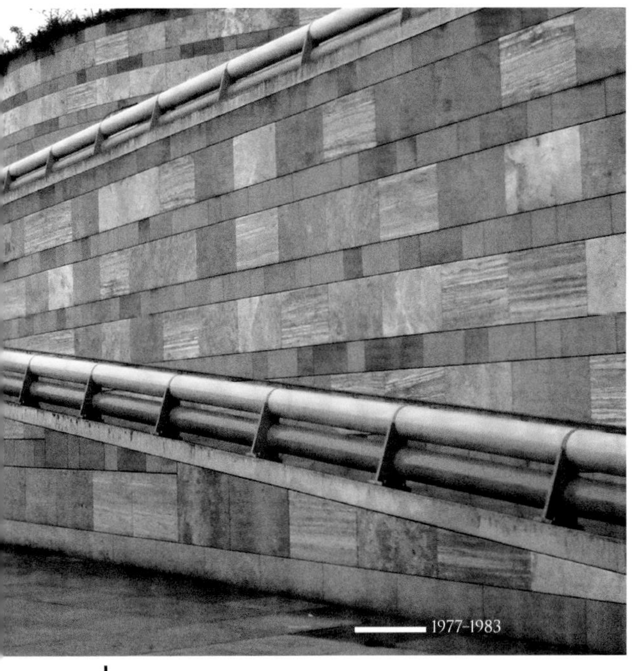

9° 11′ 11″E

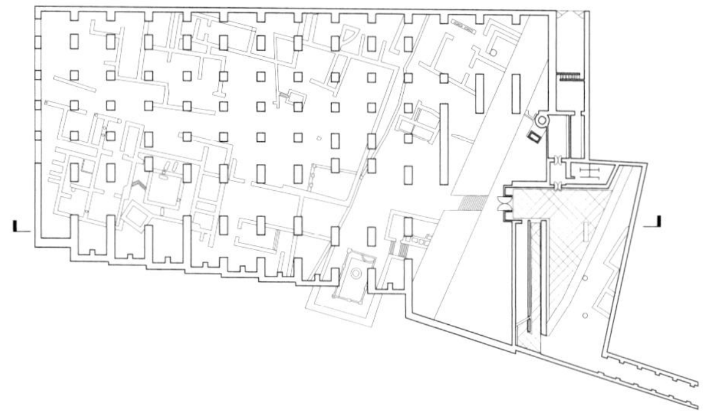

Floor Plan

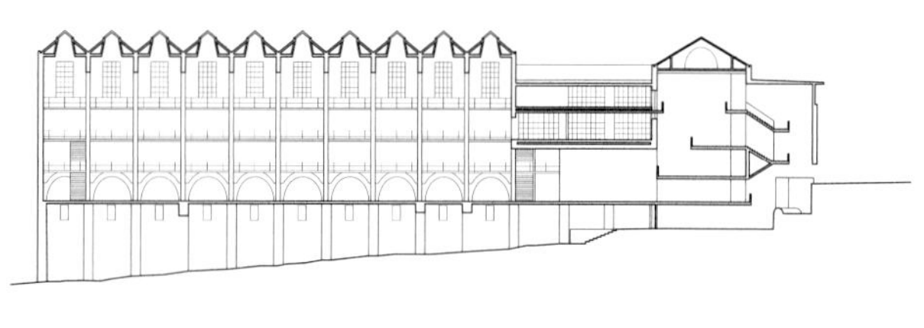

Section

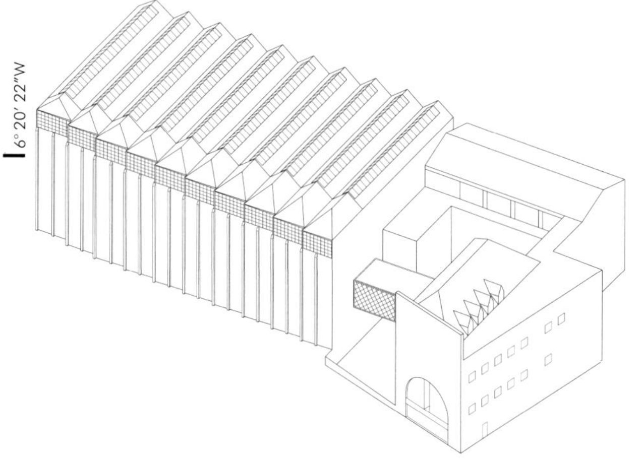

38° 55′ 02″N

61

NATIONAL MUSEUM OF ROMAN ART

RAFAEL MONEO
Mérida, Spain
1980–1986

A modern basilica cadenced by a series of soaring brick arches, this building sits adjacent to the ancient Roman complex of Mérida. Simultaneously expressing historicity and modernity, Moneo suggests ancient brickwork techniques and the resultant play of sunlight on the ruins, while stringing between these arched walls a series of light steel ambulatories, thereby creating a dialogue with the archaeological monuments and the contemporary urban surroundings, without resorting to imitation. The flank of the museum, along the Calle Mélida, has a strong resemblance, in proportion and modeling, to the proscenium of the nearby Roman theater. While the building's overall structural grid conforms to that of the existing city, in the subterranean level this grid conflicts with the grids of the excavated foundations, a disruption that clearly confronts old with new, with the new system's relatively undisturbed regularity of spacing being a measure of the ruins, objectifying them while covering them.

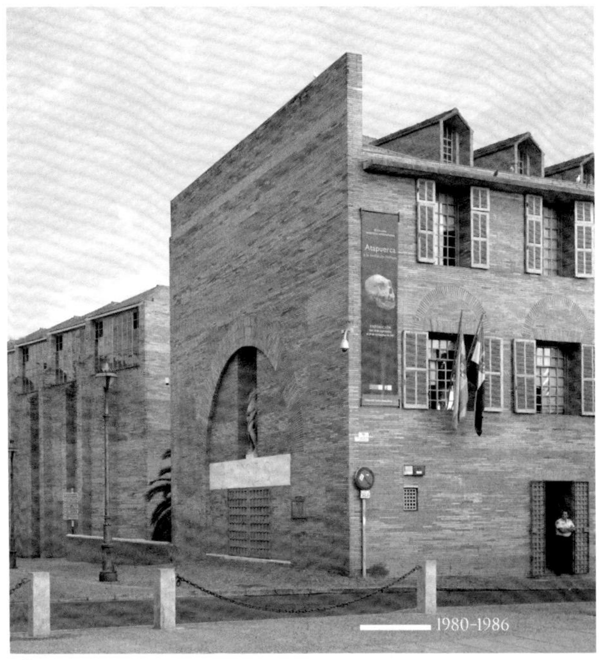

1980–1986

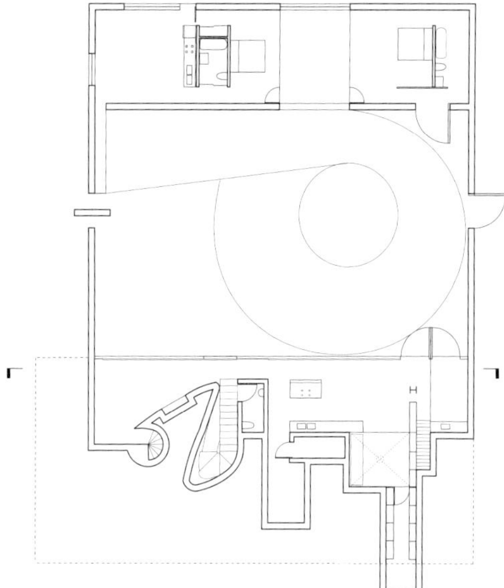

Floor Plan

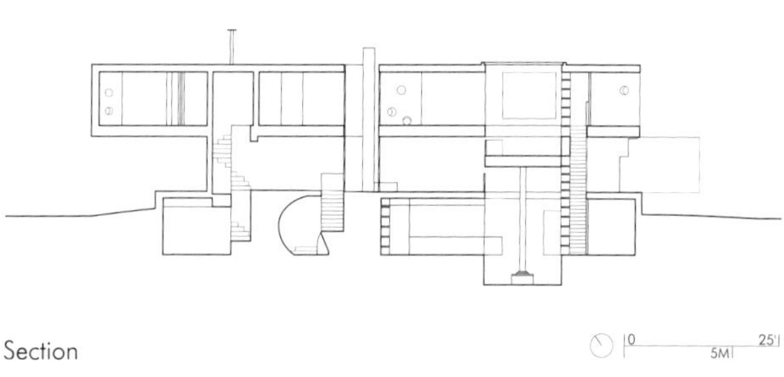

Section

0° 31' 05"W

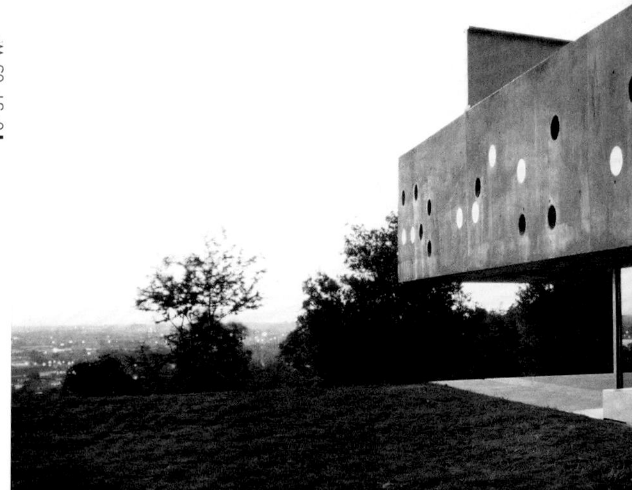

44° 49′ 42″N

62

MAISON À BORDEAUX

REM KOOLHAAS (OMA)
Bordeaux, France
1994–1998

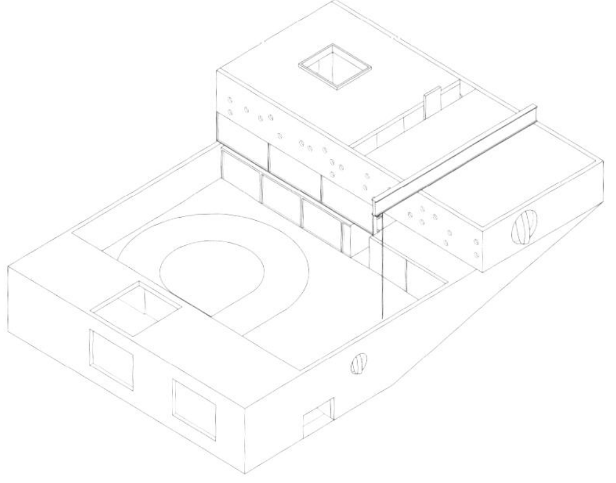

A house for a family whose patriarch is confined to a wheelchair, it is organized as three houses stacked one atop the other, the three layers "skewered"—both connected and separated—by a large platform lift elevator lined on one side by a wall of bookshelves containing "everything needed for living" and, symmetrically positioned, a tight spiral stair. By means of this machine at the heart of the plan, the owner could experience many aspects of life within the house from the platform. Sited atop a mountain, the base is treated as if it were a carved volume, two levels above is a large concrete box perforated with a series of porthole windows that frame specific views of the Bordeaux landscape. The intermediate layer is enclosed in floor-to-ceiling glass, reinforcing the structural and phenomenal "floating" aspect of the upper living volume.

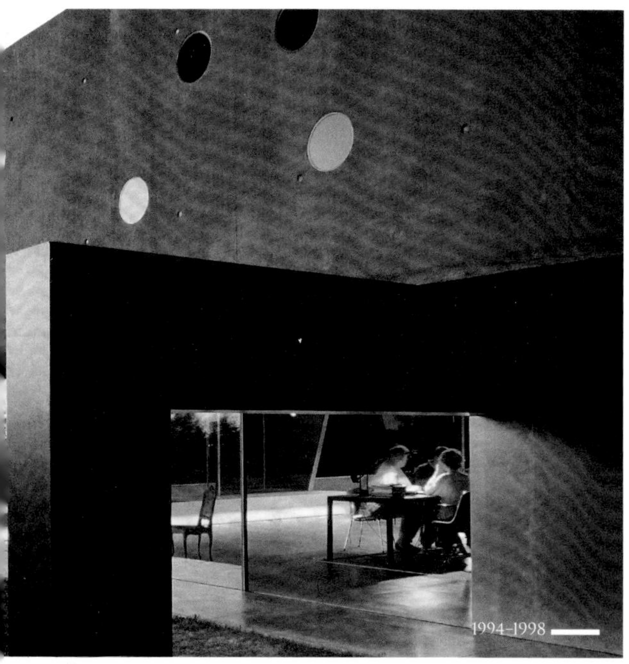

1994–1998

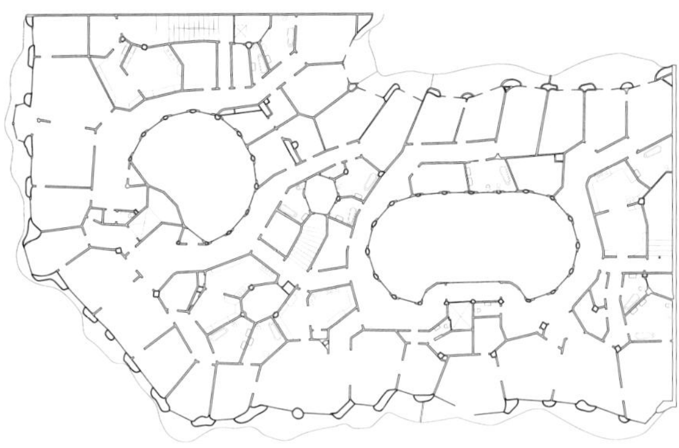

Floor Plan

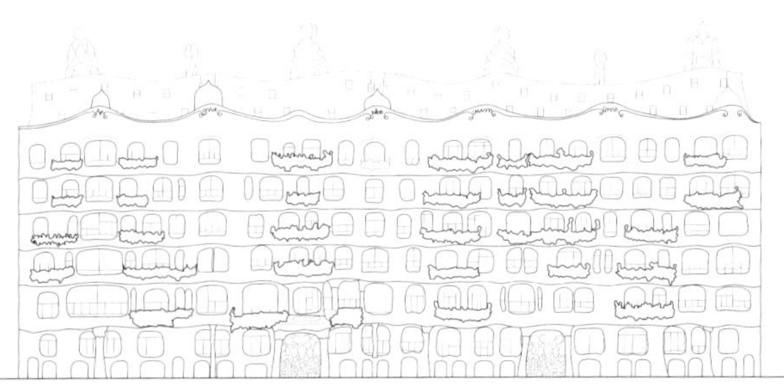

Elevation

0 10M 50'

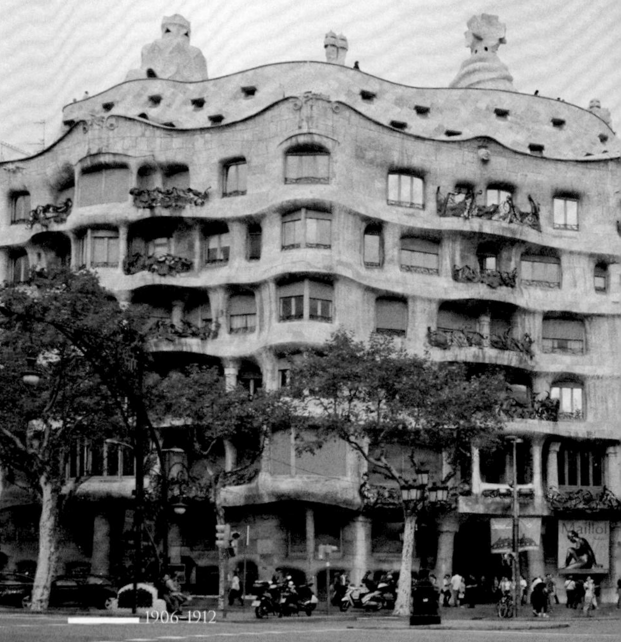

41° 23′ 44″N

63

CASA MILÀ

ANTONI GAUDÍ
Barcelona, Spain
1906–1912

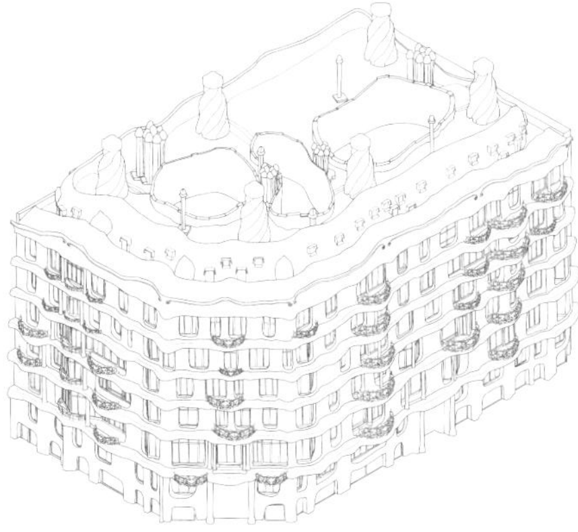

Though appearing to be random, Casa Milà's form is rooted in rational planning and structural principles, resting on pillars, arches, and steel beams that follow the curves of the facade, rather than the load-bearing walls one might expect from such an organic compilation. The facade is constructed of limestone, intricately cut to the specified curvatures, but with an irregular pattern of joints (hence the building's nickname, La Pedrera, or "The Quarry"). The sophisticated stonework is augmented with an equally elaborate program of ornamental ironwork, both plantlike and skeletal in its contours, all of which push the formal boundaries of rectilinearity, a characteristic of Catalan Art Nouveau. The roof of the building is a vast landscape of stepped terraces with monumental chimneys, skylights, access stair pavilions, and steep dormer-lined chasms that bring light to the building's two large courtyards.

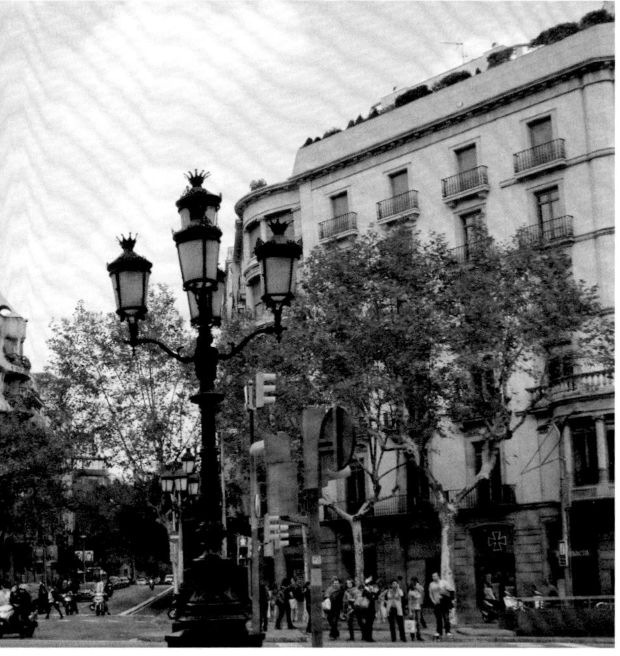

2° 09′ 43″E

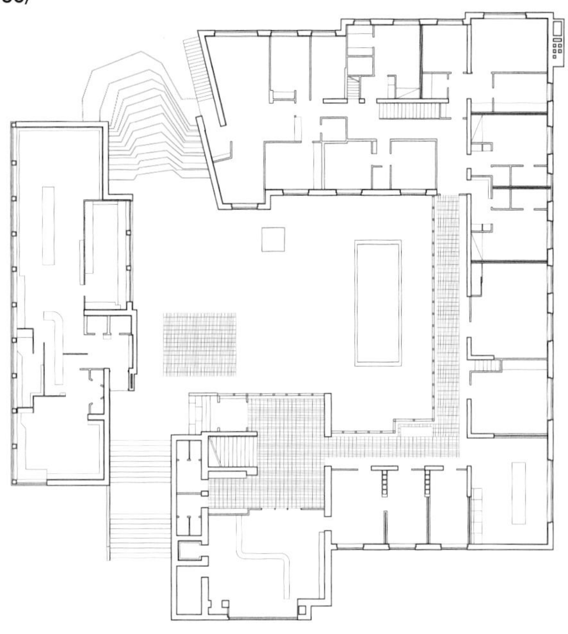

Floor Plan

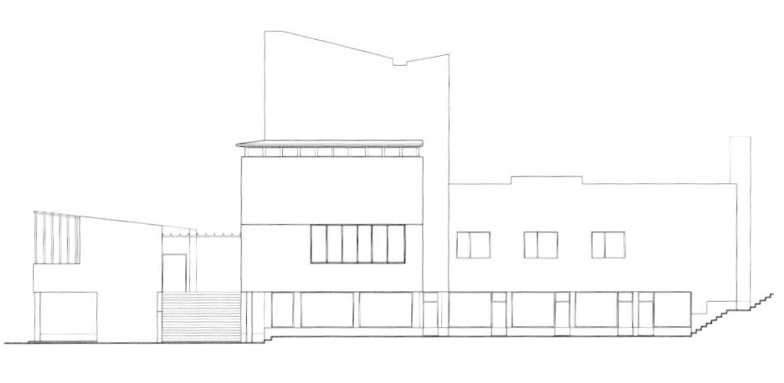

Elevation

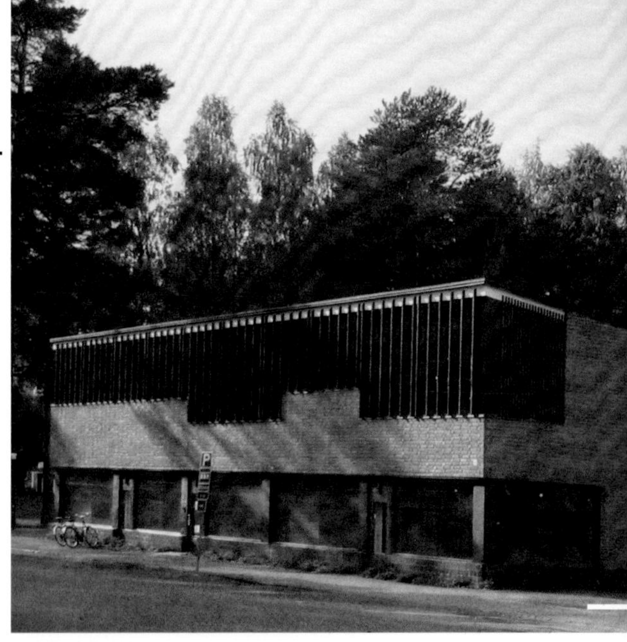

62° 08′ 25″N

64

SÄYNÄTSALO TOWN HALL

ALVAR AALTO
Säynätsalo, Finland
1949–1952

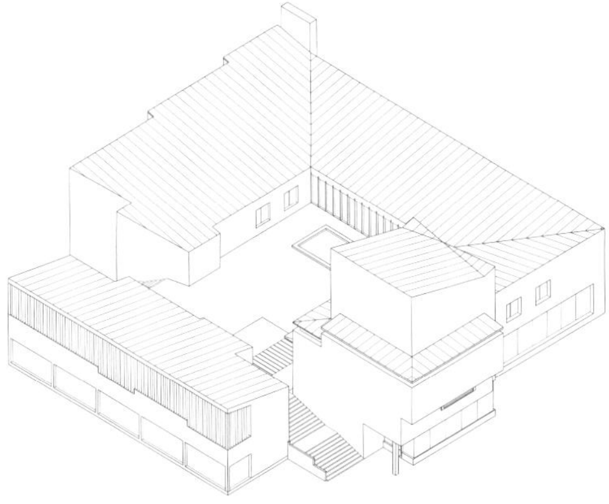

Serving the 3,000 residents of a new industrial town on an island in central Finland, this competition-winning scheme is based on a Renaissance-inspired courtyard plan, recalling traditional European civic plazas (specifically, as noted by Aalto, Siena's Piazza Pubblico). The courtyard is defined by a C-shaped administrative building of brick and wood, terminated by a truncated brick tower indicating the council chamber. The fourth side of the court contains a library with commercial spaces below. Whereas the site plan is classic, the building elevations are decidedly modern, with articulated and layered collages of forms, apertures, and landscape, including a grand "stair" that is of grass instead of stone. Aalto's partiality toward local materiality and tectonics, combined with his abstract interpretations of Western typologies, anchors his legacy as perhaps the foremost regional modernist of his generation.

25° 46′ 09″E

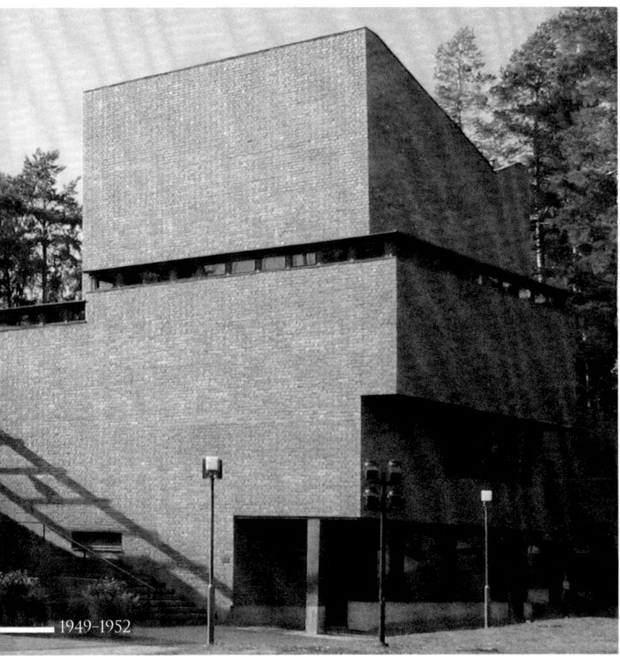

1949–1952

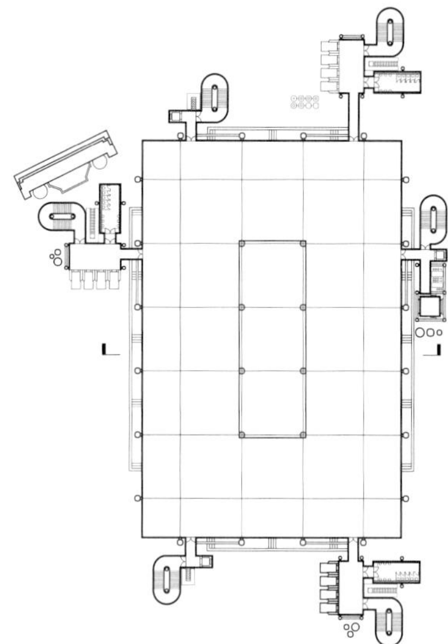

Floor Plan

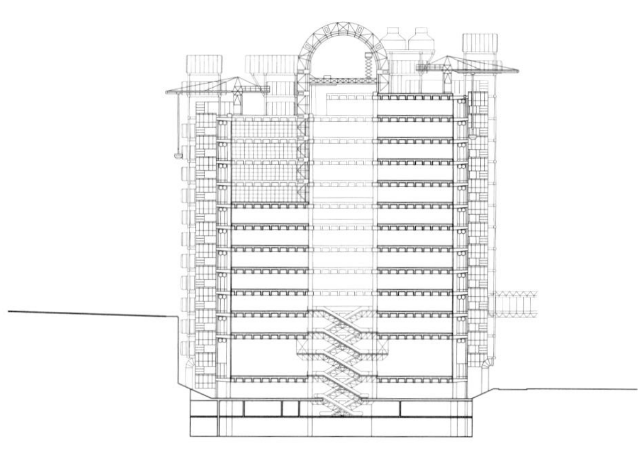

Section

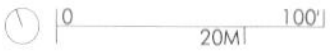

0 100' 20M

0° 04′ 56″W

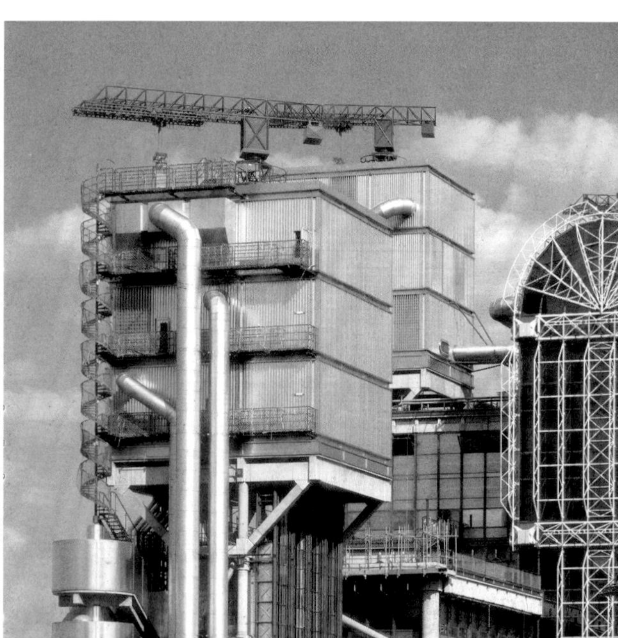

51° 30′ 48″N

65

LLOYD'S OF LONDON

RICHARD ROGERS
London, United Kingdom
1978–1986

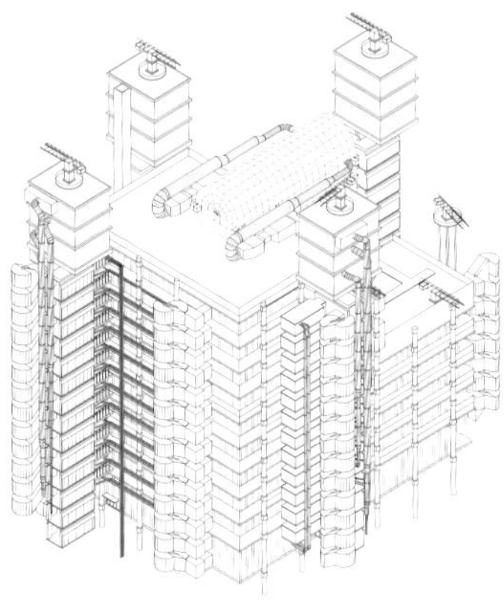

Like its predecessor, the Centre Pompidou, the Lloyd's building is another "inside-out" construction, but here designed as a tower. With an exterior composed of service components—elevators, stairs, ductwork, electrical conduits, plumbing, utility closets, and even bathrooms—visibly expressed, and clad with stainless steel panels and glass curtain walls, the design and materiality of the Lloyd's building brought a high-tech architectural aesthetic to the largely historic structures of London's financial district. A full-height sixty-meter atrium punctures through the center of the building, opening views across and diagonally through all the floors. Rogers also chose to keep the original construction cranes on the roof as symbols of the structure's potential for continuous reconstruction, techno-gargoyles for the building-as-machine.

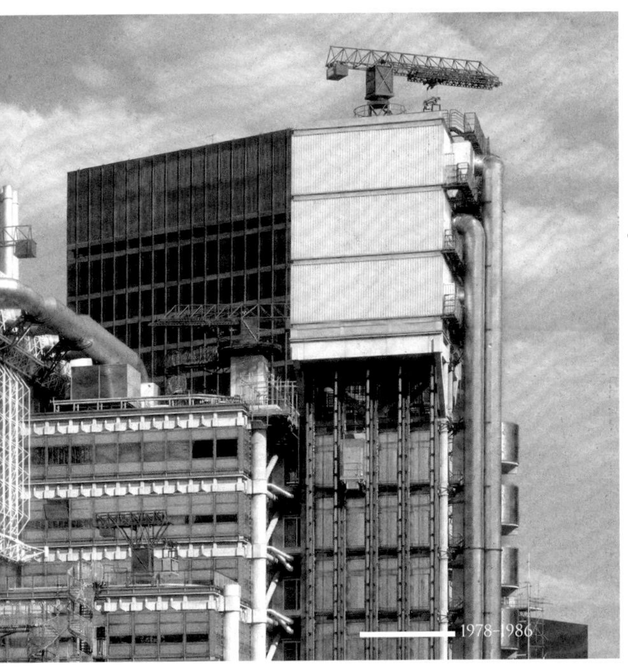

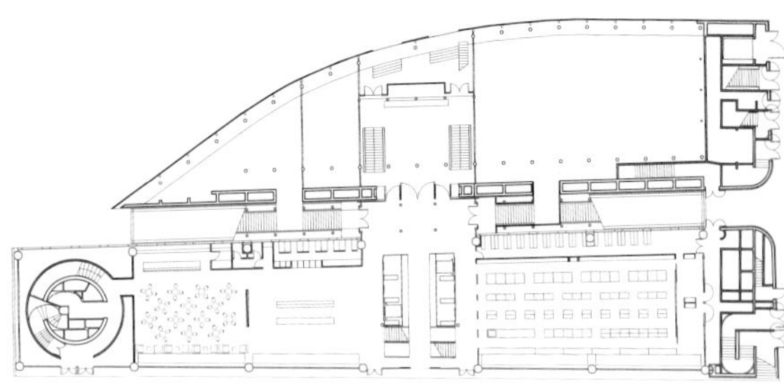

Floor Plan

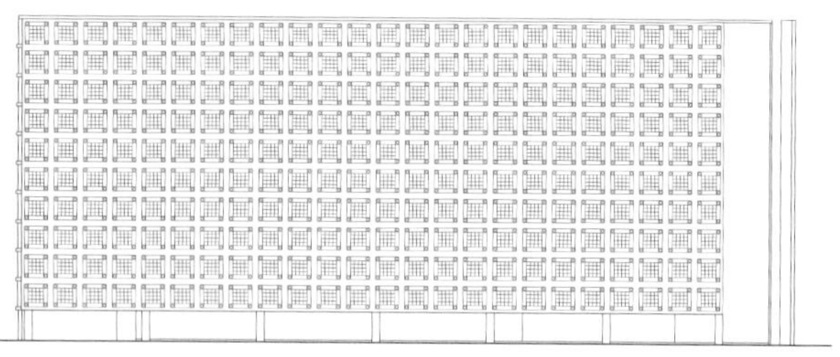

Elevation

0 50' 10M

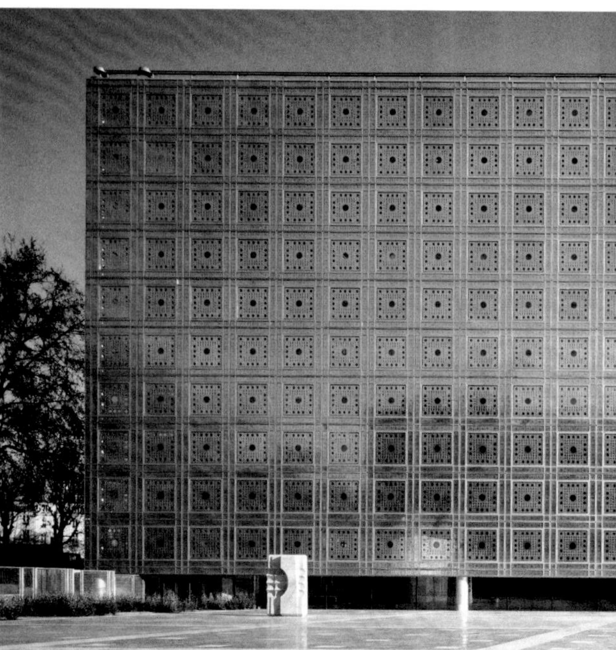

48° 50′ 56″N

66

INSTITUT DU MONDE ARABE

JEAN NOUVEL, GILBERT LÉZÉNÈS, PIERRE SORIA, ARCHITECTURE-STUDIO

Paris, France

1981–1987

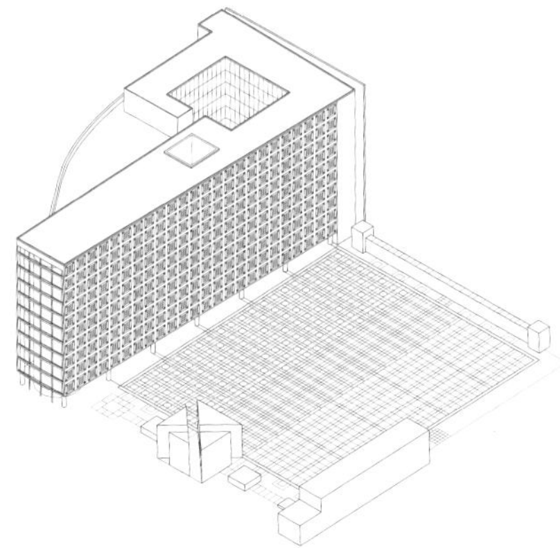

The Institut du Monde Arabe develops a series of dialectics that originate from both site and program. While appearing as two buildings on approach from the west, it resolves itself as a single structure with a large, cubic courtyard that recalls the traditional inward-looking aspects of many Arabic structures. The deceptively simple massing is embellished with intricate detail, such as its innovative dynamic metal brise-soleil on the south facade, one of the first examples of active environmental responsiveness. A network of photoelectric cells operate diaphragms that regulate day lighting by mechanically rotating metal fins to either narrow or dilate openings in the facade. The resultant patterns suggest *mashrabiya*, the wooden latticework characteristic of traditional Arabic architecture. New technology and traditional forms are combined, locating commonalities among Arab and Western cultures.

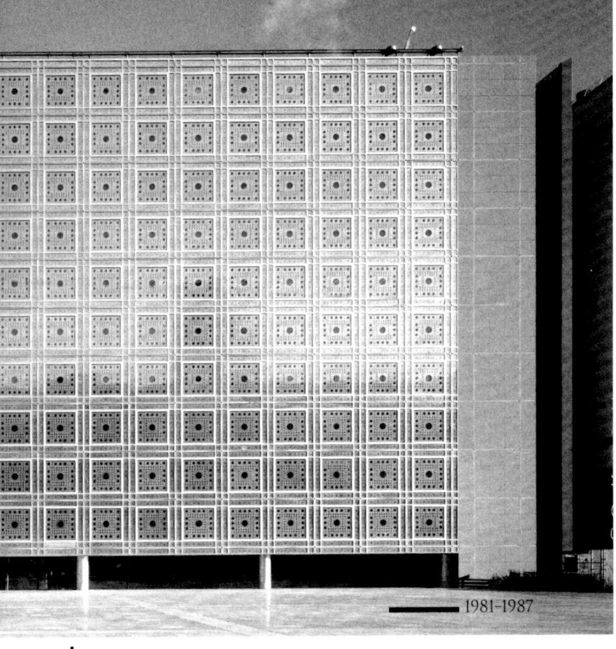

2° 21′ 26″E

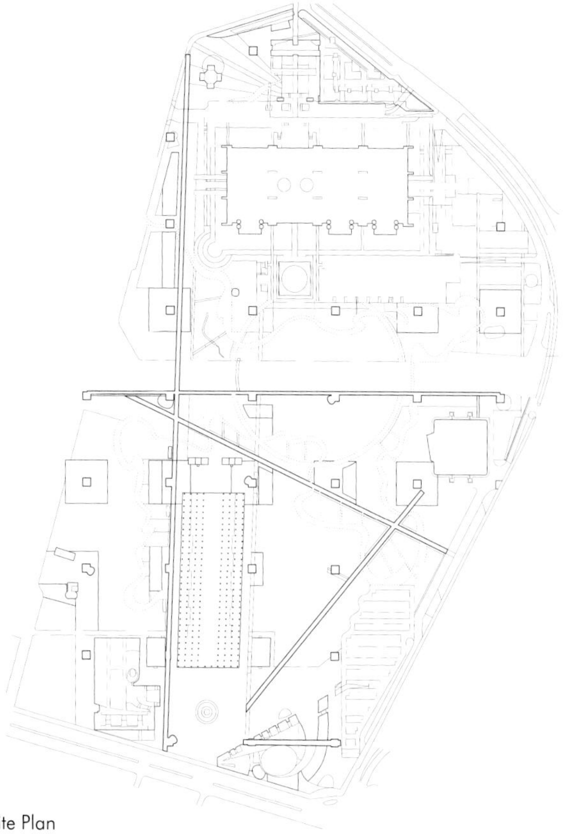

Site Plan

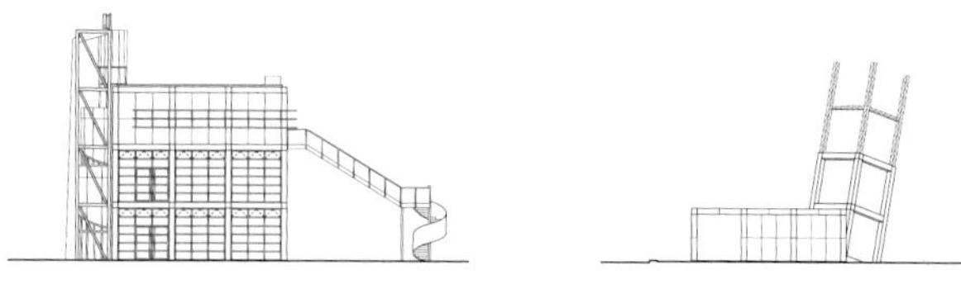

Sample Elevations

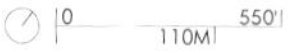

0 550' 110M

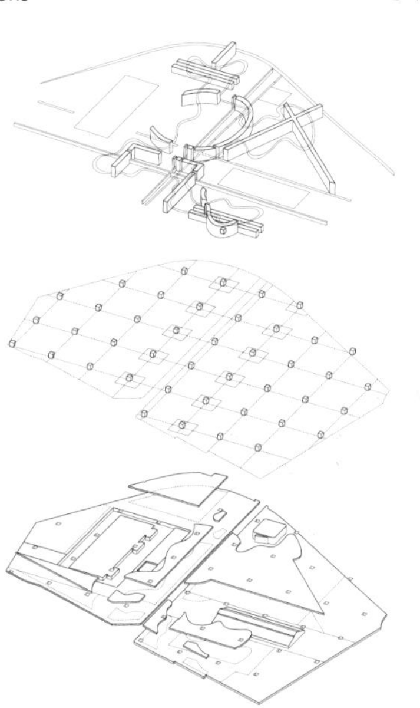

48° 53′ 37″N

67

PARC DE LA VILLETTE

BERNARD TSCHUMI
Paris, France
1982–1998

An expansive site, bisected by a canal and occupied by a massive museum as well as by the remnants of Paris's former meat markets, the Parc de la Villette posed a considerable challenge for those who entered the international competition. Given that the brief was for the "park of the twenty-first century," Bernard Tschumi decided that rather than the traditional garden, he would produce a site for interaction, discovery, and rediscovery. A series of lines is superimposed upon the park—some as curved paths, some as geometric figures—connecting various points of interest. Then a grid derived from the geometry of the largest existing slaughterhouse structure was developed. At the points of intersection on this grid, Tschumi proposed a series of "follies": bright red neo-Constructivist compositions that could expand or contract as necessary and over time. They would provide a unifying field of measure and reference for the entire park. Largely the superimposition of a series of formal, intellectual constructs, the park demonstrates that the production of abstract form has a capacity to be infinitely appropriated and interpreted by a public.

2° 23′ 26″E

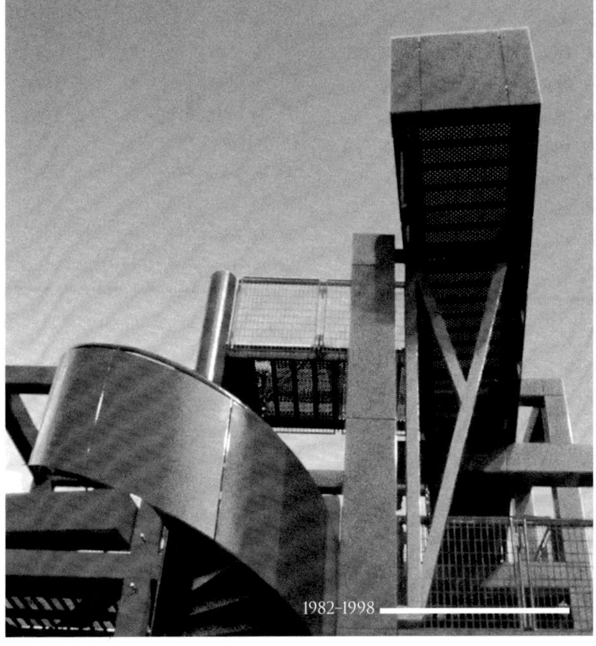
1982–1998

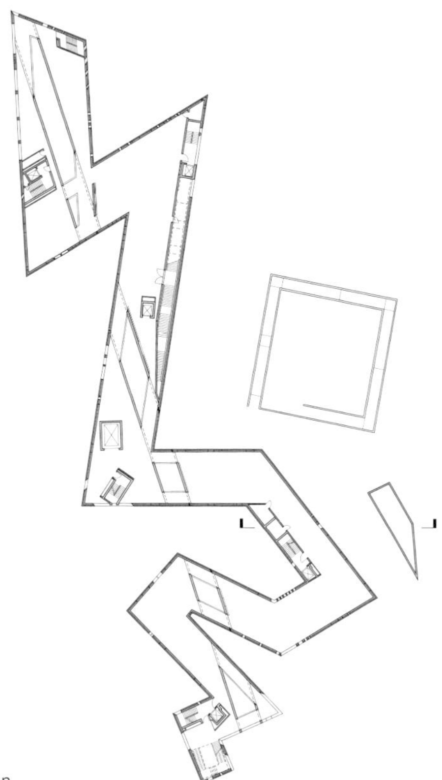

Floor Plan

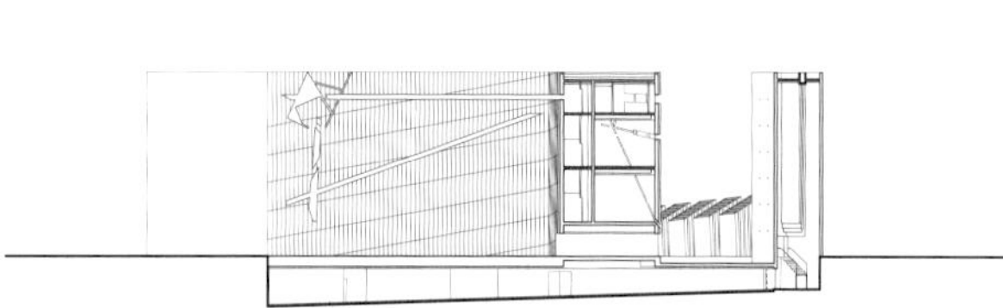

Section

0 100' 20M

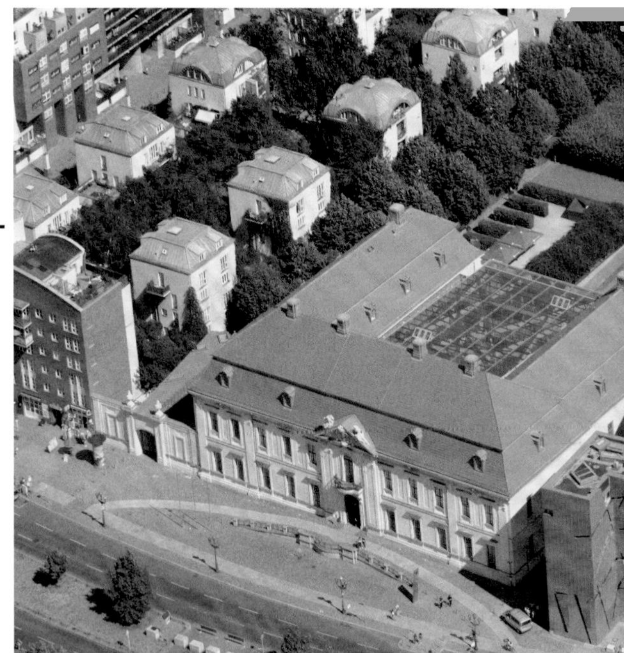

52° 30′ 08″N

68

JEWISH MUSEUM BERLIN

DANIEL LIBESKIND (STUDIO LIBESKIND)
Berlin, Germany
1989–1999

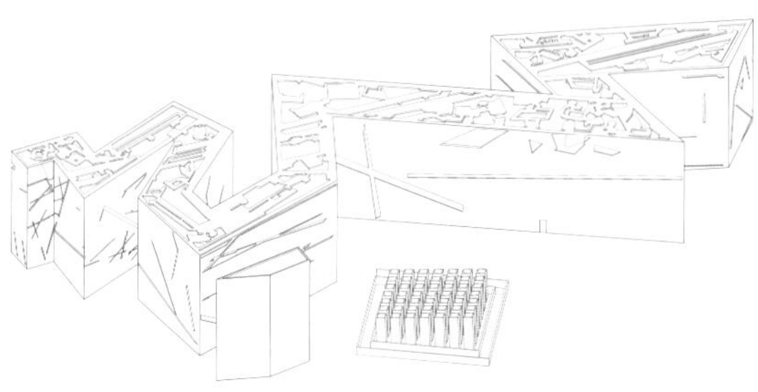

An intentionally harsh and at times alienating annex that vividly contrasts with its hosting institution, the Jewish Museum in Berlin fully represents Libeskind's design philosophy of overlaying information in multiple dimensions. The building's zigzag form is derived from a Star of David that has been stretched across the site in establishing alignments with the sites of various events in Jewish history. In representing this history, moments of regularity and stability are consistently disrupted by slots and scars of an almost graphic nature. Light and structure sometimes pour into spaces, sometimes caress surfaces, and occasionally slash through volumes. While there are three narrative promenades through the building—each representing a different period of Jewish life in Germany in relation to the Holocaust—the sequences are intentionally difficult to access with frequent dead ends, more experiential than literally didactic. Libeskind seeks to represent the complex history of Jewishness in Germany through an architecture evocative of hope, anxiety, and disappearance.

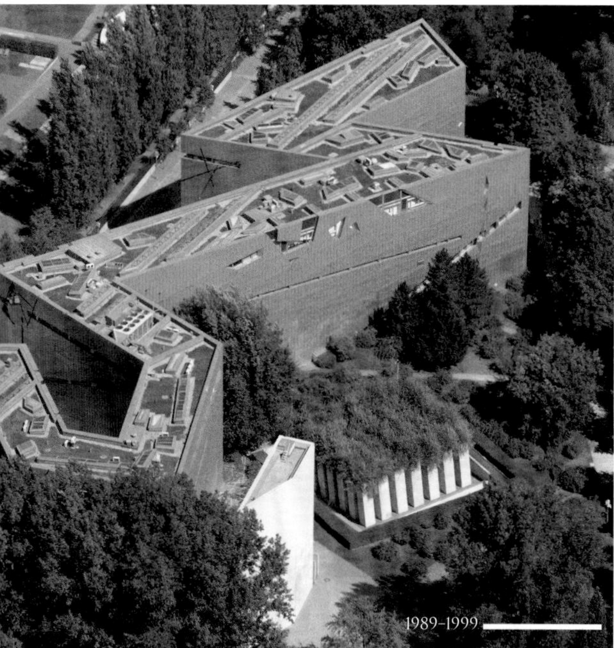
1989–1999

13° 23′ 44″E

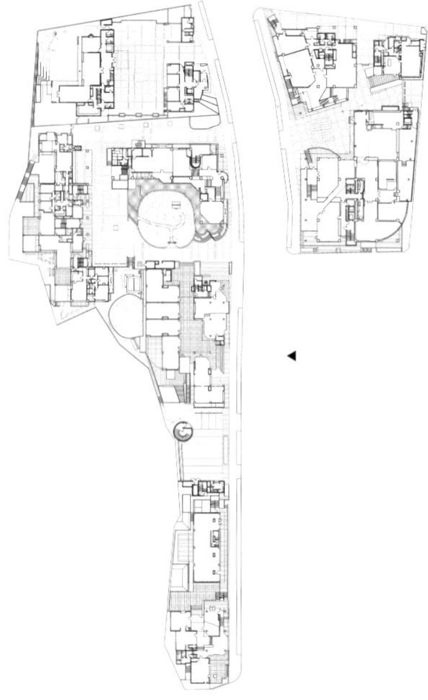

Floor Plan

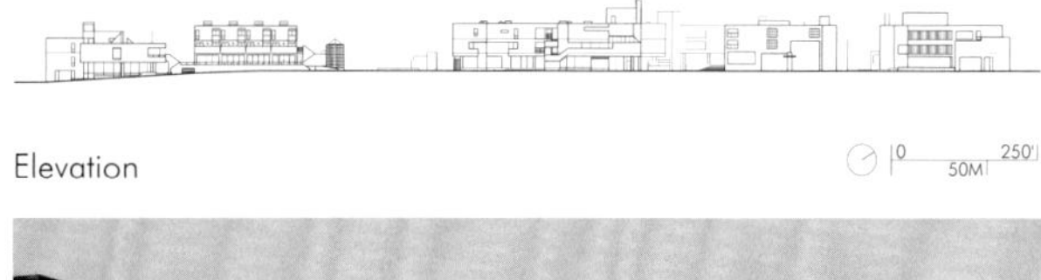

Elevation

0 250'
50M

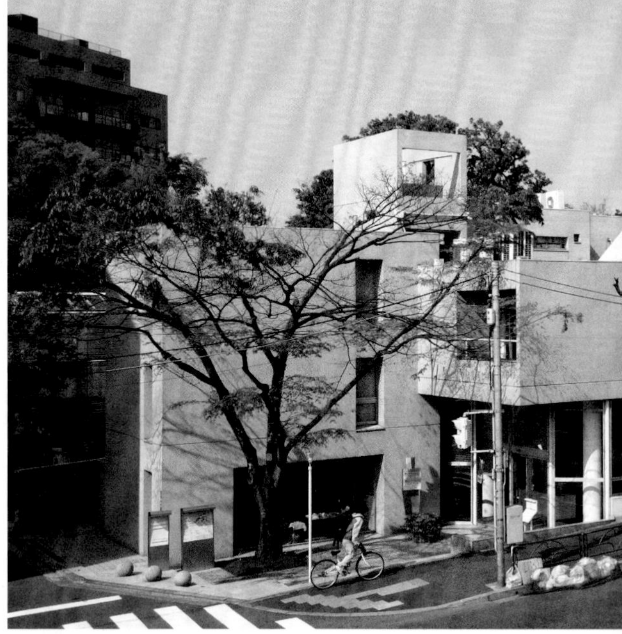

35° 38′ 55″N

69

HILLSIDE TERRACE COMPLEX I-VI

FUMIHIKO MAKI (MAKI & ASSOCIATES)
Tokyo, Japan
1967–1992

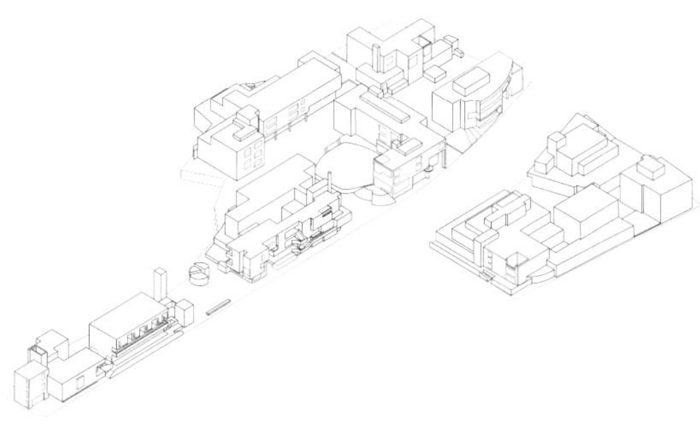

A collective form developed in numerous phases over thirty years beginning in 1969, Hillside Terrace is an urban project responsive to the continuous changes of the city. A medium-density, mixed-use experiment in urban design composed of apartments, commercial, and cultural facilities, the project presents a series of experimental design strategies relating to an attentive support of public life. The variety of architectural approaches reflect both the architect's and the culture's evolutions over time. Nevertheless, the architecture and urban intentions remain consistent in their essence, such as the use of the ground level for public functions, with living and other private activities occupying the upper levels. The design of plazas, passages, plantings, and open spaces is as carefully modulated as the masses of the buildings themselves.

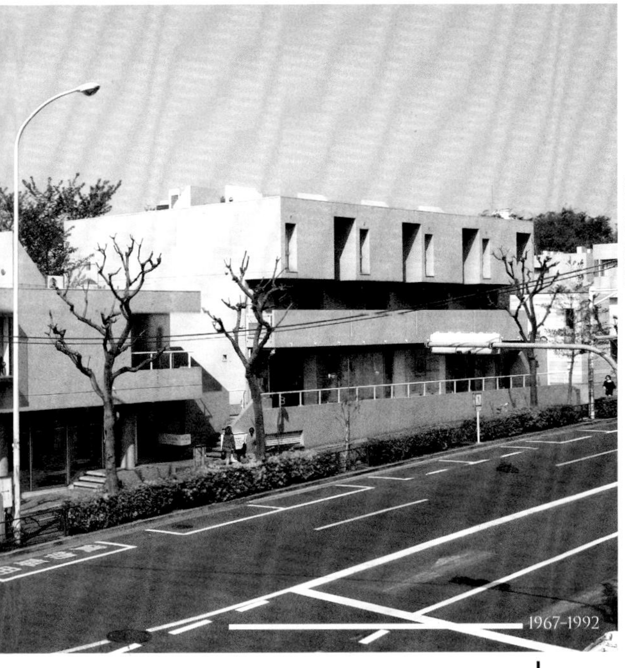

139° 42′ 00″E

41° 03′ 16″N

Floor Plan

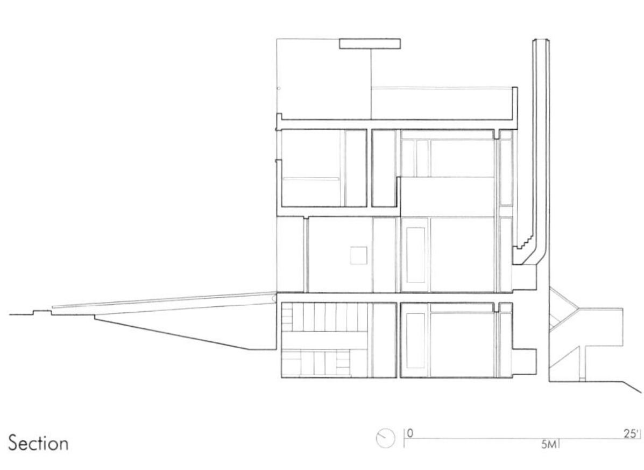

Section

73° 27′ 21″W

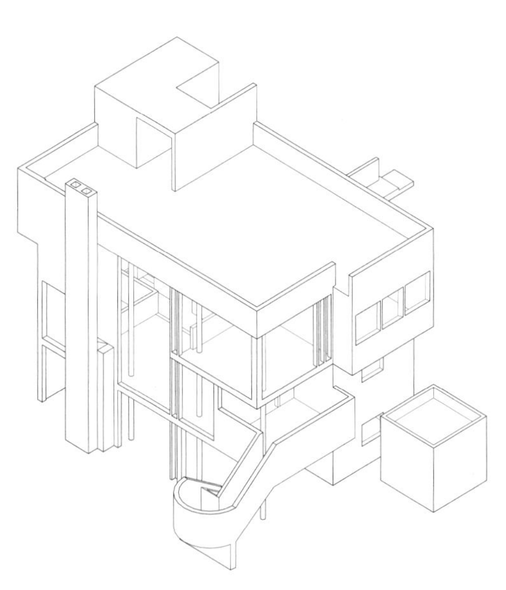

70

SMITH HOUSE

RICHARD MEIER
Darien, Connecticut, USA
1965–1967

Experimenting with concepts of abstraction and idealism, the house's whiteness and crisp geometric interplay create a striking contrast with the verdant coastline context. One approaches the house along a walkway that brings one into the center of a large wall that houses the more private elements of the program. One is then given an expansive, uninterrupted view of the nearby trees and the water's edge. Horizontal circulation is a series of stacked passages within the more solid block of the house, while vertical circulation occurs between two stairs—one inside and the other outside—that create a diagonal tension across the plan. Essentially an extension of Le Corbusier's Purist experiments adapted to an American site, material sensibility, and domestic regimen, the Smith House is both a sculpture one views from outside and a framework with which one views the surrounding nature.

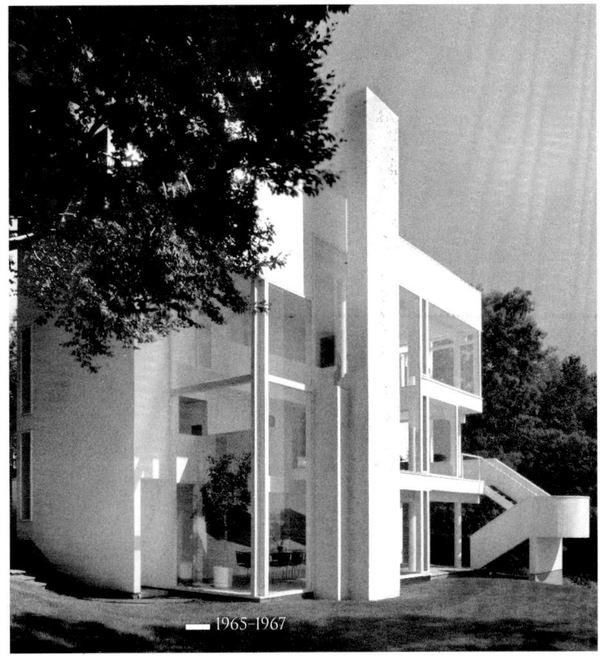
1965–1967

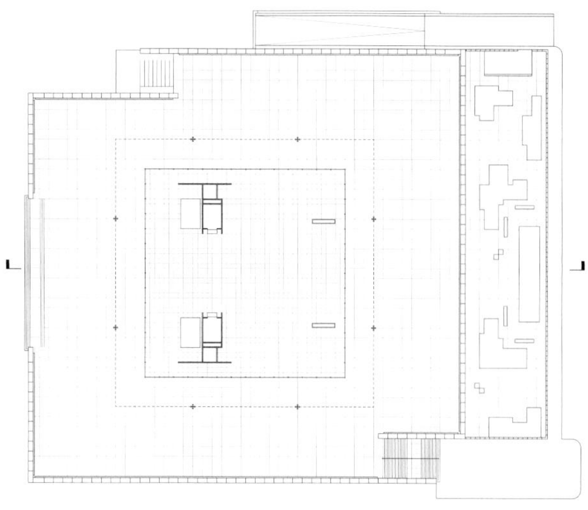

Floor Plan

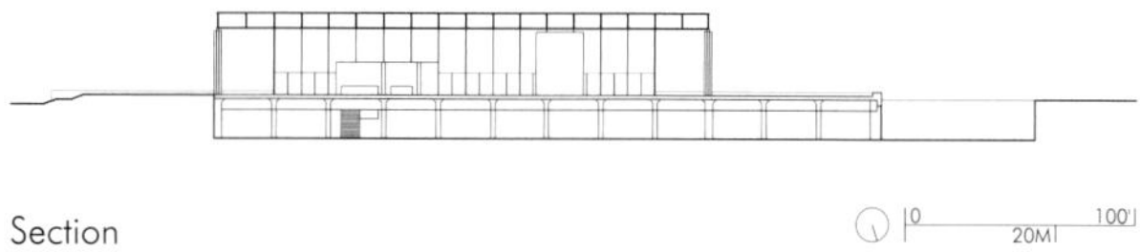

Section

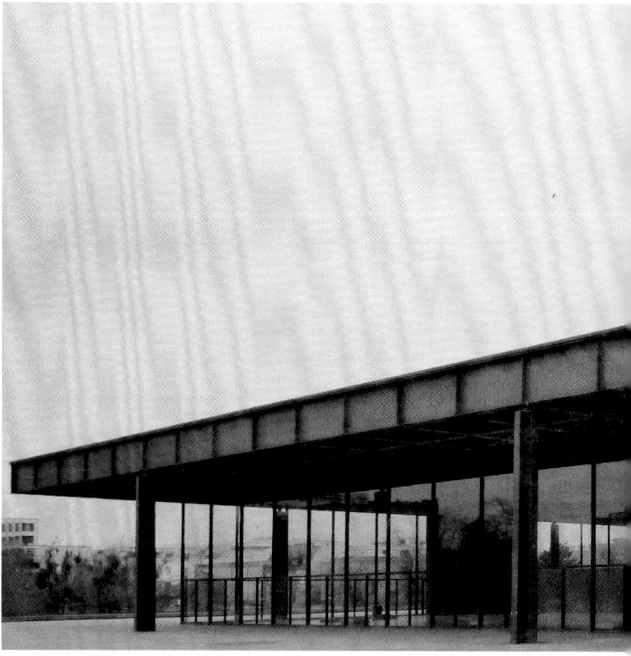

0 20M 100'

52° 30′ 25″N

71

NEW NATIONAL GALLERY

MIES VAN DER ROHE
Berlin, Germany
1962–1968

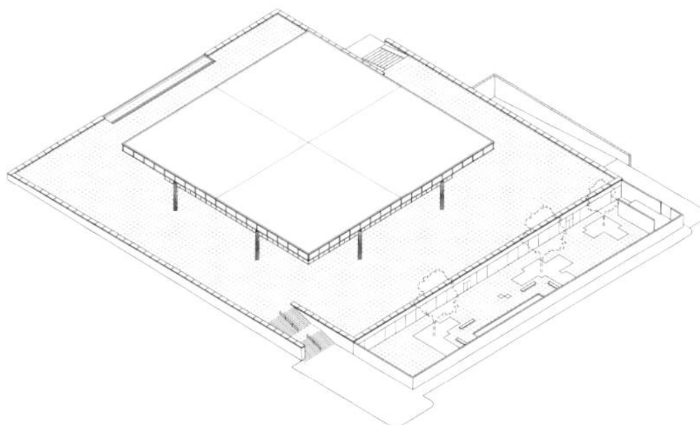

The return of Germany's native son was appropriately celebrated with the significant commission of a New National Gallery. Perfect in placement and proportions, Mies's gallery for Berlin is one of the last constructions he witnessed and one of his ultimate versions of the glass box on a podium. At a time when museums were still being treated as enclosed art fortresses, Mies conceived of the museum as a fully glazed beacon, its interior transparently linked to the public's elevated belvedere, sandwiched between the white granite of the base and the brooding black steel of the floating roof. Constructed in what was then a mostly empty field, the procession upward onto the building's plinth provides a meticulously framed vista of August Stüler's historic St. Matthew's Church—one of the few surviving prewar buildings—and of Scharoun's optimistic image of a new Berlin, the Philharmonie. Once inside the museum, one can descend into the base, with its service spaces and more traditional galleries. Since its construction, it has stoically witnessed and absorbed numerous more flamboyant late modern neighbors.

13° 22′ 03″E

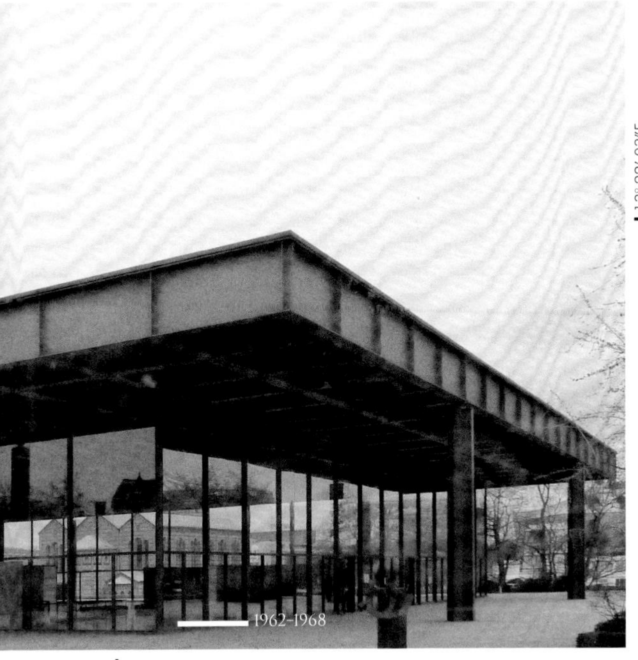
1962–1968

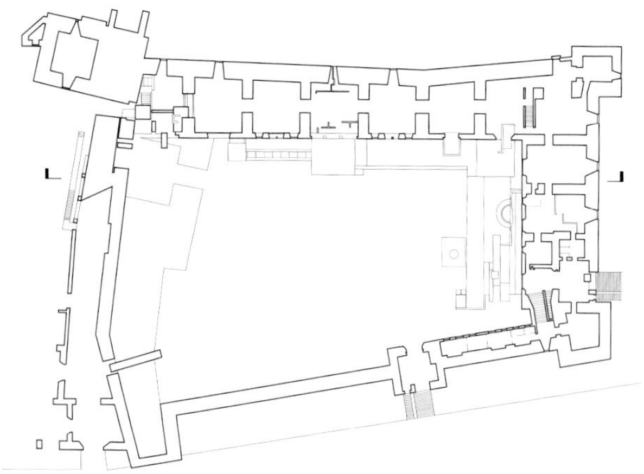

Floor Plan

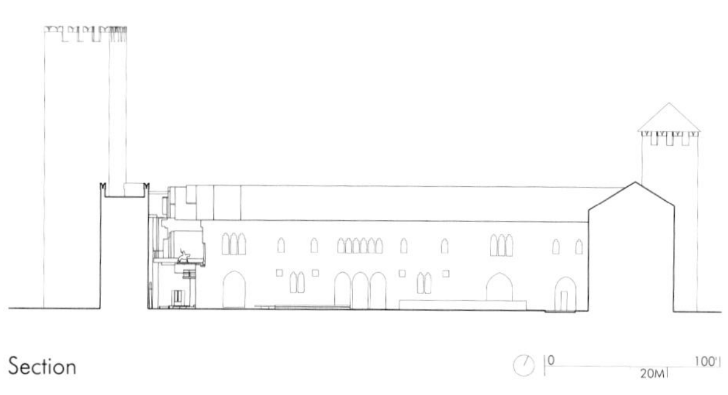

Section

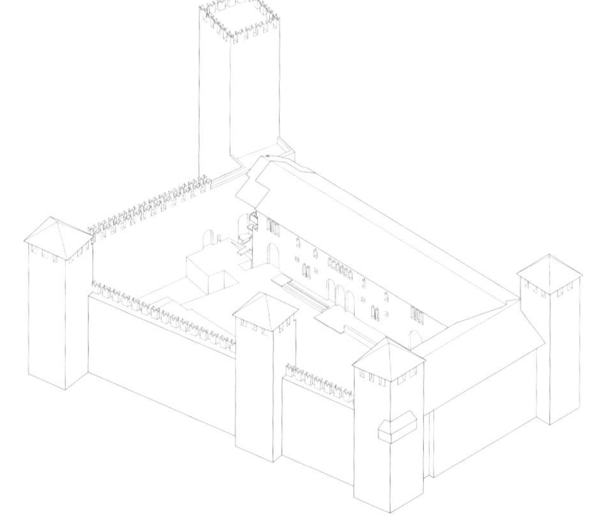

45° 26′ 23″N

72

CASTELVECCHIO MUSEUM

CARLO SCARPA
Verona, Italy
1956–1964

A civic museum located within the envelope of a historic fortress in Verona, Castelvecchio reflects a careful dialogue between the restoration of the existing building fabric and the introduction of a modern grammar, using traditional and new materials of marble, steel, brass, wood, and glass. Scarpa's controversial decision to remove a somewhat clumsy historic construction in the building became vindicated by his erecting a sculptural concrete platform in its place, which lifts a medieval equestrian statue so as to be viewable in three dimensions at the intersection of a pedestrian bridge crossing the river and from circulation above and below. Louis Kahn's maxim, "Detail is the adoration of the joint," is everywhere in this building, from the separation of the floor from the walls in the entry galleries to the careful offsetting of the pedestrian barriers separating viewers from large scale artworks in the collection.

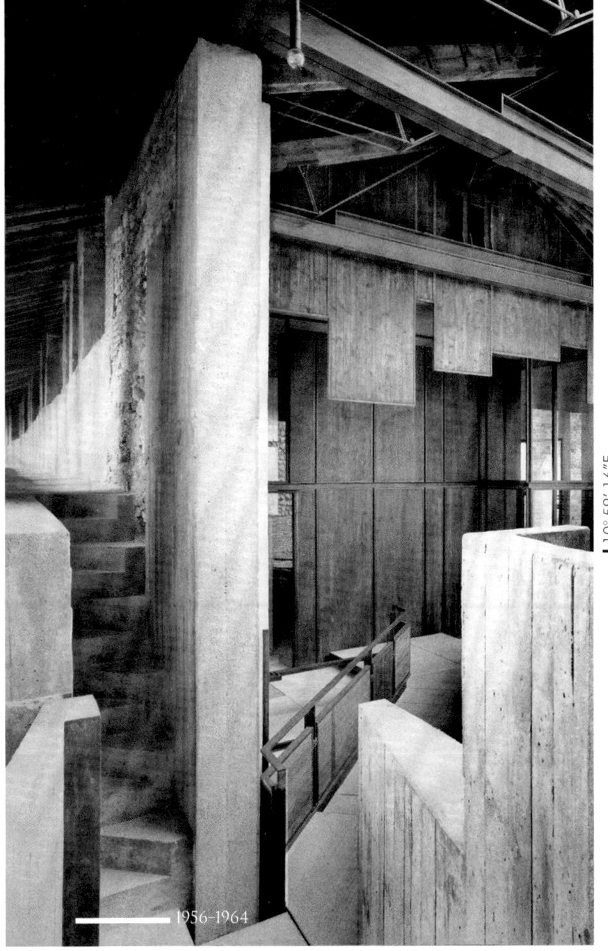
1956–1964

10° 59′ 16″E

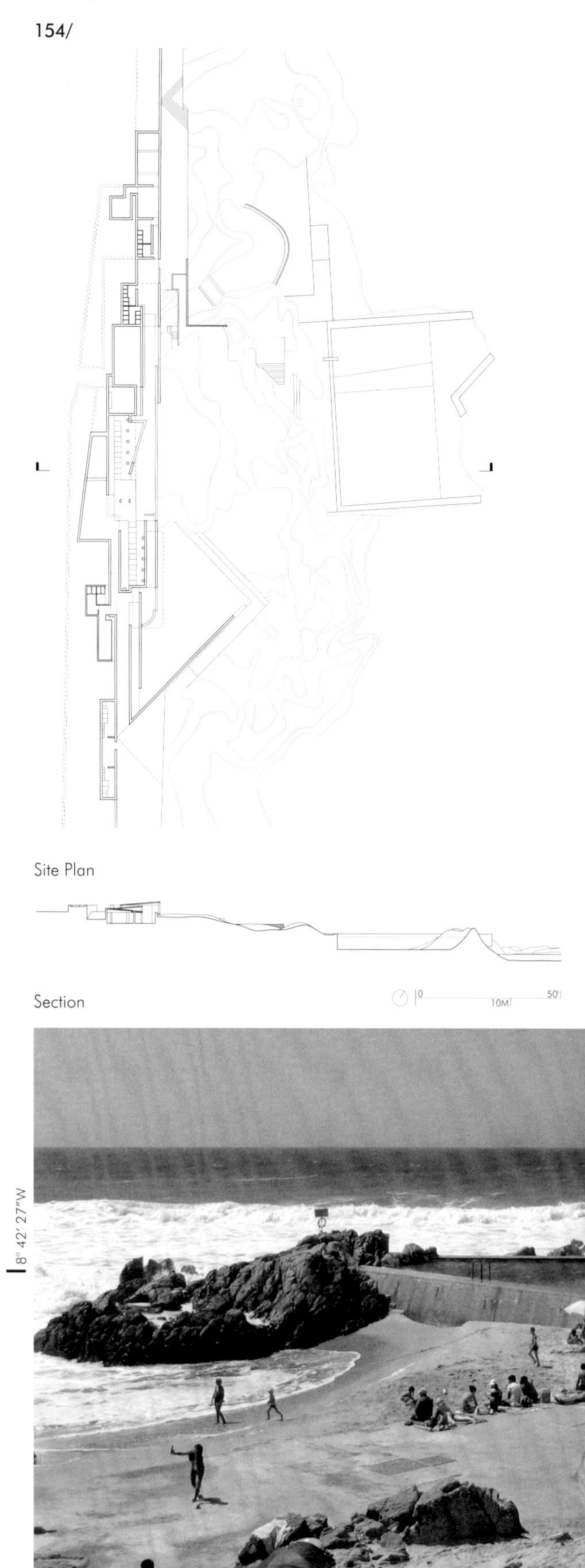

Site Plan

Section

41° 11′ 34″N

73

PISCINA DE MARÉS

ALVARO SIZA
Palmeira, Portugal
1961–1966

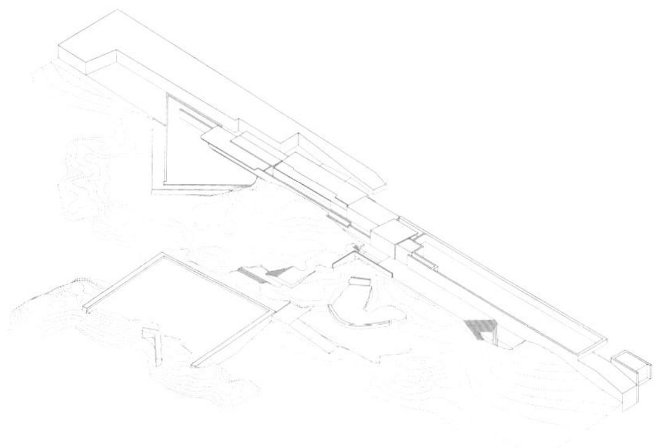

When approached from the busy coastal road in Matosinhos, the bathhouse at Piscinas de Marés is almost invisible. The long seawall gives way to a gentle ramp with a false perspective that foreshortens its depth, allowing one to descend within framed views that reveal the sea, the roof edges, and the entry to the bathhouse. One eventually arrives in a cubic room with a floor of water before moving outward toward the broad array of pools set in and among the rocks of the coastline. Concrete and wood merge with the craggy rocks of the coastline; cement steps fade into sandy terraces; and a series of pools containing fresh- and saltwater cascade downward as they become engulfed by the sea. Siza's construction at Leça da Palmeira demonstrates that architecture can be both bold and subtle, simple and complex, all while engaging all of the senses.

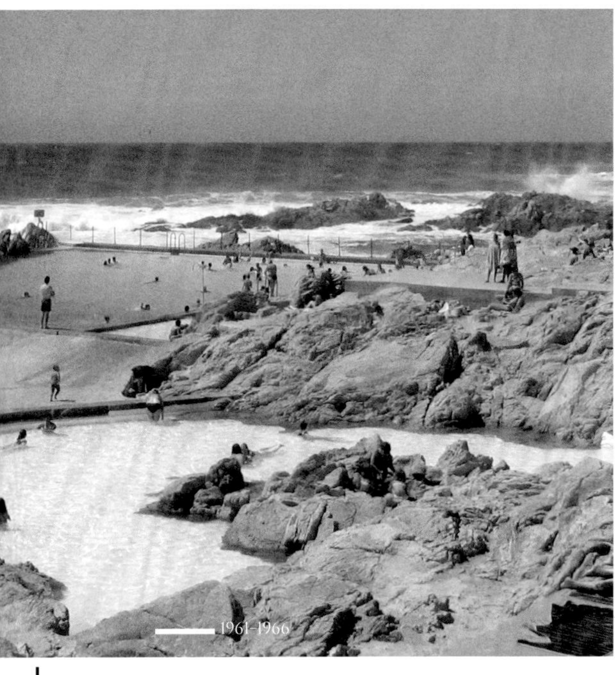
1961–1966

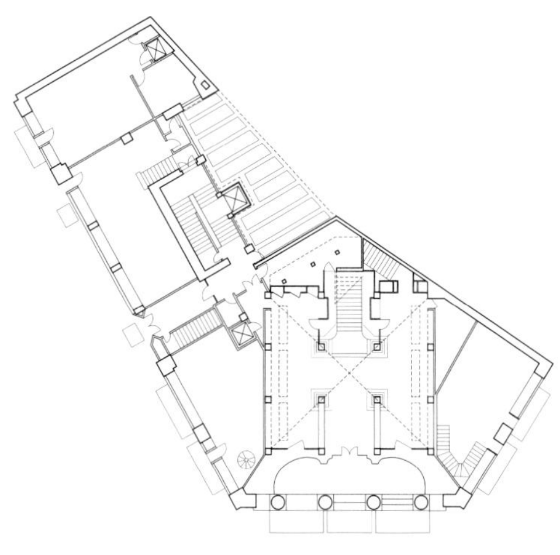

Floor Plan

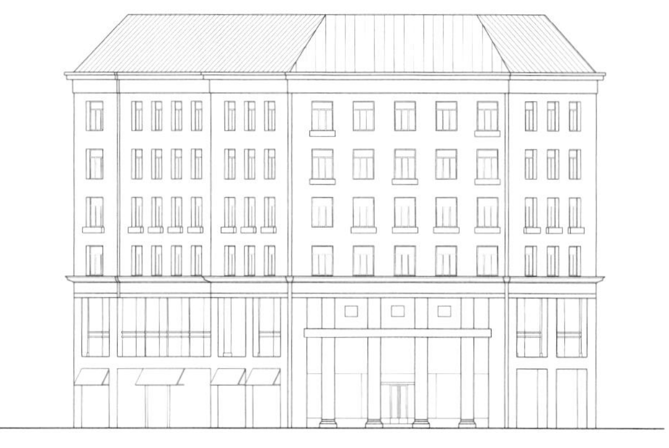

Elevation

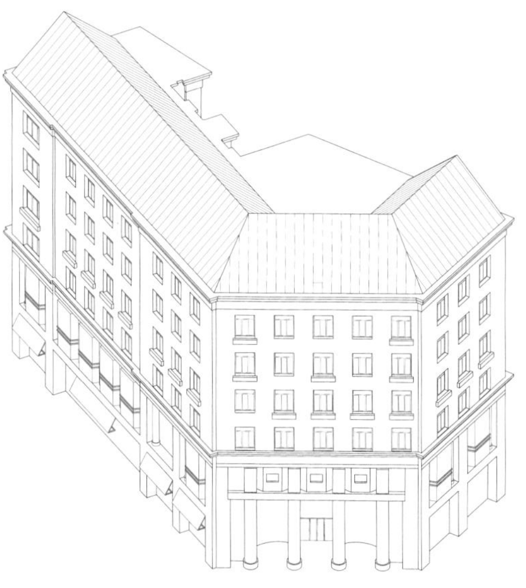

1909–1911

48° 12′ 31″N

74

MICHAELERPLATZ HOUSE
LOOSHAUS

ADOLF LOOS
Vienna, Austria
1909–1911

Controversial at the time for its starkly reductive facades in the midst of the exuberant baroqueness of Vienna's historic center, the Looshaus represents Adolf Loos's strategy of using materials—their grain, finish, colors, tones, and textures—as the sole decorative program for an architecture. Designed for Goldman & Salatsch, a luxurious clothing line (that Loos was known to promote), with a store below and offices and apartments above, the building was itself an architectural expression of Loos's theories on architectural form and fashion. Exterior marble detailing, including columns that are distinctly nonstructural—is juxtaposed with plain white stucco, while exotic and highly polished woods with few moldings and glass vitrines shape the interior. Most important is its urban presence: the Looshaus transforms Fischer von Erlach's baroque and royal Michaelerplatz into a modern space of commerce and public life.

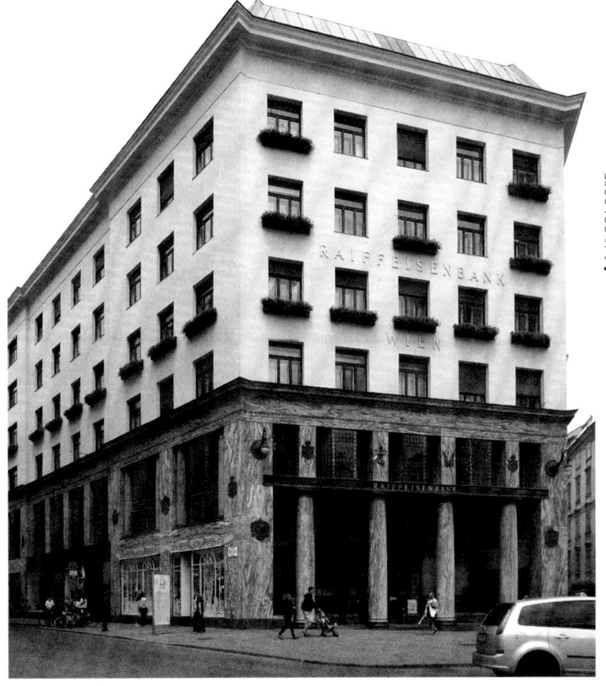

16° 22′ 00″E

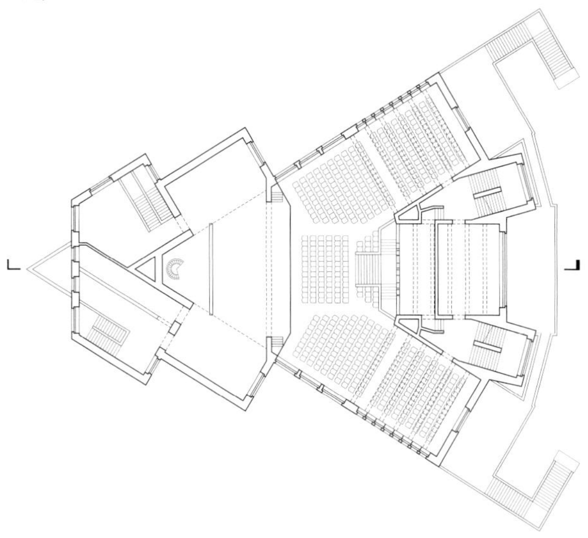

Floor Plan

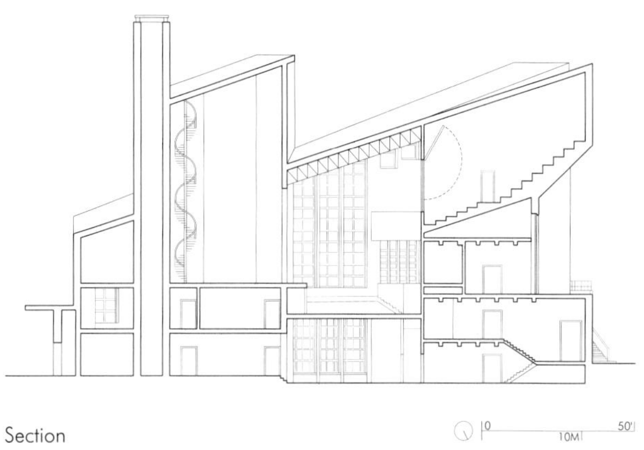

Section

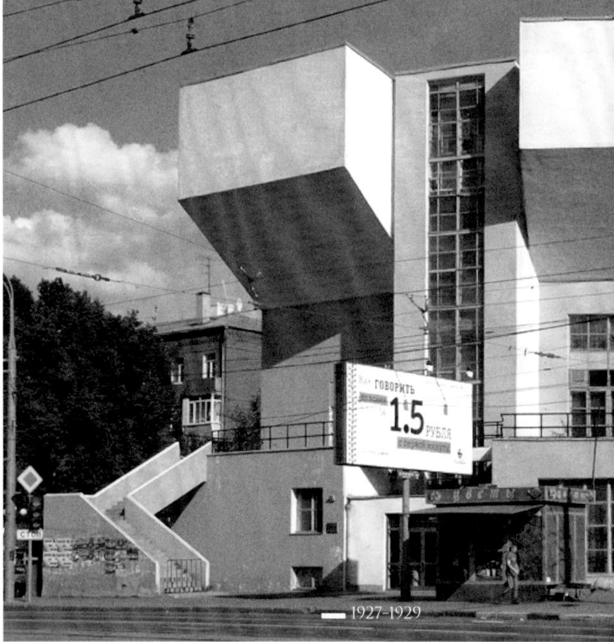

1927–1929

55° 47′ 29″N

75

RUSAKOV WORKERS' CLUB

KONSTANTIN MELNIKOV
Moscow, Russia
1927–1929

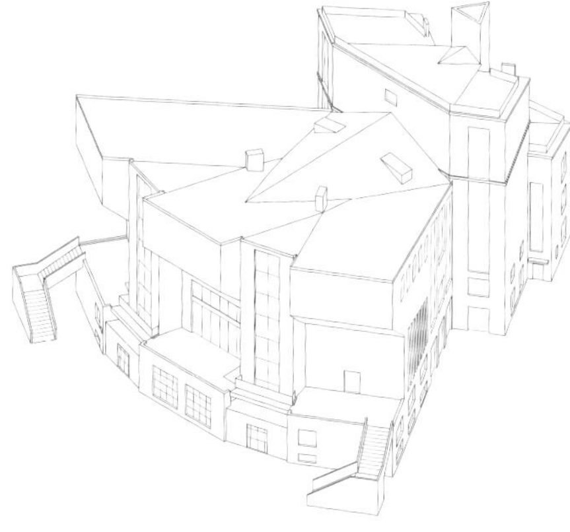

Melnikov was searching for an architecture that could express the force and resilience of popular revolution. Using the metaphor of a muscle tensed in an upward gesture, he produced one of the few remaining works of the influential yet short-lived Constructivist era. Three reinforced-concrete auditoria volumes boldly, almost defiantly, cantilever in a fanning shape from a singular central stage, with three audiences separated to view one production. On the exterior, these dramatic wedges are representative of the sloped floors within, as well as—metaphorically—of the cogs of a giant gear. Brick begins to take over in the fly loft, eventually shaping the building's back side as a domestically scaled construction, undoubtedly more familiar to the trolley-workers who were intended to be the primary occupants of the building. On the ground floor, galleries with movable partitions allow for a flexibility of uses.

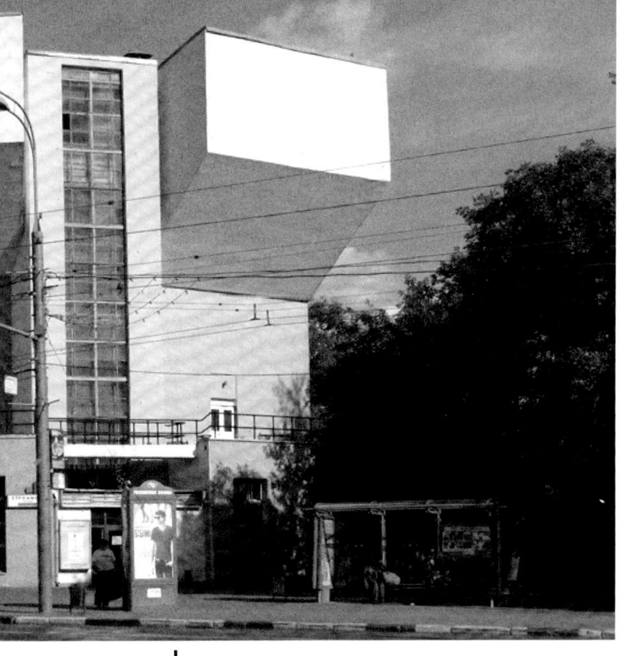

37° 41′ 14″E

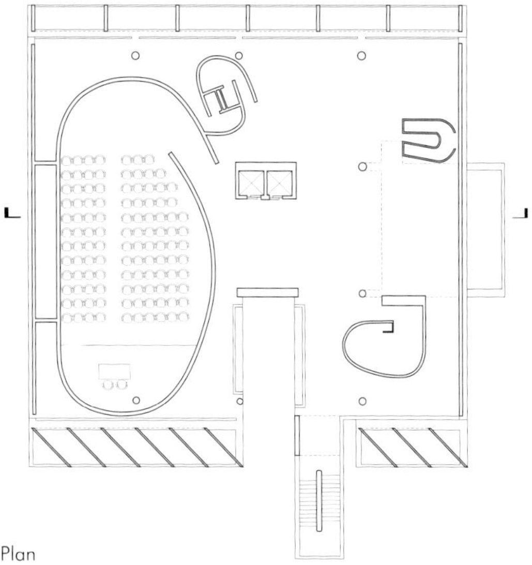

Floor Plan

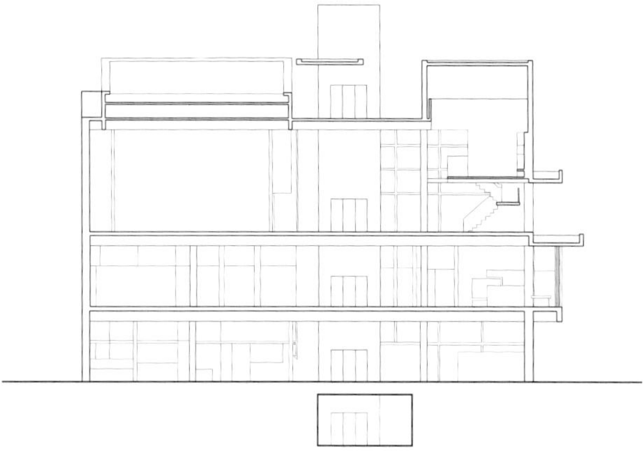

Section

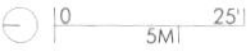

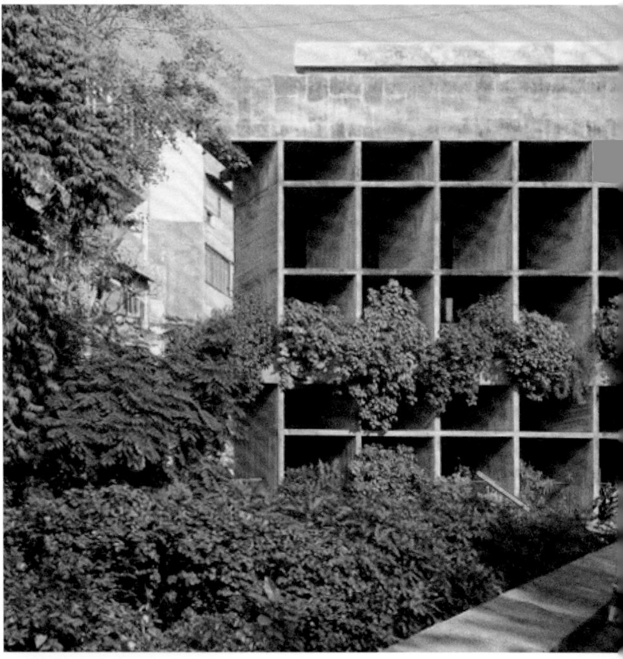

23° 01′ 57″N

76

MILL OWNERS' ASSOCIATION BUILDING

LE CORBUSIER
Ahmedabad, India
1951–1954

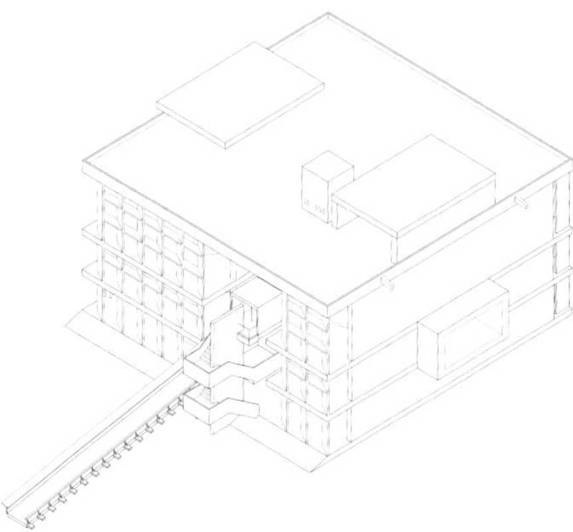

The Mill Owners' building presents a critical development of Le Corbusier's original "five points," adapted to the distinct conditions of a semi-arid area with a heavy monsoon season. A long ramp draws visitors onto an open-air piano nobile, where a generous stair leads upward to a large, free-planned plane occupied by a series of sculptural elements, one of which contains the auditorium. The west-facing entry facade has a deep, freestanding brise-soleil, with a series of concrete panels rotated to allow the low, winter sun to penetrate the building while keeping out the hotter summer sun. The east facade consists of a more shallow, rectilinear frame that allows breezes from the nearby river to move through the structure. The roof has a large, U-shaped element that allows light into the public spaces below, and that was to contain tiers of plants and a pool, so as to further help control the interior temperatures.

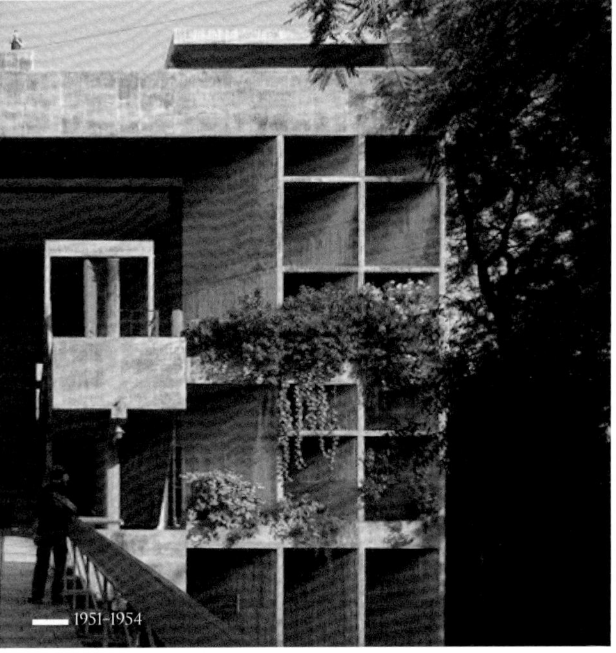

1951–1954

72° 34′ 13″E

34° 06′ 02″N

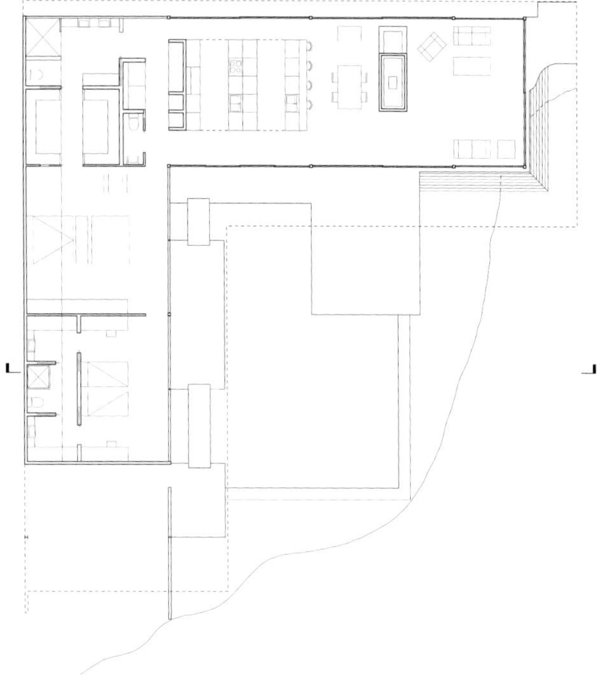

Floor Plan

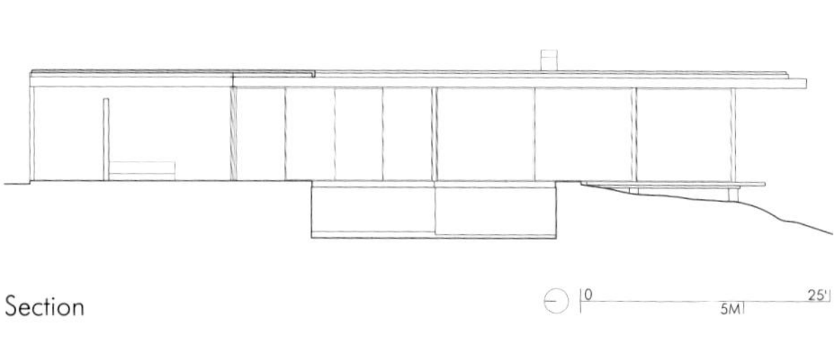

Section

0 25′ 5M

118° 22′ 13″W

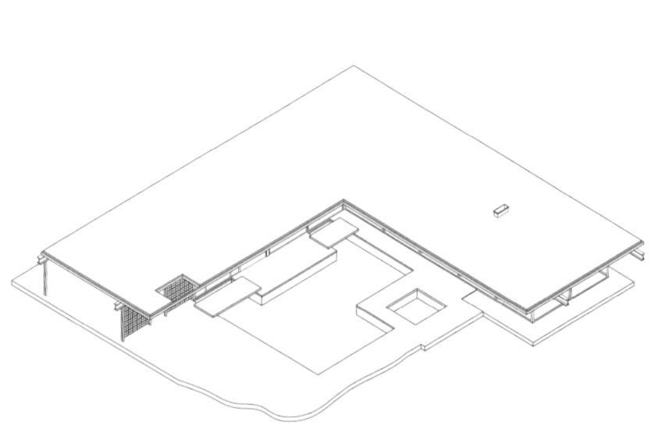

77

STAHL HOUSE
CASE STUDY HOUSE NO.22

PIERRE KOENIG
Hollywood, California, USA
1960

One of the most photogenic exemplars of the Case Study House program initiated by John Entenza, Pierre Koenig's Case Study House No. 22, from its first photographs by Julius Shulman through today represents one of the most pervasive images of casual modern living in twentieth-century Los Angeles. Conceived as a simple pavilion located on a promontory outlook in the Hollywood Hills, the Stahl House maximizes the use of extraordinarily thin sections of prefabricated steel to enclose space with a canopy of a steel-decked roof that extends to provide shade to uninterrupted glass walls. The L-shaped plan establishes the relationship between house, pool, sky, and views, locating the bedrooms along an unapologetically opaque steel wall to the street, while creating open-plan, flexible living spaces cantilevered over the site's edge that in their transparency almost dissolve into the dramatic Los Angeles skyline.

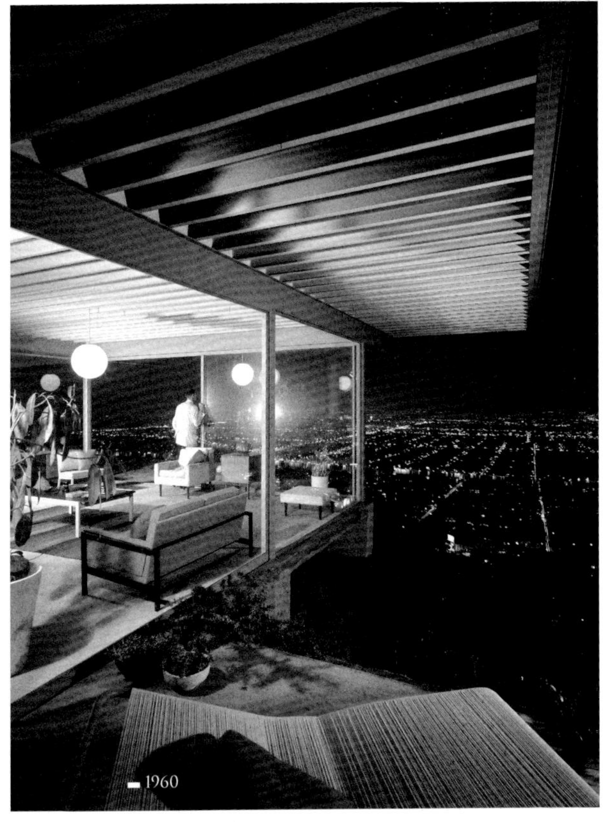

1960

164/

40° 46′ 25″N

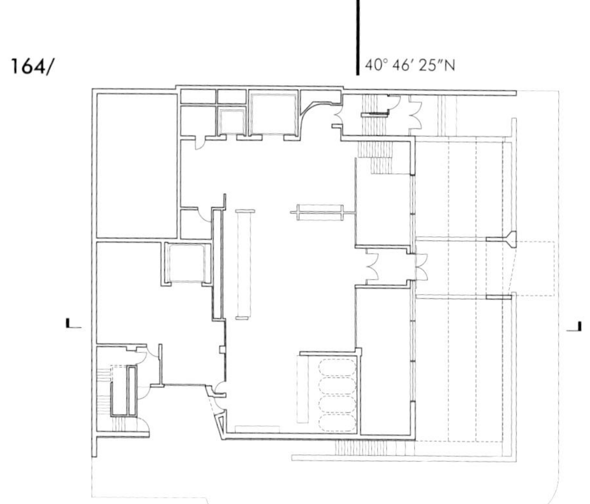

Floor Plan

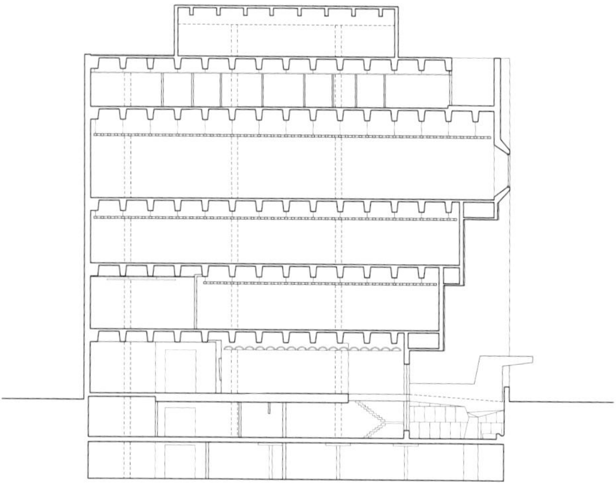

Section

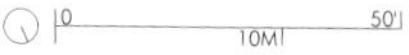

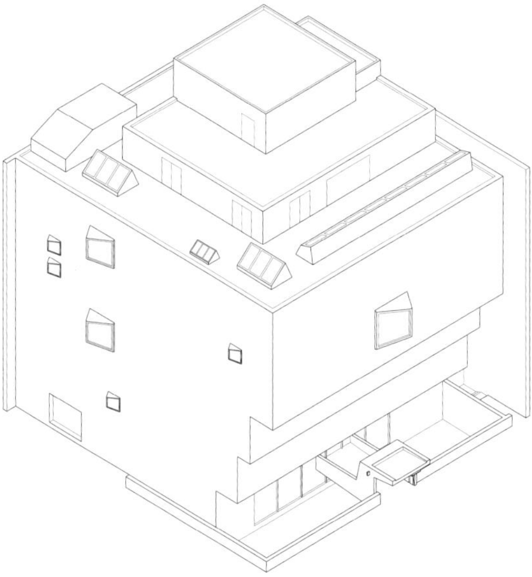

73° 57′ 50″W

78

THE BREUER BUILDING
WHITNEY MUSEUM OF AMERICAN ART

MARCEL BREUER and HAMILTON P. SMITH
New York, New York, USA
1963–1966

A boldly stacked volume of increasingly cantilevered granite masonry emerging from the brownstones that once occupied its site, with windows that appear to strain for views of the corner, the third home of the Whitney Museum as envisioned by Marcel Breuer shelters surprisingly complex open spaces that welcome the public from the street. Breuer offers an object of resistance—abstract in scale, language, intent, and iconography—to the glass towers of New York. The diagram is akin to an enormous boulder of unimaginable mass, floating above a sunken, craterlike plaza formed from its weight. The reverse-ziggurat profile emphasizes this spatial quality at the ground level, while the heavier, ascending massing previews the large exhibition spaces that await the visitor. Once inside, Breuer continues to offer open spaces to the visitor by maximizing exhibition floor spaces, with those odd windows appearing as if distorted perspectives, all linked by a gracious stair and oversize elevator to propel the adventure. In 2014, the Whitney moved operations downtown to its fourth home; as of 2016, the Breuer Building serves as "The Met Breuer," a satellite of The Metropolitan Museum of Art.

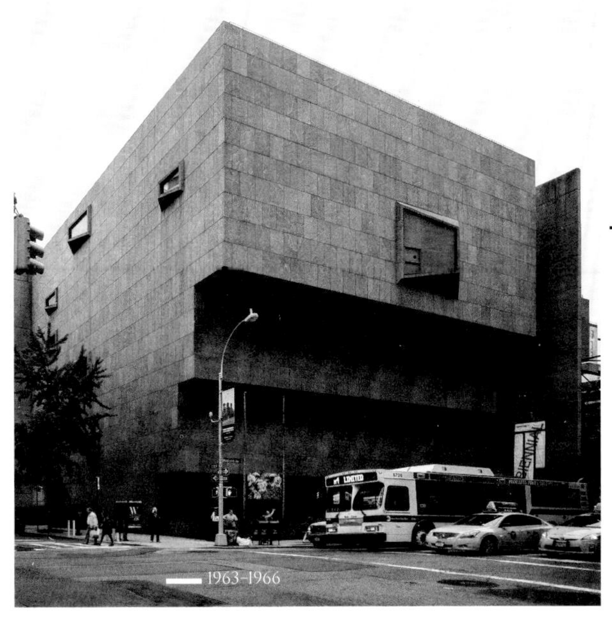

1963–1966

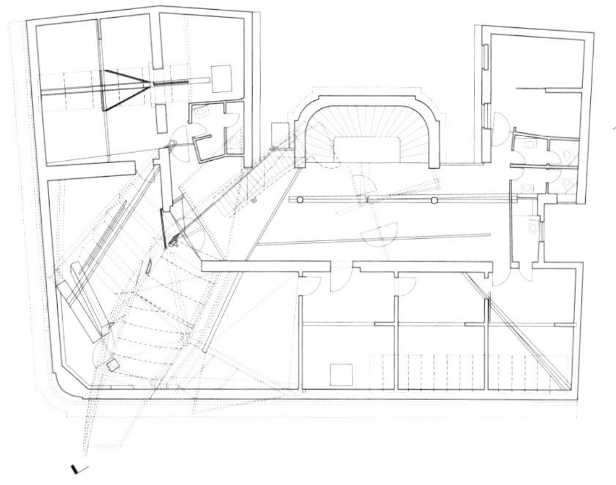

Floor Plan

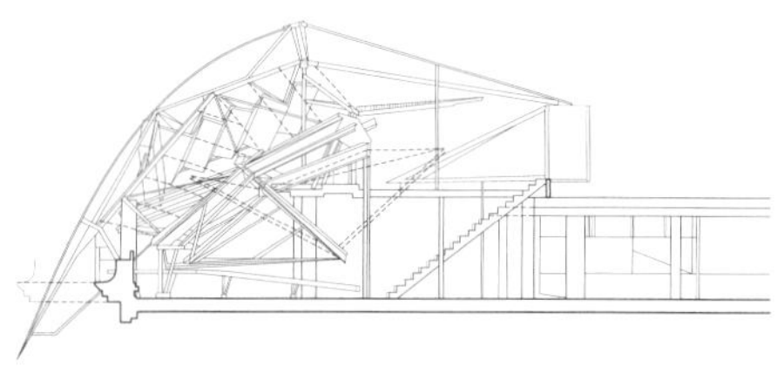

Section

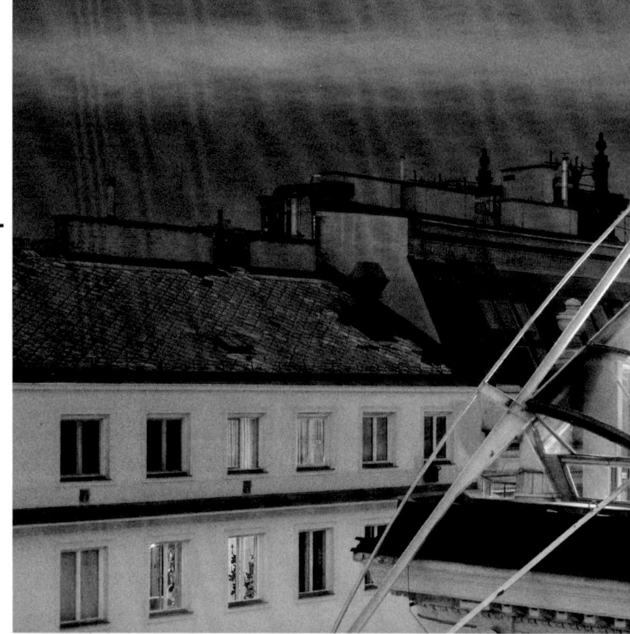

48° 12′ 31″N

79

ROOFTOP REMODELING FALKESTRASSE

COOP HIMMELB(L)AU
Vienna, Austria
1983–1988

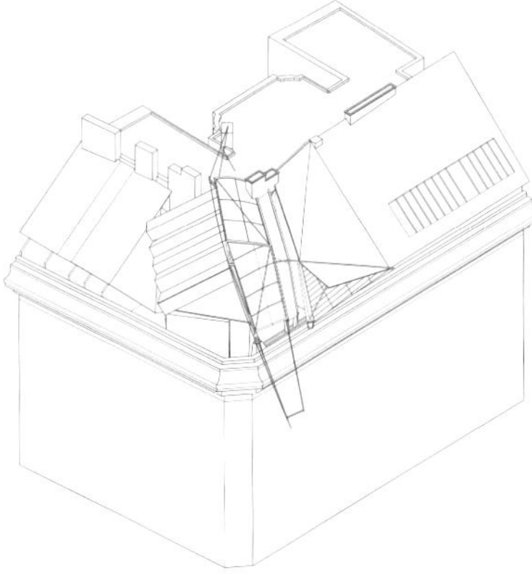

A courageous rooftop addition to a Biedermeier-era building in the historic center of Vienna (in the midst of a neo-historicist frenzy in architecture) brought a small office into prominence and encouraged architects everywhere to challenge standard procedures. Envisioned as a single, piercing "line of energy" from street to roof (and no doubt influenced by the name of the street: Falkestrasse, or Falcon Street), a taut steel arc peers over the parapet, uniting the disparate volumes of the renovated interior by penetrating and expanding the roof plane. Open, glazed surfaces alternate with closed and folded surfaces, creating the spatial and optical complexity of the experience, described by the architects as a "cross between a bridge and an airplane."

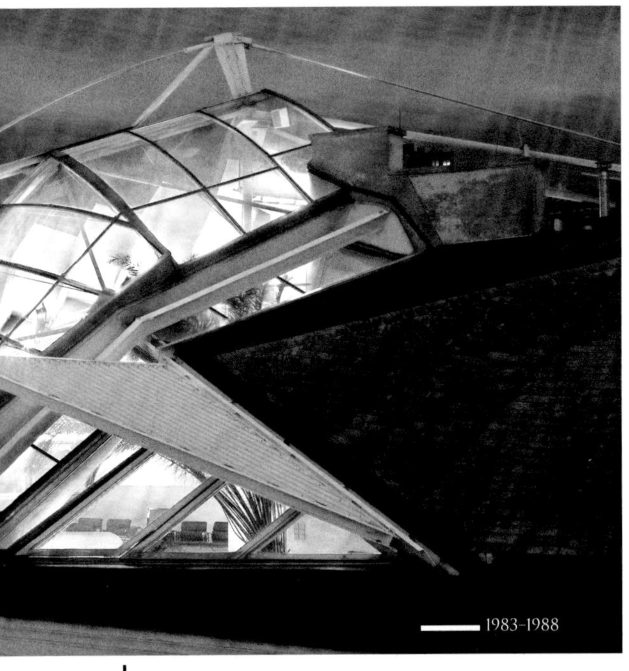

1983–1988

16° 22′ 51″E

42° 52′ 38″N

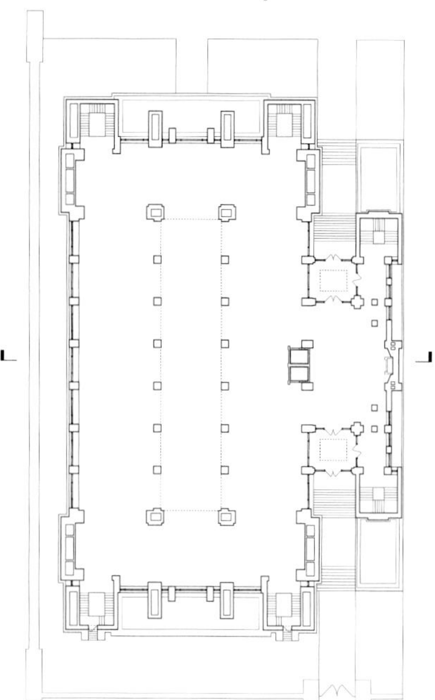

Floor Plan

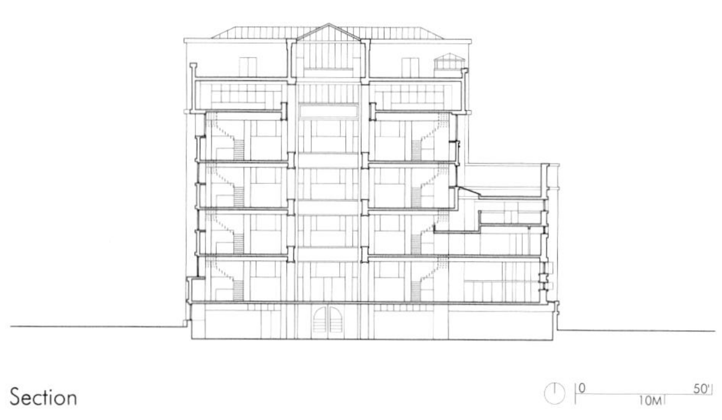

Section

0 10M 50′

78° 51′ 08″W

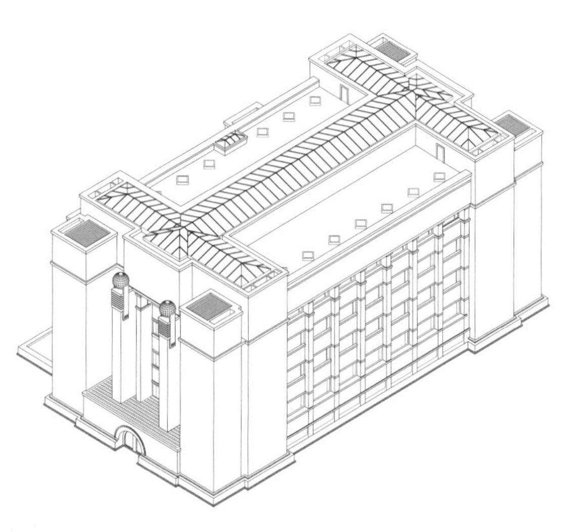

1902–1906

80

LARKIN COMPANY ADMINISTRATION BUILDING

FRANK LLOYD WRIGHT
Buffalo, New York, USA
1902–1906, destroyed 1950

The administration building of the Larkin Company illustrates Wright's and Larkin's shared vision of productive labor as the foundation of the social contract. An imposing, almost Egyptian assortment of piers from its exterior, its interior reveals the careful, organic balance of pier and wall, mass and space, compression and expansion that typified Wright's work at this time. The steel-frame structure was clad in red brick with pinkish mortar to maintain its monolithic character. After a typically circuitous entry sequence, one would finally reach the central work-space atrium, the building's full five stories in height, with a glass ceiling, and piers and recessed fascias of a cream-colored brick: a cathedral of workers in a brilliantly lit nave. Among its many innovations were air-conditioning, built-in desk furniture, suspended water closets (to facilitate cleaning), and service plena with utilities and fire stairs located within the piers.

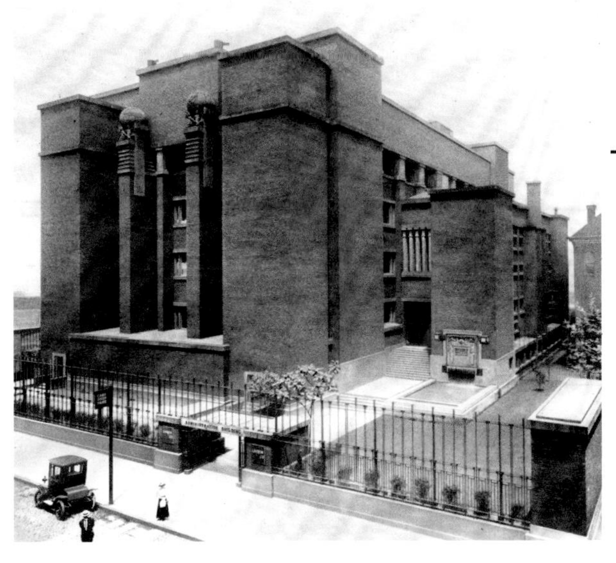

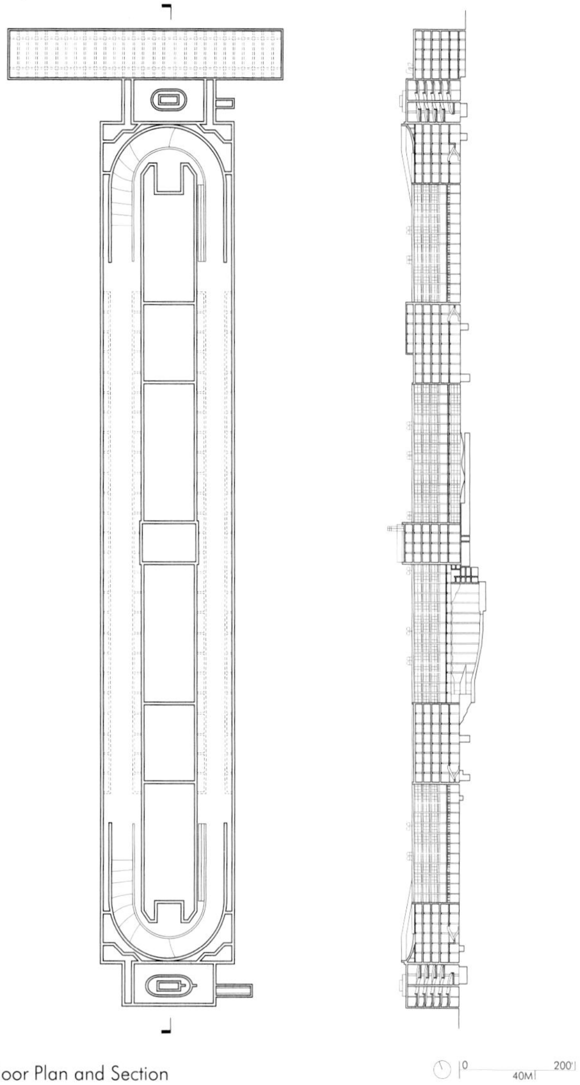

170/

Floor Plan and Section

0 40M 200'

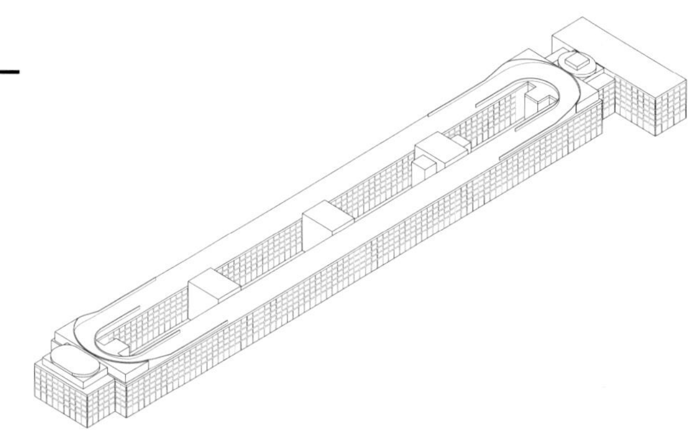

–

45° 01′ 57″N

81

FIAT WORKS

GIACOMO MATTÈ-TRUCCO
Turin, Italy
1915–1921

With a test track complete with banked shoulders on its roof, giant concrete spiral access ramps to accommodate test vehicles, and four large courtyards within an interminable facade that barely disguised its reinforced-concrete frame, the Fiat Works offered both an ambition and a legitimation to architects in the early twentieth century. Assembly would start on the ground floor, where raw-car-material shipments would arrive, gradually moving through the upper floors as the phases of assemblage were developed. Once complete and ready, the car would reach the top of the factory to be tested on the roof track. One of the first vertical urban factories, it pioneered the structural use of long-span reinforced concrete and combined the efficient circulation of a workforce with the optimal turning radius of the automobile. Born of the Futurist enthusiasm for speed and christened by Le Corbusier in his *Toward an Architecture*, it was a monument to assemblage and efficiency, representing an ideal of both gritty functionalism and romantic industrialization.

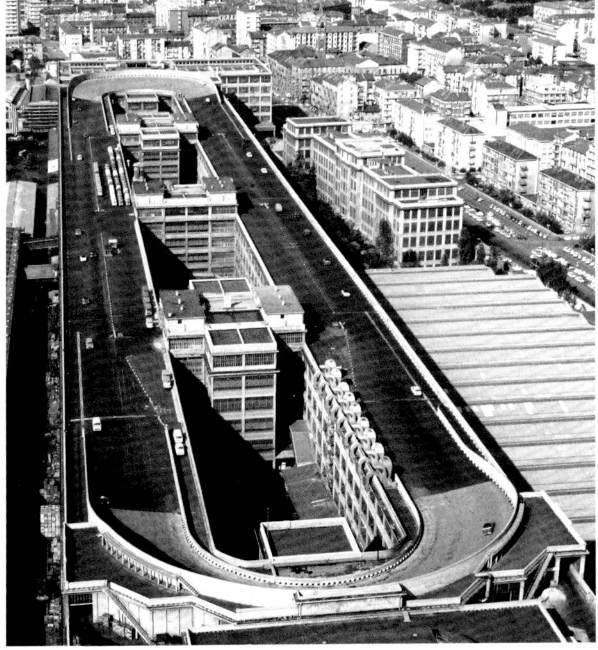

7° 39′ 57″E

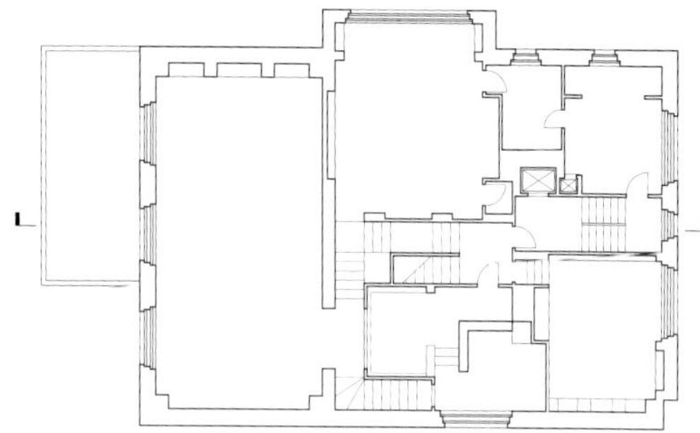

Floor Plan

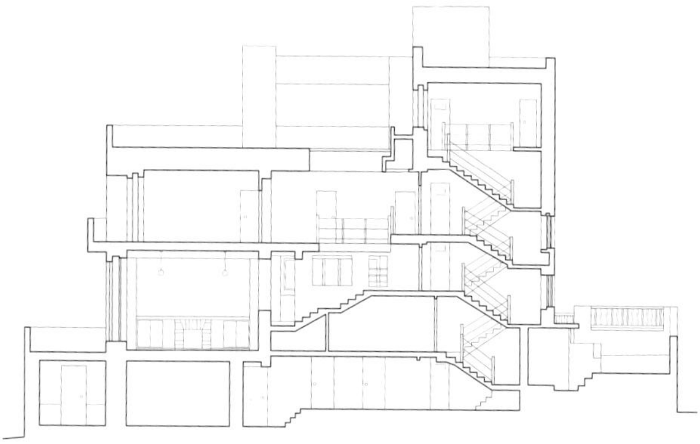

Section

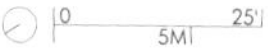

0 25' 5M

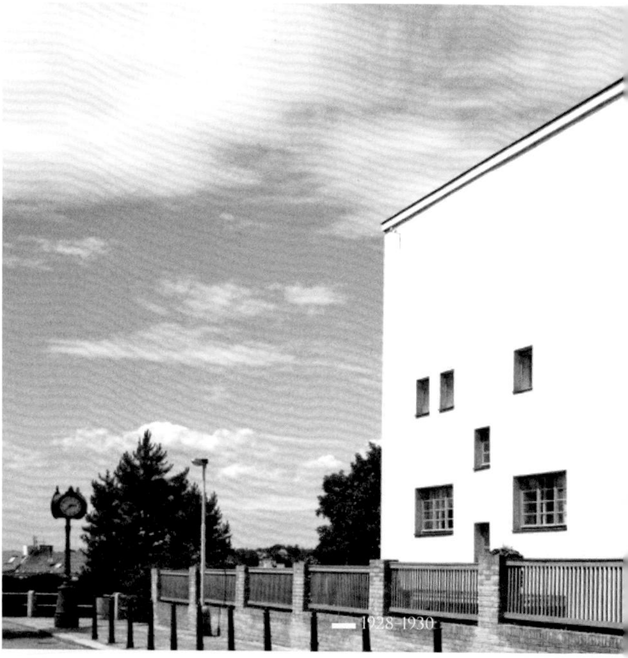

1928–1930

50° 05′ 33″N

82

VILLA MÜLLER

ADOLF LOOS
Prague, Czech Republic
1928–1930

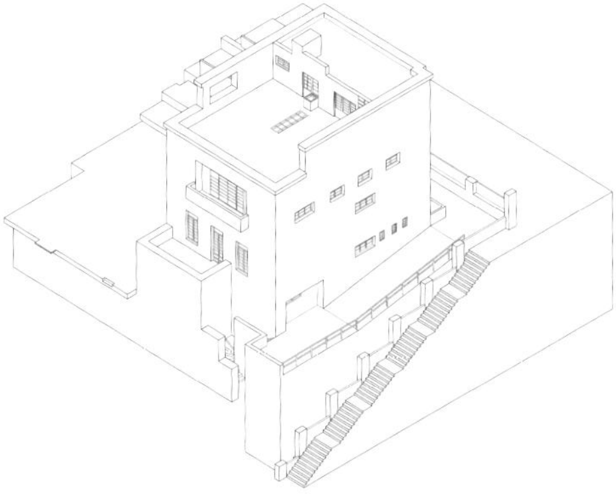

Clearly manifesting Loos's theories on architecture, from his position on ornamentation to his development of the Raumplan, the Villa Müller occupies a central role in early modernism's polemics. For Loos, the exterior of a house should be simple, almost mute, while the interior should be rich in its material and spatial expression. Here, the four facades tease but defy concepts of formal symmetry, always suggesting pure symmetries that have been disturbed by irregular fenestration or stepped massing. Once inside the tight, compressed entry, itself asymmetrically located, two staircases rise. These foster two distinct narratives: the sequential unfolding of the family's spaces from public to private, large to small; and the interwoven elements of ancillary spaces. The rooms are stark in their geometries, rich in their materials, vibrant in their colors, and visible to each other as they are staggered in a variety of levels, with the flow of stairs the principal device of revelation.

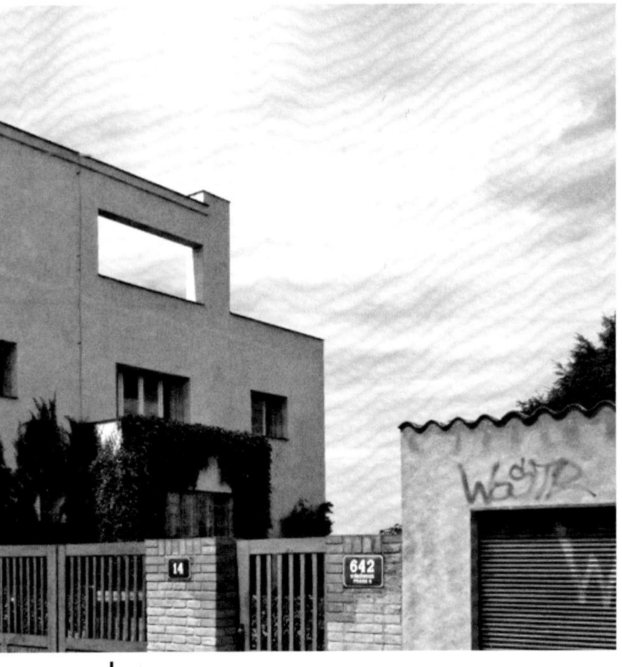

14° 22′ 42″E

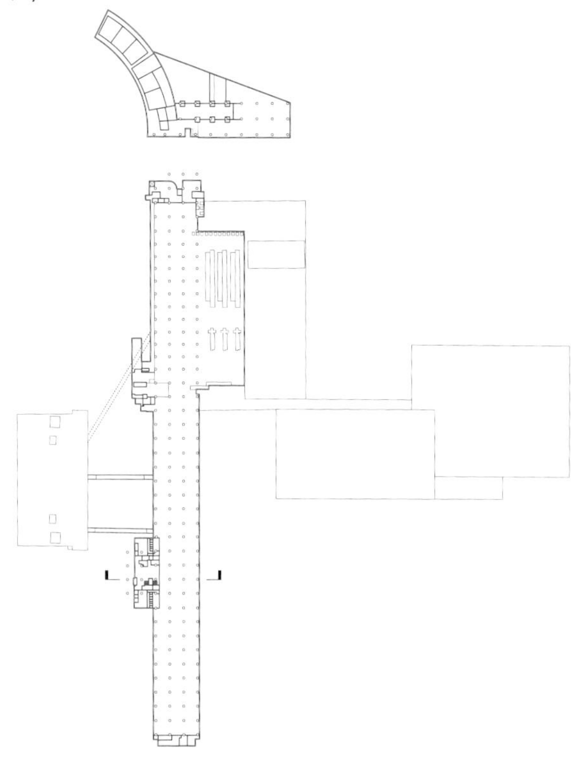

Floor Plan

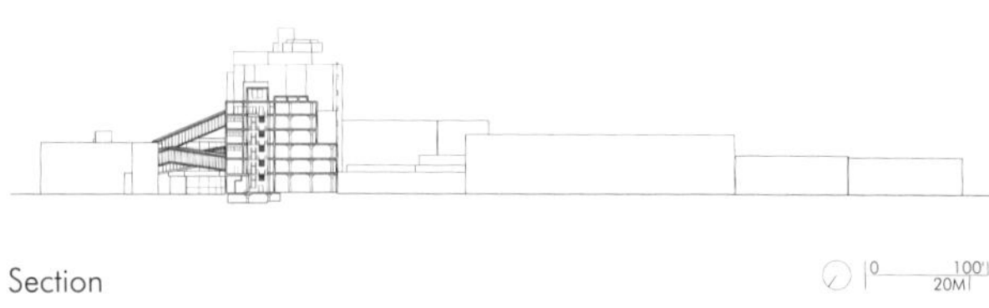

Section

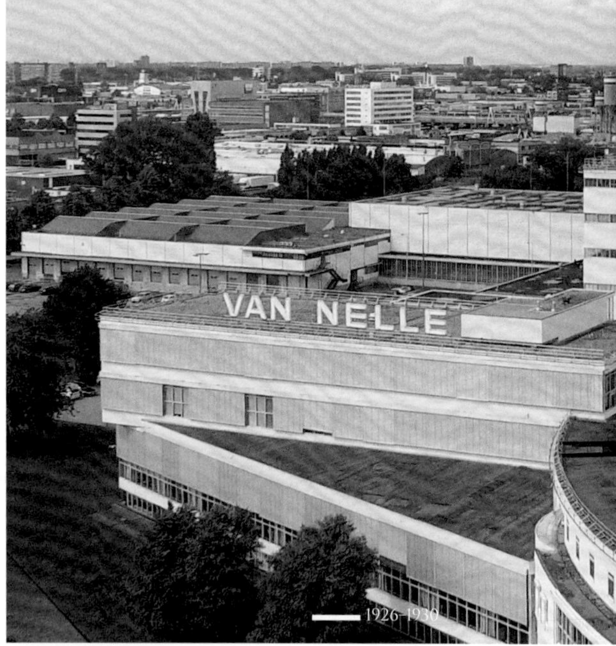

51° 55′ 24″N

83

VAN NELLE FACTORY

JOHANNES BRINKMAN, LEENDERT VAN DER VLUGT, and MART STAM

Rotterdam, The Netherlands

1926–1930

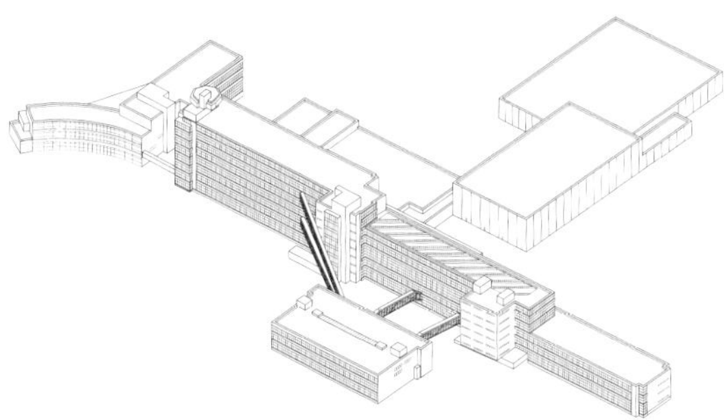

If efficiency, performance, and functionalism defined the political mission of early modernism, and light, air, and workers' welfare defined the social mission of the Dutch modernists, then the Van Nelle Factory is the poster child for such a combined ethos. Designed to process and package fine-grain products such as coffee, tea, and snuff, the factory has rigorously controlled tolerances and a very limited, prescriptive circulation system to prevent cross-contamination. The entire production cycle is showcased, from the initial delivery of raw materials at the top level through progressive processing as it descends each floor to be distributed via the expressive loading and delivery tubes containing conveyors. Its fungiform reinforced-concrete frame was clad in one of the first glass-curtain walls to display the process while offering a clean, pleasant, daylit, and safe working environment for factory employees. It is one of the rare structures that was appreciated both by those believing in functional determinism and those hoping for an expressive constructivism.

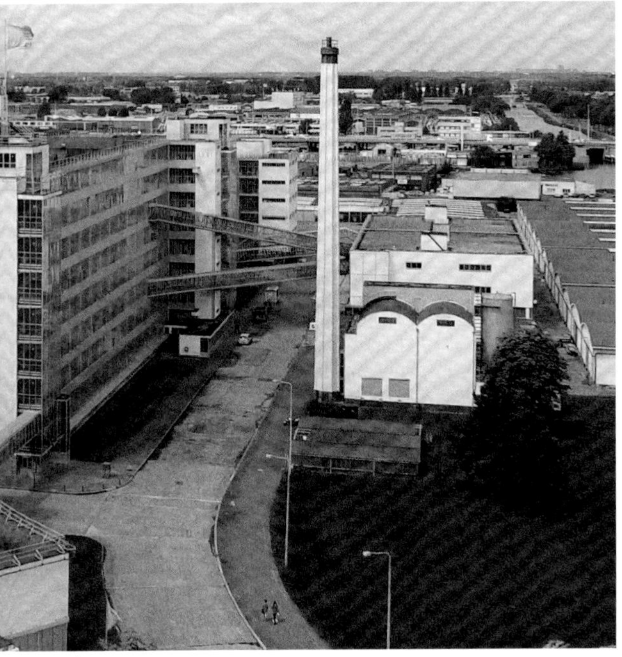

4° 25′ 36″E

42° 18′ 13″N

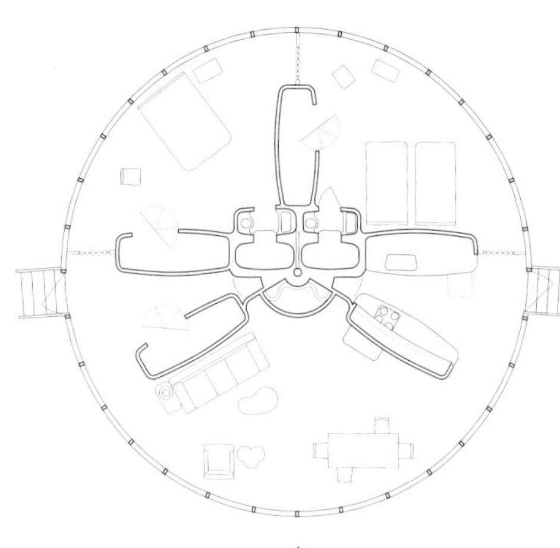

Floor Plan

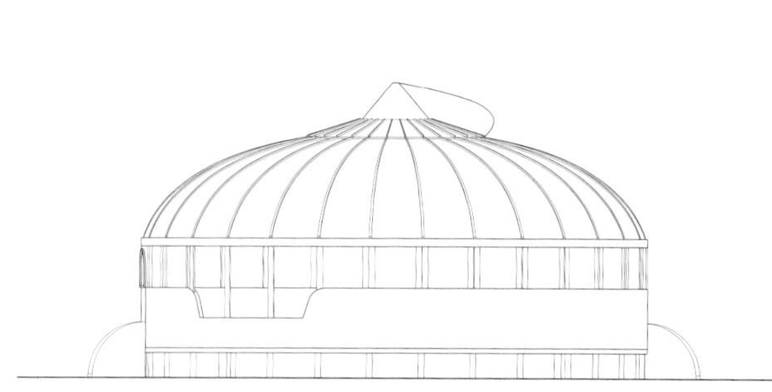

Elevation

0 5M 25′

83° 14′ 03″W

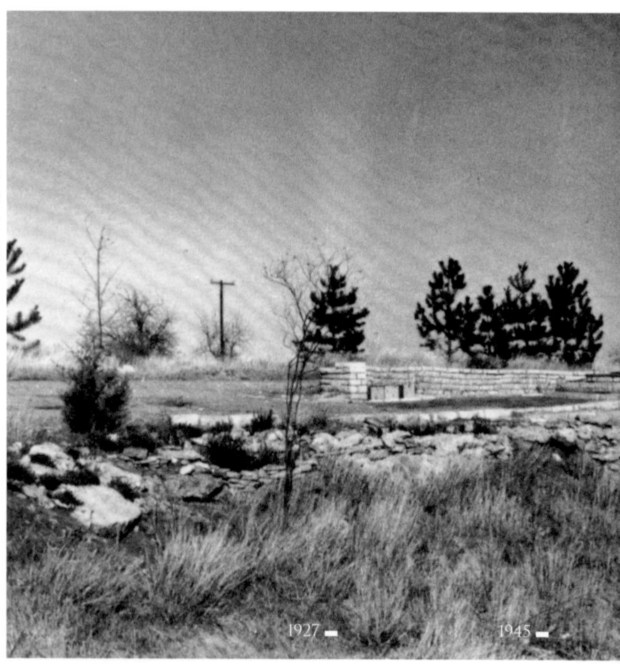

84

DYMAXION HOUSE

BUCKMINSTER FULLER
Dearborn, Michigan, USA
1927; reproduced 1945

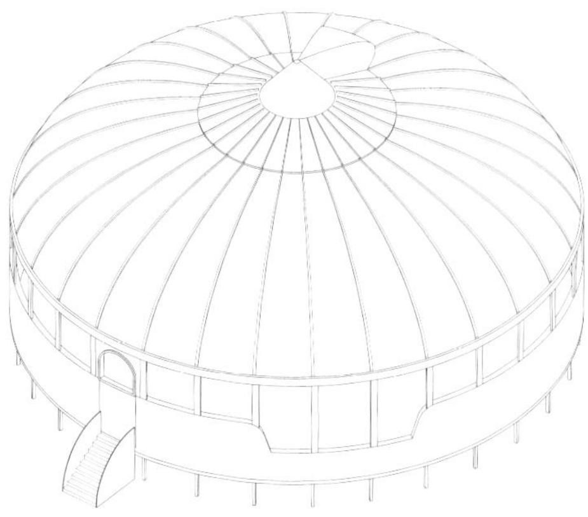

A combination of the terms *dynamic*, *maximum*, and *tension*, Buckminster Fuller's Dymaxion House was intended to introduce the automotive assembly line, materials, and financing models to domestic architecture. A visionary, sustainable structure designed as the future living machine, the house was to be self-sufficient, low-maintenance, mass-produced, and prefabricated. Earthquake proof and stormproof, the Dymaxion was made of engineered materials—primarily aluminum—that required no periodic painting or reroofing. The circular plan was organized around a central core that included the primary structural mast (minimizing foundations) and utilities, with movable service pods allowing for different spatial configurations as needed. The round shape minimized heat loss as well as the amount of materials required, reducing the house weight to one and half tons, just 1 percent of that of an average home.

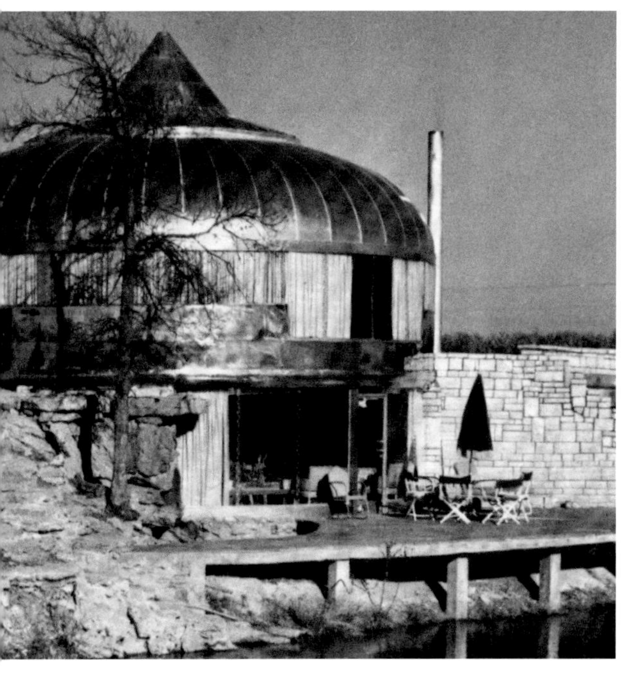

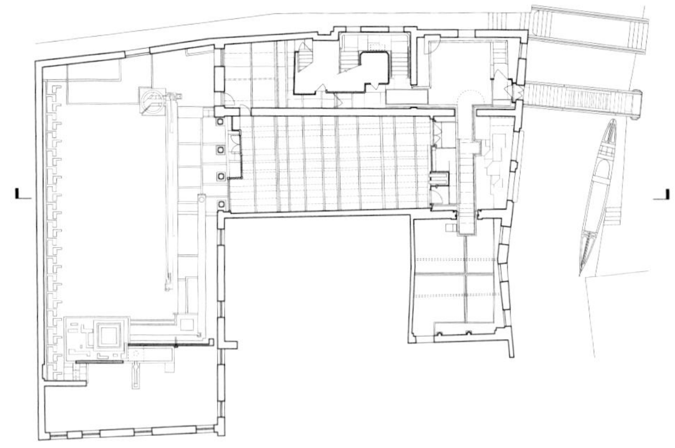

Floor Plan

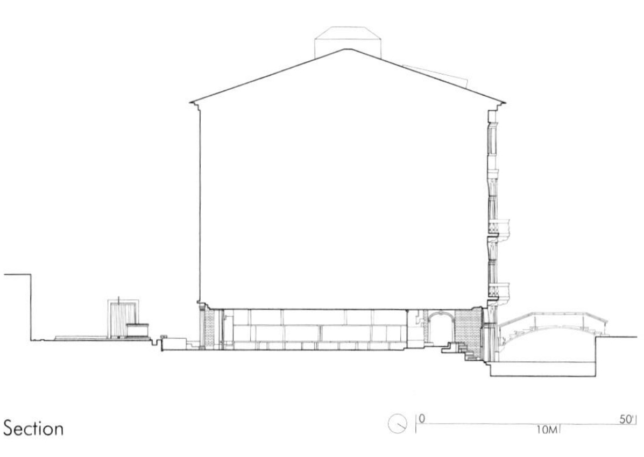

Section

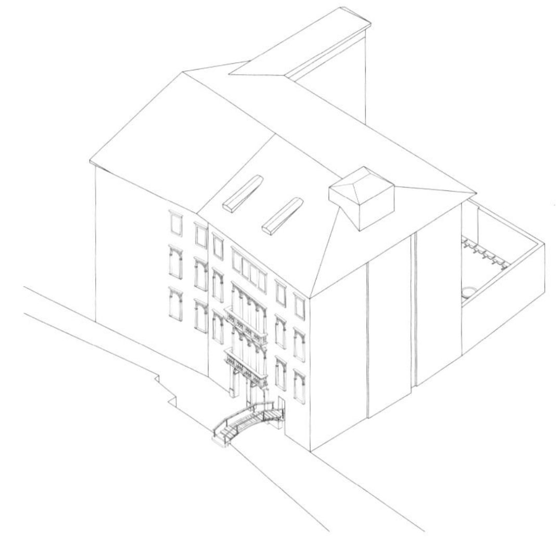

45° 26′ 13″N

85

QUERINI STAMPALIA RENOVATION

CARLO SCARPA and CARLO MASCHIETTO
Venice, Italy
1961–1963

Sharing a similar set of concerns as the Castelvecchio project, this renovation of the ground floor of a historic sixteenth-century Venetian palazzo is both within, and about, water. Next to a canal and subject to the periodic flooding of the city, all of the public areas on the lowest level are designed to passively withstand and accept the intrusion of floodwater. The project begins with a connection to the existing piazza: an arched wood-and-steel pedestrian bridge connecting to the building entry. A series of new public rooms are nested within the existing structure, in which new floors are held free from old walls, embellished with Scarpa's characteristic three-toned mosaic composition. The public rooms open onto a modest garden in the rear of the site in which a narrow runnel of water from a well spans the length of the space before being collected in a small basin and then disappearing.

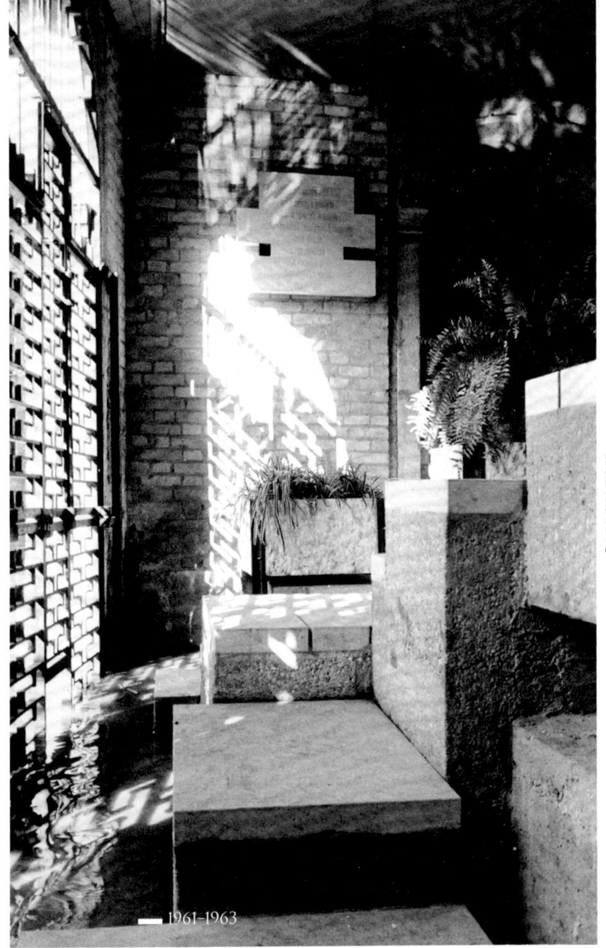
1961–1963

12° 20′ 30″E

41° 50′ 01″N

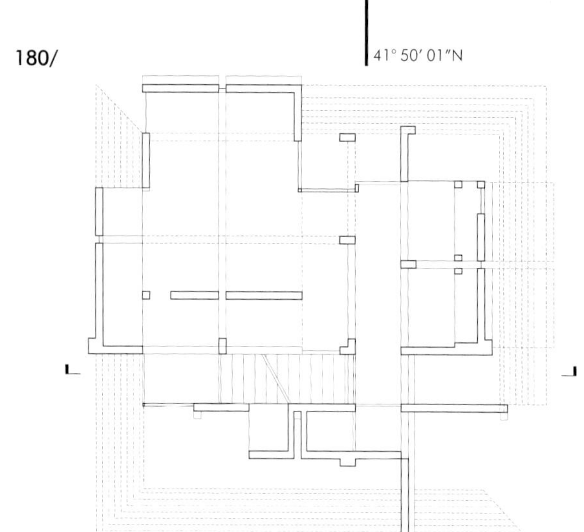

Floor Plan

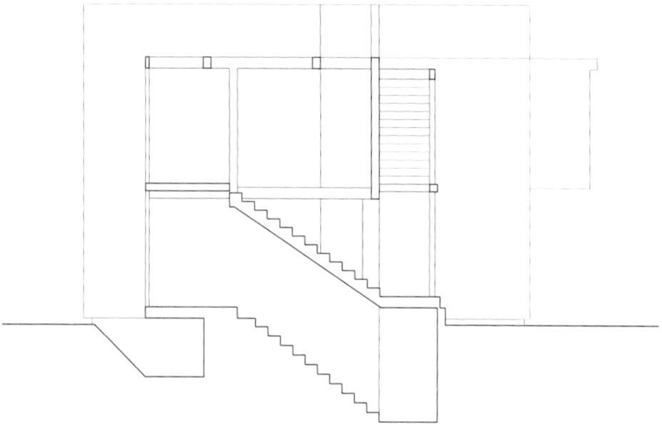

Section

0 10′
2M

73° 19′ 21″W

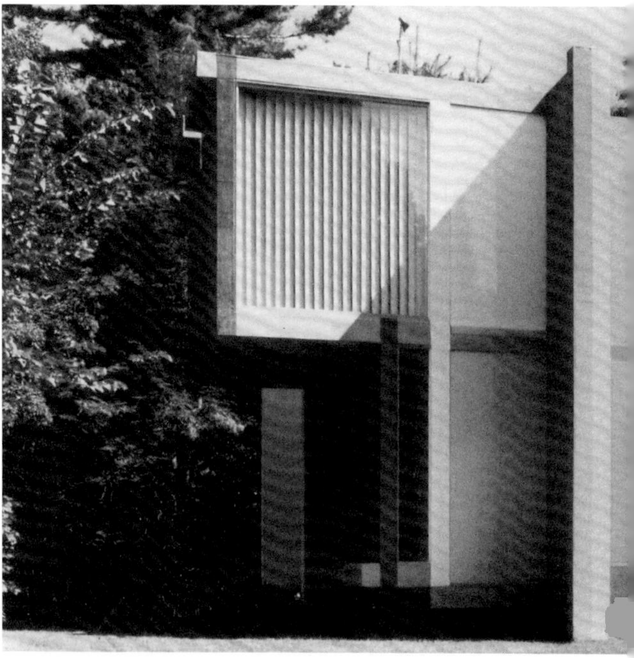

86

HOUSE VI

PETER EISENMAN
Cornwall, Connecticut, USA
1972–1975

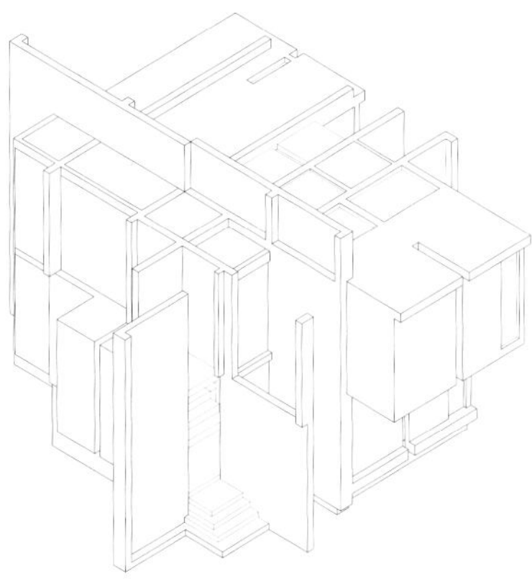

Constructed more in the way one might construct a series of drawings than a building, Eisenman's House VI ushered in the second wave of postmodernity by exploring the possibilities of an architecture that is "autonomous": that is, with a language that can be arbitrary and unique within its own disciplinarity, yet understood through a decoding of the building as a whole. Its autonomy is reinforced by the way it appears to not even touch the ground. Colors and grids, solids and voids help articulate the formal operations that began with a chevron of four walls that eventually came to form the house. In order to provoke understanding, the house manages to defamiliarize and disrupt some of the basic functions of the domestic environment: a column that interrupts the dining room table, slots of glass that bisect the master bed itself, a stair that is inverted, inaccessible slots, and so on.

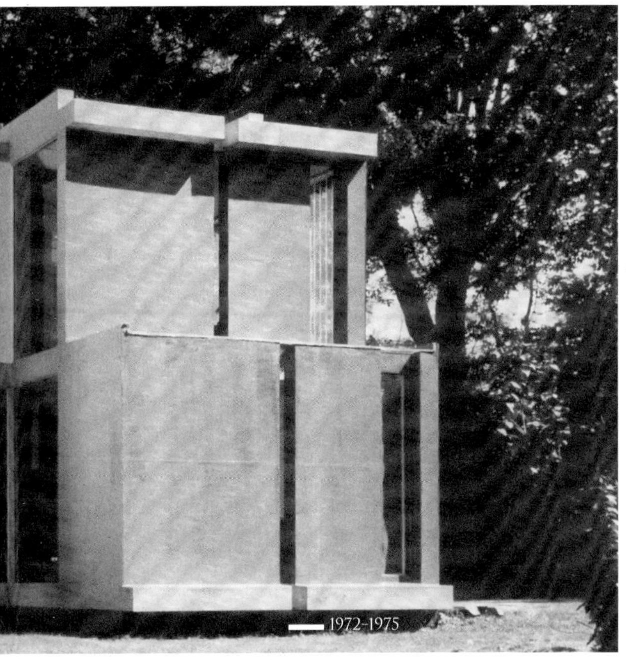

1972–1975

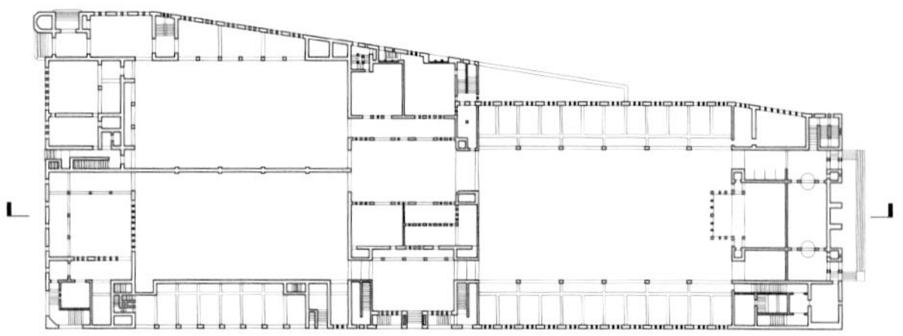

Floor Plan

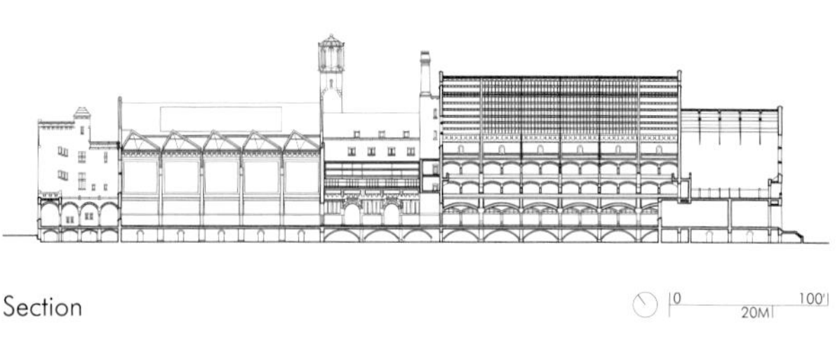

Section

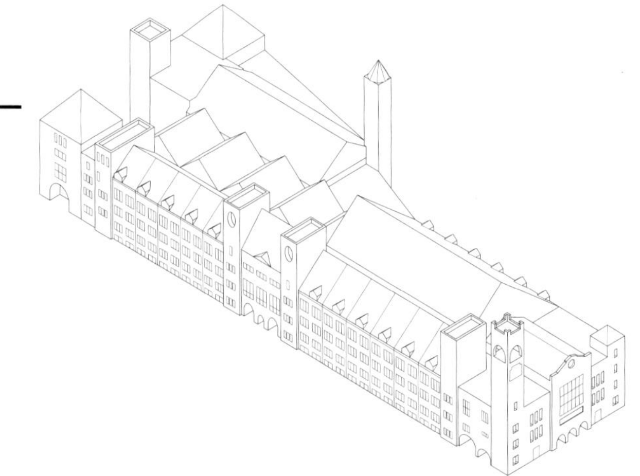

1896–1903

52° 22′ 31″N

87

BEURS VAN BERLAGE

HENDRIK PETRUS BERLAGE
Amsterdam, The Netherlands
1896–1903

Uncomfortable with the stylistic mimicry that characterized the architectural aesthetics of the nineteenth century, and of the Netherlands in particular, Hendrik Petrus Berlage chose what has been described as a neo-Romanesque style for the design of the Amsterdam Stock Exchange, one of the largest buildings in the city. Feeling the necessity to convey a sense of security, but with an equal compulsion to demonstrate freedom and openness, Berlage created a building that clearly articulates its basic programmatic volumes while demonstrating his deeply held worldview of "unity in diversity." Throughout the building and its three huge halls, plain bricks contrast with glazed bricks, polished stone with rough-hewn, and structural piers of brick and stone give way to exposed iron with articulated points of structural bearing and transference: an application of the rationalist techniques advocated by Viollet-le-Duc. Eschewing excessive decoration while maintaining a simple and rational plan, Berlage was able to move the Netherlands away from their capitalist-driven eclecticism toward Dutch Realism and, ultimately, modernism.

4° 53′ 46″E

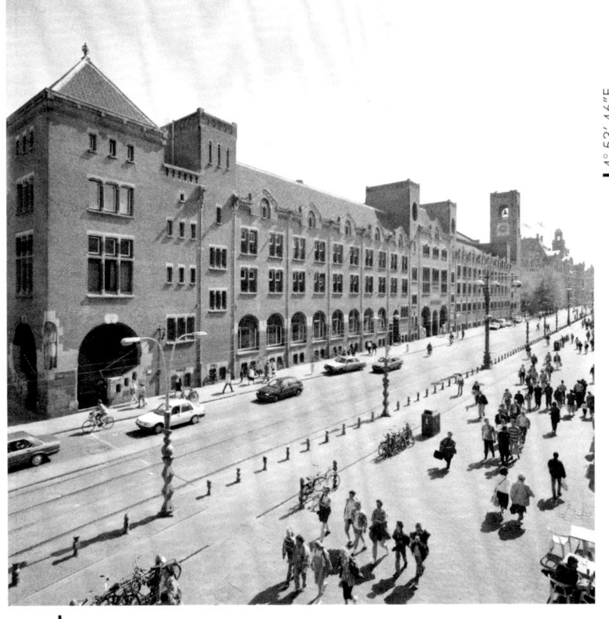

34° 09′ 07″N

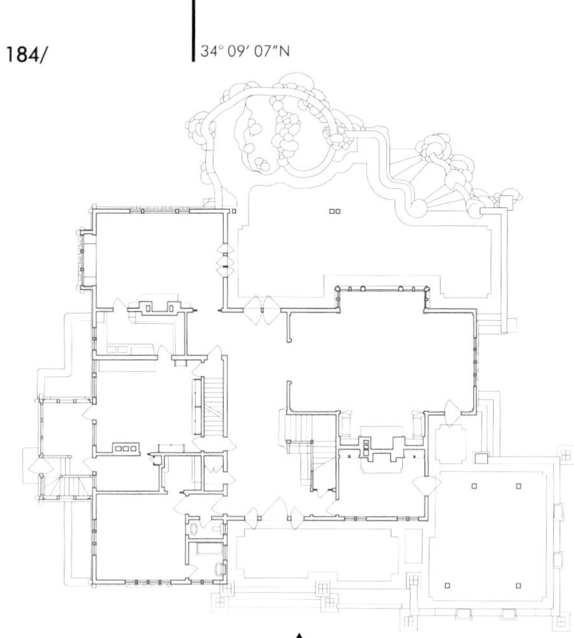

Floor Plan

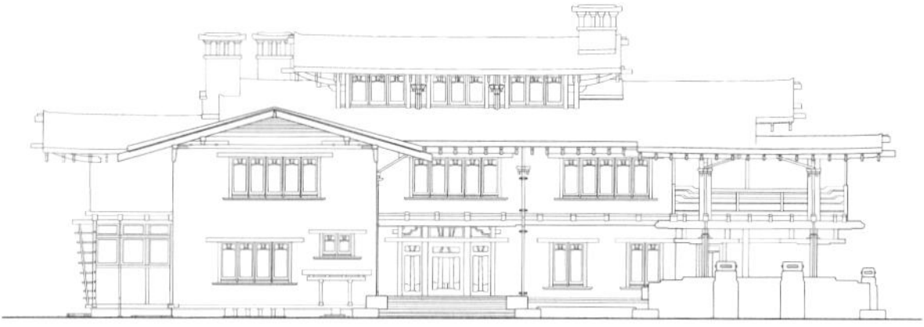

Elevation

0 25′ 5M

118° 09′ 39″W

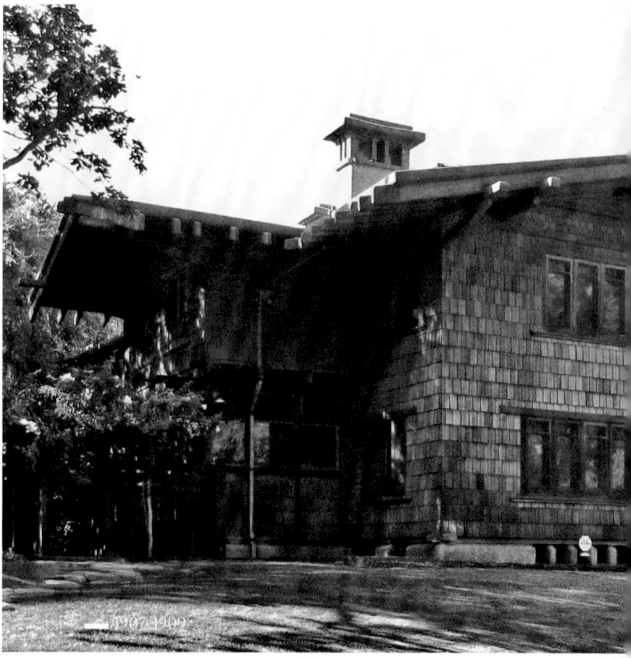

1907–1909

88

GAMBLE HOUSE

GREENE & GREENE
Pasadena, California, USA
1907–1909

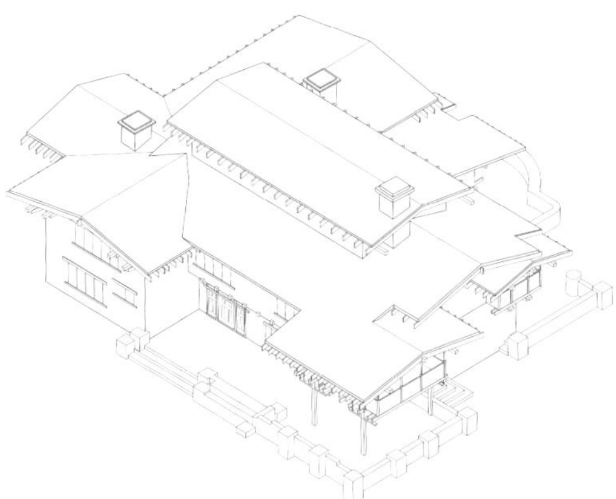

Designed by the brothers Greene & Greene as a health retreat for the Gamble family (half of the consumer-goods giant Procter & Gamble), the Gamble House represents the apotheosis of the Arts and Crafts movement in America. Inspired by the concept of the *gesamtkunstwerk*—the "total work of art"— every element of the house was custom-designed by the Greenes, from the carved and formed wood at the grand staircase to the custom Tiffany stained-glass windows, the lantern fixtures, light-switch plates, and furnishings. The house exhibits a combination of Californian openness in plan with the influence of Japanese traditional architecture, particularly noticeable in the details of the fine wood joinery. To take advantage of the healthful California climate, the house is organized with close relationships between interior and exterior spaces, including features such as sleeping porches and patios.

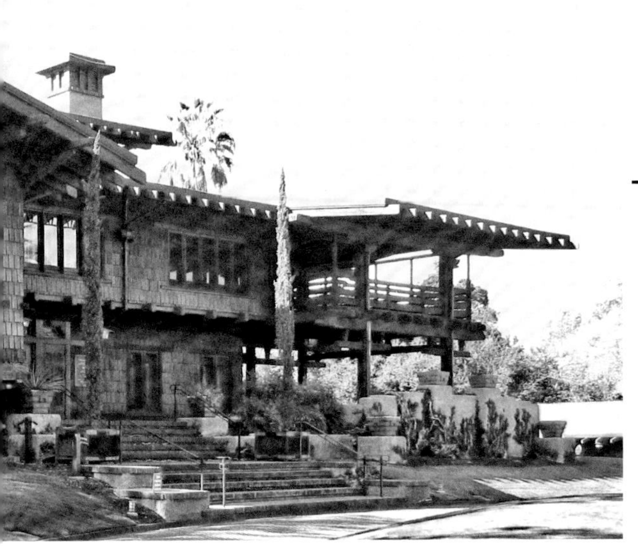

33° 36′ 21″N

Floor Plan

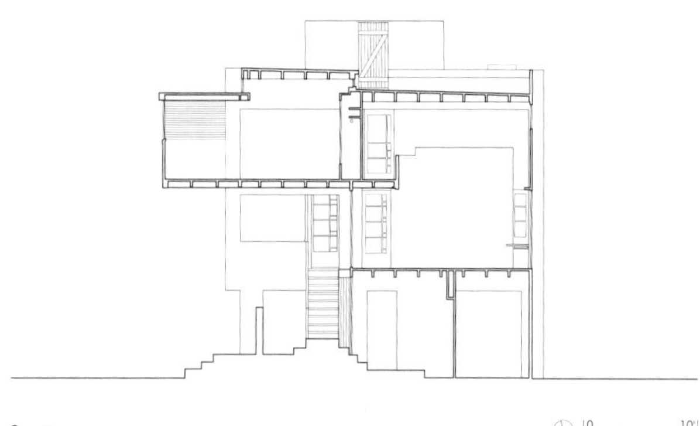

Section

0 10′
2M

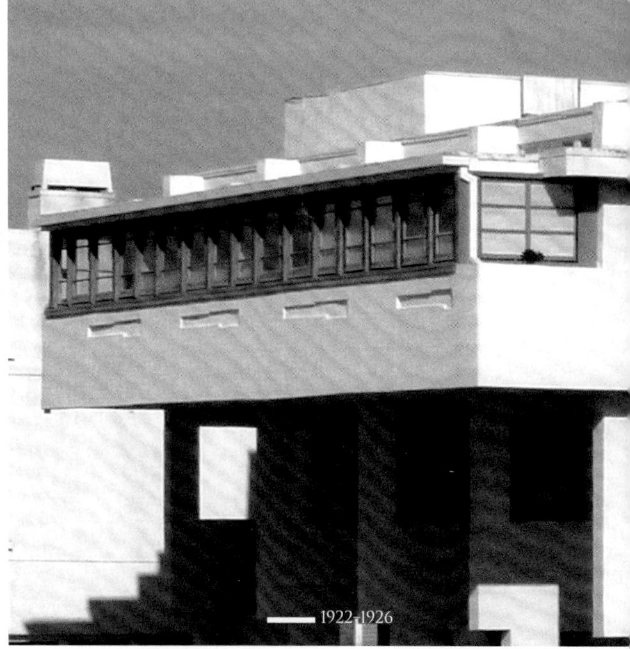

117° 55′ 04″W

89

LOVELL BEACH HOUSE

RUDOLF SCHINDLER
Newport Beach, California, USA
1922–1926

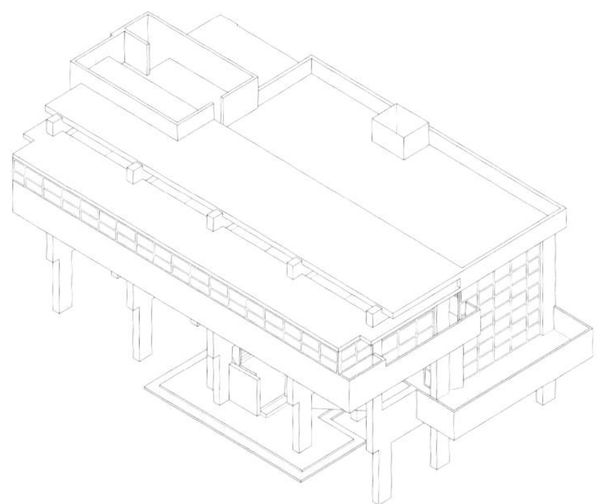

Built four years after Schindler's own manifesto of a residence, the Lovell Beach House continues the architect's exploration into structure, living volume, and circulation, while experimenting with concrete as an a priori material for residential construction. The house was built for Dr. Philip Lovell, a popular media figure who advocated clean living through healthy environments, and who would later commission Richard Neutra for the Lovell Health House. Five parallel poured-in-place structural piers become the spatial and functional templates for the house. They lift the residential volume into the air, with the resultant portico mediating public and private space. Between the defining piers, living spaces—like the generous two-story volume in the center—are determined by weaving wooden volumes through the piers, while private spaces occur on the upper level, in cellular spaces on trays supported by the piers.

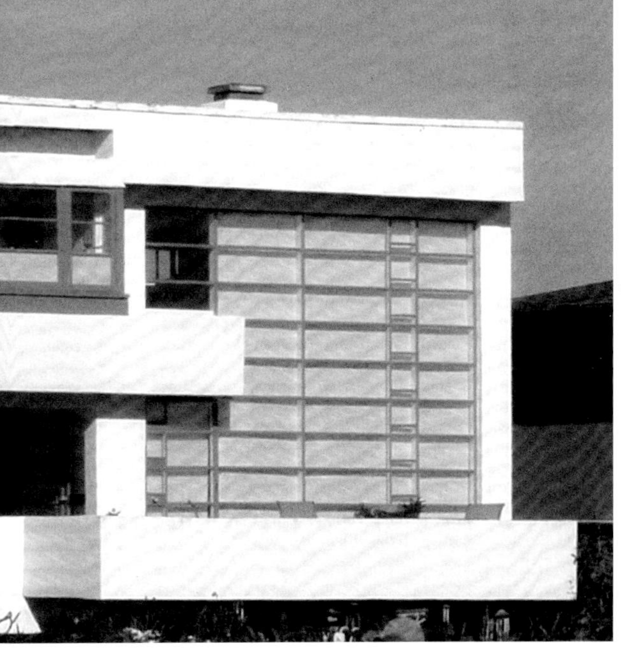

188/

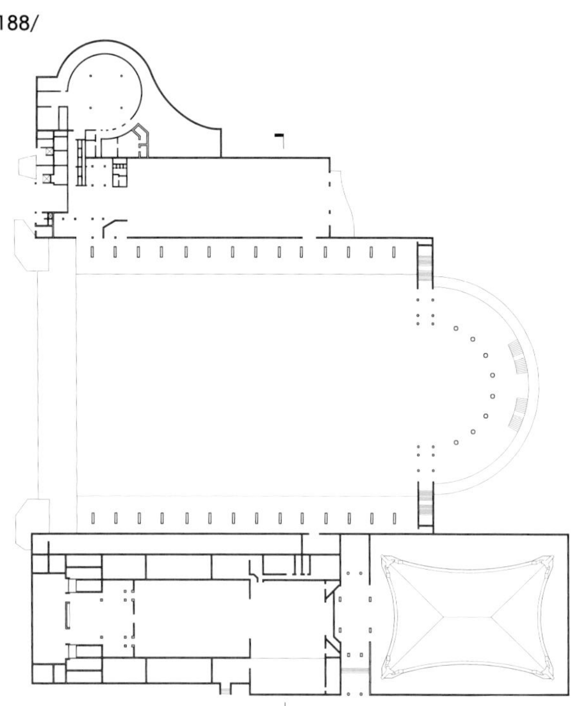

Floor Plan

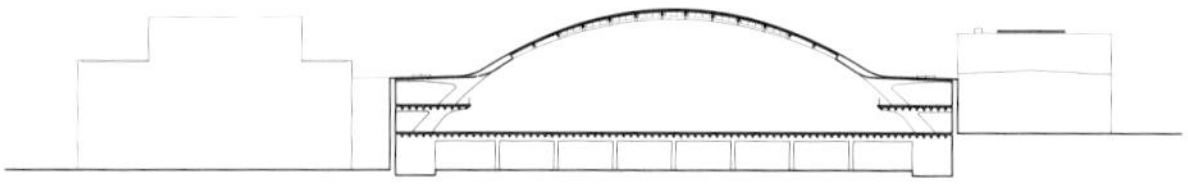

Section

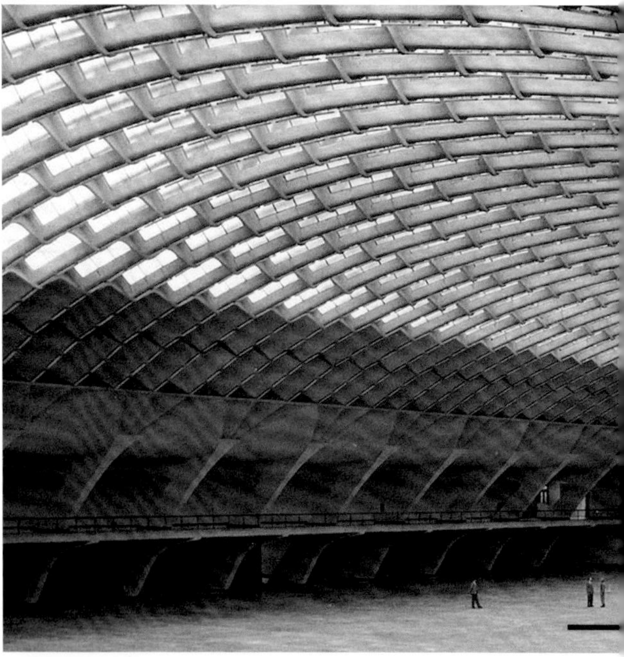

0 20M 100'

45° 02′ 58″N

90

TURIN EXHIBITION HALL

PIER LUIGI NERVI
Turin, Italy
1948–1954

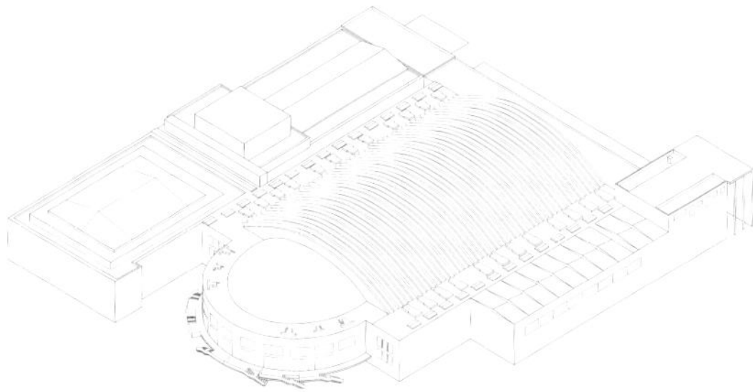

For an exhibition hall that was 94 meters in width, Nervi designed a top-lit, column-free, modular ferro-cement vault with a shallow arch configuration. Poured-in-place abutments begin the vaulted spans, spreading so that each supports three arches. These arches are composed of a series of wave-shaped, prefabricated ferro-cement elements, approximately 5 meters by 2.5 meters in dimension, 5 centimeters in thickness, and with window openings cast in their diagonal sides to admit light. V-shaped triangular stiffeners are used between panels to achieve rigidity in the transverse direction. Cast-in-place concrete at the apex and trough of each of the corrugated units functions as the unit-to-unit connector, locking the overall assembly into place. In addition to collecting the arches, the abutments support a continuous balcony overlooking the main hall. A domed apse, 40 meters in diameter, constructed of reinforced concrete cast over diamond-shaped pans, ends the space.

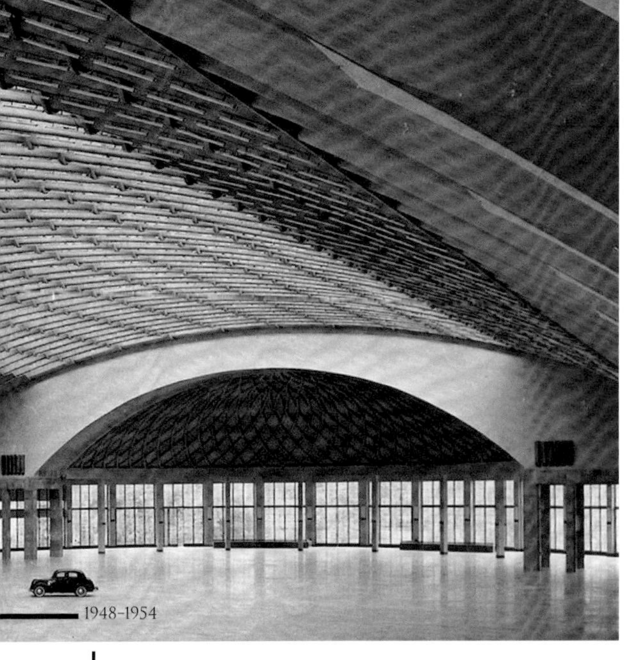

1948–1954

7° 40′ 53″E

190/

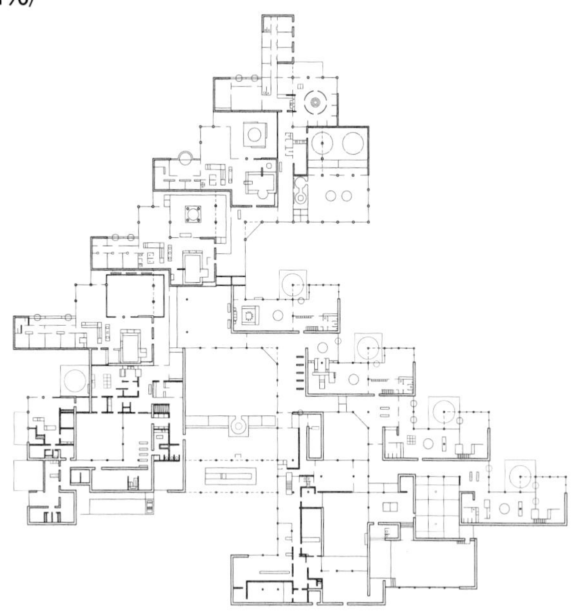

Floor Plan

Elevation

0 20M 100'

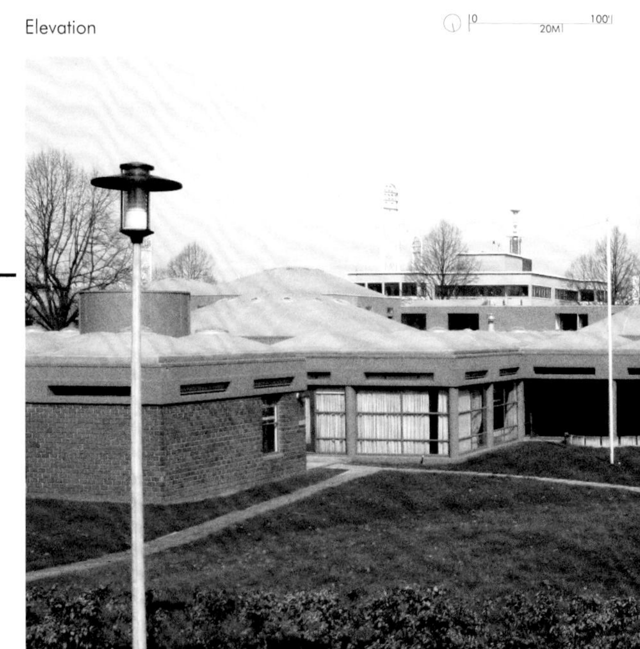

52° 20′ 28″N

91

MUNICIPAL ORPHANAGE, AMSTERDAM

ALDO VAN EYCK
Amsterdam, The Netherlands
1955–1960

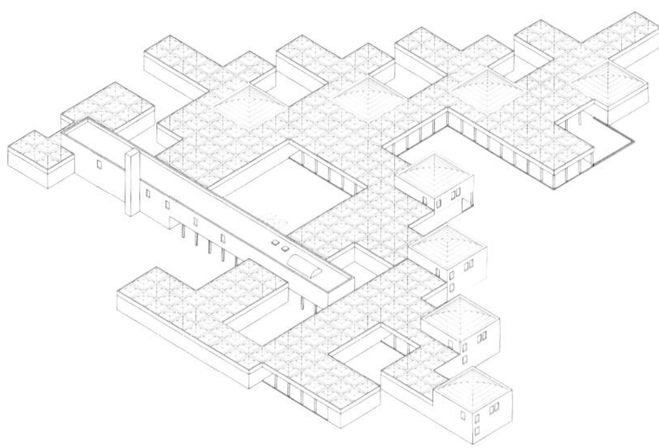

As one of the founding members of Team 10, Aldo van Eyck found the perfect program in an orphanage on the outskirts of Amsterdam: it required an architecture that was related to community and that could invoke the humanist aspects of the city—markets, streets, and squares—all within the protected confines of a singular mat building. Composed primarily of brick, with prefabricated concrete roof modules in 1x1 and 3x3 proportions, the building sets out these modules so as to contain interior public spaces and a series of exterior courtyards. Each wing accommodates living spaces and classrooms for each age and gender. While machinelike in its overall precision, its components—such as benches, stoops, archways, and ledges—relate to the scale of its young residents. Mirrors and windows are placed in unexpected locations, many of which are invisible to adults. Van Eyck produced a microcosm of a village, with many open and even unassigned spaces, and with a program that traditionally valued efficiency over vitality.

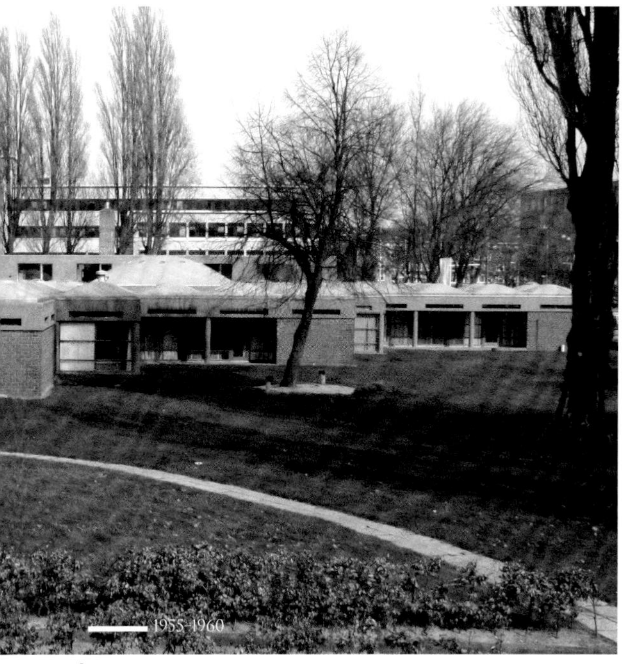

1955–1960

4° 51′ 22″E

42° 22′ 25″N

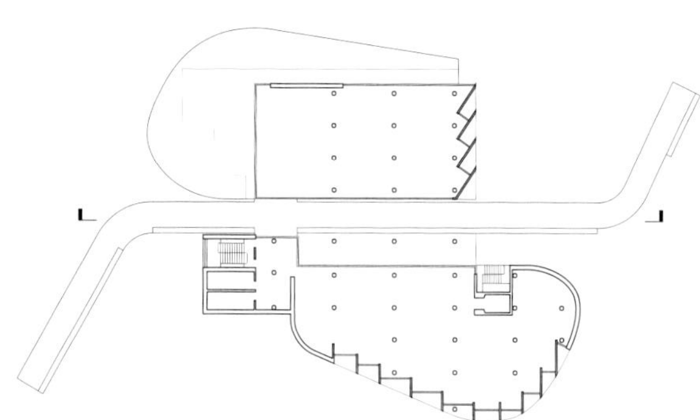

Floor Plan

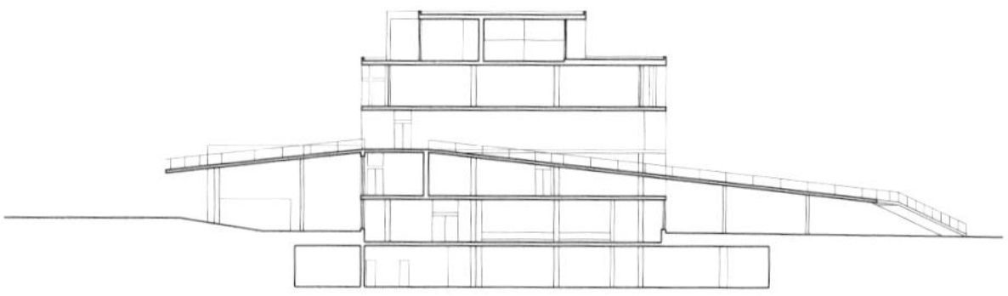

Section

0 10M 50′

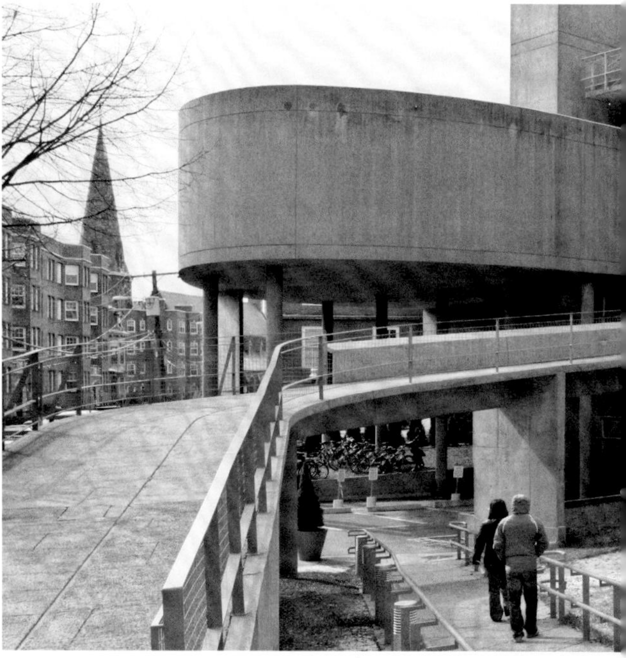

71° 06′ 52″W

92

CARPENTER CENTER FOR THE VISUAL ARTS

LE CORBUSIER
Harvard University, Cambridge, Massachusetts, USA
1959–1962

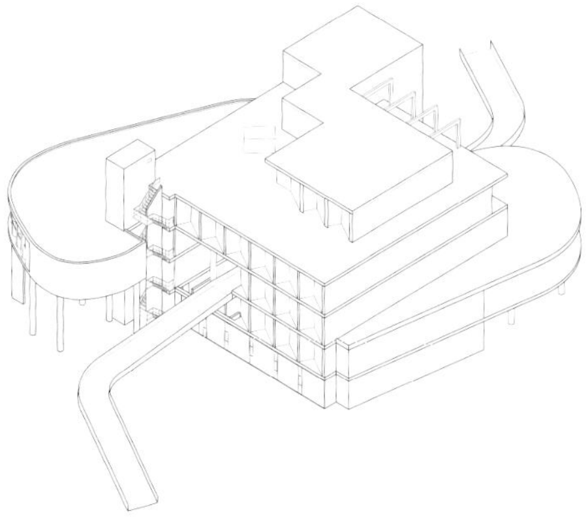

For his first building in the United States, Le Corbusier presents a virtual *œuvre complète* of his principles and designs. Brilliantly sited on a street bordering Harvard Yard, the main cubic volume—dressed in brise-soleils turned parallel to the bounding streets—is rotated, mediating between the volumes of a museum and a small faculty club. A grand, sinuous ramp provides the public with a promenade that bisects the building in the center of its mass, affording everyone on the campus an opportunity to witness the activities of the new visual arts center while traversing the block. As this S-shaped ramp penetrates the poured-in-place concrete cube of the building, two lobe-shaped volumes emerge, as if generated from the combined dynamism of movement and form, and shape exterior exhibition and secondary entries in the piloti zones beneath their masses. An apartment for a visiting artist occupies the roof terrace.

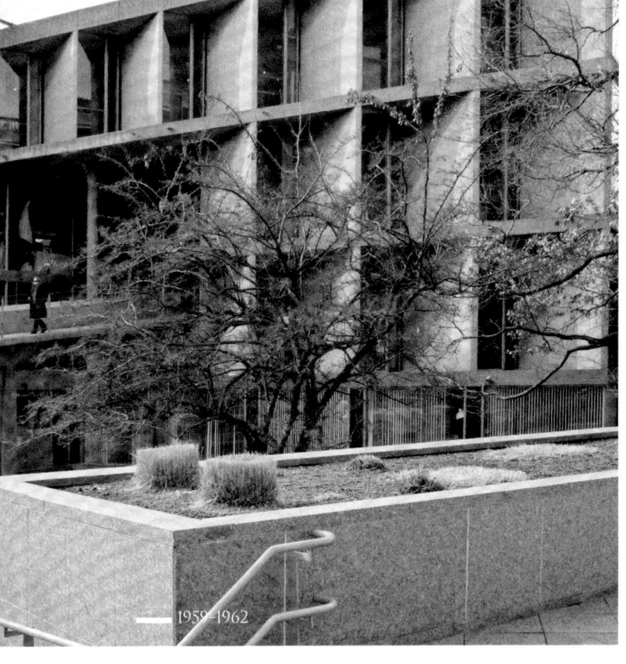

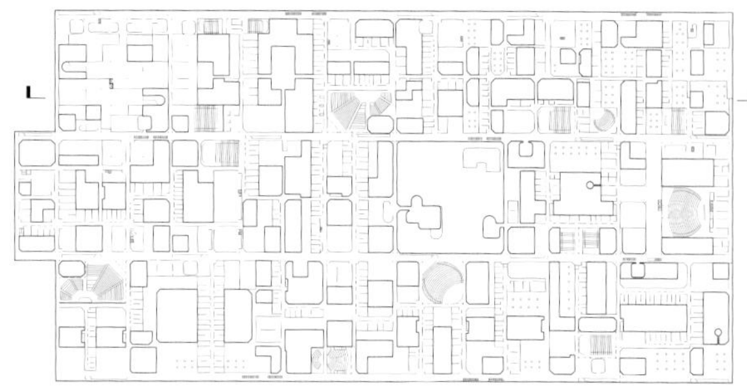

Floor Plan

Section

0 100M 500'

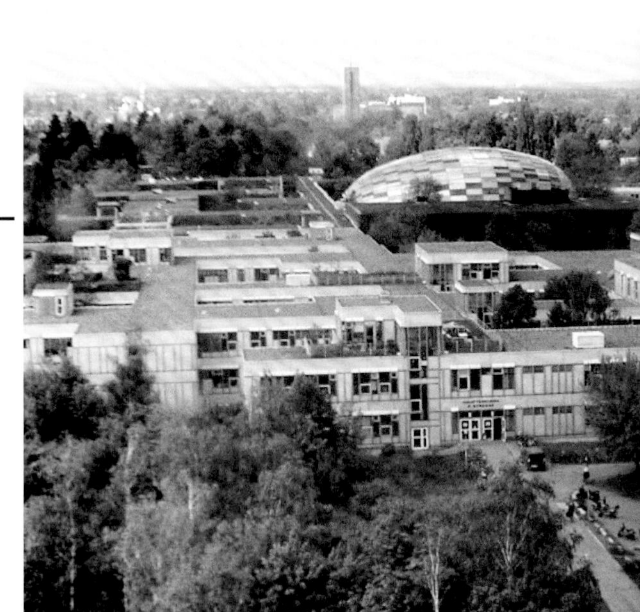

52° 27′ 10″N

93

FREE UNIVERSITY OF BERLIN

CANDILIS-JOSIC-WOODS and MANFRED SCHIEDHELM

Berlin, Germany

1963–1973

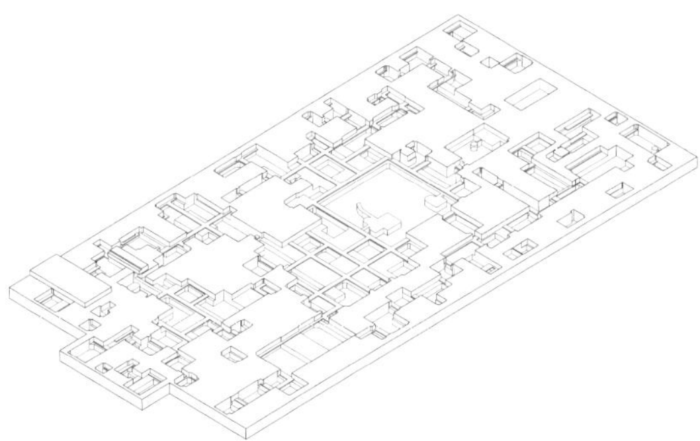

One of the first of Team 10's city/buildings to have been built, and still one of the most cited among constructed mat buildings, the Free University of Berlin is a distinct application of Shadrach Woods's concepts of "stem" and "web." A horizontally arranged "network" building intended to replicate the scalar and experiential variety one might find in a casbah or a dense city rendered in microcosm, the project echoes Aldo van Eyck's call for "labyrinthine clarity" through the programmatic medium of a university campus. The two- and three-story buildings sometimes shape and at other times infill a potentially endless grid of layered courtyard gardens intended to admit light to the building's central spaces. Conceived as a nonheirarchical matrix building, the design intent was predicated on modular flexibility of both structure and cladding, enabling extensive future flexibility by means of easily reconfigurable partitions and even structure, including columns, precast floor slabs, and a Cor-Ten exterior enclosure engineered and fabricated by Jean Prouvé.

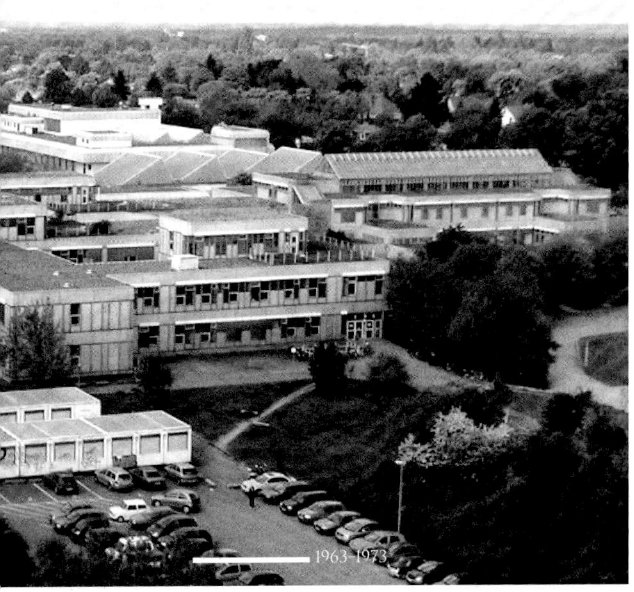

1963–1973

13° 17′ 23″E

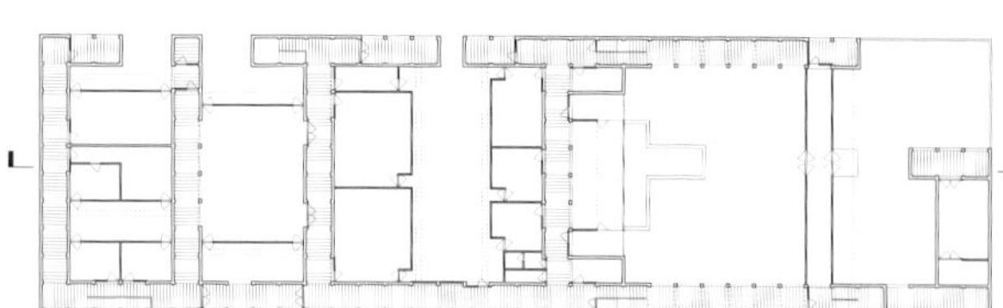

Floor Plan

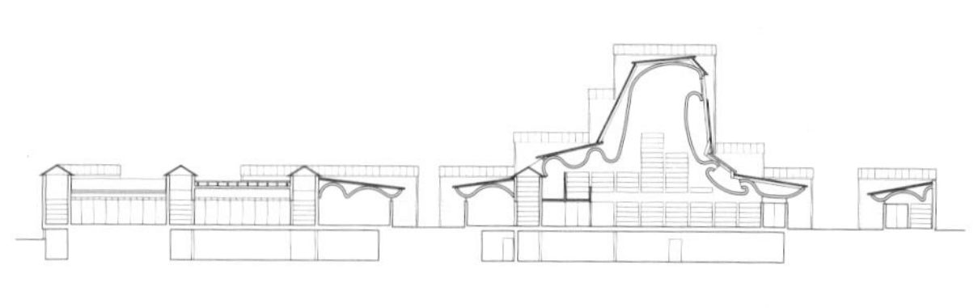

Section

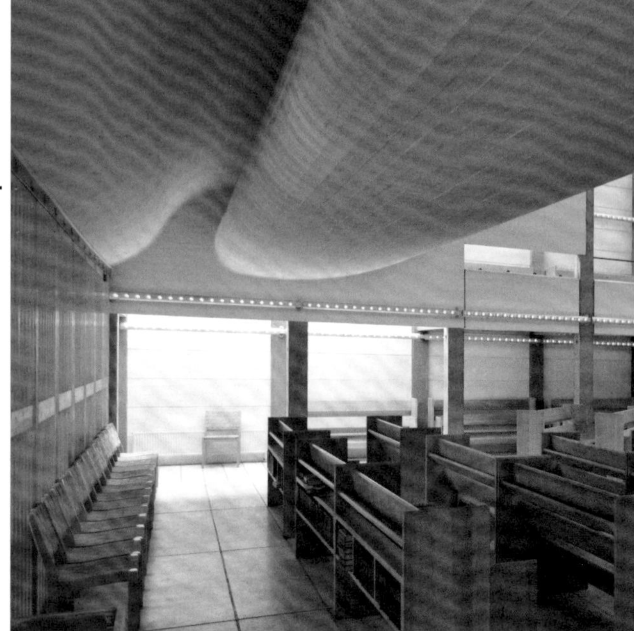

55° 45′ 42″N

94

BAGSVÆRD CHURCH

JØRN UTZON
Copenhagen, Denmark
1969–1976

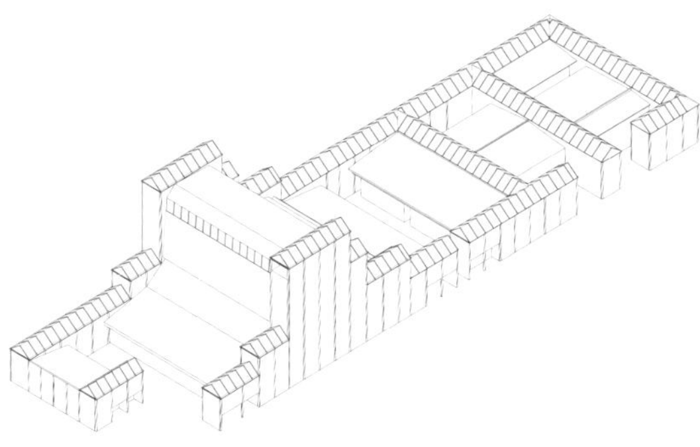

In elevation and materials, it is slightly reminiscent of the local agricultural and industrial buildings; in plan, it is suggestive of a Danish castle or courtyard farm—the Bagsværd Church uses section to express its divinity. Its orthogonal, stepped exterior elevations are clad in white precast concrete panels that give way to glazed ceramic tiles, subtly suggesting the church's section. The corrugated aluminum of the roofs further suggests an industrial calmness. The section, however, incorporates a series of curved, billowing cast-in-place shell vaults that are extruded across the section and that build to a crescendo before the altar, reaching toward the sky above and capturing the Nordic light to be drawn deeply into the spaces of the church. As Utzon had hoped, through the use of modest materials and the adept manipulation of light, the Bagsværd Church replicates the most primal experience of worshipping outdoors beneath the clouds.

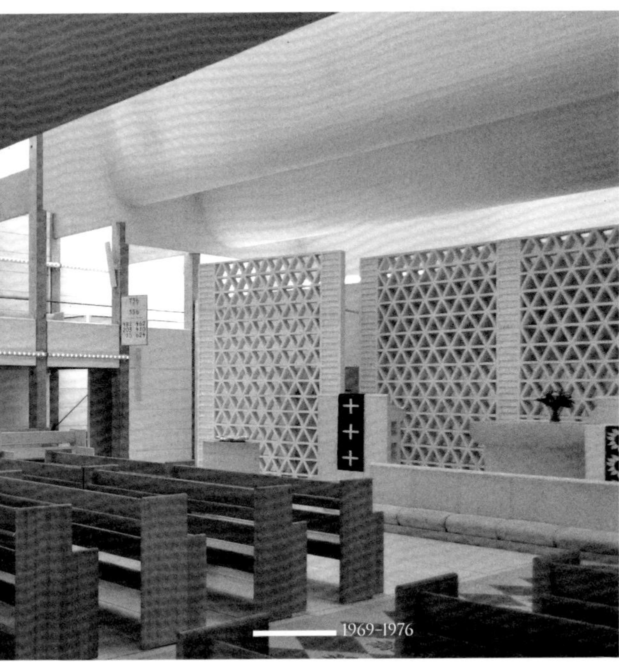

1969–1976

12° 26′ 41″E

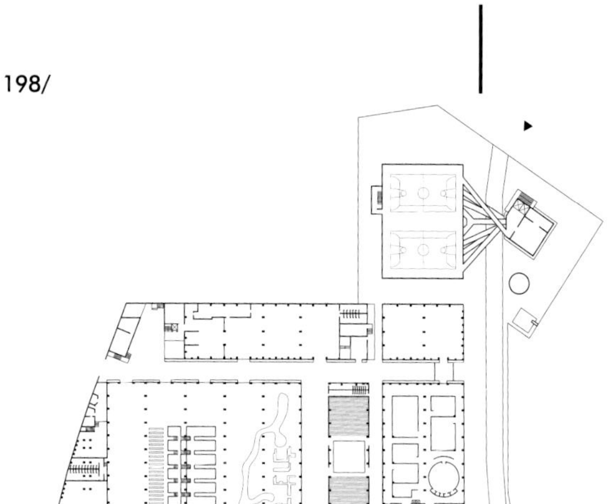

Floor Plan

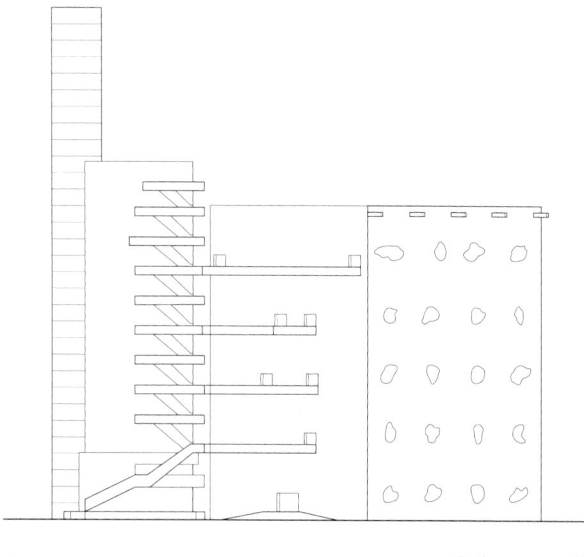

Elevation

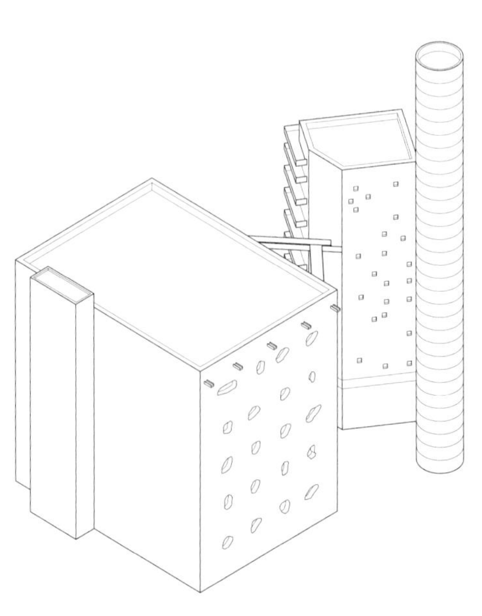

46° 41′ 00″W

23° 31′ 31″S

95

SESC POMPÉIA

LINA BO BARDI
São Paulo, Brazil
1977–1986

An existing barrel-manufacturing complex is renovated into a community center with a rich tapestry of programs for members of a very large employees' union. In the lower buildings, a combination of libraries, cafeterias, exhibition spaces, and meeting rooms are kept as open as possible, with rivulets of water and shelving units suggesting the divisions of spaces. Distinguished by red-screened irregular window apertures, the twin gymnasium towers are approached along a long, winding wooden sunning deck. The smokestack-like water tower stands as an adjacent third member of the composition. It is made of cast-in-place concrete utilizing an "oozing joint" technique between pours, creating an irregular layering that telegraphs the process of its own making. In her SESC Pompéia, Bo Bardi fully demonstrates her philosophy of placing social interaction at the center of all architectural compositions.

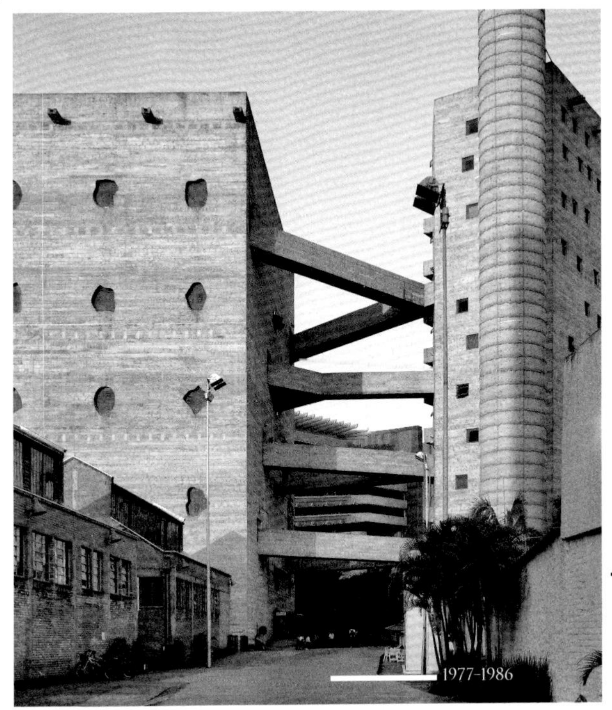
1977–1986

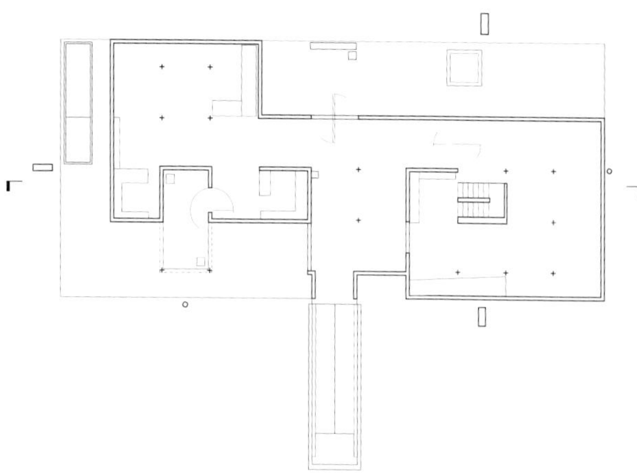

Floor Plan

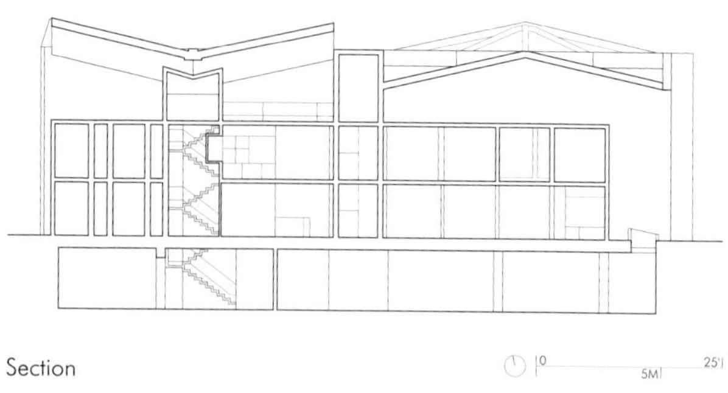

Section

0 5M 25'

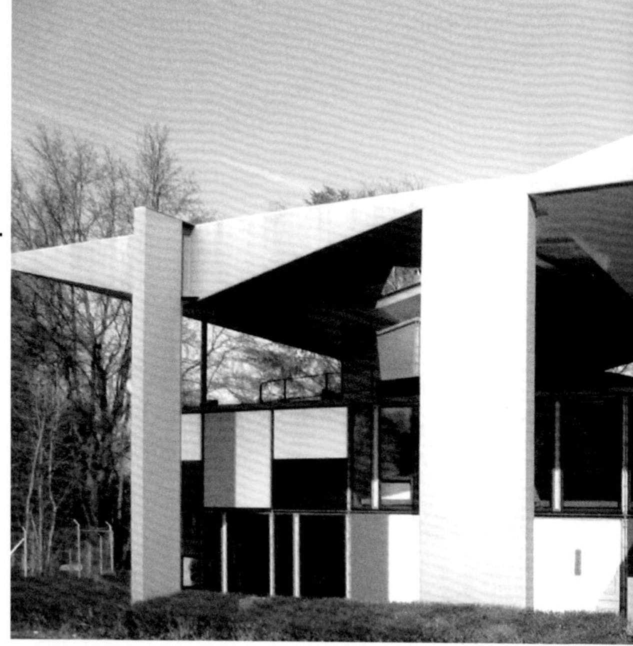

47° 21′ 22″N

96

CENTRE LE CORBUSIER
HEIDI WEBER HOUSE

LE CORBUSIER
Zürich, Switzerland
1965–1967

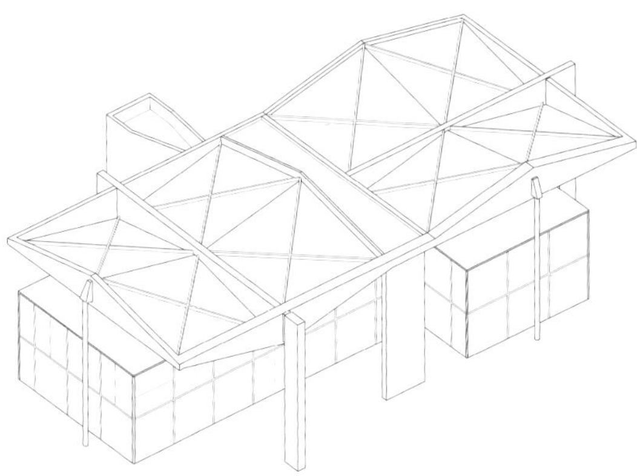

One of the last designed projects by Le Corbusier, the Heidi Weber House was conceived as a park pavilion, home, and gallery for the collection of Le Corbusier's art, to accommodate the collector and curator, Heidi Weber. The only Le Corbusier building that was almost completely steel, the structure was designed to be modular (and using his Modulor proportioning system), consisting of a clearly articulated system of L-shaped steel channels that could be combined to form composite L-shaped, T-shaped, and cruciform columns. Enameled steel panels combine with glass to make the walls; floors consist of steel panels with rubber tiles. This prefabrication system merges earlier studies and explorations from his career: the prefabricated pavilion proposed for Liège and San Francisco in 1939, the Roq and Rob housing from 1949, and the project for an Exposition at the Porte Maillot of 1950.

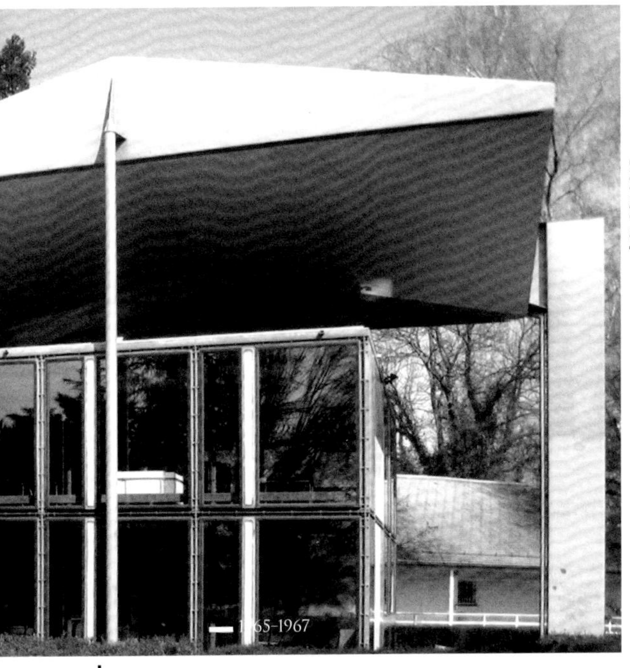

8° 33′ 03″E

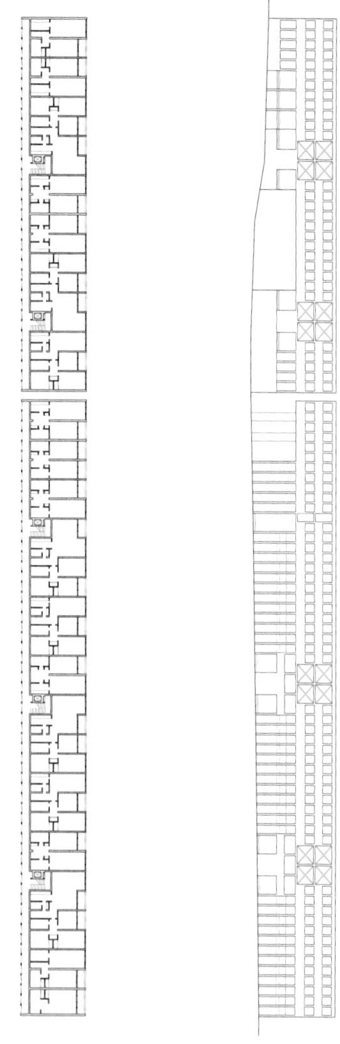

Floor Plan and Section

0 50'
10M

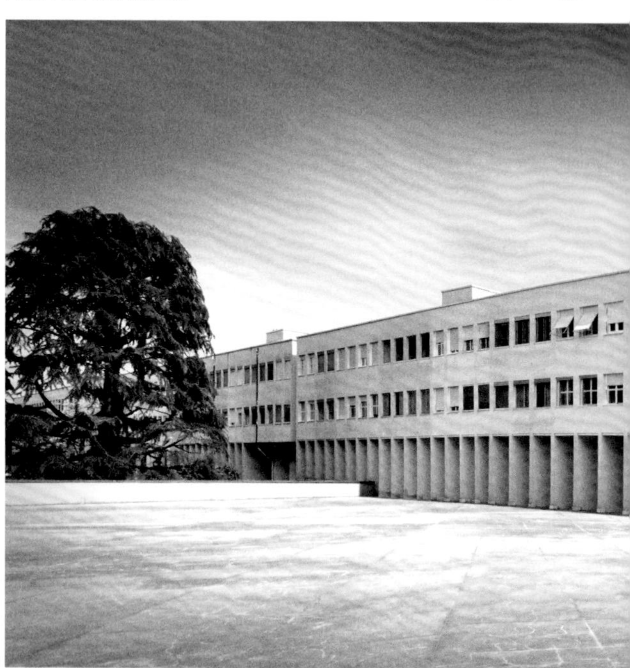

45° 29′ 54″N

97

GALLARATESE II APARTMENTS

ALDO ROSSI and CARLO AYMONINO
Milan, Italy
1969–1974

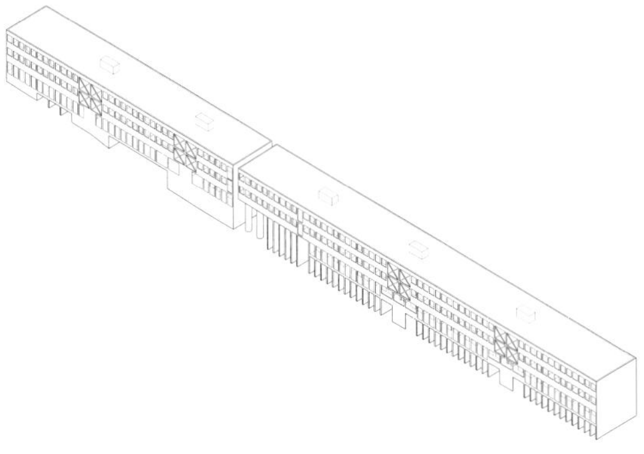

Rossi advocated an "architecture of silence," and in Milan's Gallaratese II, the silence finally became deafening. Rossi was selected by Carlo Aymonino, architect of the Gallaratese quarter, in an insightful move that was intended to provide both a dialogue with Aymonino's complex take on the modern galleria, a datum—more like a Rosetta Stone—against which that architecture could be interpreted, and a porous public space through which all residents of the entire complex would pass. Silent, perhaps, but not mute, his Gallaratese reflects Rossi's philosophy that architecture should be like a Brechtian stage set within which the occupants are free to enact whatever dramas they chose, using a "degree zero" of architectural forms to stimulate the individuality of the residents. The Gallaratese II Apartments epitomize and synthesize Aldo Rossi's theory on the responsibility of architecture to reiterate and elaborate on the most fundamental elements of architectural form.

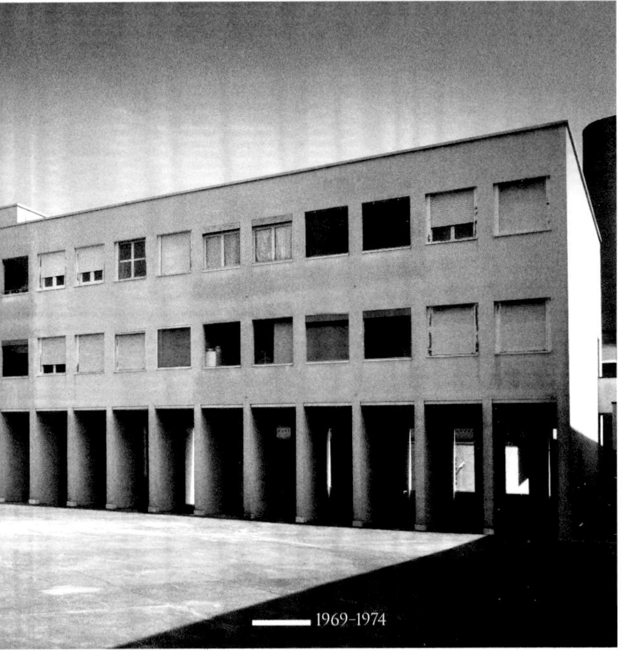

9° 06′ 03″E

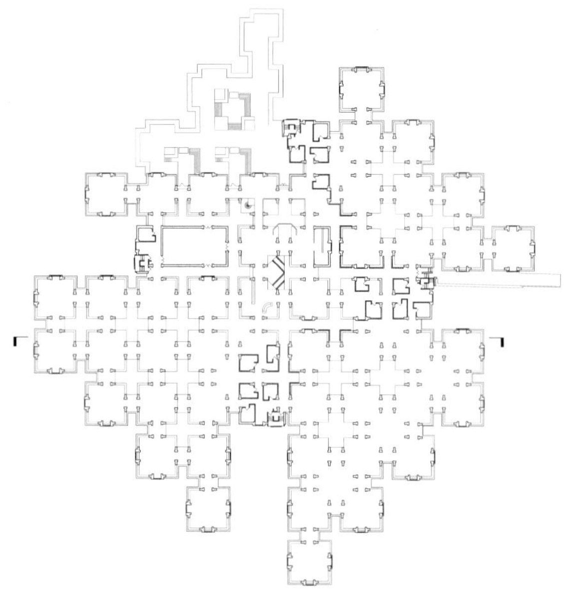

Floor Plan

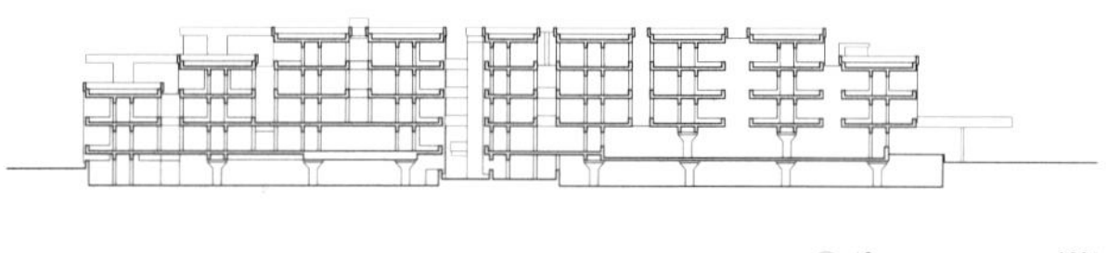

Section

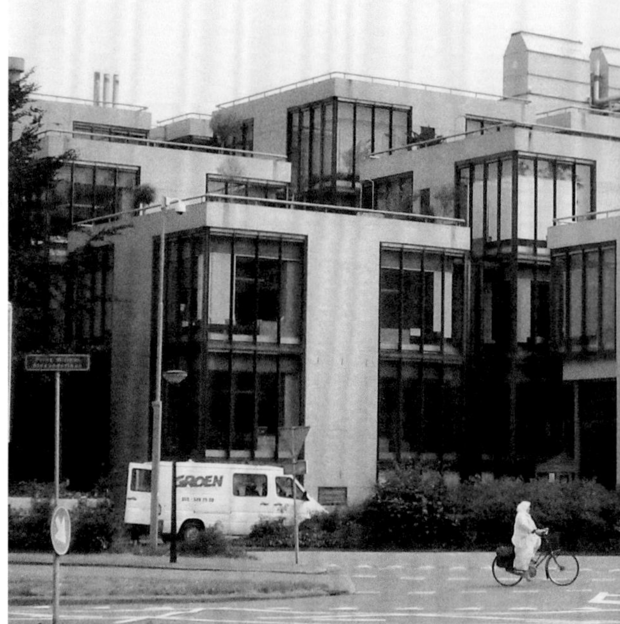

52° 12′ 37″N

98

CENTRAAL BEHEER BUILDING

HERMAN HERTZBERGER
Apeldoorn, The Netherlands
1968–1972

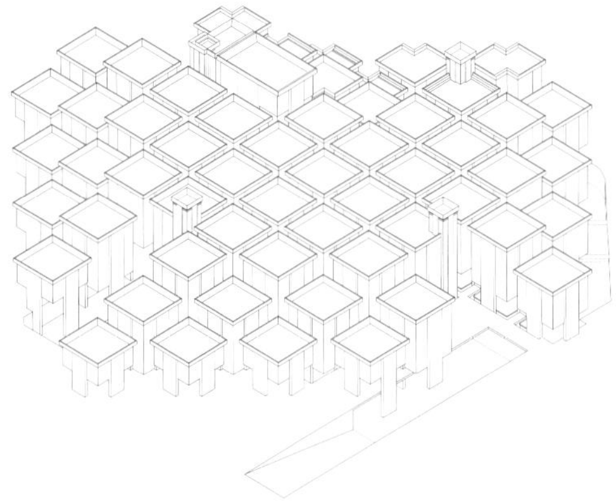

Initiating a new trajectory in office design and workplace culture, the Centraal Beheer insurance company's office building represents Hertzberger's theories that every public building should be a communal structure—in effect a small village, with streets, plazas, and spaces for rendezvous. The building contains more than thirty-five small office towers, 9x9 meters, open on the corners, and within a few meters of one another. The structure of the modules allows a flexibility of partitioning as needs change. A mat building that challenges traditional aspects of hierarchy, the Centraal Beheer became one of the most representative constructions of Team 10's desire to see each building as a village, where social interactions are the ultimate determinant of spatial configurations.

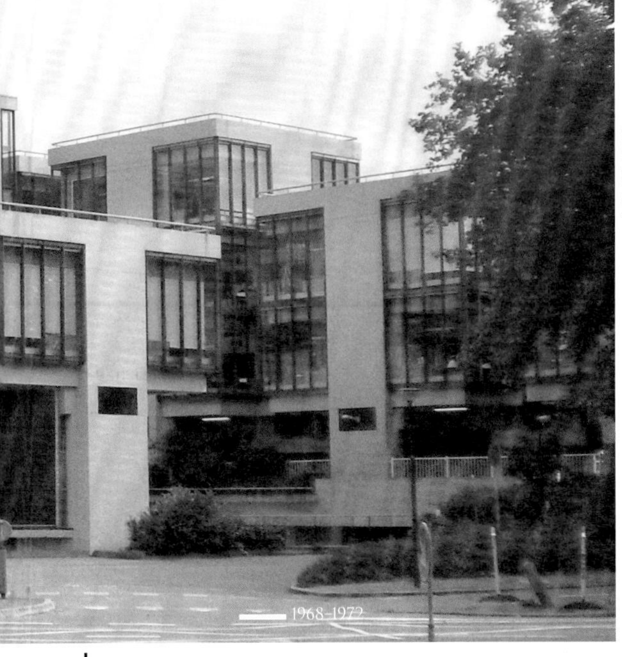

5° 57′ 38″E

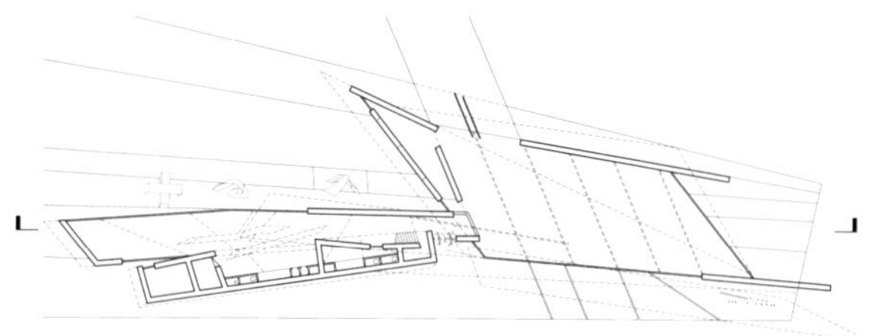

Floor Plan

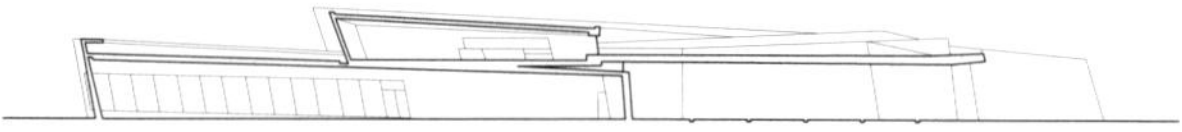

Section

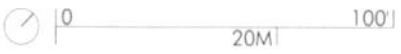

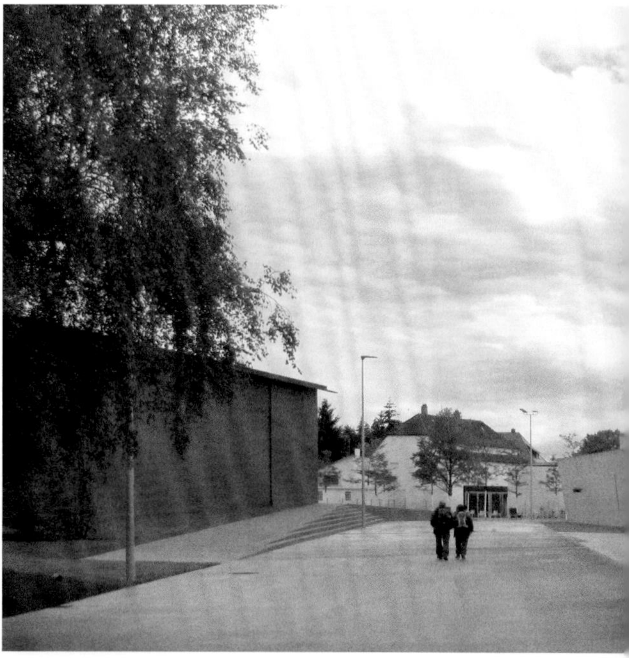

0 20M 100'

47° 36′ 01″N

99

VITRA FIRE STATION

ZAHA HADID ARCHITECTS
Weil am Rhein, Germany
1990–1993

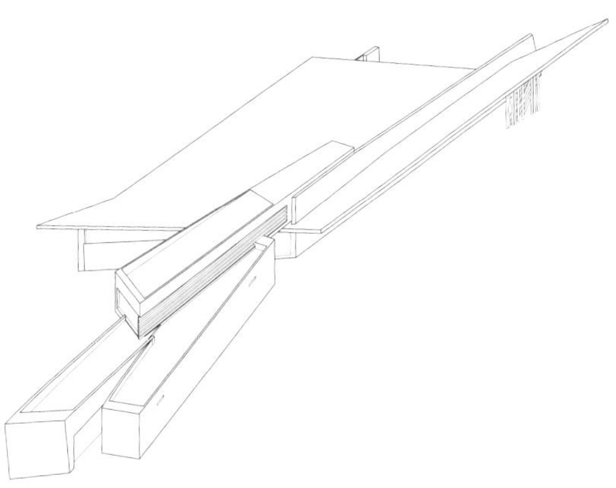

The first of Hadid's realized projects that demonstrated the neo-Constructivist language present in her paintings and the associated theories of tension and dynamism, the fire station she designed for the Vitra furniture complex experiments with space and form, relating architecture to its surrounding context. The narrow, horizontal profile created by the concrete planes instigates a sense of instability, provoked by the constant tilting and bending of the shapes, responsive to conceptual dynamic forces that connect landscape and architecture. Additionally, the angles and colors contribute to optical illusions and false perspectives that accentuate this abstract tension. The building is notable for its insistent abstraction of detail, with mullions and various copings eliminated throughout. Now an exhibition pavilion, the Vitra Fire Station remains one of the most provocative and studied buildings of Hadid's career.

7° 36′ 52″E

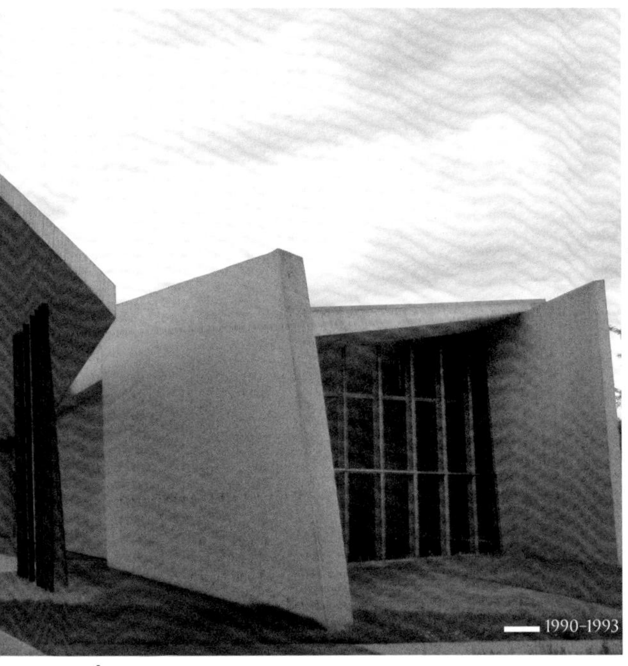

1990–1993

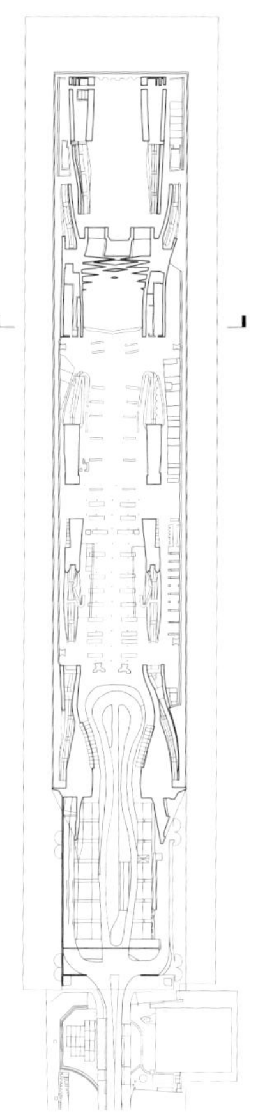

Floor Plan

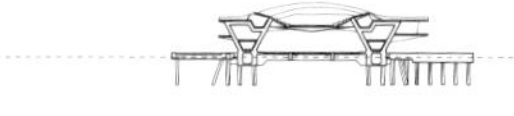

Section

0 10M 50'

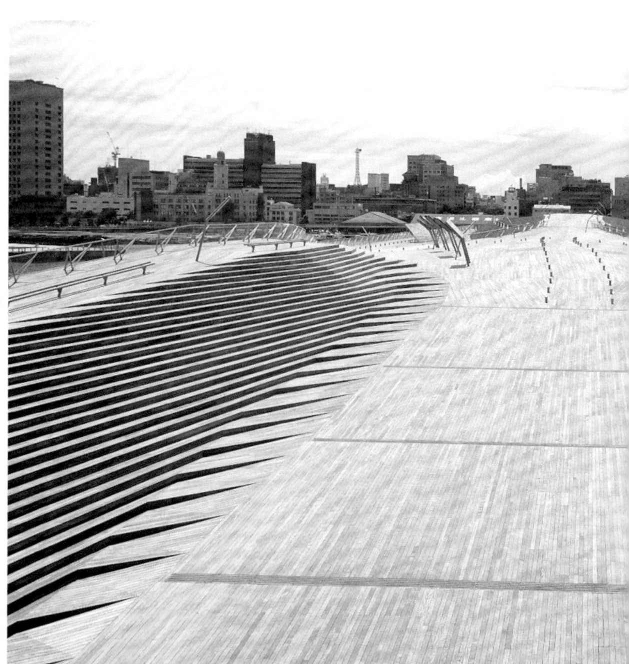

35° 27′ 04″N

100

YOKOHAMA INTERNATIONAL PORT TERMINAL

FOREIGN OFFICE ARCHITECTS
Yokohama, Japan
1995–2002

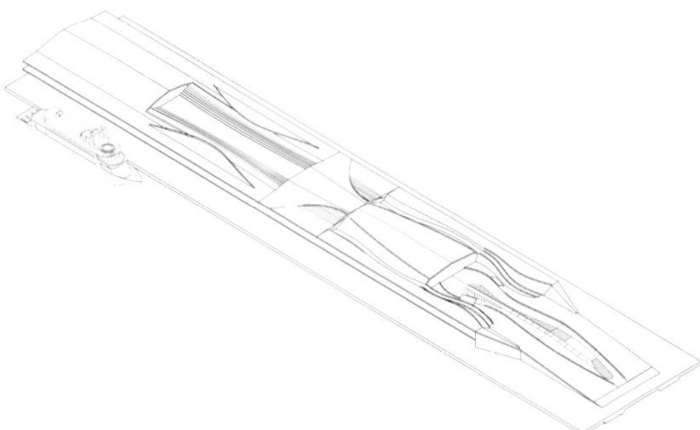

The first impression of the Yokohama terminal is that of a vast, 430-meter-long fluid topography of ramps, steps, terraces, and earthen mounds. The circulation on this landscape resists the typical singular directionality of most pier structures in favor of a loop with a network of variable paths, moments for viewing, and constantly shifting horizons. Structurally, the main building employs a hybrid system of concrete girders supported on two parallel pairs of pilings, spanned with folded steel plates that not only permit the development of folds and fissures that accommodate the numerous programs—parking, shops, restaurants, a civic hall, and all of the accoutrements of an international transportation hub—but also help the structure successfully resist lateral seismic movements. Simple in its diagram yet complex in its implementation, the Yokohama terminal is one of the first constructions that depended heavily on digital computation and modeling for every aspect of its development and was largely accomplished through the mutation of a series of sections that are elaborate both spatially and structurally.

139° 38′ 50″E

building
-
architect matrix

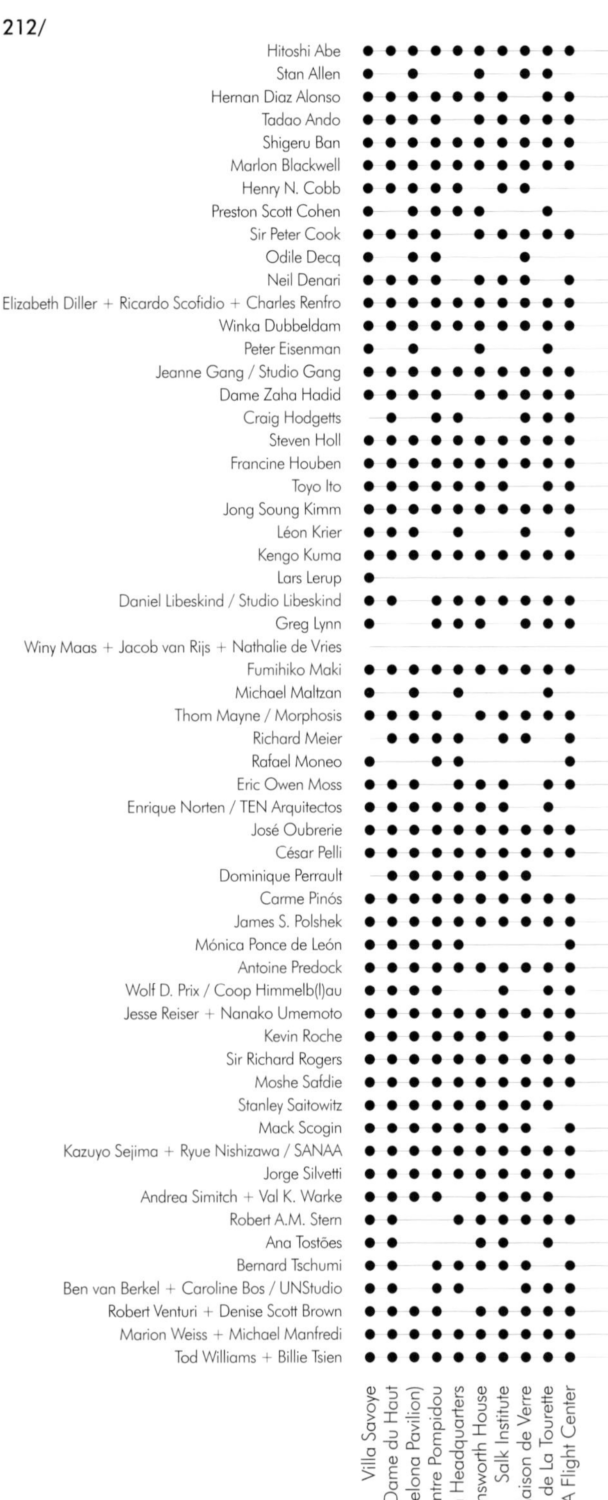

	Villa Savoye	Chapelle Notre-Dame du Haut	German Pavilion (Barcelona Pavilion)	Centre Pompidou	S.C. Johnson & Son Headquarters	Farnsworth House	Salk Institute	La Maison de Verre	Couvent Sainte-Marie de La Tourette	TWA Flight Center
Hitoshi Abe	●	●	●	●	●	●	●	●	●	●
Stan Allen	●		●			●		●	●	
Hernan Diaz Alonso	●	●	●	●	●	●	●		●	●
Tadao Ando	●	●	●	●		●	●	●	●	●
Shigeru Ban	●	●	●	●	●	●	●	●	●	●
Marlon Blackwell	●	●	●	●	●	●	●	●	●	●
Henry N. Cobb	●	●	●	●	●		●	●		
Preston Scott Cohen	●		●	●	●	●			●	
Sir Peter Cook	●	●	●	●		●	●	●	●	●
Odile Decq	●		●	●				●		
Neil Denari	●	●	●	●		●	●	●		●
Elizabeth Diller + Ricardo Scofidio + Charles Renfro	●	●	●	●	●	●	●	●	●	●
Winka Dubbeldam	●	●	●	●	●	●	●	●	●	●
Peter Eisenman	●		●			●			●	
Jeanne Gang / Studio Gang	●	●	●	●	●	●	●	●	●	●
Dame Zaha Hadid	●	●	●	●		●	●	●	●	●
Craig Hodgetts		●		●	●			●	●	●
Steven Holl	●	●	●	●	●	●	●	●	●	●
Francine Houben	●	●	●	●	●	●	●	●	●	●
Toyo Ito	●	●	●	●	●	●	●		●	●
Jong Soung Kimm	●	●	●	●	●	●	●	●	●	●
Léon Krier	●	●	●		●			●		●
Kengo Kuma	●	●	●	●	●	●	●	●	●	●
Lars Lerup	●									
Daniel Libeskind / Studio Libeskind	●	●		●	●	●	●	●	●	●
Greg Lynn	●			●	●	●		●	●	●
Winy Maas + Jacob van Rijs + Nathalie de Vries										
Fumihiko Maki	●	●	●	●	●	●	●	●	●	●
Michael Maltzan	●		●		●				●	
Thom Mayne / Morphosis	●	●	●	●		●	●	●	●	●
Richard Meier		●	●	●	●		●	●		●
Rafael Moneo	●			●	●					●
Eric Owen Moss	●	●	●		●	●	●		●	●
Enrique Norten / TEN Arquitectos	●	●	●	●	●	●	●		●	
José Oubrerie	●	●	●	●	●	●	●	●	●	●
César Pelli	●	●	●	●	●	●	●	●	●	●
Dominique Perrault		●	●	●	●	●	●	●		
Carme Pinós	●	●	●	●	●	●	●	●	●	●
James S. Polshek	●	●	●	●	●	●	●	●	●	●
Mónica Ponce de León	●	●	●	●	●					●
Antoine Predock	●	●	●	●	●	●	●	●	●	●
Wolf D. Prix / Coop Himmelb(l)au	●	●	●	●			●		●	●
Jesse Reiser + Nanako Umemoto	●	●	●	●	●	●	●	●	●	●
Kevin Roche	●	●	●	●	●	●	●		●	●
Sir Richard Rogers	●	●	●	●	●	●	●	●	●	●
Moshe Safdie	●	●	●	●	●	●	●	●	●	●
Stanley Saitowitz	●	●	●	●	●	●	●	●	●	
Mack Scogin	●	●	●	●	●	●	●	●		●
Kazuyo Sejima + Ryue Nishizawa / SANAA	●	●	●	●	●	●	●	●	●	●
Jorge Silvetti	●	●	●	●	●	●	●	●	●	●
Andrea Simitch + Val K. Warke	●	●	●	●		●	●	●	●	
Robert A.M. Stern	●	●			●	●	●	●	●	●
Ana Tostões	●	●				●	●		●	
Bernard Tschumi	●	●		●	●	●	●	●		●
Ben van Berkel + Caroline Bos / UNStudio	●	●		●	●			●	●	●
Robert Venturi + Denise Scott Brown	●	●	●	●		●	●	●	●	●
Marion Weiss + Michael Manfredi	●	●	●	●	●	●	●	●	●	●
Tod Williams + Billie Tsien	●	●	●	●	●	●	●	●	●	●

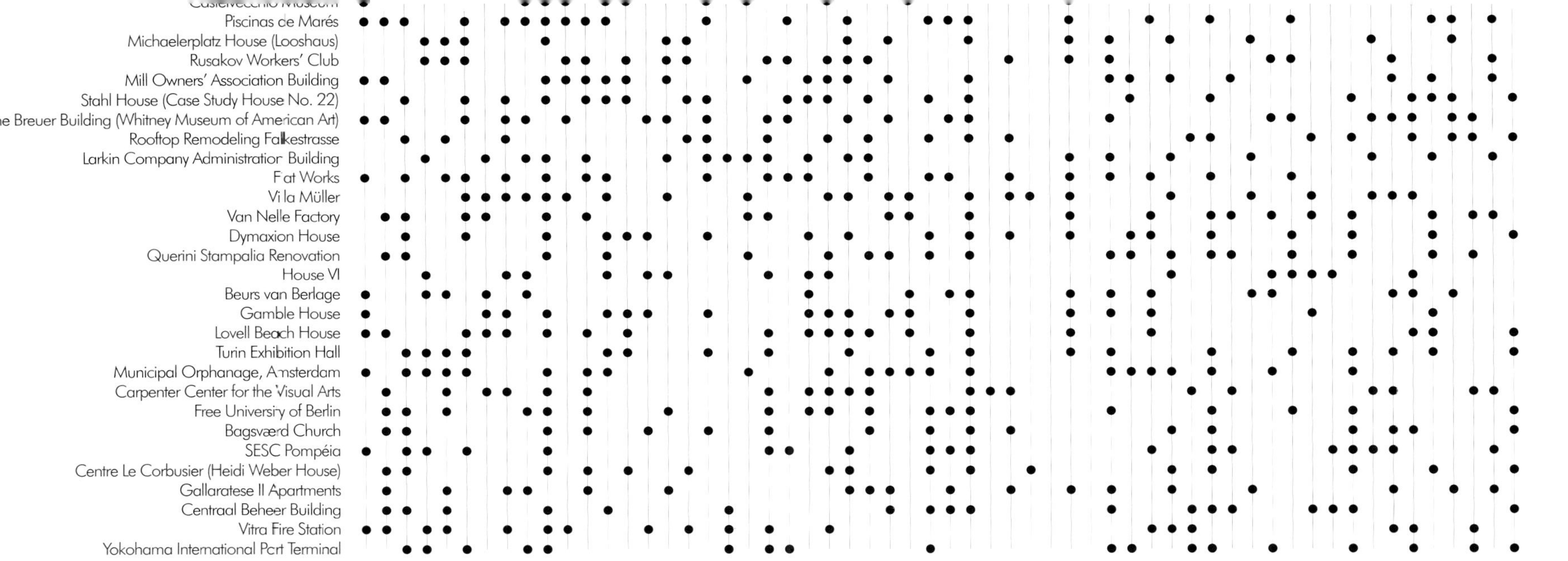
Piscinas de Marés
Michaelerplatz House (Looshaus)
Rusakov Workers' Club
Mill Owners' Association Building
Stahl House (Case Study House No. 22)
The Breuer Building (Whitney Museum of American Art)
Rooftop Remodeling Falkestrasse
Larkin Company Administration Building
Fiat Works
Villa Müller
Van Nelle Factory
Dymaxion House
Querini Stampalia Renovation
House VI
Beurs van Berlage
Gamble House
Lovell Beach House
Turin Exhibition Hall
Municipal Orphanage, Amsterdam
Carpenter Center for the Visual Arts
Free University of Berlin
Bagsværd Church
SESC Pompéia
Centre Le Corbusier (Heidi Weber House)
Gallaratese II Apartments
Centraal Beheer Building
Vitra Fire Station
Yokohama International Port Terminal

architects' selections

Hitoshi Abe

Thomas Edison Concrete House
AEG Turbine Factory
Frederick C. Robie House
Posen Tower
Postsparkasse
Schindler House
Schröderhuis
Lovell Beach House
Bauhaus Dessau
Karl-Marx-Hof
Lovell Health House
Stockholm Public Library
German Pavilion (Barcelona Pavilion)
Stockholm Exhibition of 1930
Villa Savoye
La Maison de Verre
Edgar J. Kaufmann House (Fallingwater)
Casa del Fascio
S.C. Johnson & Son Headquarters
Villa Mairea
The Woodland Cemetery
Casa Malaparte
Dymaxion House
Turin Exhibition Hall
The Eames House (Case Study House No. 8)
Kaufmann House
Farnsworth House
L'Unité d'Habitation
Lever House
Muuratsalo Experimental House
Iglesia de la Medalla Milagrosa
Chapelle Notre-Dame du Haut
Sydney Opera House
Crown Hall
Seagram Building
Philips Pavilion
National Congress, Brazil
Solomon R. Guggenheim Museum
Church of the Three Crosses
Stahl House (Case Study House No. 22)
Chemosphere
Couvent Sainte-Marie de La Tourette
TWA Flight Center
The Beinecke Rare Book & Manuscript Library
Nissay Theatre
Berliner Philharmonie
Leicester University Engineering Building
National Olympic Gymnasium, Tokyo
Kagawa Prefectural Government Hall
Rudolph Hall
Shrine of the Book
Centre Le Corbusier (Heidi Weber House)
Salk Institute
Sea Ranch Condominium Complex
Oita Prefectural Library
Kuwait Embassy, Tokyo
Sonsbeek Pavilion
Habitat '67
Ford Foundation Headquarters
Art Center College of Design, Pasadena
Hillside Terrace Complex I–VI
Nakagin Capsule Tower
Olympic Stadium, Munich
Kimbell Art Museum
Castelvecchio Museum
Free University of Berlin
Casa Bianchi
Museum of Modern Art, Gunma
Tanikawa House
Centraal Beheer Building
Bagsværd Church
Sumiyoshi Row House
World Trade Center Towers
Centre Pompidou
Brion Family Tomb
Gehry House
Teatro del Mondo
Kyungdong Presbyterian Church, Seoul
Tanimura Art Museum
Spiral, Tokyo
Steinhaus, Lake Ossiach
Lloyd's of London
Hongkong and Shanghai Bank Headquarters
Institut du Monde Arabe
Kate Mantilini, Beverly Hills
Tokyo Institute of Technology Centennial Hall
Rooftop Remodeling Falkestrasse
Igualada Cemetery
SYNTAX, Kyoto
Umeda Sky Building
UFA Cinema Centre
Maison à Bordeaux
Guggenheim Museum Bilbao
Jewish Museum Berlin
Expo 2000, Netherlands Pavilion
Sendai Mediatheque
Yokohama International Port Terminal
Diamond Ranch High School
Gifu Kitagata Apartment Building
Louis Vuitton Nagoya

Stan Allen

Ozenfant House
Villa Stein
Villa Savoye
Carpenter Center for the Visual Arts
Mill Owners' Association Building
Curutchet House
Couvent Sainte-Marie de La Tourette
Saint-Pierre, Firminy
Lange and Esters Houses
Tugendhat House
German Pavilion (Barcelona Pavilion)
Farnsworth House
New National Gallery
Norman Fisher House
First Unitarian Church of Rochester
National Assembly Building, Bangladesh
Franklin D. Roosevelt Four Freedoms Park
Studio Aalto
Säynätsalo Town Hall
Leicester University Engineering Building
Neue Staatsgalerie
Frederick C. Robie House
Larkin Company Administration Building
Solomon R. Guggenheim Museum
Stadtbad Mitte, Berlin
AEG Turbine Factory
Vanna Venturi House
Trubek and Wislocki Houses
National Gallery, Sainsbury Wing
Seattle Central Library
Plantahof Auditorium
DRLG Zentrale
Umlauftank
Barclay-Vesey Building
Commonwealth Building, Portland
Rusakov Workers' Club
Hunstanton School
The Economist Building, London
Casa Malaparte
Stockholm Public Library
The Woodland Cemetery
Woodland Chapel
Chapel of the Resurrection
Flower Kiosk, Malmö Cemetery
Hedmark Cathedral Museum
Nordic Pavillion, Venice
House I, Princeton
Berlin Memorial to the Murdered Jews of Europe
Benacerraf House Project
Town Hall, Logroño
Teatro del Mondo
Gallaratese II Apartments
Schröderhuis
Van Nelle Factory
PSFS Building
Arve Bridge
Gatti Wool Factory
La Maison de Verre
Robert Motherwell Quonset House
The Eames House (Case Study House No. 8)
Schindler House
Rockefeller Center
Municipal Bus Terminal, Salto
Bacardi Bottling Plant
Civil Government Building, Tarragona
Gimansio del Colegio Maravillas
Edificio de viviendas en la Barceloneta
Center for Hydrographic Studies, Madrid
Instituto de Nuestra Señora de la Victoria
Villa Belloti, Milan
Casa al Parco
Casa del Fascio
Museum Insel Hombroich, Gallery Pavilions
Benedictine Monastery Chapel, Santiago
FAU, University of São Paulo
Museu de Arte de São Paulo
SESC Pompéia
Casa Butantã
Capela São Pedro Apóstolo
Museum of Sculpture, São Paulo
Igualada Cemetery
Torre Velasca
Padiglione d'Arte Contemporanea
Pirelli Tower
Gut Garkau Farm
Wall House II
Sky House, Tokyo
House with an Earthen Floor
White U
Tama Art University Library
21st Century Museum, Kanazawa
Piscinas de Marés
Iberê Camargo Foundation
Ricola Storage Building
House in Leymen
Laurenz-Stiftung Schaulager
Elbphilharmonie
Museo de Arte Contemporáneo de Castilla y León
Ron Davis House, Malibu
Frog Hollow

Hernan Diaz Alonso

Igualada Cemetery
Barcelona Olympic Archery Range
Sports Center in Huesca
Scottish Parliament Building
Bank of London and South America
Villa La Roche
Curutchet House
Villa Savoye
Couvent Sainte-Marie de La Tourette
Saint-Pierre, Firminy
Carpenter Center for the Visual Arts
Chapelle Notre-Dame du Haut
Casa del Puente
Rooftop Remodeling Falkestrasse
Musée des Confluences
Louis Vuitton Foundation
Guggenheim Museum Bilbao
German Pavilion (Barcelona Pavilion)
Tugendhat House
New National Gallery
Farnsworth House
Glass House
Pantheon, Rome
Querini Stampalia Renovation
Quinta da Conceição, Swimming Pool
Maison à Bordeaux
The Woodland Cemetery
Mare de Déu de Montserrat de Montferri
Casa Iglesias, Barcelona
Church of Colònia Güell
Casa Batlló
Gimansio del Colegio Maravillas
Edificio Altamira
Église Sainte-Bernadette du Banlay
Einstein Tower
Jewelry Store Schullin
Zentralsparkasse Bank, Vienna
The Breuer Building (Whitney Museum)
Majolikahaus
Berlin Memorial to the Murdered Jews of Europe
San Carlo alle Quattro Fontane
Maison Coilliot
Mobius House
Wexner Center for the Visual Arts
Hôtel Tassel
Burgos Cathedral
Santa Maria del Mar, Barcelona
Vitra Fire Station
Ford Foundation Headquarters
The Beinecke Rare Book & Manuscript Library
Gardens of Versailles
Sir John Soane's Museum
Centre Pompidou
Lloyd's of London
Mosque–Cathedral of Córdoba
TWA Flight Center
S.C. Johnson & Son Headquarters
Palacio de los Deportes
Igreja da Pampulha
Walt Disney Concert Hall
Palais Garnier
MAXXI
Berliner Philharmonie
CCTV Headquarters
Rudolph Hall
Lippo Centre
RV (Room Vehicle) House Prototype
Water Pavilion H2O Expo
Vitra Design Museum
Beijing National Stadium
Sendai Mediatheque
41 Cooper Square
BMW Welt
Pterodactyl, Culver City
Villa dall'Ava
Emerson College Los Angeles
Church of Cristo Obrero
Villa Foscari
Stealth, Culver City
Torre Velasca
James R. Thompson Center
Vanna Venturi House
Van Nelle Factory
Karl-Marx-Hof
Glasgow School of Art
Post Office, Piazza Bologna
Teatro Regio
Solomon R. Guggenheim Museum
Robin Hood Gardens
History Faculty Building, Cambridge
Salk Institute
Elbphilharmonie
Mercedes-Benz Museum
Yokohama International Port Terminal
Parc de la Villette
Four Seasons Restaurant, Seagram Building
Seagram Building
Opéra Nouvel
Pérgolas en la Avenida de Icària
Storefront for Art and Architecture

Tadao Ando

Beurs van Berlage
Glasgow School of Art
Casa Milà
Michaelerplatz House (Looshaus)
Fagus Factory
Postsparkasse
Imperial Hotel, Tokyo
Stockholm City Hall
Église Notre-Dame du Raincy
Schröderhuis
Bauhaus Dessau
Sagrada Família
Stockholm Public Library
German Pavilion (Barcelona Pavilion)
Villa Savoye
La Maison de Verre
Edgar J. Kaufmann House (Fallingwater)
Casa del Fascio
Villa Mairea
The Woodland Cemetery
Casa Malaparte
Kaufmann House
Barragán House and Studio
Glass House
The Eames House (Case Study House No. 8)
Farnsworth House
Säynätsalo Town Hall
L'Unité d'Habitation
Lever House
Chapelle Notre-Dame du Haut
MIT Chapel
Sydney Opera House
Crown Hall
Otaniemi Chapel
Seagram Building
Louisiana Museum of Modern Art
National Congress, Brazil
Solomon R. Guggenheim Museum
Capilla de las Capuchinas
Stahl House (Case Study House No. 22)
Couvent Sainte-Marie de La Tourette
Halen Estate
TWA Flight Center
The Beinecke Rare Book & Manuscript Library
Berliner Philharmonie
Leicester University Engineering Building
National Olympic Gymnasium, Tokyo
Rudolph Hall
Vanna Venturi House
Salk Institute
Sea Ranch Condominium Complex
Piscinas de Marés
The Breuer Building (Whitney Museum)
Habitat '67
Smith House
Norman Fisher House
Hyatt Regency, San Francisco
Ford Foundation Headquarters
History Faculty Building, Cambridge
Cuadra San Cristóbal
Montreal Biosphère
Hillside Terrace Complex I–VI
Cubic Forest
Nakagin Capsule Tower
Olympic Stadium, Munich
Kimbell Art Museum
Gund Hall
Castelvecchio Museum
Douglas House
Marquette Plaza
Casa Bianchi
Museum of Modern Art, Gunma
Gallaratese II Apartments
Town Hall, Logroño
Marie Short House
La Fábrica, Sant Just Desvern
Sumiyoshi Row House
Sainsbury Center for Visual Arts
World Trade Center Towers
Centre Pompidou
Brion Family Tomb
Gehry House
Teatro del Mondo
Koshino House
Abteiberg Museum
Neue Staatsgalerie
Lloyd's of London
Hongkong and Shanghai Bank Headquarters
Church of the Light
The Menil Collection
Rooftop Remodeling Falkestrasse
Parc de la Villette
Goetz Collection
Maison à Bordeaux
Therme Vals
Kunsthaus Bregenz
Guggenheim Museum Bilbao
Diamond Ranch High School
Jewish Museum Berlin
Sendai Mediatheque

Shigeru Ban

Larkin Company Administration Building
AEG Turbine Factory
Glasgow School of Art
Gamble House
Frederick C. Robie House
Casa Milà
Palais Stoclet
Postsparkasse
Schindler House
Ozenfant House
Stockholm City Hall
Van Nelle Factory
Schröderhuis
Lovell Beach House
Sagrada Família
Bauhaus Dessau
Villa Stein
Lovell Health House
Stockholm Public Library
German Pavilion (Barcelona Pavilion)
Tugendhat House
Villa Savoye
Paimio Sanatorium
La Maison de Verre
Edgar J. Kaufmann House (Fallingwater)
Casa del Fascio
Asilo Sant'Elia
S.C. Johnson & Son Headquarters
Villa Mairea
The Woodland Cemetery
Dymaxion House
Barragán House and Studio
Turin Exhibition Hall
Glass House
The Eames House (Case Study House No. 8)
Farnsworth House
Säynätsalo Town Hall
L'Unité d'Habitation
Lever House
Muuratsalo Experimental House
Gatti Wool Factory
Iglesia de la Medalla Milagrosa
Chapelle Notre-Dame du Haut
MIT Chapel
Villa Sarabhai
Crown Hall
Maisons Jaoul
Mill Owners' Association Building
Studio Aalto
Richards Medical Research Laboratories
Palazzetto dello Sport
Seagram Building
Philips Pavilion
National Congress, Brazil
Solomon R. Guggenheim Museum
Church of the Three Crosses
Los Manantiales
Capilla de las Capuchinas
Bacardi Bottling Plant
Stahl House (Case Study House No. 22)
Couvent Sainte-Marie de La Tourette
TWA Flight Center
Ena de Silva House
Querini Stampalia Renovation
Berliner Philharmonie
Leicester University Engineering Building
National Olympic Gymnasium, Tokyo
Otaniemi Technical University
Centre Le Corbusier (Heidi Weber House)
Salk Institute
The Assembly, Chandigarh
Piscinas de Marés
Edifício Copan
Habitat '67
Smith House
Norman Fisher House
Hyatt Regency, Atlanta
Ford Foundation Headquarters
New National Gallery
History Faculty Building, Cambridge
Kappe Residence
Cuadra San Cristóbal
Montreal Biosphère
Charles De Gaulle Airport, Terminal 1 & 2A–2F
Nakagin Capsule Tower
Olympic Stadium, Munich
Phillips Exeter Academy Library
Kimbell Art Museum
Castelvecchio Museum
Museum of Modern Art, Gunma
Sumiyoshi Row House
Centre Pompidou
Brion Family Tomb
Hedmark Cathedral Museum
Koshino House
National Assembly Building, Bangladesh
Lloyd's of London
Hongkong and Shanghai Bank Headquarters
Institut du Monde Arabe
Kunsthaus Bregenz

Marlon Blackwell

Beurs van Berlage
Frederick C. Robie House
Fagus Factory
Merchants' National Bank, Grinnell
Schindler House
Sagrada Família
Lovell Beach House
Bauhaus Dessau
Stockholm Public Library
Villa Stein
German Pavilion (Barcelona Pavilion)
Villa Müller
Villa Savoye
Paimio Sanatorium
La Maison de Verre
Edgar J. Kaufmann House (Fallingwater)
Casa del Fascio
S.C. Johnson & Son Headquarters
Villa Mairea
Casa Malaparte
The Woodland Cemetery
Barragán House and Studio
The Eames House (Case Study House No. 8)
Glass House
Säynätsalo Town Hall
Farnsworth House
L'Unité d'Habitation
Lever House
Miller House, Columbus
MIT Chapel
The Assembly, Chandigarh
Chapelle Notre-Dame du Haut
Sydney Opera House
Crown Hall
Palazzetto dello Sport
Solomon R. Guggenheim Museum
National Library, Brasília
Haystack Mountain School of Crafts
Couvent Sainte-Marie de La Tourette
Capilla de las Capuchinas
Stahl House (Case Study House No. 22)
Prairie Chicken House
Esherick House
TWA Flight Center
Nordic Pavillion, Venice
Boa Nova Tea House
Berliner Philharmonie
Sheats Goldstein Residence
Rudolph Hall
Salk Institute
Sea Ranch Condominium Complex
The Breuer Building (Whitney Museum)
Habitat '67
Cuadra San Cristóbal
Kappe Residence
Flower Kiosk, Malmö Cemetery
Phillips Exeter Academy Library
Kimbell Art Museum
Castelvecchio Museum
San Cataldo Cemetery
Bagsværd Church
Centre Pompidou
Brion Family Tomb
Atheneum, New Harmony
Thorncrown Chapel
Magney House
Neue Staatsgalerie
Wexner Center for the Visual Arts
National Museum of Roman Art
Inn at Middleton Place
Ricola Storage Building
House VI
Stone House, Tavole
Saint Benedict Chapel, Sumvitg
Rooftop Remodeling Falkestrasse
Void Space/Hinged Space Housing
Igualada Cemetery
Goetz Collection
Kunsthal, Rotterdam
Signal Box Auf dem Wolf
Maison à Bordeaux
Vitra Fire Station
Yokohama International Port Terminal
Dominus Winery
Bruton Barr Library
Neurosciences Institute, La Jolla
Therme Vals
Burnette Residence
Kunsthaus Bregenz
Kew House, Victoria
Chapel of St. Ignatius
Palmer House, Tucson
Jewish Museum Berlin
Boyd Art Center, Riversdale
Diamond Ranch High School
Church of the Light
Keenan TowerHouse
Glass Chapel, Alabama
Gifu Kitagata Apartment Building
Sendai Mediatheque

Henry N. Cobb

Flatiron Building
Beurs van Berlage
Darwin D. Martin House
Postsparkasse
Unity Temple
National Farmers Bank
Glasgow School of Art
Frederick C. Robie House
Casa Milà
New York Public Library
Palais Stoclet
Park Güell
Aircraft Hangars, Orly
The Cenotaph, Whitehall
Het Schip
Einstein Tower
Schindler House
L'Esprit Nouveau Pavilion
Schröderhuis
Bauhaus Dessau
Los Angeles Public Library
Villa Stein
Rusakov Workers' Club
Barclay-Vesey Building
Karl-Marx-Hof
Stockholm Public Library
German Pavilion (Barcelona Pavilion)
Villa Müller
Tugendhat House
Villa Savoye
PSFS Building
La Maison de Verre
Schwandbach Bridge
Rockefeller Center
Viipuri Municipal Library
Casa del Fascio
Göteborg Town Hall
S.C. Johnson & Son Headquarters
Edgar J. Kaufmann House (Fallingwater)
Villa Mairea
Chamberlain Cottage
Lloyd Lewis House
Turin Exhibition Hall
The Eames House (Case Study House No. 8)
Glass House
Casa Il Girasole
860–880 Lake Shore Drive
Säynätsalo Town Hall
Borsalino Housing
L'Unité d'Habitation
Coyoacán Market Hall
Chapelle Notre-Dame du Haut
National Pensions Building, Helsinki
Mill Owners' Association Building
Crown Hall
Richards Medical Research Laboratories
Edificio de viviendas en la Barceloneta
Seagram Building
Solomon R. Guggenheim Museum
McMath-Pierce Solar Telescope
The Assembly, Chandigarh
Carpenter Center for the Visual Arts
Berliner Philharmonie
Leicester University Engineering Building
Rudolph Hall
Vanna Venturi House
Salk Institute
The Breuer Building (Whitney Museum)
Fire Station No. 4, Columbus
Habitat '67
New National Gallery
Oakland Museum of California
Mummers Theater
House II (Vermont House)
Phillips Exeter Academy Library
Kimbell Art Museum
Douglas House
Gallaratese II Apartments
Whig Hall, Princeton University
Bagsværd Church
Centre Pompidou
Brion Family Tomb
Gehry House
Vietnam Veterans Memorial
Gordon Wu Hall
Neue Staatsgalerie
Loyola Law School Campus
Hongkong and Shanghai Bank Headquarters
SESC Pompéia
National Museum of Roman Art
Ricola Storage Building
Church of the Light
Kunsthal, Rotterdam
Vitra Fire Station
Neurosciences Institute, La Jolla
Chapel of St. Ignatius
Guggenheim Museum Bilbao
Murcia Town Hall
Diamond Ranch High School
Jewish Museum Berlin

Preston Scott Cohen

Guaranty Building
National Farmers Bank
Union Bank, Columbus, Wisconsin
Peoples Savings Bank, Cedar Rapids
AEG Turbine Factory
Stockholm Public Library
Petersdorff Department Store
Barclay-Vesey Building
Flatiron Building
Downtown Athletic Club, New York
Glasgow School of Art
Larkin Company Administration Building
Frederick C. Robie House
Solomon R. Guggenheim Museum
S.C. Johnson & Son Headquarters
David and Gladys Wright House
Beth Sholom Congregation, Elkins Park
Rue Franklin Apartments
Villa Savoye
Villa Stein
Swiss Pavilion
Carpenter Center for the Visual Arts
The Assembly, Chandigarh
Couvent Sainte-Marie de La Tourette
L'Unité d'Habitation
Schröderhuis
Soviet Pavilion
Het Schip
Palais Stoclet
American Bar, Vienna
Villa Müller
Michaelerplatz House (Looshaus)
German Pavilion (Barcelona Pavilion)
Tugendhat House
Hubbe House
Seagram Building
Crown Hall
Farnsworth House
Inland Steel Building
Lever House
John Hancock Center
Casa Milà
Park Güell
Viipuri Municipal Library
Baker House
Aalto-Hochhaus, Bremen
Berliner Philharmonie
Palazzetto dello Sport
Saint Mary's Cathedral, San Francisco
San Juan de Ávila, Alcalá de Henares
The Breuer Building (Whitney Museum)
Centre Pompidou
The Pagoda, Madrid
Iglesia de la Medalla Milagrosa
Edificio de CEPAL
FAU, University of São Paulo
Nordic Pavillion, Venice
Sydney Opera House
SESC Pompéia
Richards Medical Research Laboratories
Kimbell Art Museum
Yale Center for British Art
Phillips Exeter Academy Library
National Assembly Building, Bangladesh
Rudolph Hall
Temple Street Parking Garage, New Haven
Boston City Hall
National Olympic Gymnasium, Tokyo
Marina City, Chicago
Casa del Fascio
Casa Il Girasole
CBS Building, New York
John Hancock Tower
Ford Foundation Headquarters
Hyatt Regency, Atlanta
Torre Velasca
Leicester University Engineering Building
Neue Staatsgalerie
AT&T Building, New York
Pennzoil Place
Vanna Venturi House
Brant House, Greenwich
Allen Memorial Art Museum, Oberlin
San Cataldo Cemetery
Wexner Center for the Visual Arts
Maison à Bordeaux
Zentrum für Kunst und Medientechnologie
Carlos Ramos Pavilion
Galician Center of Contemporary Art
Gehry House
Binoculars Building
Vitra Design Museum
Neuer Zollhof
National Museum of Roman Art
The Menil Collection
Signal Box Auf dem Wolf
Koechlin House
The Woodland Cemetery
House on a Curved Road
Bank of Georgia headquarters, Tbilisi

Sir Peter Cook

Melnikov House
Boots Pharmaceutical Factory
Samfunnshuset, Oslo
Bavinger House
Church of St. Michael, Frankfurt
Edifício Copan
Church of St. Peter, Klippan
Umlauftank
Tower of Winds, Yokohama
Spiral Apartment House, Ramat Gan
Shonandai Cultural Center
UFA Cinema Centre
Postsparkasse
Schindler House
Karl-Marx-Hof
Lovell Health House
Stockholm Public Library
Villa Moller
German Pavilion (Barcelona Pavilion)
Villa Savoye
Van Nelle Factory
La Maison de Verre
Villa Girasole
Edgar J. Kaufmann House (Fallingwater)
Casa del Fascio
The Woodland Cemetery
Casa Malaparte
Dymaxion House
Turin Exhibition Hall
Glass House
The Eames House (Case Study House No. 8)
Baker House
Muuratsalo Experimental House
Farnsworth House
L'Unité d'Habitation
Lever House
Crown Hall
Maisons Jaoul
Chapelle Notre-Dame du Haut
Seagram Building
National Congress, Brazil
Philips Pavilion
Solomon R. Guggenheim Museum
Cité d'Habitacion of Carrières Centrales
Stahl House (Case Study House No. 22)
Couvent Sainte-Marie de La Tourette
Municipal Orphanage, Amsterdam
Halen Estate
TWA Flight Center
Querini Stampalia Renovation
Berliner Philharmonie
Leicester University Engineering Building
Vanna Venturi House
National Olympic Gymnasium, Tokyo
Rudolph Hall
Salk Institute
The Assembly, Chandigarh
Centre Le Corbusier (Heidi Weber House)
Kuwait Embassy, Tokyo
Bank of London and South America
Habitat '67
Smith House
Museu de Arte de São Paulo
Ford Foundation Headquarters
Benacerraf House Project
Flower Kiosk, Malmö Cemetery
The Beinecke Rare Book & Manuscript Library
House III (Miller House)
Nakagin Capsule Tower
Olympic Stadium, Munich
Worker's Housing Estate, Hoek van Holland
Phillips Exeter Academy Library
Kimbell Art Museum
Free University of Berlin
Byker Wall
Centraal Beheer Building
Bagsværd Church
Brion Family Tomb
Centre Pompidou
SESC Pompéia
Hedmark Cathedral Museum
Gehry House
Koshino House
National Assembly Building, Bangladesh
Neue Staatsgalerie
Lloyd's of London
Hongkong and Shanghai Bank Headquarters
Rooftop Remodeling Falkestrasse
National Museum of Roman Art
Igualada Cemetery
Parc de la Villette
Maison à Bordeaux
Samitaur Tower
Guggenheim Museum Bilbao
Jewish Museum Berlin
Bordeaux Law Courts
Diamond Ranch High School
Yokohama International Port Terminal
Sendai Mediatheque
Einstein Tower

Odile Decq

Charles De Gaulle Airport, Terminal 1 & 2A–2F
Centre Pompidou
La Maison de Verre
Palazzetto dello Sport
German Pavilion (Barcelona Pavilion)
Casa del Fascio
French Communist Party Headquarters, Paris
Jewish Museum Berlin
UFA Cinema Centre
Berliner Philharmonie
Casa Malaparte
Villa Savoye
Maison Bernard
Maison Drusch
Zevaco Dome
Schröderhuis
Lloyd's of London
Robin Hood Gardens
Cave of Museum of Graffiti
Hundertwasserhaus
Nemausus
Narkomfin Building
Heinz-Galinski School
SAS Royal Hotel, Copenhagen
Torre Velasca
Berkeley City Club
Quartier de la Maladrerie, Aubervilliers
SESC Pompéia
London Stansted Airport
Habitat '67
Shrine of the Book
Bergiselschanze
Sydney Opera House
Eglise Sainte-Bernadette du Banlay
Climat de France, Algiers
University of Constantine
Hongkong and Shanghai Bank Headquarters
Banque Populaire de l'Ouest, Rennes
Nakagin Capsule Tower
Yamanashi Museum of Fruit
Olympic Stadium, Munich
American Bar, Vienna
Sheats Goldstein Residence
Atomium
Jewelry Store Schullin
Montreal Biosphère
Phillips Exeter Academy Library
Igualada Cemetery
Crematorium Baumschulenweg
Lord's Media Centre
Cathedral of Brasília
Guggenheim Museum Bilbao
Solomon R. Guggenheim Museum
Parc de la Villette
New National Gallery
Pavilion for World Design Exposition, Nagoya
Bauhaus Dessau
UNESCO Headquarters, Paris
Pilgrimage Church, Neviges
The Eames House (Case Study House No. 8)
Einstein Tower
Maison Jean Prouvé, Nancy
Babylon Apartments, Miami
Marina City, Chicago
Balfron Tower
B 018
University of Urbino
Glass House
Bavinger House
Centraal Beheer Building
Maison d'Iran
Maison Bloc
L'Unité d'Habitation
Philips Pavilion
Alexandra Road Housing
Walden 7
Croulebarbe Tower
Amiraux Swimming Pool
Säynätsalo Town Hall
Shukhov Tower
Cardiff Bay Visitor Center
Signal Box Auf dem Wolf
Library Delft University of Technology
Bank of London and South America
Zolani Multi Purpose Centre
New Gourna Village Mosque
Ville évolutive, La Douvaine
Sawchu
Plastic House, Paris
Port la Galère
Gehry House
Montreal Biosphère
Maison Gonflable
House VI
E-1027
Maison à Bordeaux
Snowdon Aviary
Gratte-ciel, Villeurbanne
Melnikov House
Kunsthaus Graz

Neil Denari

Postsparkasse
Gamble House
Casa Milà
Palais Stoclet
Fagus Factory
Frederick C. Robie House
Park Güell
Het Schip
German Pavilion (Barcelona Pavilion)
Schindler House
Goetheanum
Einstein Tower
Bauhaus Dessau
Schröderhuis
Van Nelle Factory
Villa Cook
La Maison de Verre
Tugendhat House
Villa Müller
Villa Savoye
Edgar J. Kaufmann House (Fallingwater)
Casa del Fascio
Casa Malaparte
The Eames House (Case Study House No. 8)
Baker House
Ariston Hotel, Mar del Plata
Lever House
Solomon R. Guggenheim Museum
Chapelle Notre-Dame du Haut
Farnsworth House
Ginásio do Clube Atlético Paulistano
Hunstanton School
Crown Hall
Richards Medical Research Laboratories
L'Unité d'Habitation
Studio Aalto
Sky House, Tokyo
National Congress, Brazil
Olivetti Factory, Merlo
US Air Force Academy Cadet Chapel
Leicester University Engineering Building
Salk Institute
TWA Flight Center
Pepsi-Cola Building
Bank of London and South America
Torre Blancas
Snowdon Aviary
Gwathmey Residence
Edifício Copan
Lieb House
Fire Station No. 4, Columbus
Kappe Residence
Smith House
Balfron Tower
New National Gallery
Rogers House
Wyss Garden Center
Pilgrimage Church, Neviges
Olivetti Training Center
Nibankan
The Pagoda, Madrid
Mummers Theater
Zentralsparkasse Bank, Vienna
Yamanashi Press and Broadcasting Center
Nakagin Capsule Tower
Olivetti Headquarters, Frankfurt
Centre Pompidou
White U
Florey Building
Kuwait Embassy, Tokyo
House VI
Willis Faber and Dumas Headquarters
Kimbell Art Museum
Olympic Stadium, Munich
House on a Curved Road
Charles De Gaulle Airport, Terminal 1 & 2A–2F
Bass Residence
Gehry House
Brant House, Greenwich
Centraal Beheer Building
Sainsbury Center for Visual Arts
Pennzoil Place
Rooftop Remodeling Falkestrasse
El Helicoide
Hongkong and Shanghai Bank Headquarters
Lloyd's of London
Allied Bank Tower
Brühl Sports Center
Venice III House
Vitra Design Museum
The Menil Collection
Guggenheim Museum Bilbao
Suzuki House
Barcelona Olympic Archery Range
Villa VPRO
Diamond Ranch High School
Miyagi Stadium
Goetz Collection
Signal Box Auf dem Wolf
Igualada Cemetery

Elizabeth Diller + Ricardo Scofidio + Charles Renfro

Rue Franklin Apartments
AEG Turbine Factory
Glasgow School of Art
Casa Milà
Frederick C. Robie House
Detroit Arsenal
Posen Tower
Postsparkasse
Fiat Works
Shukhov Tower
Schröderhuis
Villa Moller
German Pavilion (Barcelona Pavilion)
Rusakov Workers' Club
Downtown Athletic Club, New York
Salginatobel Bridge
Villa Savoye
La Maison de Verre
Haus Schminke
London Zoo Penguin Pool
Villa Girasole
Casa del Fascio
Merzbau
S.C. Johnson & Son Headquarters
Villa Mairea
The Woodland Cemetery
Casa Malaparte
Dymaxion House
Barragán House and Studio
8x8 Demountable House
Turin Exhibition Hall
The Eames House (Case Study House No. 8)
Bavinger House
Farnsworth House
L'Unité d'Habitation
Das Canoas House
Miller House, Columbus
Chapelle Notre-Dame du Haut
House of the Future, 1956
Los Manantiales
Seagram Building
Philips Pavilion
Museum of Modern Art, Rio de Janeiro
Solomon R. Guggenheim Museum
Church of the Three Crosses
Palácio do Planalto
Church of Cristo Obrero
Couvent Sainte-Marie de La Tourette
US Air Force Academy Cadet Chapel
TWA Flight Center
Sheats Goldstein Residence
Gateway Arch
Querini Stampalia Renovation
The Beinecke Rare Book & Manuscript Library
Berliner Philharmonie
Leicester University Engineering Building
National Museum of Anthropology
Chiesa dell'Autostrada del Sole
National Olympic Gymnasium, Tokyo
Shrine of the Book
The Pagoda, Madrid
Salk Institute
National Art Schools of Cuba
The Breuer Building (Whitney Museum)
Église Sainte-Bernadette du Banlay
Piscinas de Marés
Montessori School, Delft
German Pavilion, Expo '67
Hyatt Regency, Atlanta
Villa Rosa, 1966–1970
Museu de Arte de São Paulo
FAU, University of São Paulo
Art Center College of Design, Pasadena
Nakagin Capsule Tower
Oase Nr. 7
Kimbell Art Museum
Castelvecchio Museum
Free University of Berlin
House VI
Charles De Gaulle Airport, Terminal 1 & 2A–2F
Marina City, Chicago
Bank of Georgia headquarters, Tbilisi
InterAction Centre, Kentish Town
White U
World Trade Center Towers
Centre Pompidou
Hedmark Cathedral Museum
Sítio Roberto Burle Marx
Hongkong and Shanghai Bank Headquarters
The Menil Collection
Institut du Monde Arabe
Kunsthal, Rotterdam
Maison à Bordeaux
Therme Vals
Schouwburgplein
Guggenheim Museum Bilbao
Diamond Ranch High School
Jewish Museum Berlin
Sendai Mediatheque
Expo 2000, Netherlands Pavilion

Winka Dubbeldam

TWA Flight Center
Alhambra, Granada
Community Centre, Bak
German Pavilion (Barcelona Pavilion)
Bass Residence
Rudolph Residence, 23 Beekman Place
Berlin State Library
Berliner Philharmonie
Beurs van Berlage
Le Saint James, Bouliac
Palácio da Alvorada
Petah Tikva
Brion Family Tomb
CaixaForum Madrid
California Academy of Sciences
Museo Canova
Capilla de las Capuchinas
Casa da Música
Casa Malaparte
Centre Pompidou
Chapelle Notre-Dame du Haut
Chiesa dell'Autostrada del Sole
Chrysler Building
Church of the Light
Glass Chapel, Alabama
Couvent Sainte-Marie de La Tourette
41 Cooper Square
Cuadra San Cristóbal
Das Canoas House
Diamond Ranch High School
Dominus Winery
Netherlands Embassy, Berlin
De Admirant Entrance Building
Edgar J. Kaufmann House (Fallingwater)
Farnsworth House
Saint-Pierre, Firminy
Glass House
Casa de Vidro
497 Greenwich Building
Guggenheim Museum Bilbao
High Line 23
Holy Spirit Church, Paks
Hongkong and Shanghai Bank Headquarters
House VI
Chapel of St. Ignatius
Ingalls Rink
Jean-Marie Tjibaou Cultural Centre
S.C. Johnson & Son Headquarters
Institut du Monde Arabe
Kiefhoek Housing Development
Casa Milà
Lincoln Center
La Maison de Verre
Marina City, Chicago
Sendai Mediatheque
Melnikov House
Mercedes-Benz Museum
Musée des Confluences
Yale Center for British Art
Nakagin Capsule Tower
Netherlands Dance Theatre, Hague
New National Gallery
Nine Bridges Country Club
No Mass House
NORD/LB Hanover
Olympic Stadium, Munich
Municipal Orphanage
Parco Acqua Santa
Parco della Musica
Perot Museum of Nature and Science
Phaeno Science Center
Potala Palace Renovation
Prada Aoyama
Reichstag Dome
Schröderhuis
Frederick C. Robie House
Yokohama International Port Terminal
Rusakov Workers' Club
Sagrada Família
Salk Institute
Zonnenstraal
Seattle Central Library
History Faculty Building, Cambridge
Serpentine Gallery Pavilion, 2002
Sydney Opera House
Sonneveld House
Spanish Pavilion at Shanghai Expo 2010
Steinhaus, Lake Ossiach
Tate Modern
Igreja da Pampulha
Sheats Goldstein Residence
Therme Vals
National Congress, Brazil
Van Nelle Factory
Villa Savoye
Tugendhat House
Walt Disney Concert Hall
The Breuer Building (Whitney Museum)
Vitra Design Museum
520 West 28th Street

Peter Eisenman

Palais de la musique et des congrès
Maison Dom-ino
Maison Citrohan
Villa Savoye
Villa Stein
Swiss Pavilion
City of Refuge, Paris
Couvent Sainte-Marie de La Tourette
German Pavilion (Barcelona Pavilion)
Brick Country House
New National Gallery
Crown Hall
Farnsworth House
Villa Müller
Villa Moller
Michaelerplatz House (Looshaus)
Larkin Company Administration Building
Darwin D. Martin House
Solomon R. Guggenheim Museum
Palicka Villa
Basel Petersschule
Zonnenstraal
Werkbundsiedlung, Vienna
Berliner Philharmonie
Proposal for the Bank of Dresden
Casa del Fascio
Casa Giuliani Frigerio
Asilo Sant'Elia
Casa Cattaneo a Cernobbio
Fencing Academy, Rome
Casa Il Girasole
Corso Italia Complex, Milan
Casa Rustici
Istituto Marchiondi Spagliardi
AEG Turbine Factory
Goetheanum
Einstein Tower
Narkomfin Building
History Faculty Building, Cambridge
Leicester University Engineering Building
Florey Building
Neue Staatsgalerie
Braun AG Headquarters, Melsungen
Enschede Dormitory
San Cataldo Cemetery
Gallaratese II Apartments
The Economist Building, London
Golden Lane Housing
Robin Hood Gardens
Vanna Venturi House
Yale Mathematics Building Competition 1970
National Gallery, Sainsbury Wing
College Football Hall of Fame Proposal, VSBA
Smith House
Hanselmann House
Benacerraf House Project
Snyderman House
Whitney Museum Expansion Proposal, M. Graves
Fargo-Moorhead Cultural Center Bridge
Gwathmey Residence
Berlin Masque
Wall House II
House II (Vermont House)
Berlin Memorial to the Murdered Jews of Europe
Wexner Center for the Visual Arts
Design, Architecture, Art & Planning Building
Rudolph Hall
Sarasota High School
Glass House
Kline Biology Tower
Léon Krier (overall oeuvre)
Town Hall, Logroño
Bankinter Building
Bouça Saal Housing Complex
Jewelry Store Schullin
Museum of Modern Art, Gunma
Naoshima Contemporary Art Museum
Sendai Mediatheque
Austrian Cultural Forum
Boston City Hall
Miller House, Columbus
Knights of Columbus Building
Pacific Design Center
Très Grande Bibliothèque
Jussieu – Two Libraries
Parc de La Villette, OMA proposal
Eurodisney, Marne-la-Vallée, OMA Proposal
Peak Leisure Club
Rosenthal Center for Contemporary Art
Herta and Paul Amir Building
6th Street House, Santa Monica
2-4-6-8 House
Chapel of St. Ignatius
Peter B. Lewis Building, CWRU
Guggenheim Museum Bilbao
Ron Davis House, Malibu
Schröderhuis
Beurs van Berlage
Säynätsalo Town Hall
Tallinn Art Museum Proposal

Jeanne Gang / Studio Gang

SESC Pompéia
S.C. Johnson & Son Headquarters
Sydney Opera House
German Pavilion (Barcelona Pavilion)
Crown Hall
Sagrada Família
Chapelle Notre-Dame du Haut
Phillips Exeter Academy Library
Yale Center for British Art
The Beinecke Rare Book & Manuscript Library
Casa de Vidro
Villa Mairea
Tugendhat House
Casa del Fascio
University of Virginia
Viipuri Municipal Library
Church of Cristo Obrero
Centraal Beheer Building
Querini Stampalia Renovation
National Assembly Building, Bangladesh
Salk Institute
Edgar J. Kaufmann House (Fallingwater)
Centre Pompidou
La Maison de Verre
Louisiana Museum of Modern Art
Millard House
Berliner Philharmonie
Olympic Stadium, Munich
Habitat '67
E-1027
The Eames House (Case Study House No. 8)
Farnsworth House
New National Gallery
Frederick C. Robie House
Göteborg Town Hall
Park Güell
Santuario Dom Bosco
TWA Flight Center
Mill Owners' Association Building
Van Nelle Factory
The Assembly, Chandigarh
Casa Milà
Flatiron Building
Castelvecchio Museum
Montreal Biosphère
Auditorium Building, Chicago
Finlandia Hall
Kimbell Art Museum
Casa Butantã
Rudolph Hall
Villa Savoye
Museu de Arte de São Paulo
Säynätsalo Town Hall
Unity Temple
Schindler House
Indian Institute of Management, Ahmedabad
Edifício Jaraguá
Cathedral of Brasília
Itamaraty Palace
Postsparkasse
Ford Motor Company Glass Manufacturing Plant
Couvent Sainte-Marie de La Tourette
Carpenter Center for the Visual Arts
Gateway Arch
Bibliothèque nationale de France
Torres del Parque
Bulgwang-dong Catholic Church
Sir John Soane's Museum
Apolloscholen
National Art Schools of Cuba
Edifício Copan
FAU, University of São Paulo
Marquette Building
L'Unité d'Habitation
Sangath
The Woodland Cemetery
Carson, Pirie, Scott and Company Building
Studio Aalto
Palazzetto dello Sport
Monticello
Neutra Research House
Pantheon, Rome
Chand Baori
Notre Dame de Paris
Igualada Cemetery
Elbphilharmonie
MAXXI
Casa da Música
Beijing Airport
The Menil Collection
Universita Luigi Bocconi
Heydar Aliyev Center
UC Campus Recreation Center
Berlin Memorial to the Murdered Jews of Europe
Maison à Bordeaux
Ricola Storage Building
Louis Vuitton Foundation
Tama Art University Library
Sendai Mediatheque
Nexus World Housing

Dame Zaha Hadid

American Bar, Vienna
Einstein Tower
Zuev Workers' Club
Svoboda Factory Club
Melnikov House
Nikolaev's House
London Zoo Penguin Pool
Highpoint Apartment Blocks
Finsbury Health Centre
BLPS Housing
Rockefeller Center
Gustavo Capanema Palace
Igreja da Pampulha
Boavista Bank Headquarters, Rio de Janeiro
Royal Festival Hall
Das Canoas House
Usk Street Estate
UNESCO Headquarters, Paris
Marina City, Chicago
Royal College of Physicians
Trellick Tower
Willis Faber and Dumas Headquarters
Royal National Theatre
Casa Gilardi
Sainsbury Center for Visual Arts
Qatar University
Vitra Campus
National Library of the Argentine Republic
Lord's Media Centre
Postsparkasse
Schindler House
Fiat Works
Schröderhuis
Cité Frugès Housing Complex
Karl-Marx-Hof
Lovell Health House
Stockholm Public Library
Villa Moller
German Pavilion (Barcelona Pavilion)
Villa Savoye
Van Nelle Factory
La Maison de Verre
Villa Girasole
Edgar J. Kaufmann House (Fallingwater)
Casa del Fascio
The Woodland Cemetery
Casa Malaparte
Dymaxion House
Turin Exhibition Hall
Glass House
The Eames House (Case Study House No. 8)
Baker House
Muuratsalo Experimental House
Farnsworth House
L'Unité d'Habitation
Lever House
Pedregulho Housing Complex
Crown Hall
Maisons Jaoul
Chapelle Notre-Dame du Haut
Seagram Building
National Congress, Brazil
Philips Pavilion
Solomon R. Guggenheim Museum
Cité d'Habitacion of Carrières Centrales
Stahl House (Case Study House No. 22)
Couvent Sainte-Marie de La Tourette
Municipal Orphanage
Halen Estate
TWA Flight Center
Querini Stampalia Renovation
Berliner Philharmonie
Leicester University Engineering Building
Vanna Venturi House
National Olympic Gymnasium, Tokyo
Peabody Terrace
Rudolph Hall
Salk Institute
The Assembly, Chandigarh
Centre Le Corbusier (Heidi Weber House)
Piscinas de Marés
Kuwait Embassy, Tokyo
Bank of London and South America
Habitat '67
Smith House
Museu de Arte de São Paulo
Ford Foundation Headquarters
Kowloon Walled City
Benacerraf House Project
Flower Kiosk, Malmö Cemetery
Petrobras Headquarters
The Beinecke Rare Book & Manuscript Library
House III (Miller House)
Nakagin Capsule Tower
Olympic Stadium, Munich
Phillips Exeter Academy Library
Kimbell Art Museum
Free University of Berlin
Byker Wall
Centraal Beheer Building

Dame Zaha Hadid (Continued)

Whig Hall, Princeton University
Bagsværd Church
Brion Family Tomb
Centre Pompidou
SESC Pompéia
Hedmark Cathedral Museum
Gehry House
Atheneum, New Harmony
Koshino House
Vietnam Veterans Memorial
National Assembly Building, Bangladesh
Neue Staatsgalerie
Lloyd's of London
Hongkong and Shanghai Bank Headquarters
Rooftop Remodeling Falkestrasse
National Museum of Roman Art
Void Space/Hinged Space Housing
Igualada Cemetery
Parc de la Villette
Maison à Bordeaux
Samitaur Tower
Guggenheim Museum Bilbao
UFA Cinema Centre
Jewish Museum Berlin
Bordeaux Law Courts
Diamond Ranch High School
Yokohama International Port Terminal
Sendai Mediatheque

Craig Hodgetts

TWA Flight Center
General Motors Technical Center
Washington Dulles International Airport
MIT Chapel
Rudolph Hall
Dipoli
Säynätsalo Town Hall
Riola Parish Church
Otaniemi Technical University
Maison du Brésil
Chapelle Notre-Dame du Haut
L'Unité d'Habitation
City of Refuge, Paris
Philips Pavilion
Couvent Sainte-Marie de La Tourette
Carpenter Center for the Visual Arts
History Faculty Building, Cambridge
Florey Building
Southgate Estate
Neue Staatsgalerie
Leicester University Engineering Building
Bank of London and South America
Berlin State Library
Berliner Philharmonie
Renault Distribution Centre
Centre Pompidou
Lloyd's of London
Richards Medical Research Laboratories
Centraal Beheer Building
Expo '70 Osaka, Festival Plaza
National Olympic Gymnasium, Tokyo
Habitat '67
2-4-6-8 House
UC Campus Recreation Center
41 Cooper Square
Santa Caterina Market
Scottish Parliament Building
Chrysler Building
PSFS Building
Rockefeller Center
United Nations Headquarters
Cincinnati Union Terminal Station
The Menil Collection
The Shard
Nakagin Capsule Tower
Maison Tropicale
Taliesin West
S.C. Johnson & Son Headquarters
Edgar J. Kaufmann House (Fallingwater)
Towell Library
Vitra Fire Station
Rooftop Remodeling Falkestrasse
Groninger Museum
The Eames House (Case Study House No. 8)
Pepsi-Cola Building
Inland Steel Building
Blur Building
Bibliotheca Alexandrina
Prada Aoyama
Dominus Winery
Signal Box Auf dem Wolf
Linked Hybrid
Chapel of St. Ignatius
Nelson-Atkins Museum of Art Addition
Horton Plaza
Canal City Hakata, Fukuoka
Olympic Stadium, Munich
German Pavilion, Expo '67
Seattle Central Library
House in Leymen
Guggenheim Museum Bilbao
Gehry House
Binoculars Building
Neutra Research House
Reiner-Burchill Residence
El Pueblo Ribera
High Line 23
Bauhaus Dessau
La Maison de Verre
Marie Short House
Einstein Tower
Futurama, 1939 New York World's Fair
National Congress, Brazil
Edifício Copan
Mercado de Colón
St. John's Abbey, Collegeville
IBM France
Palazzetto dello Sport
Orvieto Aircraft Hangars
Glass Pavilion
Sydney Opera House
Chiesa dell'Autostrada del Sole
Hayden Tract
Parc de la Villette
Le Fresnoy Art Center
Church on the Water
Yokohama International Port Terminal
Institut du Monde Arabe
Mimesis Museum
Gare do Oriente

Steven Holl

Glasgow School of Art
Larkin Company Administration Building
Unity Temple
Frederick C. Robie House
Steiner House
Postsparkasse
Michaelerplatz House (Looshaus)
Merchants' National Bank, Grinnell
Imperial Hotel, Tokyo
Einstein Tower
Schindler House
Ozenfant House
Villa La Roche
Schröderhuis
Tristan Tzara House
Cranbrook Academy of Art
Bauhaus Dessau
Villa Moller
Melnikov House
German Pavilion (Barcelona Pavilion)
Villa Müller
Villa Savoye
La Maison de Verre
Rockefeller Center
Edgar J. Kaufmann House (Fallingwater)
Casa del Fascio
S.C. Johnson & Son Headquarters
Casa Malaparte
Villa Mairea
The Eames House (Case Study House No. 8)
Farnsworth House
L'Unité d'Habitation
Baker House
Barragán House and Studio
Chapelle du Rosaire de Vence
Säynätsalo Town Hall
Crown Hall
Mill Owners' Association Building
The Assembly, Chandigarh
Chapelle Notre-Dame du Haut
House of Culture
St. Mark's Church in Björkhagen
Municipal Orphanage
National Congress, Brazil
Berliner Philharmonie
Torres de Satélite
Church of the Three Crosses
Couvent Sainte-Marie de La Tourette
Richards Medical Research Laboratories
Sydney Opera House
Seagram Building
Philips Pavilion
Rudolph Hall
Museu de Arte de São Paulo
Salk Institute
Solomon R. Guggenheim Museum
Leicester University Engineering Building
TWA Flight Center
National Assembly Building, Bangladesh
Indian Institute of Management, Ahmedabad
Querini Stampalia Renovation
The Beinecke Rare Book & Manuscript Library
Ford Foundation Headquarters
National Olympic Gymnasium, Tokyo
History Faculty Building, Cambridge
Phillips Exeter Academy Library
Church of St. Peter, Klippan
Centre Le Corbusier (Heidi Weber House)
Habitat '67
Hanselmann House
Smith House
Gallaratese II Apartments
Olympic Stadium, Munich
Bagsværd Church
Brion Family Tomb
Kimbell Art Museum
Nakagin Capsule Tower
Museum of Modern Art, Gunma
Centre Pompidou
House VI
San Cataldo Cemetery
Beires House
Athenaeum, New Harmony
Uehara House
Neue Staatsgalerie
Institut du Monde Arabe
The Menil Collection
Parc de la Villette
Tokyo Institute of Technology Centennial Hall
Faculty of Architecture of the University of Porto
Jewish Museum Berlin
Church of the Light
Void Space/Hinged Space Housing
Norwegian Glacier Museum
Vitra Fire Station
Maison à Bordeaux
UFA Cinema Centre
Guggenheim Museum Bilbao
Diamond Ranch High School
Sendai Mediatheque

Francine Houben

Villa Savoye
L'Unité d'Habitation
Chapelle Notre-Dame du Haut
The Assembly, Chandigarh
Couvent Sainte-Marie de La Tourette
Edgar J. Kaufmann House (Fallingwater)
S.C. Johnson & Son Headquarters
Taliesin West
Jacobs First House
Solomon R. Guggenheim Museum
Villa Mairea
Villa Moller
Das Canoas House
National Congress, Brazil
Ibirapuera Park
Casa de Vidro
SESC Pompéia
Museu de Arte de São Paulo
Sydney Opera House
Saint Catherine's College, Oxford
Old Faithful Inn
Farnsworth House
German Pavilion (Barcelona Pavilion)
Seagram Building
Tugendhat House
The Eames House (Case Study House No. 8)
Bailey House (Case Study House No. 21)
Salk Institute
Phillips Exeter Academy Library
Kimbell Art Museum
Rudolph Hall
Dymaxion House
National Olympic Gymnasium, Tokyo
Nakagin Capsule Tower
Igualada Cemetery
Sagrada Família
Casa Milà
Bauhaus Dessau
TWA Flight Center
Gateway Arch
UNESCO Headquarters, Paris
Schindler House
Lovell Health House
Lovell Beach House
Gamble House
Chemosphere
Kaufmann House
Van Nelle Factory
Vanna Venturi House
Centre Pompidou
Ford Foundation Headquarters
National Gallery of Art, East Building
Haus Schminke
Berliner Philharmonie
Hyatt Regency, Atlanta
The Beinecke Rare Book & Manuscript Library
La Maison de Verre
Zonnenstraal
Beurs van Berlage
Het Schip
Postsparkasse
Barragán House and Studio
Glasgow School of Art
Stockholm Public Library
Hilversum Town Hall
Casa del Fascio
Vitra Fire Station
Kunsthal, Rotterdam
Library Delft University of Technology
Piscinas de Marés
Therme Vals
Chrysler Building
Empire State Building
World Trade Center Towers
Melnikov House
Jean Prouvé Housing Elements & Façades
Brion Family Tomb
Municipal Museum, The Hague
Guggenheim Museum Bilbao
John Hancock Center
Casa Malaparte
Glass House
Silver Hut
Sendai Mediatheque
Hongkong and Shanghai Bank Headquarters
Tate Modern
Royal Festival Hall
Kanchanjunga Apartments
Hufeisensiedlung
Papaverhof
Highpoint Apartment Blocks
Huis Van der Leeuw
Schröderhuis
Fiat Works
Café De Unie
Auditorium of the Technical University in Delft
Kasbah Housing, Hengelo
Municipal Orphanage, Amsterdam
Mobius House
Villa VPRO

Toyo Ito

Postsparkasse
Villa Savoye
The Eames House (Case Study House No. 8)
L'Unité d'Habitation
Chapelle Notre-Dame du Haut
Sydney Opera House
Villa Sarabhai
National Congress, Brazil
Church of the Three Crosses
Couvent Sainte-Marie de La Tourette
Municipal Orphanage
TWA Flight Center
Berliner Philharmonie
National Olympic Gymnasium, Tokyo
Vanna Venturi House
Salk Institute
The Assembly, Chandigarh
Glasgow School of Art
Frederick C. Robie House
Schindler House
Stockholm Public Library
Villa Moller
German Pavilion (Barcelona Pavilion)
Edgar J. Kaufmann House (Fallingwater)
S.C. Johnson & Son Headquarters
Villa Mairea
Dymaxion House
Glass House
Farnsworth House
Mill Owners' Association Building
Solomon R. Guggenheim Museum
Stahl House (Case Study House No. 22)
Toulouse-le-Mirail Housing
Halen Estate
Querini Stampalia Renovation
John Deere World Headquarters
Otaniemi Technical University
Rudolph Hall
Sea Ranch Condominium Complex
Habitat '67
Montreal Biosphère
Nakagin Capsule Tower
Olympic Stadium, Munich
Kimbell Art Museum
Castelvecchio Museum
Museum of Modern Art, Gunma
World Trade Center Towers
Centre Pompidou
Brion Family Tomb
Gehry House
Teatro del Mondo
Sumiyoshi Row House
National Assembly Building, Bangladesh
Hongkong and Shanghai Bank Headquarters
Institut du Monde Arabe
Void Space/Hinged Space Housing
Maison à Bordeaux
Guggenheim Museum Bilbao
Diamond Ranch High School
Sendai Mediatheque
Yokohama International Port Terminal

Jong Soung Kimm

Beurs van Berlage
Postsparkasse
Glasgow School of Art
Rue Franklin Apartments
Gamble House
AEG Turbine Factory
Michaelerplatz House (Looshaus)
Carson, Pirie, Scott and Company Building
Larkin Company Administration Building
Frederick C. Robie House
Edgar J. Kaufmann House (Fallingwater)
S.C. Johnson & Son Headquarters
Unity Temple
Solomon R. Guggenheim Museum
German Pavilion (Barcelona Pavilion)
Tugendhat House
860–880 Lake Shore Drive
Farnsworth House
Crown Hall
Seagram Building
New National Gallery
Villa Stein
Villa Savoye
L'Unité d'Habitation
Chapelle Notre-Dame du Haut
Couvent Sainte-Marie de La Tourette
The Assembly, Chandigarh
Mill Owners' Association Building
Einstein Tower
Bauhaus Dessau
La Maison de Verre
Sagrada Família
Park Güell
Casa Milà
Casa del Fascio
Schröderhuis
Stockholm Public Library
The Woodland Cemetery
St. Mark's Church in Björkhagen
Fiat Works
Schindler House
Lovell Health House
Rusakov Workers' Club
Säynätsalo Town Hall
Baker House
The Eames House (Case Study House No. 8)
Richards Medical Research Laboratories
Salk Institute
Kimbell Art Museum
Phillips Exeter Academy Library
Yale Center for British Art
National Assembly Building, Bangladesh
Lever House
The Beinecke Rare Book & Manuscript Library
Glass House
Rudolph Hall
Sydney Opera House
Berliner Philharmonie
National Congress, Brazil
Leicester University Engineering Building
TWA Flight Center
John Deere World Headquarters
Ford Foundation Headquarters
Vanna Venturi House
Querini Stampalia Renovation
Brion Family Tomb
Palazzo del Lavoro
Turin Exhibition Hall
Free University of Berlin
National Olympic Gymnasium, Tokyo
The Breuer Building (Whitney Museum)
Hillside Terrace Complex I–VI
Centraal Beheer Building
San Cataldo Cemetery
Gallaratese II Apartments
Municipal Orphanage
National Gallery of Art, East Building
Pyramide du Louvre
Bank of China Tower, Hong Kong
Richard J. Daley Center
Sears Tower
Smith House
Getty Center
Olympic Stadium, Munich
Centre Pompidou
The Menil Collection
Gehry House
Guggenheim Museum Bilbao
Hongkong and Shanghai Bank Headquarters
Lloyd's of London
Parc de la Villette
National Museum of Roman Art
Institut du Monde Arabe
Jewish Museum Berlin
Yokohama International Port Terminal
Igualada Cemetery
Maison à Bordeaux
Naoshima Contemporary Art Museum
Sendai Mediatheque
Diamond Ranch High School

Léon Krier

Kirche am Steinhof
Postsparkasse
Pan American Union Building
The House of the Temple
Sanatorium Purkersdorf
Palais Stoclet
Panama–California Exposition
Colonial Williamsburg Reconstructions
Hydro-Electric Plant, Riva del Garda
Vittoriale degli italiani
Hydroelectric Plant, Pienza
Prague Castle Interventions
Lincoln Memorial
Zeppelinfeld
Villa Savoye
Midland Bank, Manchester
Rue Mallet-Stevens
Siedlung Margarethenhöhe
Palazzo della Civiltà Italiana
Palazzo dei Congressi
Villa Bianca, Seveso
Firenze Santa Maria Novella
Kallithea Springs
Arco della Vittoria
Garbatella Quarter
French Embassy, Belgrade
The Woodland Cemetery
Lister County Courthouse, Sölvesborg
Copenhagen Police Headquarters
Faaborg Museum
Hilversum Town Hall
Villa Becker, Munich
Königsplatz, Munich
Texas Centennial Exposition
Chapelle Notre-Dame du Haut
The Assembly, Chandigarh
Plaza de España, Seville
Ibero-American Exposition of 1929
Petit Palais
Grand Palais
Pont Alexandre III
Aula Palatina
Villa Kerylos
Ise Grand Shrine
Davenport and Pierson Colleges, Yale
Hoover Dam
La Maison de Verre
Zonnenstraal
Leicester University Engineering Building
Pasadena City Hall
Charles De Gaulle Airport, Terminal 1 & 2A–2F
Baikonur Cosmodrome Launch Site 250
Miami Biltmore Hotel
Grand Central Terminal
Pennsylvania Station
Union Station, Washington, D.C.
Adolphe Bridge
Eccles Building
Villa Wagner II
Casa Malaparte
Reconstruction of Old Warsaw
Frauenkirche Dresden Reconstruction
German Pavilion (Barcelona Pavilion)
Windsor, Vero Beach
Seaside Chapel, Ruskin Square
Flak Towers, Vienna
Golden Gate Bridge
Festspielhaus Hellerau
S.C. Johnson & Son Headquarters
Celebration Masterplan
Il villaggio Cesare Battisti
All-Union Agricultural Exhibition
New Gouma Village Mosque
Island Mosque, Jeddah
Via Roma, Torino
1939 Reconstruction of Devastated Regions, Spain
Kongresshalle
Hoover Building
Detroit Arsenal
De La Warr Pavilion
Halen Estate
Barragán House and Studio
TWA Flight Center
Palm Beach Town Hall Square
San Francisco Maritime Museum
Richmond Riverside Development
Grundtvig Memorial Church
Vilanova House, Key Biscayne
Stockholm Public Library
New Reich Chancellery
Plečnik Žale Cemetery
Ljubljana Central Market
Triple Bridge
Søndermark Chapel and Crematorium
Øregård Gymnasium
Atlantic Wall Bunkers & Towers
McMillan Plan
Staaken Garden City, Berlin
Foro Italico
Port Grimaud

Kengo Kuma

Métropolitain Entrance
Beurs van Berlage
Rue Franklin Apartments
Larkin Company Administration Building
AEG Turbine Factory
Glasgow School of Art
Gamble House
Unity Temple
Frederick C. Robie House
Casa Milà
Palais Stoclet
Posen Tower
Fagus Factory
Postsparkasse
Park Güell
Het Schip
Einstein Tower
Schindler House
Fiat Works
Monument to the March Dead
Stockholm City Hall
Van Nelle Factory
Schröderhuis
Café De Unie
Lovell Beach House
Schocken Department Store, Stuttgart
Sagrada Família
Bauhaus Dessau
Barclay-Vesey Building
Karl-Marx-Hof
Lovell Health House
Stockholm Public Library
Villa Moller
E-1027
Goetheanum
German Pavilion (Barcelona Pavilion)
Rusakov Workers' Club
Narkomfin Building
Stockholm Exhibition of 1930
Villa Müller
Tugendhat House
Villa Savoye
Hilversum Town Hall
Paimio Sanatorium
La Maison de Verre
Haus Schminke
Villa Girasole
Edgar J. Kaufmann House (Fallingwater)
Casa del Fascio
Michaelerplatz House (Looshaus)
Asilo Sant'Elia
S.C. Johnson & Son Headquarters
Villa Mairea
Arve Bridge
The Woodland Cemetery
Casa Malaparte
National and University Library of Slovenia
Dymaxion House
Golconde, Pondicherry
Baker House
Barragán House and Studio
Turin Exhibition Hall
The Eames House (Case Study House No. 8)
Architect's Second House, São Paulo
Farnsworth House
Säynätsalo Town Hall
L'Unité d'Habitation
Iglesia de la Medalla Milagrosa
Chapelle Notre-Dame du Haut
MIT Chapel
Villa Sarabhai
Sydney Opera House
Palazzetto dello Sport
Seagram Building
Louisiana Museum of Modern Art
National Congress, Brazil
Solomon R. Guggenheim Museum
Los Manantiales
Bacardi Bottling Plant
Couvent Sainte-Marie de La Tourette
TWA Flight Center
Berliner Philharmonie
National Olympic Gymnasium, Tokyo
Salk Institute
The Assembly, Chandigarh
Museu de Arte de São Paulo
Nakagin Capsule Tower
Phillips Exeter Academy Library
Kimbell Art Museum
Castelvecchio Museum
Gallaratese II Apartments
Centre Pompidou
Gehry House
Hongkong and Shanghai Bank Headquarters
Ricola Storage Building
Institut du Monde Arabe
Parc de la Villette
Congrexpo
Guggenheim Museum Bilbao
Piscinas de Marés

Lars Lerup

Villa Snellman
Stockholm Public Library
The Woodland Cemetery
Göteborg Town Hall
Stockholm Exhibition of 1930
Chapel of the Resurrection
Court of the National Social Insurance Building
St. Mark's Church in Björkhagen
Church of St. Peter, Klippan
Stockholm Concert Hall
Flower Kiosk, Malmö Cemetery
Vårby Gårds Kyrka
Kulturhuset, Stockholm
The Riksbank Building, Stockholm
Villa Klockberga
Filmhuset, Stockholm
Lunds Konsthall
Malmö Konsthall
Göteborgs Konstmuseum
Svappavaara Housing
Byker Wall
The Ark, London
Brittgården Housing Estate
Allhuset
Villa Erskine
School Churwalden
House Räth
Shelters for Roman Archaeological Site
Saint Benedict Chapel, Sumvitg
Bündner Kunstmuseum, Chur
Gugalun House
Therme Vals
Kunsthaus Bregenz
Bruder Klaus Field Chapel
Serpentine Gallery Pavilion, 2011
Synthes Headquarters, Solothurn
Museum La Congiunta
Novartis Campus, 6 Fabrikstrasse
Swiss Re Tüfihaus
Gartenbad und Schule, Wohlen
Eliot Hall, Washington University
Palestra, Losone
Casa Rezzonico
Edificio Postale, Locarno
Casa Aurora, Lugano
House of Three Women, Beinwil am See
Augustinian Monte Carasso Monastery
Palestra, Monte Carasso
Casa Guidotti
Casa Grossi
Casa Bianchi
Goetz Collection
Signal Box Auf dem Wolf
Dominus Winery
Tate Modern
Laban Dance Centre, London
Forum Building
166 Cottbus Library
De Young
Allianz Arena
Beijing National Stadium
CaixaForum Madrid
1111 Lincoln Road
Museum der Kulturen
Parrish Art Museum
Congrexpo
Netherlands Dance Theatre, Hague
Villa dall'Ava
Nexus World Housing
Kunsthal, Rotterdam
Maison à Bordeaux
Netherlands Embassy, Berlin
Prada Epicenters
Seattle Central Library
Casa da Música
Shenzhen Stock Exchange
Dee and Charles Wyly Theatre
Milstein Hall
CCTV Headquarters
New Court Rothschild Bank
Villa Savoye
Münster City Library
Luxor Theater, Rotterdam
Jewish Museum Berlin
Berlin Memorial to the Murdered Jews of Europe
1234 Howard Street
Architecture and Art Building, Prairie View A&M U.
Guggenheim Museum Bilbao
San Francisco Federal Building
Casa del Fascio
Pabellón de España, Zaragoza
Municipal Auditorium of Teulada
Murcia Town Hall
Viviendas en la Calle Prior
Gimansio del Colegio Maravillas
Casa Ugalde
Peabody Terrace
Igualada Cemetery
BMW Welt
Samitaur Tower

Daniel Libeskind / Studio Libeskind

Church of the Three Crosses
Säynätsalo Town Hall
Villa Mairea
Paimio Sanatorium
Church of the Light
Barragán House and Studio
AEG Turbine Factory
La Maison de Verre
Le Palais ideal
Het Schip
Steinhaus, Lake Ossiach
Simon Fraser University
Norwegian Glacier Museum
Villa Kise
Hedmark Cathedral Museum
Hongkong and Shanghai Bank Headquarters
Montreal Biosphère
Casa alle Zattere, Venice
Casa Batlló
Casa Milà
Park Güell
Sagrada Família
Guggenheim Museum Bilbao
Hanselmann House
E-1027
Bauhaus Dessau
Gut Garkau Farm
Kreuzberg Tower
Palais Stoclet
Chilehaus
Maison & Atelier Horta
The Woodland Cemetery
SAS Royal Hotel, Copenhagen
National Assembly Building, Bangladesh
Kimbell Art Museum
Salk Institute
Chapelle Notre-Dame du Haut
The Assembly, Chandigarh
Centre Le Corbusier (Heidi Weber House)
Couvent Sainte-Marie de La Tourette
Villa Stein
Villa Savoye
Männistö Church, Kuopio
Church of St. Peter, Klippan
Casa Malaparte
Villa Müller
Glasgow School of Art
Israel Museum
High Museum of Art
Melnikov House
Einstein Tower
Schaubühne
Chiesa dell'Autostrada del Sole
Corso Italia Complex, Milan
Palazzetto dello Sport
Lovell Health House
National Congress, Brazil
Maison Drusch
Bank of China Tower, Hong Kong
Église Notre-Dame du Raincy
Centre Pompidou
Sulphuric Acid Factory, Lubon
Großes Schauspielhaus
Maison Tropicale
Toronto City Hall
Schröderhuis
Fagnano Olona Elementary School
San Cataldo Cemetery
Rudolph Hall
Gateway Arch
TWA Flight Center
Helsinki Central Railway Station
Habitat '67
Museo Canova
Berlin State Library
Sears Tower
Goetheanum
Neue Staatsgalerie
Leicester University Engineering Building
Braun AG Headquarters, Melsungen
Carson, Pirie, Scott and Company Building
Krause Music Store
National Olympic Gymnasium, Tokyo
Hufeisensiedlung
Casa del Fascio
Sydney Opera House
Farnsworth House
New National Gallery
Seagram Building
Tugendhat House
Vanna Venturi House
Mostorg Department Store
Palace of Labor
Kaiser Pavilion, Stadtbahn Station
Edgar J. Kaufmann House (Fallingwater)
Solomon R. Guggenheim Museum
S.C. Johnson & Son Headquarters
Frederick C. Robie House
Unity Temple
Philips Pavilion

Greg Lynn

Viipuri Municipal Library
House of the Century
The Woodland Cemetery
Futurama, 1939 New York World's Fair
Maison Bloc
Casa de Vidro
Museu de Arte de São Paulo
Alcuin Library
The Beinecke Rare Book & Manuscript Library
La Maison de Verre
Pacific Design Center
Steinhaus, Lake Ossiach
IBM Pavillion, NY World's Fair
The Eames House (Case Study House No. 8)
Design, Architecture, Art & Planning Building
Art Center College of Design, Pasadena
Dymaxion House
Casa Batlló
Vitra Design Museum
Hanselmann House
Bal Harbor Shops
Gwathmey Residence
Phaeno Science Center
Wall House II
Elbphilharmonie
Palais Stoclet
Retti Candle Shop
Hôtel Solvay
Villa Girasole
Expo '70 Osaka, Festival Plaza
Sendai Mediatheque
Langham Place, Hong Kong
Glass House
Performing Arts Theater, Fort Wayne
Endless House
Seattle Central Library
Maison à Bordeaux
Nakagin Capsule Tower
Bob and Dolores Hope Estate
Carpenter Center for the Visual Arts
Couvent Sainte-Marie de La Tourette
Villa Savoye
Casa Malaparte
Regional Council, Trento
Jewish Museum Berlin
Villa Müller
London Zoo Penguin Pool
Castle Drogo
Hill House, Helensburgh
Splitting, 1974
Fiat Works
Diamond Ranch High School
Rusakov Workers' Club
Petersdorff Department Store
Teatro Regio
Watergate Complex
Hayden Tract
US Air Force Academy Cadet Chapel
Kaufmann House
Das Canoas House
Gustavo Capanema Palace
Fondation Cartier pour l'Art Contemporain
Secession Building
Weissenhof Estate, Haus 5–9
Église Sainte-Bernadette du Banlay
Centre Pompidou
Westin Bonaventure Hotel
Snowdon Aviary
Rooftop Remodeling Falkestrasse
BMW Welt
Maison Tropicale
Schröderhuis
Knights of Columbus Building
Rogers House
Gallaratese II Apartments
Rudolph Residence, 23 Beekman Place
TWA Flight Center
First Christian Church, Columbus
Habitat '67
Berlin State Library
Schindler House
MLC Centre
Shukhov Tower
House of the Future, 1956
Solimene Ceramics Factory
Leicester University Engineering Building
Futuro House
Asilo Sant'Elia
Parc de la Villette
Bagsværd Church
Farnsworth House
Seagram Building
Tugendhat House
Gordon Wu Hall
Postsparkasse
Norris Dam
Indeterminate Façade Building
Solomon R. Guggenheim Museum
S.C. Johnson & Son Headquarters
George Sturges House

Winy Maas + Jacob van Rijs + Nathalie de Vries / MVRDV

Glass Pavilion
Helsinki Central Railway Station
Großes Schauspielhaus
Einstein Tower
Imperial Hotel, Tokyo
Liverpool Cathedral
Schröderhuis
Zuev Workers' Club
Chrysler Building
Milano Centrale Railway Station
Reichsparteitagsgelände
Battersea Power Station
Molitor Building
New Reich Chancellery
Barragán House and Studio
Glass House
Skylon, Festival of Britain
Royal Festival Hall
Bankside Power Station
Groothandselgebouw
Hiroshima Peace Memorial Museum
Taliesin West
Unité d'Habitation, Berlin
Maison Louis Carré
Esherick House
Michael Faraday Memorial
National Art Schools of Cuba
La Rinascente, Milan
Nordic Pavillion, Venice
New Saint Michael's Cathedral, Coventry
Carpenter Center for the Visual Arts
Vanna Venturi House
BT Tower
Marina City, Chicago
St. Peter's Seminary, Cardross
History Faculty Building, Cambridge
Orange County Government Centre, Goshen
Kafka Castle
Bensberg Town Hall
Toronto-Dominion Centre
Diagoon Housing
Pimlico Academy
Embassy of the United Kingdom, Rome
Olympic Stadium, Munich
Corviale
Trellick Tower
Brunswick Centre
Robin Hood Gardens
Douglas House
InterAction Centre, Kentish Town
Robarts Library
Sears Tower
Bank of Georgia headquarters, Tbilisi
Jewelry Store Schullin
Hirshhorn Museum
Retti Candle Shop
Yale Center for British Art
Cube Houses, Rotterdam
Prentice Women's Hospital Building
1 United Nations Plaza
Barbican Centre and Estate
CN Tower
Muziekcentrum Vredenburg
Crystal Cathedral
AT&T Building, New York
San Cataldo Cemetery
Bolwoningen
Venetian City Garden
Brixton Recreation Centre
Hongkong and Shanghai Bank Headquarters
Hundertwasserhaus
Tower of Winds, Yokohama
Nemausus
Central Research Institute of Robotics & Cybernetics
French Ministry for the Economy and Finance
Church on the Water
Pyramide du Louvre
Teatro Carlo Felice
Nexus World Housing
Allen Lambert Galleria
Fondation Cartier pour l'Art Contemporain
Paper Church, Kobe
The Hague City Hall
Maggie's Edinburgh
Dancing House
WoZoCo
Getty Center
Blades Residence
British Library
Castalia, The Hague
Maison à Bordeaux
O-Museum, Nagano
Zurichtoren
Borneo 12
Millennium Dome
Kunsthaus Graz
Eden Project
London Millennium Footbridge
Tate Modern
Sagrada Família

Fumihiko Maki

Beurs van Berlage
Glasgow School of Art
Postsparkasse
Frederick C. Robie House
AEG Turbine Factory
Gamble House
Casa Milà
Michaelerplatz House (Looshaus)
Einstein Tower
Schindler House
Schröderhuis
Lovell Beach House
Bauhaus Dessau
Stockholm Public Library
Villa Moller
German Pavilion (Barcelona Pavilion)
Van Nelle Factory
Villa Stein
Tugendhat House
Stockholm Exhibition of 1930
Villa Müller
Villa Savoye
La Maison de Verre
Casa del Fascio
Edgar J. Kaufmann House (Fallingwater)
S.C. Johnson & Son Headquarters
Villa Mairea
The Woodland Cemetery
Dymaxion House
L'Unité d'Habitation
The Eames House (Case Study House No. 8)
Farnsworth House
Baker House
Barragán House and Studio
Turin Exhibition Hall
Glass House
Crown Hall
Säynätsalo Town Hall
Lever House
The Assembly, Chandigarh
Muuratsalo Experimental House
Chapelle Notre-Dame du Haut
St. Mark's Church in Björkhagen
Municipal Orphanage
Sydney Opera House
Mill Owners' Association Building
Berliner Philharmonie
Couvent Sainte-Marie de La Tourette
Seagram Building
Museu de Arte de São Paulo
National Congress, Brazil
Solomon R. Guggenheim Museum
Leicester University Engineering Building
Salk Institute
Stahl House (Case Study House No. 22)
Halen Estate
TWA Flight Center
US Air Force Academy Cadet Chapel
Carpenter Center for the Visual Arts
Vanna Venturi House
John Deere World Headquarters
Querini Stampalia Renovation
The Beinecke Rare Book & Manuscript Library
Ford Foundation Headquarters
Free University of Berlin
National Olympic Gymnasium, Tokyo
Peabody Terrace
Sea Ranch Condominium Complex
Centre Le Corbusier (Heidi Weber House)
The Breuer Building (Whitney Museum)
Piscinas de Marés
Habitat '67
Hillside Terrace Complex I–VI
Smith House
New National Gallery
Olympic Stadium, Munich
Brion Family Tomb
House III (Miller House)
Nakagin Capsule Tower
Museum of Modern Art, Gunma
Centre Pompidou
Kimbell Art Museum
Phillips Exeter Academy Library
Centraal Beheer Building
Bagsværd Church
World Trade Center Towers
SESC Pompéia
Teatro del Mondo
Gehry House
Hongkong and Shanghai Bank Headquarters
Lloyd's of London
Parc de la Villette
National Assembly Building, Bangladesh
Neue Staatsgalerie
National Museum of Roman Art
The Menil Collection
Institut du Monde Arabe
Rooftop Remodeling Falkestrasse
Guggenheim Museum Bilbao
Sendai Mediatheque

Michael Maltzan

Leicester University Engineering Building
Beurs van Berlage
National Farmers Bank
AEG Turbine Factory
Posen Tower
Postsparkasse
Fagus Factory
Park Güell
Fiat Works
Schindler House
Ozenfant House
Schröderhuis
Schocken Department Store, Stuttgart
Bauhaus Dessau
Stockholm Public Library
Karl-Marx-Hof
Villa Moller
Melnikov House
German Pavilion (Barcelona Pavilion)
Open-air School, Amsterdam
Villa Savoye
Boots Pharmaceutical Factory
London Zoo Penguin Pool
Viipuri Municipal Library
Casa del Fascio
S.C. Johnson & Son Headquarters
W.E. Oliver House
Casa Malaparte
The Woodland Cemetery
Casa del Puente
Baker House
Barragán House and Studio
Glass House
Lever House
L'Unité d'Habitation
Muuratsalo Experimental House
Yale University Art Gallery
General Motors Technical Center
Villa Planchart
Gávea Housing Complex
Torre Velasca
860–880 Lake Shore Drive
Inland Steel Building
National Congress, Brazil
Couvent Sainte-Marie de La Tourette
The Beinecke Rare Book & Manuscript Library
Berliner Philharmonie
Vanna Venturi House
Peabody Terrace
National Olympic Gymnasium, Tokyo
National Museum of Anthropology
Sea Ranch Condominium Complex
The Economist Building, London
Gwathmey Residence
Piscinas de Marés
The Breuer Building (Whitney Museum)
Habitat '67
Hanselmann House
New National Gallery
Ford Foundation Headquarters
Art Center College of Design, Pasadena
Andrew Melville Hall
Mummers Theater
House II (Vermont House)
Nakagin Capsule Tower
Government Service Center, Boston
Robin Hood Gardens
Phillips Exeter Academy Library
Center for the Arts, Wesleyan University
Kresge College
Free University of Berlin
Gallaratese II Apartments
Centraal Beheer Building
Whig Hall, Princeton University
Willis Faber and Dumas Headquarters
Uehara House
John Hancock Tower
SESC Pompéia
Neue Staatsgalerie
Loyola Law School Campus
National Museum of Roman Art
Capela São Pedro Apóstolo
The Menil Collection
Institut du Monde Arabe
Museum of Sculpture, São Paulo
Vitra Design Museum Void
Space/Hinged Space Housing
Santa Maria Church de Canaveses
Nexus World Housing
Santa Caterina Market
Fondation Cartier pour l'Art Contemporain
Hayden Tract
Educatorium
21st Century Museum, Kanazawa
Nelson-Atkins Museum of Art Addition
Tama Art University Library
Iberê Camargo Foundation
Teshima Art Museum
1111 Lincoln Road
Madrid Public Housing

Thom Mayne / Morphosis

Postsparkasse
Schindler House
Fiat Works
Schröderhuis
Cité Frugès Housing Complex
Karl-Marx-Hof
Lovell Health House
Stockholm Public Library
Villa Moller
German Pavilion (Barcelona Pavilion)
Villa Savoye
La Maison de Verre
Villa Girasole
Edgar J. Kaufmann House (Fallingwater)
Casa del Fascio
The Woodland Cemetery
Casa Malaparte
Dymaxion House
Turin Exhibition Hall
Glass House
The Eames House (Case Study House No. 8)
Baker House
Muuratsalo Experimental House
Farnsworth House
L'Unité d'Habitation
Lever House
Pedregulho Housing Complex
Crown Hall
Maisons Jaoul
Chapelle Notre-Dame du Haut
Seagram Building
National Congress, Brazil
Philips Pavilion
Solomon R. Guggenheim Museum
Cité d'Habitacion of Carrières Centrales
Stahl House (Case Study House No. 22)
Couvent Sainte-Marie de La Tourette
Municipal Orphanage
Halen Estate
TWA Flight Center
Querini Stampalia Renovation
Berliner Philharmonie
Vanna Venturi House
National Olympic Gymnasium, Tokyo
Peabody Terrace
Rudolph Hall
Salk Institute
The Assembly, Chandigarh
Centre Le Corbusier (Heidi Weber House)
Piscinas de Marés
Bank of London and South America
Habitat '67
Smith House
Museu de Arte de São Paulo
Ford Foundation Headquarters
Kowloon Walled City
History Faculty Building, Cambridge
Benacerraf House Project
Flower Kiosk, Malmö Cemetery
Petrobras Headquarters
The Beinecke Rare Book & Manuscript Library
House III (Miller House)
Florey Building
Nakagin Capsule Tower
Olympic Stadium, Munich
Phillips Exeter Academy Library
Kimbell Art Museum
Free University of Berlin
Byker Wall
Centraal Beheer Building
Whig Hall, Princeton University
Bagsværd Church
Brion Family Tomb
Centre Pompidou
SESC Pompéia
Hedmark Cathedral Museum
Gehry House
Teatro del Mondo
Atheneum, New Harmony
Koshino House
Vietnam Veterans Memorial
National Assembly Building, Bangladesh
Neue Staatsgalerie
Lloyd's of London
Hongkong and Shanghai Bank Headquarters
Steinhaus, Lake Ossiach
Rooftop Remodeling Falkestrasse
National Museum of Roman Art
Void Space/Hinged Space Housing
Igualada Cemetery
Parc de la Villette
Maison à Bordeaux
Samitaur Tower
Guggenheim Museum Bilbao
UFA Cinema Centre
Jewish Museum Berlin
Bordeaux Law Courts
Diamond Ranch High School
Yokohama International Port Terminal
Sendai Mediatheque

Richard Meier

Sydney Opera House
Maison Louis Carré
Hongkong and Shanghai Bank Headquarters
Church of the Light
Magney House
Tate Modern
Centre Pompidou
Lloyd's of London
Barragán House and Studio
Camino Real Hotel, Mexico City
Nara Centennial Hall
Kaze-no-Oka Crematorium
Slither Housing
Petronas Towers
Kiasma
Wall House II
Serralves Museum of Contemporary Art
National Gallery of Art, East Building
BMW Central Building
De Blas House
Neuer Zollhof
Jewish Museum Berlin
Alfonse M. D'Amato United States Courthouse
Neugebauer House
National Farmers Bank
Chrysler Building
The Woodland Cemetery
Bauhaus Dessau
AEG Turbine Factory
Beurs van Berlage
Open-air School, Amsterdam
Van Nelle Factory
Flatiron Building
La Maison de Verre
Museum of the Great War
Zuev Workers' Club
Kanchanjunga Apartments
Gustavo Capanema Palace
Van Doesburg House
Palau de la Música Catalana
Hilversum Town Hall
The Eames House (Case Study House No. 8)
Berlin Memorial to the Murdered Jews of Europe
Municipal Orphanage
Figini House
Josef Frank House, Vienna
Casa Milà
Guggenheim Museum Bilbao
Woolworth Building
E-1027
Gamble House
Métropolitain Entrance
Palais Stoclet
Chapel of St. Ignatius
Glass House
Seagram Building
Rockefeller Center
Villa Stein
Chapelle Notre-Dame du Haut
Salk Institute
Villa dall'Ava
East Bohemian Museum
Casa Malaparte
Villa Müller
Castle Drogo
Glasgow School of Art
Villa Allatini and Villa de Daniel Dreyfuss
Bingham House, Santa Barbara
Pennsylvania Station
Getty Center
Melnikov House
Einstein Tower
German Pavilion (Barcelona Pavilion)
National Museum of Roman Art
Lovell Health House
Palácio do Planalto
Joseph Maria Olbrich's House
Weissenhof Estate, Haus 5-9
Church of the Most Sacred Heart of Our Lord
Großes Schauspielhaus
Schröderhuis
Ford Foundation Headquarters
Rudolph Hall
TWA Flight Center
Cranbrook Academy of Art
Castelvecchio Museum
Berliner Philharmonie
Lovell Beach House
Fundació Joan Miró
Lever House
The Economist Building, London
Leicester University Engineering Building
Glass Pavilion
Casa del Fascio
Postsparkasse
Unity Temple
Frederick C. Robie House
Edgar J. Kaufmann House (Fallingwater)
S.C. Johnson & Son Headquarters
Solomon R. Guggenheim Museum

Rafael Moneo

Secession Building
Rue Franklin Apartments
Glasgow School of Art
Gamble House
AEG Turbine Factory
Frederick C. Robie House
Michaelerplatz House (Looshaus)
Posen Tower
Palais Stoclet
Postsparkasse
Festival Hall, Hellerau
Spaarndammerplantsoen
Rashtrapati Bhavan
Schindler House
Ca' Brutta
Casa Milà
Schröderhuis
Bauhaus Dessau
Villa Müller
Lovell Health House
Weiße Stadt, Berlin
Villa Savoye
Van Nelle Factory
ADGB Trade Union School
Schocken Department Store, Stuttgart
Boots Pharmaceutical Factory
Hilversum Town Hall
Casa Malaparte
Tugendhat House
Casa de las Flores, Madrid
Edificio Carrión
Cineac
Casa del Fascio
Villa Mairea
Rockefeller Center
The Woodland Cemetery
Göteborg Town Hall
S.C. Johnson & Son Headquarters
National and University Library of Slovenia
Resurrection Chapel, Turku
Casa del Puente
XYZ Buildings, New York
Lever House
Borsalino Housing
Capilla de las Capuchinas
Pedregulho Housing Complex
Casa Il Girasole
Mill Owners' Association Building
Munkegaard School
Civil Government Building, Tarragona
Torre Velasca
Sydney Opera House
Seagram Building
Municipal Orphanage
Yale University Art Gallery
The Breuer Building (Whitney Museum)
Casa Ugalde
National Congress, Brazil
Kline Biology Tower
Rudolph Hall
Retti Candle Shop
TWA Flight Center
La Rinascente, Milan
Leicester University Engineering Building
Berliner Philharmonie
Querini Stampalia Renovation
Vanna Venturi House
Peabody Terrace
National Olympic Gymnasium, Tokyo
The Economist Building, London
Sea Ranch Condominium Complex
Torre Blancas
Museu de Arte de São Paulo
Ford Foundation Headquarters
John Hancock Tower
Indian Institute of Management, Ahmedabad
House II (Vermont House)
Centraal Beheer Building
Twin Parks Northeast Housing
Tokyo Metropolitan Art Museum
Gallaratese II Apartments
Centre Pompidou
Sainsbury Center for Visual Arts
Hedmark Cathedral Museum
Faculty of Architecture of the University of Porto
Portland Building
Neue Staatsgalerie
Loyola Law School Campus
Church of the Light
Bank of China Tower, Hong Kong
Igualada Cemetery
Private House, Corrubedo
Portuguese National Pavilion
Maison à Bordeaux
Therme Vals
Dominus Winery
Guggenheim Museum Bilbao
Kiasma
Gifu Kitagata Apartment Building
Sendai Mediatheque

Eric Owen Moss

Larkin Company Administration Building
AEG Turbine Factory
Glasgow School of Art
Park Güell
Großes Schauspielhaus
Einstein Tower
Fiat Works
Shukhov Tower
Schindler House
Hutfabrik Friedrich Steinberg, Herrmann & Co.
Imperial Hotel, Tokyo
Schröderhuis
Magazzini Generali, Chiasso
Lovell Beach House
Bauhaus Dessau
Gut Garkau Farm
Weissenhof Estate, Exhibition of 1927
Villa Moller
Rusakov Workers' Club
Narkomfin Building
Melnikov House
Lovell Health House
German Pavilion (Barcelona Pavilion)
Villa Savoye
Ogonyok Magazine Printing Plant
Edgar J. Kaufmann House (Fallingwater)
Casa del Fascio
S.C. Johnson & Son Headquarters
Aarhus City Hall
The Eames House (Case Study House No. 8)
Glass House
Farnsworth House
Säynätsalo Town Hall
Lever House
Capilla de las Capuchinas
Watts Towers
Iglesia de la Medalla Milagrosa
Chapelle Notre-Dame du Haut
Sydney Opera House
National Congress, Brazil
National Library, Brasília
North Shore Beach and Yacht Club
Church of the Three Crosses
Municipal Orphanage
Couvent Sainte-Marie de La Tourette
Stahl House (Case Study House No. 22)
St. John's Abbey, Collegeville
TWA Flight Center
Querini Stampalia Renovation
John Deere World Headquarters
Berliner Philharmonie
Leicester University Engineering Building
Palm Springs Aerial Tramway Valley Station
Sheats Goldstein Residence
Carpenter Center for the Visual Arts
Peabody Terrace
Rudolph Hall
Vanna Venturi House
National Olympic Gymnasium, Tokyo
Frey House II
The Assembly, Chandigarh
Salk Institute
National Art Schools of Cuba
Retti Candle Shop
Shizuoka Press and Broadcasting Center
Habitat '67
Knights of Columbus Building
Benacerraf House Project
Geisel Library
Expo' 70 Tower, Osaka
Phillips Exeter Academy Library
Florey Building
Aula Paolo VI
Nakagin Capsule Tower
Olympic Stadium, Munich
Free University of Berlin
San Francisco State Student Center
Douglas House
Museum of Modern Art, Gunma
Gallaratese II Apartments
Kitakyushu International Conference Center
Indian Institute of Management, Ahmedabad
Bagsværd Church
Transvaal House
Gehry House
Ramot Polin
Steinhaus, Lake Ossiach
National Museum of Roman Art
Marina City, Chicago
House of the Suicide
Rooftop Remodeling Falkestrasse
Wexner Center for the Visual Arts
Igualada Cemetery
Berliner Philharmonie
Diamond Ranch High School
Chapel of St. Ignatius
Jean-Marie Tjibaou Cultural Centre
Stealth, Culver City
Sagrada Família
MIT Chapel

Enrique Norten / TEN Arquitectos

Rue Franklin Apartments
Larkin Company Administration Building
AEG Turbine Factory
Glasgow School of Art
Gamble House
Frederick C. Robie House
Casa Milà
Fagus Factory
Park Güell
Michaelerplatz House (Looshaus)
Einstein Tower
Ozenfant House
Soviet Pavilion
Lovell Beach House
Sagrada Família
Bauhaus Dessau
Stockholm Public Library
German Pavilion (Barcelona Pavilion)
Rusakov Workers' Club
Narkomfin Building
Casa Estudio Diego Rivera y Frida Kahlo
Villa Müller
Villa Savoye
Edgar J. Kaufmann House (Fallingwater)
Casa del Fascio
Asilo Sant'Elia
S.C. Johnson & Son Headquarters
Villa Mairea
Súper Servicio Lomas
Centro Urbano Presidente Alemán
Dymaxion House
New Gouma Village Mosque
Barragán House and Studio
Turin Exhibition Hall
The Eames House (Case Study House No. 8)
Museo Experimental El Eco
Biblioteca Central, UNAM
Rectoría Building, UNAM
Olympic University Stadium, UNAM
Faculty of Philosophy and Letters, UNAM
Gante Indoor Garage
Torre Latinoamericana
Conjunto Aristos
Torres de Satélite
Farnsworth House
Lever House
Muuratsalo Experimental House
Iglesia de la Medalla Milagrosa
Chapelle Notre-Dame du Haut
The Assembly, Chandigarh
MIT Chapel
Sydney Opera House
Mill Owners' Association Building
Palazzetto dello Sport
Cube House, Köln
National Congress, Brazil
Los Manantiales
Conjunto Urbano Nonoalco Tlatelolco
Palacio de los Deportes
Celanese Mexicana
Capilla de las Capuchinas
Couvent Sainte-Marie de La Tourette
Carpenter Center for the Visual Arts
Berliner Philharmonie
Otaniemi Technical University
Vanna Venturi House
Centre Le Corbusier (Heidi Weber House)
Salk Institute
Piscinas de Marés
Edifício Copan
The Breuer Building (Whitney Museum)
Habitat '67
Museu de Arte de São Paulo
New National Gallery
Cuadra San Cristóbal
Art Center College of Design, Pasadena
Itamaraty Palace
Kimbell Art Museum
Castelvecchio Museum
Gallaratese II Apartments
Marie Short House
SESC Pompéia
Centre Pompidou
Teatro del Mondo
Museo Rufino Tamayo
Koshino House
Hongkong and Shanghai Bank Headquarters
National Museum of Roman Art
The Menil Collection
Televisa Mixed Use Building
Escuela Nacional de Teatro
Casa LE
Hotel Habita, Mexico City
Igualada Cemetery
Kunsthal, Rotterdam
Goetz Collection
Therme Vals
Kunsthaus Bregenz
Chapel of St. Ignatius
Guggenheim Museum Bilbao

José Oubrerie

L'Esprit Nouveau Pavilion
Villa La Roche
Villa Savoye
L'Unité d'Habitation
Chapelle Notre-Dame du Haut
Villa Sarabhai
Villa Shodhan
Mill Owners' Association Building
Maisons Jaoul
Couvent Sainte-Marie de La Tourette
The Assembly, Chandigarh
Carpenter Center for the Visual Arts
Centre Le Corbusier (Heidi Weber House)
German Pavilion (Barcelona Pavilion)
Tugendhat House
Weissenhof Estate, Exhibition of 1927
Farnsworth House
Crown Hall
New National Gallery
Villa Mairea
Studio Aalto
Stockholm Public Library
Baker House
Church of the Three Crosses
Unity Temple
Frederick C. Robie House
Edgar J. Kaufmann House (Fallingwater)
S.C. Johnson & Son Headquarters
Millard House
Richards Medical Research Laboratories
Phillips Exeter Academy Library
Kimbell Art Museum
Salk Institute
Indian Institute of Management, Ahmedabad
National Assembly Building, Bangladesh
Villa Müller
Villa Moller
Café Museum
Casa Milà
Park Güell
Gehry House
Vitra Design Museum
Guggenheim Museum Bilbao
Schindler House
Lovell Beach House
Leicester University Engineering Building
Andrew Melville Hall
Querini Stampalia Renovation
Castelvecchio Museum
Brion Family Tomb
Lever House
The Beinecke Rare Book & Manuscript Library
Wexner Center for the Visual Arts
House III (Miller House)
House VI
Kiasma
Chapel of St. Ignatius
Nelson-Atkins Museum of Art Addition
Kate Mantilini, Beverly Hills
Venice III House
Diamond Ranch High School
Villa dall'Ava
Maison à Bordeaux
Congrexpo
Kunsthal, Rotterdam
Fondation Cartier pour l'Art Contemporain
Institut du Monde Arabe
Rooftop Remodeling Falkestrasse
UFA Cinema Centre
Lloyd's of London
Vitra Fire Station
Miller House, Lexington
Free University of Berlin
Centre Pompidou
TWA Flight Center
Municipal Orphanage
Igualada Cemetery
Allied Bank Tower
Rue Franklin Apartments
Glasgow School of Art
Bauhaus Dessau
Narkomfin Building
E-1027
La Maison de Verre
The Eames House (Case Study House No. 8)
Casa Malaparte
Schröderhuis
Einstein Tower
Casa del Fascio
Lovell Health House
Gamble House
Rusakov Workers' Club
Berliner Philharmonie
The Woodland Cemetery
St. Mark's Church in Björkhagen
Barragán House and Studio
National Congress, Brazil
Glass House
Stahl House (Case Study House No. 22)
Goetheanum

César Pelli

Beurs van Berlage
Rue Franklin Apartments
AEG Turbine Factory
Glasgow School of Art
Gamble House
Union Bank, Columbus, Wisconsin
Larkin Company Administration Building
Unity Temple
Frederick C. Robie House
Fagus Factory
Pennsylvania Station
Het Schip
Schindler House
Fiat Works
Schröderhuis
Cité Frugès Housing Complex
Lovell Beach House
Karl-Marx-Hof
Lovell Health House
German Pavilion (Barcelona Pavilion)
Einstein Tower
Bauhaus Dessau
Goetheanum
Villa Savoye
La Maison de Verre
Edgar J. Kaufmann House (Fallingwater)
Casa del Fascio
S.C. Johnson & Son Headquarters
Chrysler Building
Rockefeller Center
The Woodland Cemetery
Dymaxion House
Baker House
Glass House
The Eames House (Case Study House No. 8)
Cranbrook Academy of Art
Carpenter Center for the Visual Arts
Farnsworth House
L'Unité d'Habitation
Lever House
Chapelle Notre-Dame du Haut
Sydney Opera House
Seagram Building
Solomon R. Guggenheim Museum
Crown Hall
Maisons Jaoul
Mill Owners' Association Building
Miller House, Columbus
Church of Cristo Obrero
Stahl House (Case Study House No. 22)
Couvent Sainte-Marie de La Tourette
TWA Flight Center
Snowdon Aviary
John Deere World Headquarters
Berliner Philharmonie
Leicester University Engineering Building
National Olympic Gymnasium, Tokyo
Rudolph Hall
Vanna Venturi House
Salk Institute
The Assembly, Chandigarh
Bank of London and South America
Smith House
Hyatt Regency, Atlanta
Ford Foundation Headquarters
Museu de Arte de São Paulo
Knights of Columbus Building
Andrew Melville Hall
Fire Station No. 4, Columbus
COMSAT Laboratories
Sea Ranch Condominium Complex
Nakagin Capsule Tower
Olympic Stadium, Munich
Phillips Exeter Academy Library
Snyderman House
Kimbell Art Museum
Free University of Berlin
House VI
Casa Bianchi
Whig Hall, Princeton University
Centre Pompidou
Brion Family Tomb
Gehry House
Teatro del Mondo
Very Large Array
Vietnam Veterans Memorial
National Assembly Building, Bangladesh
Lloyd's of London
Hongkong and Shanghai Bank Headquarters
National Museum of Roman Art
Steinhaus, Lake Ossiach
Igualada Cemetery
Parc de la Villette
Congrexpo
Samitaur Tower
Guggenheim Museum Bilbao
Diamond Ranch High School
Jewish Museum Berlin
Sendai Mediatheque
Petronas Towers

Dominique Perrault

Métropolitain Entrance
Park Güell
Halle Tony Garnier
AEG Turbine Factory
Glasgow School of Art
Ford Motor Company Glass Manufacturing Plant
Einstein Tower
Église Notre-Dame du Raincy
Fiat Works
Chilehaus
Tristan Tzara House
La Maison de Verre
Rusakov Workers' Club
Stockholm Public Library
Paimio Sanatorium
German Pavilion (Barcelona Pavilion)
Casa Malaparte
Chrysler Building
Gratte-ciel, Villeurbanne
Villa Cavrois
London Zoo Penguin Pool
Gustavo Capanema Palace
Palais d'Iéna
Rockefeller Center
S.C. Johnson & Son Headquarters
Palazzo della Civiltà Italiana
Glass House
Barragán House and Studio
General Motors Technical Center
Farnsworth House
United Nations Headquarters
L'Unité d'Habitation
Annakirche, Düren
St. Mary's Cathedral, Tokyo
Chapelle Notre-Dame du Haut
Maison des Jours Meilleurs
Climat de France, Algiers
Complesso Olivetti
Atomium
Seagram Building
Sky House, Tokyo
Pirelli Tower
Valle de los Caídos
Stahl House (Case Study House No. 22)
Solomon R. Guggenheim Museum
Capilla de las Capuchinas
Habitat '67
Snowdon Aviary
Palazzo del Lavoro
Nordic Pavillion, Venice
Mémorial des Martyrs de la Déportation
The Breuer Building (Whitney Museum)
Salk Institute
Église Sainte-Bernadette du Banlay
Piscinas de Marés
Montreal Biosphère
New National Gallery
John Hancock Center
Marina City, Chicago
Hew Offices, Hamburg
Maison d'Iran
FAU, University of São Paulo
Fondation Maison des sciences de l'homme
United States Pavilion Expo '70, Osaka
Danmarks Nationalbank, Copenhagen
French Communist Party Headquarters, Paris
Olympic Stadium, Munich
Phillips Exeter Academy Library
Nakagin Capsule Tower
Sydney Opera House
White U
Centre Pompidou
Berlin State Library
SESC Pompéia
Hongkong and Shanghai Bank Headquarters
Church on the Water
Lloyd's of London
Church of the Light
Bonjour Tristesse, Berlin
Stone House, Tavole
Pyramide du Louvre
Grande Arche
Fondation Cartier pour l'Art Contemporain
Kunsthal, Rotterdam
Museum of Sculpture, São Paulo
Goetz Collection
Faculty of Architecture of the University of Porto
Sofitel, Tokyo
Velodrome and Olympic Swimming Pool, Berlin
Sendai Mediatheque
National Library of France
Tate Modern
Acros Building
Yokohama International Port Terminal
Guggenheim Museum Bilbao
Therme Vals
Gifu Kitagata Apartment Building
Maison à Bordeaux
21st Century Museum Kanazawa
Jewish Museum Berlin

Carme Pinós

Larkin Company Administration Building
AEG Turbine Factory
Glasgow School of Art
Casa Milà
Park Güell
Einstein Tower
Fiat Works
Van Nelle Factory
Schröderhuis
Soviet Pavilion
Lovell Beach House
Villa Moller
E-1027
German Pavilion (Barcelona Pavilion)
Rusakov Workers' Club
Stockholm Exhibition of 1930
Villa Savoye
La Maison de Verre
Edgar J. Kaufmann House (Fallingwater)
S.C. Johnson & Son Headquarters
Arve Bridge
The Woodland Cemetery
Casa Malaparte
Baker House
Turin Exhibition Hall
The Eames House (Case Study House No. 8)
Architect's Second House, São Paulo
Farnsworth House
Säynätsalo Town Hall
L'Unité d'Habitation
Cité d'Habitacion of Carrières Centrales
Chapelle Notre-Dame du Haut
The Assembly, Chandigarh
St. Mark's Church in Björkhagen
MIT Chapel
Sydney Opera House
Richards Medical Research Laboratories
Palazzetto dello Sport
Torre Velasca
Seagram Building
Museum of Modern Art, Rio de Janeiro
Solomon R. Guggenheim Museum
Los Manantiales
Pepsi-Cola Building
Couvent Sainte-Marie de La Tourette
Snowdon Aviary
Carpenter Center for the Visual Arts
TWA Flight Center
Berliner Philharmonie
Leicester University Engineering Building
National Olympic Gymnasium, Tokyo
Otaniemi Technical University
The Economist Building, London
Gwathmey Residence
Salk Institute
High Court, Assembly, Chandigarh
Montessori School, Delft
Sonsbeek Pavilion
The Breuer Building (Whitney Museum)
Norman Fisher House
Torre Blancas
Ford Foundation Headquarters
Museu de Arte de São Paulo
New National Gallery
History Faculty Building, Cambridge
Art Center College of Design, Pasadena
Knights of Columbus Building
Mivtachim Sanitarium
Florey Building
Can Lis, Majorca
Olympic Stadium, Munich
Phillips Exeter Academy Library
Castelvecchio Museum
Free University of Berlin
Douglas House
House VI
Marie Short House
Bagsværd Church
Sainsbury Center for Visual Arts
World Trade Center Towers
SESC Pompéia
Centre Pompidou
Brion Family Tomb
Gehry House
Teatro del Mondo
Warehouse, Port of Montevideo
National Assembly Building, Bangladesh
Hongkong and Shanghai Bank Headquarters
Church of the Light
Rooftop Remodeling Falkestrasse
Igualada Cemetery
Storefront for Art and Architecture
Signal Box Auf dem Wolf
Vitra Fire Station
Therme Vals
WoZoCo
Guggenheim Museum Bilbao
Diamond Ranch High School
Yokohama International Port Terminal
American Folk Art Museum

James S. Polshek

Rose Center for Earth and Space
Clinton Presidential Center
Larkin Company Administration Building
Glasgow School of Art
Unity Temple
Casa Milà
Imperial Hotel, Tokyo
Schindler House
Van Nelle Factory
Schröderhuis
Café De Unie
Sagrada Família
Villa Stein
German Pavilion (Barcelona Pavilion)
Villa Müller
Tugendhat House
Villa Savoye
Hilversum Town Hall
Paimio Sanatorium
La Maison de Verre
Edgar J. Kaufmann House (Fallingwater)
S.C. Johnson & Son Headquarters
Villa Mairea
Aarhus City Hall
Barragán House and Studio
The Eames House (Case Study House No. 8)
Farnsworth House
L'Unité d'Habitation
Chapelle Notre-Dame du Haut
Villa Sarabhai
Sydney Opera House
Maisons Jaoul
Mill Owners' Association Building
Richards Medical Research Laboratories
Philips Pavilion
National Library, Brasília
Solomon R. Guggenheim Museum
Taliesin West
Torres de Satélite
Maison Louis Carré
Pepsi-Cola Building
Couvent Sainte-Marie de La Tourette
Municipal Orphanage, Amsterdam
Halen Estate
Nordic Pavilion, Venice
TWA Flight Center
Querini Stampalia Renovation
Gateway Arch
John Deere World Headquarters
Berliner Philharmonie
Leicester University Engineering Building
Otaniemi Technical University
Rudolph Hall
National Art Schools of Cuba
Salk Institute
The Assembly, Chandigarh
Montessori School, Delft
Retti Candle Shop
Ford Foundation Headquarters
History Faculty Building, Cambridge
National Assembly Building, Bangladesh
Indian Institute of Management, Ahmedabad
Teijin Institute for Biomedical Research
Charles De Gaulle Airport, Terminal 1 & 2A–2F
Can Lis, Majorca
Phillips Exeter Academy Library
Franklin D. Roosevelt Four Freedoms Park
Kimbell Art Museum
Castelvecchio Museum
Museum of Modern Art, Gunma
Yale Center for British Art
Town Hall, Logroño
Willis Faber and Dumas Headquarters
Centre Pompidou
Vietnam Veterans Memorial
Smith House
Lloyd's of London
Hongkong and Shanghai Bank Headquarters
The Menil Collection
Institut du Monde Arabe
Pyramide du Louvre
TEPIA Science Pavilion, Tokyo
Neue Staatsgalerie
Norwegian Glacier Museum
Fondation Cartier pour l'Art Contemporain
Neurosciences Institute, La Jolla
Therme Vals
Chapel of St. Ignatius
Jean-Marie Tjibaou Cultural Centre
Diamond Ranch High School
O-Museum, Nagano
Parco della Musica
Mercedes-Benz Museum
Tama Art University Library
CaixaForum Madrid
41 Cooper Square
Parc de la Villette
Bordeaux Law Courts
American Folk Art Museum
Kiasma

Mónica Ponce de León

Park Güell
Larkin Company Administration Building
AEG Turbine Factory
Broomfield Rowhouse
Casa Milà
Widener Memorial Library
Ford Motor Company Glass Manufacturing Plant
The Woodland Cemetery
E-1027
Schröderhuis
Bauhaus Dessau
Boston Avenue Methodist Church
Weissenhof Estate, Haus 5-9
Villa Moller
German Pavilion (Barcelona Pavilion)
Lovell Health House
Open-Air School, Amsterdam
Villa Savoye
Casa del Fascio
S.C. Johnson & Son Headquarters
Villa Mairea
Casa del Puente
The Eames House (Case Study House No. 8)
General Motors Technical Center
Lever House
Casa Il Girasole
Casa de Vidro
Pedregulho Housing Complex
L'Unité d'Habitation
Aula Magna, Caracas
Edifício Copan
The Economist Building, London
Eduardo Guinle Park Housing
Seagram Building
Chapelle Notre-Dame du Haut
St. Mark's Church in Björkhagen
Glass House
Pryor House
Villa Planchart
Los Manantiales
Bank of London and South America
Solomon R. Guggenheim Museum
Church of Cristo Obrero
Halen Estate
Ichinomiya Rowhouses
National Art Schools of Cuba
Theme Building
Aalto-Hochhaus, Bremen
TWA Flight Center
Nordic Pavillion, Venice
Rudolph Hall
Donald Pollock House
Berliner Philharmonie
Marina City, Chicago
Chiesa dell'Autostrada del Sole
University Reformed Church, Ann Arbor
Peabody Terrace
Vanna Venturi House
Phillips Exeter Academy Library
John Hancock Center
Saint Francis de Sales Church
Centraal Beheer Building
John Hancock Tower
Oakland Museum of California
World Trade Center Towers
University Art Museum, Berkeley
Sears Tower
San Cataldo Cemetery
Centre Pompidou
Nakagin Capsule Tower
Kimbell Art Museum
Sydney Opera House
Embassy of the United States, Tokyo
Casa Gilardi
Allen Memorial Art Museum, Oberlin
Thorncrown Chapel
Musée d'Orsay
National Museum of Roman Art
San Juan Capistrano Library
Hongkong and Shanghai Bank Headquarters
Parc de la Villette
Igualada Cemetery
Ricola Storage Building
Housing Schilderswijk West
Tokyo Metropolitan Gymnasium
Nexus World Housing
Void Space/Hinged Space Housing
Robert F. Wagner, Jr. Park, New York
Villa VPRO
Vitra Fire Station
Yokohama International Port Terminal
Bruton Barr Library
Santa Caterina Market
Walt Disney Concert Hall
Nomentana Residence
Diamond Ranch High School
N Museum, Wakayama
Jewish Museum Berlin
Hayden Tract
City of Culture of Galicia

Antoine Predock

Larkin Company Administration Building
AEG Turbine Factory
Glasgow School of Art
Gamble House
Unity Temple
Frederick C. Robie House
Casa Milà
Einstein Tower
Schindler House
Fiat Works
Sagrada Família
E-1027
Goetheanum
German Pavilion (Barcelona Pavilion)
Zarzuela Hippodrome
Tugendhat House
Villa Savoye
Hilversum Town Hall
La Maison de Verre
Villa Girasole
Edgar J. Kaufmann House (Fallingwater)
S.C. Johnson & Son Headquarters
Villa Mairea
Arve Bridge
The Woodland Cemetery
Casa Malaparte
Dymaxion House
New Gourna Village Mosque
Barragán House and Studio
Turin Exhibition Hall
The Eames House (Case Study House No. 8)
Farnsworth House
Säynätsalo Town Hall
Chapelle Notre-Dame du Haut
The Assembly, Chandigarh
MIT Chapel
Sydney Opera House
Seagram Building
Louisiana Museum of Modern Art
National Congress, Brazil
Solomon R. Guggenheim Museum
Hiroshima Peace Memorial Museum
Los Manantiales
Pepsi-Cola Building
Stahl House (Case Study House No. 22)
Couvent Sainte-Marie de La Tourette
Prairie Chicken House
Halen Estate
US Air Force Academy Cadet Chapel
TWA Flight Center
The Beinecke Rare Book & Manuscript Library
Berliner Philharmonie
Leicester University Engineering Building
National Museum of Anthropology
Rudolph Hall
Salk Institute
High Court, Assembly, Chandigarh
Sea Ranch Condominium Complex
Piscinas de Marés
The Breuer Building (Whitney Museum)
Habitat '67
Xanadú, Calpe
Pilgrimage Church, Neviges
Art Center College of Design, Pasadena
Sheats Goldstein Residence
Nakagin Capsule Tower
Olympic Stadium, Munich
Phillips Exeter Academy Library
Kimbell Art Museum
Castelvecchio Museum
Casa Bianchi
Bagsværd Church
World Trade Center Towers
Centre Pompidou
Brion Family Tomb
Gehry House
Teatro del Mondo
Atheneum, New Harmony
Coxe-Hayden House and Studio
Vietnam Veterans Memorial
National Assembly Building, Bangladesh
Allied Bank Tower
Hongkong and Shanghai Bank Headquarters
National Museum of Roman Art
Church of the Light
Institut du Monde Arabe
Museum of Sculpture, São Paulo
Rooftop Remodeling Falkestrasse
Evergreen Building, Vancouver
Igualada Cemetery
Goetz Collection
Villa dall'Ava
Samitaur Tower
Therme Vals
Stretto House
6th Street House, Santa Monica
Marika-Alderton House
Santa Maria Church de Canaveses
Benesse House
Mesa Laboratory

Wolf D. Prix / Coop Himmelb(l)au

Monument to the Third International
German Pavilion (Barcelona Pavilion)
Philips Pavilion
Museu de Arte de São Paulo
Centre Le Corbusier (Heidi Weber House)
Centre Pompidou
Guggenheim Museum Bilbao
Austrian Cultural Forum
Jewish Museum Berlin
Vulcania Centre Européen du Volcanisme
Walt Disney Concert Hall
Seattle Central Library
Kanno Museum
BMW Welt
City of Culture of Galicia
Sifang Art Museum
CaixaForum Zaragoza
Heydar Aliyev Center
Musée des Confluences
Sagrada Família
Great Mosque of Djenné
Goetheanum
Chapelle Notre-Dame du Haut
Couvent Sainte-Marie de La Tourette
Cathedral of Brasília
Église Sainte-Bernadette du Banlay
Brion Family Tomb
Wotruba Church
Martin Luther Church, Hainburg
Olympic Stadium, Munich
Großes Schauspielhaus
Rusakov Workers' Club
Berliner Philharmonie
Sydney Opera House
Umbrella, Culver City
Dalian International Conference Center
Elbphilharmonie
Einstein Tower
Diamond Ranch High School
41 Cooper Square
Rolex Learning Center
Lovell Health House
Villa Savoye
Edgar J. Kaufmann House (Fallingwater)
Endless House
Stahl House (Case Study House No. 22)
Fuente de los Amantes
Das Canoas House
Chemosphere
Maison Drusch
Maison Bordeaux le Pecq
Studio Baumann, Vienna
Solohouse
Steinhaus, Lake Ossiach
Gehry House
Embryological House
L'Unité d'Habitation
Pedregulho Housing Complex
Edifício Copan
Habitat '67
Nakagin Capsule Tower
Torre Cube
Linked Hybrid
7132 Hotel & Arrival
Postsparkasse
Michaelerplatz House (Looshaus)
Loos' Tribune Tower Competition
Seagram Building
Salk Institute
BMW Hochhaus Vierzylinder
Bank of Georgia headquarters, Tbilisi
Zentralsparkasse Bank, Vienna
Hongkong and Shanghai Bank Headquarters
Pterodactyl, Culver City
CCTV Headquarters
Seat of the European Central Bank
Los Manantiales
Retti Candle Shop
Rooftop Remodeling Falkestrasse
Vitra Fire Station
Santa Caterina Market
Merida Factory Youth Movement
Kaiser Pavilion, Stadtbahn Station
National Congress, Brazil
Copacabana Breach Promenade
Radical Reconstruction in Havana
The City of the Future, Los Angeles 2106
TWA Flight Center
Druzhba Holiday Center Hall
The Golem (Film)
Wolkenbügel
New Babylon
The Sin Centre, London
Aircraft Carrier City in Landscape
Walking City
Plug-In City
Unterirdische Stadt
Wingnut, Stockholm
The Continuous Monument
Inhabiting the Quake

Jesse Reiser + Nanako Umemoto

Figini House
Villa Savoye
Chapelle Notre-Dame du Haut
Couvent Sainte-Marie de La Tourette
Villa Stein
The Assembly, Chandigarh
Villa Shodhan
Villa La Roche
Mill Owners' Association Building
L'Unité d'Habitation
Gallaratese II Apartments
Società Ippica Torinese
Casa Miller, Turin
TWA Flight Center
Cleveland Museum of Art, North Entrance
De Bijenkorf, Rotterdam
The Breuer Building (Whitney Museum)
Josephine Hagerty House
Casa Malaparte
Villa Mairea
Finlandia Hall
Paimio Sanatorium
National Congress, Brazil
Palácio do Planalto
Palácio da Alvorada
Frederick C. Robie House
Solomon R. Guggenheim Museum
S.C. Johnson & Son Headquarters
Edgar J. Kaufmann House (Fallingwater)
Unity Temple
Larkin Company Administration Building
Fagus Factory
Gropius House, Lincoln
Bauhaus Dessau
Weissenhof Estate, Haus 28-30
Hellerhof Estate
Einstein Tower
Hutfabrik Friedrich Steinberg, Herrmann & Co.
Schocken Department Store, Stuttgart
Villa Müller
Michaelerplatz House (Looshaus)
Villa Karma
Steiner House
American Bar, Vienna
Sulphuric Acid Factory, Lubon
Posen Tower
AEG Turbine Factory
Kreuzberg Tower
Berliner Philharmonie
Weissenhof Estate, Haus 33
German Pavilion (Barcelona Pavilion)
860–880 Lake Shore Drive
Seagram Building
Farnsworth House
Tugendhat House
Weissenhof Estate, Exhibition of 1927
Crown Hall
New National Gallery
Free University of Berlin
Salk Institute
Kimbell Art Museum
National Assembly Building, Bangladesh
Phillips Exeter Academy Library
Gwathmey Residence
House VI
Berlin Memorial to the Murdered Jews of Europe
City of Culture of Galicia
Smith House
Douglas House
Atheneum, New Harmony
High Museum of Art
Museum Angewandte Kunst, Frankfurt am Main
Jewish Museum Berlin
Centre Pompidou
The Menil Collection
The Shard
Shukhov Tower
Nakagin Capsule Tower
National Art Center, Tokyo
White U
Sendai Mediatheque
Stockholm Public Library
The Woodland Cemetery
Villa Snellman
Sky House, Tokyo
Edo Tokyo Museum
Miyakonojo Civic Hall
Rusakov Workers' Club
Melnikov House
La Maison de Verre
St. Mark's Church in Björkhagen
Church of St. Peter, Klippan
Palazzetto dello Sport
Zentralflughafen Tempelhof-Berlin
Goetheanum
Postsparkasse
Bank of London and South America
National Library of the Argentine Republic
Chiesa dell'Autostrada del Sole
Pilgrimage Church, Neviges

Kevin Roche

Métropolitain Entrance
AEG Turbine Factory
Glasgow School of Art
Gamble House
Frederick C. Robie House
Casa Milà
Schindler House
Cité Frugès Housing Complex
Bauhaus Dessau
Lovell Health House
Stockholm Public Library
E-1027
German Pavilion (Barcelona Pavilion)
Chrysler Building
Villa Savoye
Paimio Sanatorium
Edgar J. Kaufmann House (Fallingwater)
S.C. Johnson & Son Headquarters
Villa Mairea
Dymaxion House
Baker House
Glass House
The Eames House (Case Study House No. 8)
Chapelle du Rosaire de Vence
Farnsworth House
L'Unité d'Habitation
Lever House
Muuratsalo Experimental House
Miller House, Columbus
Chapelle Notre-Dame du Haut
MIT Chapel
Sydney Opera House
Crown Hall
Maisons Jaoul
Seagram Building
Ingalls Rink
Solomon R. Guggenheim Museum
Church of the Three Crosses
Capilla de las Capuchinas
Couvent Sainte-Marie de La Tourette
US Air Force Academy Cadet Chapel
TWA Flight Center
The Beinecke Rare Book & Manuscript Library
Gateway Arch
John Deere World Headquarters
Marina City, Chicago
Olivetti Factory, Merlo
Rudolph Hall
Salk Institute
The Assembly, Chandigarh
Kuwait Embassy, Tokyo
The Breuer Building (Whitney Museum)
Habitat '67
Smith House
Hyatt Regency, Atlanta
Orange County Government Centre, Goshen
Ford Foundation Headquarters
Knights of Columbus Building
Montreal Biosphère
National Assembly Building, Bangladesh
Charles De Gaulle Airport, Terminal 1 & 2A–2F
House III (Miller House)
Aula Paolo VI
Phillips Exeter Academy Library
Kimbell Art Museum
Robin Hood Gardens
Sears Tower
Marquette Plaza
Casa Bianchi
House VI
Hirshhorn Museum
Whig Hall, Princeton University
Prentice Women's Hospital Building
1 United Nations Plaza
Bagsværd Church
World Trade Center Towers
Centre Pompidou
Gehry House
Crystal Cathedral
Koshino House
Vietnam Veterans Memorial
Vitra Design Museum
Zurichtoren
Lloyd's of London
The Menil Collection
Pyramide du Louvre
Reykjavík Town Hall
Glass Chapel, Alabama
Vitra Fire Station
Paper Church, Kobe
Guggenheim Museum Bilbao
Getty Center
Diamond Ranch High School
Church of the Light
London Millennium Footbridge
Tate Modern
Nine Bridges Country Club
Jewish Museum Berlin
American Folk Art Museum
Petronas Towers

Sir Richard Rogers

AEG Turbine Factory
Glasgow School of Art
Gamble House
Frederick C. Robie House
Posen Tower
Postsparkasse
Schindler House
Schröderhuis
Cité Frugès Housing Complex
Lovell Beach House
Bauhaus Dessau
Lovell Health House
Stockholm Public Library
German Pavilion (Barcelona Pavilion)
Rusakov Workers' Club
Villa Savoye
La Maison de Verre
Haus Schminke
Edgar J. Kaufmann House (Fallingwater)
S.C. Johnson & Son Headquarters
Villa Mairea
The Woodland Cemetery
Dymaxion House
Baker House
Barragán House and Studio
Turin Exhibition Hall
Glass House
The Eames House (Case Study House No. 8)
Farnsworth House
L'Unité d'Habitation
Lever House
Pedregulho Housing Complex
Muuratsalo Experimental House
Cité d'Habitacion of Carrières Centrales
Chapelle Notre-Dame du Haut
Sydney Opera House
Crown Hall
Maisons Jaoul
Mill Owners' Association Building
Torre Velasca
Seagram Building
Museum of Modern Art, Rio de Janeiro
National Congress, Brazil
Solomon R. Guggenheim Museum
Church of the Three Crosses
House Van den Doel
Taliesin West
Stahl House (Case Study House No. 22)
Couvent Sainte-Marie de La Tourette
Halen Estate
TWA Flight Center
Snowdon Aviary
Berliner Philharmonie
Leicester University Engineering Building
National Olympic Gymnasium, Tokyo
Otaniemi Technical University
Peabody Terrace
Salk Institute
The Assembly, Chandigarh
Smith House
Ford Foundation Headquarters
Banco Ciudad de Buenos Aires (Casa Matriz)
Art Center College of Design, Pasadena
House III (Miller House)
Nakagin Capsule Tower
Olympic Stadium, Munich
Phillips Exeter Academy Library
Kimbell Art Museum
Castelvecchio Museum
Marquette Plaza
Sainsbury Center for Visual Arts
Centre Pompidou
Atheneum, New Harmony
Koshino House
Vietnam Veterans Memorial
National Assembly Building, Bangladesh
Lloyd's of London
Hongkong and Shanghai Bank Headquarters
Guggenheim Museum Bilbao
Diamond Ranch High School
Millennium Dome
Bordeaux Law Courts
Sendai Mediatheque
Highpoint Apartment Blocks
John Hancock Center
Casa Milà
Stadio San Nicola
E-1027
Maison Jean Prouvé, Nancy
Centre Le Corbusier (Heidi Weber House)
Adolfo Madrid–Barajas Airport
The Leadenhall Building

Moshe Safdie

AEG Turbine Factory
Glasgow School of Art
Grand Palais
Gamble House
Frederick C. Robie House
Postsparkasse
Schindler House
Fiat Works
Schröderhuis
Bauhaus Dessau
Lovell Health House
Stockholm Public Library
Villa Müller
Einstein Tower
German Pavilion (Barcelona Pavilion)
Villa Savoye
La Maison de Verre
Edgar J. Kaufmann House (Fallingwater)
S.C. Johnson & Son Headquarters
Hadassah Medical Center, Mount Scopus
New Gourna Village Mosque
Barragán House and Studio
Dymaxion House
Turin Exhibition Hall
The Eames House (Case Study House No. 8)
Farnsworth House
L'Unité d'Habitation
Lever House
Cité d'Habitacion of Carrières Centrales
Highlife Textile Factory
Chapelle Notre-Dame du Haut
Sydney Opera House
Crown Hall
Maisons Jaoul
Mill Owners' Association Building
Seagram Building
National Congress, Brazil
Solomon R. Guggenheim Museum
Church of the Three Crosses
Sabarmati Ashram
Stahl House (Case Study House No. 22)
Fredensborg Housing
Couvent Sainte-Marie de La Tourette
Municipal Orphanage
TWA Flight Center
Snowdon Aviary
Querini Stampalia Renovation
The Beinecke Rare Book & Manuscript Library
John Deere World Headquarters
Berliner Philharmonie
National Olympic Gymnasium, Tokyo
Shrine of the Book
Salk Institute
The Assembly, Chandigarh
Sea Ranch Condominium Complex
Habitat '67
Smith House
Hyatt Regency, Atlanta
Ford Foundation Headquarters
Banco Ciudad de Buenos Aires (Casa Matriz)
New National Gallery
Flower Kiosk, Malmö Cemetery
Montreal Biosphère
Israel Museum
Piscinas de Marés
Golden Mile Complex
Nakagin Capsule Tower
Olympic Stadium, Munich
Phillips Exeter Academy Library
Kimbell Art Museum
Castelvecchio Museum
Casa Bianchi
House VI
Centraal Beheer Building
Centre Pompidou
Brion Family Tomb
Gehry House
Museum of Anthropology, UBC
National Gallery of Art, East Building
National Gallery of Canada
Vietnam Veterans Memorial
National Assembly Building, Bangladesh
Neue Staatsgalerie
Lloyd's of London
Hongkong and Shanghai Bank Headquarters
National Museum of Roman Art
Pyramide du Louvre
Sri Lankan Parliament Building
Water Temple, Hyogo
Beyeler Foundation
The Menil Collection
Skirball Cultural Center
Yad Vashem
Guggenheim Museum Bilbao
Bordeaux Law Courts
Sendai Mediatheque
DZ Bank Building
Therme Vals
Portuguese National Pavillion
British Museum

Stanley Saitowitz

Larkin Company Administration Building
Unity Temple
Schindler House
Fiat Works
Ozenfant House
Villa Cook
Van Nelle Factory
Schröderhuis
Cité Frugès Housing Complex
Soviet Pavilion
Shukhov Tower
Lovell Beach House
Bauhaus Dessau
Villa Stein
Lovell Health House
Weissenhof Estate, Exhibition of 1927
Melnikov House
German Pavilion (Barcelona Pavilion)
Rusakov Workers' Club
Narkomfin Building
Lange and Esters Houses
Tugendhat House
Villa Savoye
Paimio Sanatorium
La Maison de Verre
Molitor Building
Edgar J. Kaufmann House (Fallingwater)
Casa del Fascio
S.C. Johnson & Son Headquarters
Villa Mairea
The Woodland Cemetery
Aarhus City Hall
Baker House
Barragán House and Studio
Glass House
The Eames House (Case Study House No. 8)
Architect's Second House, São Paulo
Farnsworth House
Das Canoas House
Säynätsalo Town Hall
L'Unité d'Habitation
Lever House
Pedregulho Housing Complex
Hunstanton School
Chapelle Notre-Dame du Haut
The Assembly, Chandigarh
St. Mark's Church in Björkhagen
Villa Sarabhai
Sydney Opera House
Crown Hall
Maisons Jaoul
Mill Owners' Association Building
Studio Aalto
House of the Future, 1956
Capilla de las Capuchinas
Richards Medical Research Laboratories
Seagram Building
National Congress, Brazil
Unité d'Habitation, Berlin
Pepsi-Cola Building
Stahl House (Case Study House No. 22)
Couvent Sainte-Marie de La Tourette
Municipal Orphanage
Esherick House
Gimansio del Colegio Maravillas
Carpenter Center for the Visual Arts
Leicester University Engineering Building
Casa Butantã
Frey House II
Rudolph Hall
Vanna Venturi House
The Economist Building, London
Centre Le Corbusier (Heidi Weber House)
Salk Institute
Transvaal House
Piscinas de Marés
Habitat '67
Norman Fisher House
New National Gallery
Kappe Residence
FAU, University of São Paulo
Toronto-Dominion Centre
Art Center College of Design, Pasadena
National Assembly Building, Bangladesh
Indian Institute of Management, Ahmedabad
San Cataldo Cemetery
Phillips Exeter Academy Library
Franklin D. Roosevelt Four Freedoms Park
Kimbell Art Museum
Robin Hood Gardens
Free University of Berlin
Gallaratese II Apartments
Yale Center for British Art
Bagsværd Church
Centre Pompidou
Viipuri Municipal Library
Institut du Monde Arabe
Museum of Sculpture, São Paulo
Barcelona Olympic Archery Range
Dominus Winery

Mack Scogin

Palais Stoclet
Bavinger House
Stockholm Public Library
Skandia Theater
The Woodland Cemetery
Koshino House
Naoshima Contemporary Art Museum
Bauhaus Dessau
Baker House
Paimio Sanatorium
Iberê Camargo Foundation
Boa Nova Tea House
Piscinas de Marés
Faculty of Architecture of the University of Porto
Schröderhuis
Einstein Tower
S.C. Johnson & Son Headquarters
Edgar J. Kaufmann House (Fallingwater)
Taliesin West
Solomon R. Guggenheim Museum
Haus Schminke
Berliner Philharmonie
Berlin State Library
Gehry House
Guggenheim Museum Bilbao
Villa Savoye
Chapelle Notre-Dame du Haut
Mill Owners' Association Building
Villa Shodhan
Rockefeller Center
La Maison de Verre
Tristan Tzara House
American Bar, Vienna
Villa Müller
Goetheanum
Casa Milà
Flower Kiosk, Malmö Cemetery
St. Mark's Church in Björkhagen
Malmö Eastern Cemetery
National Gallery, Sainsbury Wing
Vanna Venturi House
Centre Pompidou
Neue Staatsgalerie
Wexner Center for the Visual Arts
Hongkong and Shanghai Bank Headquarters
Lloyd's of London
Portland Building
Sheats Goldstein Residence
Chemosphere
Elrod House
Arango-Marbrisa House
Levy Residence, Malibu
Villa dall'Ava
CCTV Headquarters
Casa da Música
Seattle Central Library
Brion Family Tomb
Museo Canova
Castelvecchio Museum
Igualada Cemetery
Scottish Parliament Building
Casa del Fascio
Asilo Sant'Elia
Rusakov Workers' Club
Das Canoas House
The Eames House (Case Study House No. 8)
Rudolph Residence, 23 Beekman Place
Rudolph Hall
London Zoo Penguin Pool
Church of the Most Sacred Heart of Our Lord
CBS Building, New York
TWA Flight Center
Gateway Arch
Ingalls Rink
Schindler House
Salk Institute
Kimbell Art Museum
Esherick House
National Assembly Building, Bangladesh
German Pavilion (Barcelona Pavilion)
Seagram Building
Farnsworth House
Toronto-Dominion Centre
Kluczynski Federal Building
Vitra Fire Station
John Hancock Tower
Beijing National Stadium
Tate Modern
CaixaForum Madrid
Atlanta Marriott Marquis
Hyatt Regency, Atlanta
The Breuer Building (Whitney Museum)
St. John's Abbey, Collegeville
UC Campus Recreation Center
Emerson College Los Angeles
Selfridges Birmingham
Habitat '67
Barragán House and Studio
Glass Chapel, Alabama
Guthrie Theater

Kazuyo Sejima + Ryue Nishizawa / SANAA

Larkin Company Administration Building
Glasgow School of Art
Gamble House
Frederick C. Robie House
Casa Milà
Michaelerplatz House (Looshaus)
Postsparkasse
Park Güell
Schindler House
Fiat Works
Schröderhuis
Bauhaus Dessau
Lovell Beach House
Stockholm Public Library
Lovell Health House
German Pavilion (Barcelona Pavilion)
Melnikov House
Tugendhat House
Villa Müller
Villa Savoye
Van Nelle Factory
La Maison de Verre
Edgar J. Kaufmann House (Fallingwater)
Casa del Fascio
S.C. Johnson & Son Headquarters
Villa Mairea
The Woodland Cemetery
Casa Malaparte
Dymaxion House
Barragán House and Studio
Baker House
The Eames House (Case Study House No. 8)
Glass House
Farnsworth House
Säynätsalo Town Hall
L'Unité d'Habitation
Yale University Art Gallery
Ibirapuera Park
Chapelle Notre-Dame du Haut
Villa Sarabhai
Trenton Bath House
Crown Hall
Mill Owners' Association Building
860–880 Lake Shore Drive
Seagram Building
Sky House, Tokyo
Solomon R. Guggenheim Museum
National Congress, Brazil
Couvent Sainte-Marie de La Tourette
Municipal Orphanage, Amsterdam
Stahl House (Case Study House No. 22)
TWA Flight Center
Carpenter Center for the Visual Arts
Berliner Philharmonie
Leicester University Engineering Building
The Beinecke Rare Book & Manuscript Library
Querini Stampalia Renovation
Rudolph Hall
National Olympic Gymnasium, Tokyo
Kagawa Prefectural Government Hall
Salk Institute
The Assembly, Chandigarh
Centre Le Corbusier (Heidi Weber House)
Piscinas de Marés
Habitat '67
Smith House
Montreal Biosphère
Hillside Terrace Complex I–VI
Ford Foundation Headquarters
New National Gallery
Museu de Arte de São Paulo
Toronto-Dominion Centre
Nakagin Capsule Tower
Kimbell Art Museum
Phillips Exeter Academy Library
Olympic Stadium, Munich
Castelvecchio Museum
Free University of Berlin
Centraal Beheer Building
Yale Center for British Art
Bagsværd Church
Centre Pompidou
SESC Pompéia
Brion Family Tomb
National Assembly Building, Bangladesh
Neue Staatsgalerie
Hongkong and Shanghai Bank Headquarters
Lloyd's of London
National Museum of Roman Art
Igualada Cemetery
Parc de la Villette
Santa Maria Church de Canaveses
Maison à Bordeaux
Vitra Fire Station
Guggenheim Museum Bilbao
Diamond Ranch High School
Jewish Museum Berlin
Sendai Mediatheque
Yokohama International Port Terminal
Ray and Maria Stata Center

Jorge Silvetti

Beurs van Berlage
Larkin Company Administration Building
Frederick C. Robie House
Casa Milà
Palais Stoclet
Park Güell
Ozenfant House
Schröderhuis
Villa Stein
Karl-Marx-Hof
Stockholm Public Library
Villa Moller
German Pavilion (Barcelona Pavilion)
Villa Müller
Tugendhat House
Villa Savoye
La Maison de Verre
Frontón Recoletos
Edgar J. Kaufmann House (Fallingwater)
S.C. Johnson & Son Headquarters
Villa Mairea
Arve Bridge
The Woodland Cemetery
Casa Malaparte
Casa del Puente
Baker House
Barragán House and Studio
The Eames House (Case Study House No. 8)
Farnsworth House
Säynätsalo Town Hall
L'Unité d'Habitation
Lever House
Pedregulho Housing Complex
Muuratsalo Experimental House
Chapelle Notre-Dame du Haut
The Assembly, Chandigarh
Sydney Opera House
Maisons Jaoul
St. Mark's Church in Björkhagen
Palazzetto dello Sport
Torre Velasca
Seagram Building
National Congress, Brazil
Solomon R. Guggenheim Museum
Church of Cristo Obrero
Pepsi-Cola Building
Couvent Sainte-Marie de La Tourette
Toulouse-le-Mirail Housing
US Air Force Academy Cadet Chapel
TWA Flight Center
The Beinecke Rare Book & Manuscript Library
John Deere World Headquarters
Berliner Philharmonie
Leicester University Engineering Building
National Olympic Gymnasium, Tokyo
National Museum of Anthropology
Peabody Terrace
Vanna Venturi House
The Economist Building, London
Salk Institute
Sea Ranch Condominium Complex
Piscinas de Marés
Kuwait Embassy, Tokyo
Edifício Copan
The Breuer Building (Whitney Museum)
Bank of London and South America
Habitat '67
Hyatt Regency, Atlanta
Torre Blancas
Ford Foundation Headquarters
History Faculty Building, Cambridge
Olivetti Training Center
Itamaraty Palace
Nakagin Capsule Tower
Olympic Stadium, Munich
Phillips Exeter Academy Library
Snyderman House
Kimbell Art Museum
Castelvecchio Museum
Free University of Berlin
John Hancock Tower
Gallaratese II Apartments
Centre Pompidou
House VI
Gehry House
Teatro del Mondo
Atlantis Condominium
Neue Staatsgalerie
National Museum of Roman Art
The Menil Collection
Igualada Cemetery
Goetz Collection
Maison à Bordeaux
Dominus Winery
Therme Vals
Educatorium
Guggenheim Museum Bilbao
Sendai Mediatheque
Yokohama International Port Terminal
DZ Bank Building

Andrea Simitch + Val K. Warke

Säynätsalo Town Hall
Villa Mairea
Gund Hall
Atlantis Condominium
Architect's Second House, São Paulo
Stockholm Public Library
The Woodland Cemetery
Cuadra San Cristóbal
AEG Turbine Factory
Museu de Arte de São Paulo
Casa Bianchi
The Breuer Building (Whitney Museum)
Bacardi Bottling Plant
La Maison de Verre
Rooftop Remodeling Falkestrasse
Karl-Marx-Hof
House II (Vermont House)
House VI
New Gourna Village Mosque
Center for Hydrographic Studies, Madrid
Hongkong and Shanghai Bank Headquarters
Montreal Biosphère
Il Bagno de Bellinzona
Gehry House
Guggenheim Museum Bilbao
Hanselmann House
E-1027
Gamble House
Bauhaus Dessau
Vitra Fire Station
Ricola Storage Building
Storefront for Art and Architecture
Salk Institute
Kimbell Art Museum
Stahl House (Case Study House No. 22)
Nakagin Capsule Tower
Chapelle Notre-Dame du Haut
Villa Savoye
Villa Stein
Couvent Sainte-Marie de La Tourette
L'Unité d'Habitation
Carpenter Center for the Visual Arts
The Assembly, Chandigarh
Church of St. Peter, Klippan
Casa Malaparte
Villa Müller
Glasgow School of Art
Smith House
Atheneum, New Harmony
Soviet Pavilion
Schocken Department Store, Stuttgart
Museum of Sculpture, São Paulo
Seagram Building
Farnsworth House
German Pavilion (Barcelona Pavilion)
New National Gallery
Crown Hall
National Museum of Roman Art
Igualada Cemetery
Casa Il Girasole
Diamond Ranch High School
Villa VPRO
Palazzetto dello Sport
Lovell Health House
National Congress, Brazil
Institut du Monde Arabe
Kunsthal, Rotterdam
Educatorium
Stockholm City Hall
Rue Franklin Apartments
Centre Pompidou
National and University Library of Slovenia
Villa Planchart
Teatro del Mondo
Gallaratese II Apartments
Rudolph Hall
MIT Chapel
Habitat '67
Berliner Philharmonie
Lovell Beach House
Peabody Terrace
Piscinas de Marés
Galician Center of Contemporary Art
Hunstanton School
Lever House
The Beinecke Rare Book & Manuscript Library
House at the Bom Jesus, Braga
Leicester University Engineering Building
History Faculty Building, Cambridge
Neue Staatsgalerie
Reykjavík Town Hall
Casa del Fascio
Asilo Sant'Elia
Fiat Works
Parc de la Villette
T-House, Wilton
Can Lis, Majorca
Postsparkasse
Edgar J. Kaufmann House (Fallingwater)
Solomon R. Guggenheim Museum

Robert A.M. Stern

Chapelle Notre-Dame du Haut
Couvent Sainte-Marie de La Tourette
Villa Savoye
Farnsworth House
Glass House
TWA Flight Center
Guggenheim Museum Bilbao
S.C. Johnson & Son Headquarters
Leicester University Engineering Building
La Maison de Verre
Edgar J. Kaufmann House (Fallingwater)
Seagram Building
Postsparkasse
Salk Institute
The Woodland Cemetery
Kimbell Art Museum
AEG Turbine Factory
Lovell Beach House
Solomon R. Guggenheim Museum
Rudolph Hall
Stockholm Public Library
Frederick C. Robie House
Phillips Exeter Academy Library
Villa Mairea
Ford Foundation Headquarters
Baker House
Crown Hall
Glasgow School of Art
Vanna Venturi House
Neue Staatsgalerie
National Museum of Roman Art
Larkin Company Administration Building
Carpenter Center for the Visual Arts
Casa Milà
Park Güell
Karl-Marx-Hof
Tugendhat House
Villa Müller
Van Nelle Factory
Casa Il Girasole
Säynätsalo Town Hall
Sea Ranch Condominium Complex
Posen Tower
Beurs van Berlage
New National Gallery
Miller House, Columbus
Gamble House
Hilversum Town Hall
Rockefeller Center
Torre Velasca
Gordon Wu Hall
Unity Temple
Schocken Department Store, Stuttgart
MIT Chapel
John Deere World Headquarters
Knights of Columbus Building
National Farmers Bank
Skandia Theater
Villa La Roche
Castle Drogo
Yale Center for British Art
Imperial Hotel, Tokyo
Chrysler Building
National Museum of Anthropology
Kresge College
United Nations Headquarters
American Bar, Vienna
Großes Schauspielhaus
Stockholm City Hall
Worker's Housing Estate, Hoek van Holland
Cranbrook Academy of Art
Memorial Quadrangle, Yale University
Barclay-Vesey Building
General Motors Technical Center
Hirsch Residence
Taliesin West
Taliesin East
Town Hall, Logroño
National Gallery of Art, Washington, D.C.
Kirche am Steinhof
Villa Kerylos
PSFS Building
National and University Library of Slovenia
Ingalls Rink
Dixwell Fire Station
Bass Residence
National Gallery, Sainsbury Wing
Rashtrapati Bhavan
Union Station, Washington, D.C.
Helsinki Central Railway Station
Stuttgart Hauptbahnhof
Grand Central Terminal
Lincoln Memorial
Chicago Tribune Tower
Grundtvig Memorial Church
Église Notre-Dame du Raincy
Garbatella Quarter
Pasadena City Hall
Arco della Vittoria
Triple Bridge

Ana Tostões

Studio Aalto
AEG Turbine Factory
Rádio Nacional de Angola
Postsparkasse
Barragán House and Studio
Bauhaus Dessau
Beira Railroad Station
Berliner Philharmonie
Boa Nova Tea House
Estádio Municipal de Braga
Museum of Sculpture, São Paulo
Brion Family Tomb
Casa Butantã
Calouste Gulbenkian Foundation
Das Canoas House
Casa de Vidro
Casa del Fascio
Castelvecchio Museum
Edificio de CEPAL
The Assembly, Chandigarh
Chapelle Notre-Dame du Haut
Hotel Chuabo
Le Lignon
Gimansio del Colegio Maravillas
Couvent Sainte-Marie de La Tourette
Dymaxion House
Edgar J. Kaufmann House (Fallingwater)
FAU, University of São Paulo
Farnsworth House
Fiat Works
Bank of London and South America
Guggenheim Museum Bilbao
Hizuchi Elementary School
Hotel do Mar, Sesimbra
Institut du Monde Arabe
International House of Japan
Pueblo de colonización El Realengo
Kagawa Prefectural Government Hall
Kimbell Art Museum
L'Unité d'Habitation
Los Manantiales
Lovell Beach House
Casa Malaparte
Michaelerplatz House (Looshaus)
Gustavo Capanema Palace
Olympic Stadium, Munich
Municipal Orphanage, Amsterdam
Niterói Contemporary Art Museum
Museum of Modern Art, Rio de Janeiro
Nakagin Capsule Tower
National Assembly Building, Bangladesh
National Congress, Brazil
National Museum of Roman Art
National Olympic Gymnasium, Tokyo
New Gourna Village Mosque
New National Gallery
Nissay Theatre
Cathedral of Brasília
Quinta da Conceição
Residência Tomie Ohtake
Rusakov Workers' Club
Crown Hall
Salk Institute
Museu de Arte de São Paulo
Säynätsalo Town Hall
Schindler House
Schröderhuis
Seagram Building
Sendai Mediatheque
SESC Pompéia
Shiba Ryotaro Memorial Museum
Halen Estate
Hufeisensiedlung
The Woodland Cemetery
Smiling Lion Apartment Building
Stahl House (Case Study House No. 22)
Stockholm Public Library
Sydney Opera House
Civil Government Building, Tarragona
The Breuer Building (Whitney Museum)
The Eames House (Case Study House No. 8)
Einstein Tower
Hillside Terrace Complex I–VI
St. Mark's Church in Björkhagen
Museum of Modern Art, Kamakura & Hayama
National Museum of Western Art
Resurrection Chapel, Turku
Therme Vals
Piscinas de Marés
Tugendhat House
Turin Exhibition Hall
Casa Ugalde
Van Nelle Factory
Viipuri Municipal Library
Architect's Second House, São Paulo
Villa Mairea
Villa Müller
Villa Savoye
Weissenhof Estate, Exhibition of 1927
Yokohama International Port Terminal

Bernard Tschumi

Beurs van Berlage
AEG Turbine Factory
Postsparkasse
Glasgow School of Art
Rue Franklin Apartments
Casa Milà
Fagus Factory
Glass Pavilion
Michaelerplatz House (Looshaus)
Großes Schauspielhaus
Fiat Works
Grand Central Terminal
Narkomfin Building
Open-air School, Amsterdam
Rusakov Workers' Club
Einstein Tower
Schindler House
Schröderhuis
Kiefhoek Housing Development
Co-op Zimmer
Hufeisensiedlung
Stockholm Public Library
Paimio Sanatorium
Karl-Marx-Hof
Villa Savoye
Casa del Fascio
Rockefeller Center
La Maison de Verre
S.C. Johnson & Son Headquarters
Casa Malaparte
London Zoo Penguin Pool
The Eames House (Case Study House No.8)
L'Unité d'Habitation
Farnsworth House
Glass House
Casa del Puente
Turin Exhibition Hall
Municipal Orphanage
Nestlé Headquarters
Robin Hood Gardens
Sydney Opera House
Seagram Building
Salk Institute
Leicester University Engineering Building
Los Manantiales
Chapelle Notre-Dame du Haut
National Congress, Brazil
Solomon R. Guggenheim Museum
Snowdon Aviary
Free University of Berlin
Berliner Philharmonie
Centraal Beheer Building
Église Sainte-Bernadette du Banlay
TWA Flight Center
Carpenter Center for the Visual Arts
Oita Prefectural Library
Gallaratese II Apartments
German Pavilion, Expo '67
Montreal Biosphère
Rudolph Hall
Vanna Venturi House
Smith House
Shrine of the Book
Habitat '67
Ford Foundation Headquarters
Museu de Arte de São Paulo
Umlauftank
Nakagin Capsule Tower
San Cataldo Cemetery
Hirshhorn Museum
Westin Bonaventure Hotel
Wall House II
Willis Faber and Dumas Headquarters
Centre Pompidou
Gehry House
Beires House
White U
House III (Miller House)
World Trade Center Towers
Byker Wall
La Fábrica, Sant Just Desvern
Neue Staatsgalerie
Church of the Light
Netherlands Dance Theatre, Hague
Parc de la Villette
Wexner Center for the Visual Arts
Institut du Monde Arabe
National Museum of Roman Art
Rooftop Remodeling Falkestrasse
Goetz Collection
Diamond Ranch High School
Expo 2000, Netherlands Pavilion
Kunsthal, Rotterdam
Kiasma
Guggenheim Museum Bilbao
Vitra Fire Station
Le Fresnoy Art Center
Igualada Cemetery
Jewish Museum Berlin
Sendai Mediatheque

Ben van Berkel + Caroline Bos / UNStudio

Maison & Atelier Horta
Beurs van Berlage
Larkin Company Administration Building
Riehl House
AEG Turbine Factory
Casa Milà
Posen Tower
Michaelerplatz House (Looshaus)
Park Güell
Glass Pavilion
Großes Schauspielhaus
Einstein Tower
Soviet Pavilion
Villa Stein
Goetheanum
Rusakov Workers' Club
Villa Savoye
La Maison de Verre
Haus Schminke
Villa Girasole
Orvieto Aircraft Hangars
Casa del Fascio
S.C. Johnson & Son Headquarters
Casa Malaparte
Palazzo della Civiltà Italiana
Baker House
Turin Exhibition Hall
Säynätsalo Town Hall
Casa de Vidro
Gatti Wool Factory
Iglesia de la Medalla Milagrosa
Catalano House
Chapelle Notre-Dame du Haut
Hiroshima Peace Memorial Museum
Corso Italia Complex, Milan
Ginásio do Clube Atlético Paulistano
Palazzetto dello Sport
National Congress, Brazil
Los Manantiales
Palazzo del Lavoro
Couvent Sainte-Marie de La Tourette
Municipal Orphanage
National Library of the Argentine Republic
TWA Flight Center
Leicester University Engineering Building
Berliner Philharmonie
National Olympic Gymnasium, Tokyo
Olivetti Factory, Merlo
Rudolph Hall
Kuwait Embassy, Tokyo
Oita Prefectural Library
Sonsbeek Pavilion
Bank of London and South America
Musmeci Bridge
Shizuoka Press and Broadcasting Center
Habitat '67
Smith House
Kowloon Walled City
Pilgrimage Church, Neviges
Museu de Arte de São Paulo
Mivtachim Sanitarium
FAU, University of São Paulo
Itamaraty Palace
House II (Vermont House)
House III (Miller House)
White U
Nakagin Capsule Tower
Kimbell Art Museum
House VI
Museum of Modern Art, Gunma
Teatro Regio
Town Hall, Logroño
Sumiyoshi Row House
SESC Pompéia
Centre Pompidou
Atheneum, New Harmony
Koshino House
Venice III House
Lloyd's of London
Hongkong and Shanghai Bank Headquarters
National Museum of Roman Art
Ricola Storage Building
The Menil Collection
Church of the Light
Institut du Monde Arabe
TEPIA Science Pavilion, Tokyo
Vitra Design Museum
Erasmus Bridge
Parc de la Villette
T-House, Wilton
House at the Bom Jesus, Braga
Villa Wilbrink
Mobius House
Galician Center of Contemporary Art
Vitra Fire Station
Therme Vals
Villa VPRO
Bordeaux Law Courts
Yokohama International Port Terminal
Miyagi Stadium

Robert Venturi + Denise Scott Brown

Postsparkasse
Schindler House
Fiat Works
Schröderhuis
Cité Frugès Housing Complex
Karl-Marx-Hof
Lovell Health House
Stockholm Public Library
Villa Moller
German Pavilion (Barcelona Pavilion)
Villa Savoye
Van Nelle Factory
La Maison de Verre
Villa Girasole
Edgar J. Kaufmann House (Fallingwater)
Casa del Fascio
The Woodland Cemetery
Casa Malaparte
Dymaxion House
Turin Exhibition Hall
Glass House
The Eames House (Case Study House No. 8)
Baker House
Muuratsalo Experimental House
Farnsworth House
L'Unité d'Habitation
Lever House
Pedregulho Housing Complex
Crown Hall
Maisons Jaoul
Chapelle Notre-Dame du Haut
Seagram Building
National Congress, Brazil
Philips Pavilion
Solomon R. Guggenheim Museum
Cité d'Habitacion of Carrières Centrales
Stahl House (Case Study House No. 22)
Couvent Sainte-Marie de La Tourette
Municipal Orphanage
Halen Estate
TWA Flight Center
Querini Stampalia Renovation
Berliner Philharmonie
Leicester University Engineering Building
Vanna Venturi House
National Olympic Gymnasium, Tokyo
Peabody Terrace
Rudolph Hall
Salk Institute
The Assembly, Chandigarh
Centre Le Corbusier (Heidi Weber House)
Piscinas de Marés
Kuwait Embassy, Tokyo
Bank of London and South America
Habitat '67
Smith House
Museu de Arte de São Paulo
Ford Foundation Headquarters
Kowloon Walled City
Benacerraf House Project
Flower Kiosk, Malmö Cemetery
Petrobras Headquarters
The Beinecke Rare Book & Manuscript Library
House III (Miller House)
Nakagin Capsule Tower
Olympic Stadium, Munich
Phillips Exeter Academy Library
Kimbell Art Museum
Free University of Berlin
Byker Wall
Centraal Beheer Building
Whig Hall, Princeton University
Bagsværd Church
Brion Family Tomb
Centre Pompidou
SESC Pompéia
Hedmark Cathedral Museum
Gehry House
Atheneum, New Harmony
Koshino House
Vietnam Veterans Memorial
National Assembly Building, Bangladesh
Neue Staatsgalerie
Lloyd's of London
Hongkong and Shanghai Bank Headquarters
Rooftop Remodeling Falkestrasse
National Museum of Roman Art
Void Space/Hinged Space Housing
Igualada Cemetery
Parc de la Villette
Maison à Bordeaux
Samitaur Tower
Guggenheim Museum Bilbao
UFA Cinema Centre
Jewish Museum Berlin
Bordeaux Law Courts
Diamond Ranch High School
Yokohama International Port Terminal
Sendai Mediatheque
Empty Sky

Marion Weiss + Michael Manfredi

Greywalls
Postsparkasse
Glasgow School of Art
Frederick C. Robie House
Park Güell
Schindler House
Lovell Beach House
Villa Stein
Stockholm Public Library
Lovell Health House
Tugendhat House
Villa Savoye
German Pavilion (Barcelona Pavilion)
Triple Bridge
Van Nelle Factory
Rockefeller Center
La Maison de Verre
City of Refuge, Paris
Casa Rustici
S.C. Johnson & Son Headquarters
Casa del Fascio
Taliesin West
Edgar J. Kaufmann House (Fallingwater)
Strathmore Apartments
Casa Malaparte
Villa Mairea
The Woodland Cemetery
L'Unité d'Habitation
Kaufmann House
Farnsworth House
Barragán House and Studio
Baker House
Casa Il Girasole
Crown Hall
Säynätsalo Town Hall
Maisons Jaoul
The Assembly, Chandigarh
Capilla de las Capuchinas
Chapelle Notre-Dame du Haut
Sydney Opera House
Mill Owners' Association Building
Olivetti Showroom
Church of the Three Crosses
Couvent Sainte-Marie de La Tourette
House of Culture
Seagram Building
United States Embassy, New Delhi
Rudolph Hall
Solomon R. Guggenheim Museum
Leicester University Engineering Building
Castelvecchio Museum
Church of Cristo Obrero
Salk Institute
TWA Flight Center
Carpenter Center for the Visual Arts
Querini Stampalia Renovation
Centre Le Corbusier (Heidi Weber House)
George Washington Bridge Bus Station
Free University of Berlin
National Olympic Gymnasium, Tokyo
Marina City, Chicago
Andrew Melville Hall
Piscinas de Marés
Norman Fisher House
Smith House
Habitat '67
Museu de Arte de São Paulo
Ford Foundation Headquarters
New National Gallery
Gallaratese II Apartments
FAU, University of São Paulo
Hillside Terrace Complex I–VI
House III (Miller House)
Penn Mutual Tower
Centre Pompidou
Saint-Pierre, Firminy
Phillips Exeter Academy Library
Kimbell Art Museum
Centraal Beheer Building
Yale Center for British Art
Casa Gilardi
Bagsværd Church
Neue Staatsgalerie
Gehry House
University of Urbino
National Museum of Roman Art
Parliament House, Canberra
National Assembly Building, Bangladesh
Parc de la Villette
The Menil Collection
Saint Benedict Chapel, Sumvitg
Igualada Cemetery
Kunsthal, Rotterdam
Vitra Fire Station
Chapel of St. Ignatius
Guggenheim Museum Bilbao
Sendai Mediatheque
Diamond Ranch High School
Nakagin Capsule Tower
Serralves Museum of Contemporary Art

Tod Williams + Billie Tsien

Beurs van Berlage
Rue Franklin Apartments
AEG Turbine Factory
Glasgow School of Art
Gamble House
Unity Temple
Frederick C. Robie House
Postsparkasse
Schindler House
Fiat Works
Schröderhuis
Lovell Beach House
Sagrada Família
Stockholm Public Library
German Pavilion (Barcelona Pavilion)
Villa Savoye
Paimio Sanatorium
La Maison de Verre
Edgar J. Kaufmann House (Fallingwater)
Casa del Fascio
S.C. Johnson & Son Headquarters
Villa Mairea
The Woodland Cemetery
Casa Malaparte
Glass House
Golconde, Pondicherry
Barragán House and Studio
The Eames House (Case Study House No. 8)
Farnsworth House
L'Unité d'Habitation
Lever House
Kresge College
Chapelle Notre-Dame du Haut
Sydney Opera House
Crown Hall
Mill Owners' Association Building
St. Mark's Church in Björkhagen
Seagram Building
National Congress, Brazil
Louisiana Museum of Modern Art
Solomon R. Guggenheim Museum
Capilla de las Capuchinas
Couvent Sainte-Marie de La Tourette
Municipal Orphanage
TWA Flight Center
Ena de Silva House
The Beinecke Rare Book & Manuscript Library
Berliner Philharmonie
Sabarmati Ashram
Leicester University Engineering Building
National Museum of Anthropology
National Olympic Gymnasium, Tokyo
Rudolph Hall
Vanna Venturi House
Salk Institute
The Assembly, Chandigarh
Sea Ranch Condominium Complex
Piscinas de Marés
Montessori School, Delft
Habitat '67
Ford Foundation Headquarters
Museu de Arte de São Paulo
FAU, University of São Paulo
Itamaraty Palace
Phillips Exeter Academy Library
Kimbell Art Museum
Castelvecchio Museum
Douglas House
Marie Short House
SESC Pompéia
Centre Pompidou
Brion Family Tomb
Gehry House
Hedmark Cathedral Museum
Warehouse, Port of Montevideo
Koshino House
National Assembly Building, Bangladesh
Kate Mantilini, Beverly Hills
Hongkong and Shanghai Bank Headquarters
National Museum of Roman Art
Ricola Storage Building
Church of the Light
Institut du Monde Arabe
Museum of Sculpture, São Paulo
Kiasma
Igualada Cemetery
Parc de la Villette
Vitra Fire Station
Maison à Bordeaux
Neurosciences Institute, La Jolla
Therme Vals
Guggenheim Museum Bilbao
Kunsthaus Bregenz
Signal Box Auf dem Wolf
Chapel of St. Ignatius
Diamond Ranch High School
Jewish Museum Berlin
Boyd Art Center, Riversdale
Sendai Mediatheque
American Folk Art Museum

references

REFERENCES

VILLA SAVOYE

1/ Benton, Tim. *The Villas of Le Corbusier, 1920–1930: With Photographs in the Lucien Hervé Collection*. New Haven: Yale University Press, 1987. **2/** Corbusier, Le. *Towards a New Architecture*. New York: Dover Publications, 1986. **3/** Curtis, William J. *Le Corbusier, Ideas and Forms*. Oxford: Phaidon, 1986. **4/** Davies, Colin. *Key Houses of the Twentieth Century: Plans, Sections and Elevations*. New York: W.W. Norton, 2006. **5/** Corbusier, Le, Pierre Jeanneret, Willy Boesiger, Oscar Stonorov, and Max Bill. *Œuvre Complète*. Basel: Birkhäuser, 1999. **6/** Frampton, Kenneth, and Yukio Futagawa. *Modern Architecture1920–1945*. New York: Rizzoli, 1983.

CHAPELLE NOTRE-DAME DU HAUT

1/ Corbusier, Le. *The Chapel at Ronchamp*. United Kingdom: Architectural Press London, 1957. **2/** Crippa, Maria Antonietta, Françoise Caussé, and Caroline Beamish. *Le Corbusier: The Chapel of Notre-Dame Du Haut at Ronchamp*. London: Royal Academy of Arts, 2015. **3/** Pauly, Danièle. *Le Corbusier: The Chapel at Ronchamp*. Paris: Fondation Le Corbusier, 2008. **4/** Curtis, William J. R. *Le Corbusier: Ideas and Forms*. Oxford: Phaidon, 1986. **5/** Palmes, J. C. and Maurice Jardot. *Le Corbusier: Creation Is a Patient Search*. New York: Praeger, 1960.

GERMAN PAVILION (BARCELONA PAVILION)

1/ Neumeyer, Fritz. *Global Architecture*. Japan: A.D.A. EDITA Tokyo Co. Ltd, 1995. **2/** Solà-Morales, Ignasi De, Cristian Cirici, and Fernando Ramos. *Mies Van Der Rohe: Barcelona Pavilion*. Barcelona: Gili, 1993. **3/** Dodds, George. *Building Desire: On the Barcelona Pavilion*. London: Routledge, 2005. **4/** Frampton, Kenneth, and Yukio Futagawa. *Modern Architecture 1920–1945*. New York: Rizzoli, 1983. **5/** Johnson, Philip. *Mies Van Der Rohe*. New York: Museum of Modern Art, 1978. **6/** Fritz Neumeyer. *Mies Van Der Rohe: German Pavilion, International Exposition, Barcelona, Spain, 1928–29 (reconstructed 1986), Tugendhat House, Brno, Czechoslovakia, 1928–30*. Tokyo: A.D.A. EDITA Tokyo, 1995. **7/** Evans, Robin, "Mies van der Rohe's Paradoxical Symmetries," in *Translations from Drawing to Building and Other Essays*. **8/** Quetglas, Josep, *Fear of Glass*, Birkhauser, 2001.

CENTRE POMPIDOU

1/ Piano, Renzo. *Du plateau Beaubourg au Centre Georges Pompidou*. Paris: Éditions du Centre Pompidou, 1987. **2/** Rattenbury, Kester. *Richard Rogers: The Pompidou Center*. England: Oxon; New York: Routledge, 2012. **3/** Futagawa, Yukio. *Global Architecture 44: Piano + Rogers Architects ONE ARUP Engineers*. Tokyo, A.D.A. EDITA, 1975. **4/** Weston, Richard. *Key Buildings of the 20th Century: Plans, Sections and Elevations*. New York: W.W. Norton & Co., 2010.

S.C. JOHNSON & SON HEADQUARTERS

1/ Hertzberg, Mark. *Frank Lloyd Wright's SC Johnson Research Tower*. San Francisco: Pomegranate, 2010. **2/** Carter, Brian. *Johnson Wax Administration Building and Research Tower*. London: Phaidon Press, 1998. **3/** Wright, Frank Lloyd. *Johnson & Son, Administration Building and Research Tower*. Tokyo: A.D.A. EDITA Tokyo, 1970, 1974 printing. **4/** Weston, Richard. *Key buildings of the 20th Century*. New York: W.W. Norton & Co., 2010. **5/** Lipman, Jonathan. *Frank Lloyd Wright & The Johnson Wax Building*. NY: Rizzoli, 1986.

FARNSWORTH HOUSE

1/ Goldberger, Paul; Phyllis Lambert, and Sylvia Lavin. *Modern Views: Inspired by the Mies Van Der Rohe Farnsworth House and the Philip Johnson Glass House*. New York, NY, USA: Assouline Pub., 2010. **2/** Jenna Cellini, Elizabeth Milnarik, Brad Roeder. Farnsworth House Recording Project. United States: National Trust For Historic Preservation, 2009. **3/** Rohe, Ludwig Mies Van Der, and Dirk Lohan. *Mies Van Der Rohe: Farnsworth House, Plano, Illinois, 1945–50*. Tokyo, Japan: A.D.A. EDITA Tokyo, 2000. **4/** Clemence, Paul. *Mies Van Der Rohe's Farnsworth House*. Atglen, PA: Schiffer Pub., 2006. **5/** Vandenberg, Maritz. *Farnsworth House: Ludwig Mies Van Der Rohe*. London: Phaidon, 2003. **6/** Wagner, George, "The Lair of the Bachelor," in *Architecture and Feminism*, ed. Coleman, Danze, and Henderson. Princeton: Princeton Architectural Press, 1997.

SALK INSTITUTE

1/ Stoller, Ezra. *The Salk Institute*. New York: Princeton Architectural Press, 1999. **2/** James Steele. *Salk Institute*. London: Phaidon, 1993. **3/** Savio, Andrea, and Louis Isidore. *Louis I. Kahn: Salk Institute*. Firenze: Alinea, 1994. **4/** Goldhagen, Sarah Williams. *Louis Kahn's Situated Modernism*. New Haven, CT: Yale University Press, 2001.

LA MAISON DE VERRE

1/ Bauchet, Bernard, and Marc Vellay, with Yukio Futagawa (ed.). *La Maison de Verre*. Tokyo: A.D.A. EDITA, 1988. **2/** Cinqualbre, Olivier. *Pierre Chareau, la Maison de verre, 1928–1933: un objet singulier*. Paris: J.-M. Place, 2001. **3/** Frampton, Kenneth, and Yukio Futagawa. *Modern Architecture 1920–1945*. New York: Rizzoli, 1983. **4/** Chareau, Pierre. *Pierre Chareau: Architecte, Un Art Interieur*. Paris: Centre Georges Pompidou, 1993. **5/** Taylor, Brian Brace. *Pierre Chareau: Designer and Architect*. Köln: Benedikt Taschen, 1992. **6/** Vellay, Marc, and Kenneth Frampton. *Pierre Chareau: Architect and Craftsman, 1883–1950*. New York: Rizzoli, 1985.

COUVENT SAINTE-MARIE DE LA TOURETTE

1/ Petit, Jean. *Un couvent de Le Corbusier: Volume réalisé*. Paris: Cahiers Forces Vives-Editec, 1961. **2/** Pirazzoli, Giacomo. *Le Corbusier a La Tourette:*

qualche congettura. Firenze: All'insegna del giglio, 2000. **3/** Potié, Philippe. *Le Corbusier: le Couvent Sainte Marie de La Tourette = the Monastery of Sainte Marie de La Tourette*. Paris: Fondation le Corbusier; Boston: Birkhäuser Publishers, 2001. **4/** Corbusier, Le; Yukio Futagawa, and Arata Isozaki. *Couvent Sainte Marie De La Tourette, Eveux-sur-l'Arbresle, France 1957–60*. Tokyo: A.D.A. EDITA, 1971. **5/** Cohen, Jean-Louis. *Le Corbusier: Le Grand*. London: Phaidon, 2008. **6/** Hervé, Lucien, *The Architecture of Truth: The Cistercian Abbey of Le Thoronet*. Introduction by Le Corbusier. London: Thames and Hudson, 1957. **7/** Rowe, Colin, "La Tourette," in *The Mathematics of the Ideal Villa and Other Essays*. Cambridge: The MIT Press, 1976.

TWA FLIGHT CENTER

1/ Saarinen, Eero. *TWA Terminal Building, Kennedy Airport, New York, 1956–62: Dulles International Airport (Washington, D.C.)*. Tokyo: A.D.A. EDITA Tokyo, 1973. **2/** Stoller, Ezra. *The TWA Terminal*. New York: Princeton Architectural Press, 1999. **3/** Weston, Richard. *Key Buildings of the 20th Century: Plans, Sections, and Elevations*. New York: W.W. Norton & Company, 2010. **4/** Ringli, Kornel. *Designing TWA: Eero Saarinen's Terminal in New York*. Zürich: Park, 2015.

BERLINER PHILHARMONIE

1/ Scharoun, Hans, Yukio Futagawa, and Hiroshi Sasaki. *The Berlin Philharmonic Concert Hall, Berlin, West Germany, 1956, 1960–63*. Tokyo: A.D.A. EDITA Tokyo, 1973. **2/** Barnbeck, Ulla. *Architekten, Hans Scharoun*. Stuttgart: IRB Verlag, 1987. **3/** Weston, Richard. *Key Buildings of the 20th Century: Plans, Sections and Elevations*. New York: W.W. Norton, 2010. **4/** Forsyth, Michael. *Buildings for Music*. Cambridge: MIT Press, 1985.

GUGGENHEIM MUSEUM BILBAO

1/ Museo Guggenheim (Bilbao). *Guggenheim Museum Bilbao Collection*. Madrid: TF Editores, 2009. **2/** Gehry, Frank O. *GA Document; 54: Guggenheim Bilbao Museoa*. New York: GA Intl Company Limited, 1998. **3/** Bruggen, Coosje Van. *Frank O. Gehry: Guggenheim Museum Bilbao*. New York, NY: Guggenheim Museum Publications, 1998. **4/** Gilbert-Rolfe, Jeremy, and Frank O. Gehry. *Frank Gehry: The City and Music*. London: Routledge, 2002. **5/** Isenberg, Barbara, and Frank O. Gehry. *Conversations with Frank Gehry*. New York: Alfred A. Knopf, 2009. **6/** Gehry, Frank O., and Germano Celant. *Frank O. Gehry*. N.p.: n.p., n.d. **7/** Gehry, Frank O., Fernando Márquez Cecilia, and Richard C. Levene. *Frank Gehry, 1987–2003*. Madrid: El Croquis Editorial, 2006. **8/** Mathewson, Casey C. M., and Frank O. Gehry. *Frank O. Gehry: Selected Works: 1969 to Today*. Richmond Hill, Ont.: Firefly, 2007.

EDGAR J. KAUFMANN HOUSE (FALLINGWATER)

1/ Wright, Frank Lloyd. *Kaufmann House, Fallingwater, Bear Run Pennsylvania, 1936*. Tokyo: A.D.A. EDITA Tokyo, 1970. **2/** Davis, Colin. *Key Houses of the Twentieth Century*. New York: W.W. Norton, 2006. **3/** Kaufmann, Edgar. *Fallingwater, a Frank Lloyd Wright Country House*. New York: Abbeville, 1986. **4/** Frampton, Kenneth, and Yukio Futagawa. *Modern Architecture 1920–1945*. New York: Rizzoli, 1983.

THE WOODLAND CEMETERY

1/ Asplund, Erik Gunnar; Dan Cruickshank, and Martin Charles. *Erik Gunnar Asplund*. London: Architects Journal, 1988. **2/** Caldenby, C. *Asplund*. Stockholm: Arkitektur Förl., 1986. Print. **3/** Caldenby, Claes, and Olof Hultin. *Asplund*. New York: Rizzoli, 1986. **4/** Lewerentz, Sigurd; Claes Dymling, Wilfried Wang, and Fabio Galli. *Architect Sigurd Lewerentz*. Stockholm: Byggförlaget, 1997. **5/** Frampton, Kenneth, and Yukio Futagawa. *Modern Architecture,1920–1945*. New York: Rizzoli, 1983. **6/** Holmdahl, Gustav; Sven Ivar Lind, and Kjell Ödeen. *Gunnar Asplund Architect, 1885–1940*. Stockholm: AB Tidskriften Byggmästaren, 1950. **7/** Wrede, Stuart. *The Architecture of Erik Gunnar Asplund*. Cambridge: The MIT Press, 1980. **8/** Jones, Peter Blundell. *Gunnar Asplund*. New York: Phaidon Press Inc., 2006. **9/** Ahlin, Janne. *Sigurd Lewerentz, Architect; 1885–1975*. Cambridge: The MIT Press, 1987.

SEAGRAM BUILDING

1/ Weston, Richard. Key Buildings of the 20th Century: Plans, Sections and Elevations. New York: W.W. Norton, 2010. **2/** Zimmerman, Claire. Mies Van Der Rohe, 1886–1969: The Structure of Space. Hong Kong: Taschen, 2006. **3/** Gössel, Peter, and Gabriele Leuthäuser. Architecture in the Twentieth Century. Köln: Benedikt Taschen, 1991. **4/** Lambert, Phyllis, and Barry Bergdoll. Building Seagram. London: Yale University Press, 2013.

SOLOMON R. GUGGENHEIM MUSEUM

1/ Muto, Akira, and Yukio Futagawa. *Global Architecture 12: Frank Lloyd Wright 1887–1959*. Tokyo, A.D.A. EDITA, 1975. **2/** Pfeiffer, Bruce Brooks. *Frank Lloyd Wright. Complete Works. Vol. 3, 1943–1959*. Hong Kong; Los Angeles, Taschen, 2009. **3/** Pfeiffer, Bruce Brooks. *Frank Lloyd Wright, the Guggenheim Correspondence*. Fresno Press at California State University, 1986. **4/** Ballon, Hilary. *The Guggenheim: Frank Lloyd Wright and the Making of the Modern Museum*. New York, London, Guggenheim Museum, 2009. **5/** Solomon R. Guggenheim Museum. *The Solomon R. Guggenheim Museum*. New York: Guggenheim Museum Publications, 1995.

THE EAMES HOUSE (CASE STUDY HOUSE NO. 8)

1/ Koenig, Gloria, and Peter Gössel. *Eames*. Köln: Taschen, 2015. **2/** Steele, James; Charles Eames, and Ray Eames. *Eames House: Charles and Ray Eames*. London: Phaidon, 2002. **3/** Davies, Colin. *Key Houses of the Twentieth Century: Plans, Sections and Elevations*. New York: W.W. Norton,

2006. **4/** Gamboa, Pablo. *La Casa Californiana Años 50*. Bogota: Universidad Nacional De Colombia, 2007. **5/** Smith, Elizabeth A.T. *Case Study Houses*. Cologne: Taschen, 2007.

LEICESTER UNIVERSITY ENGINEERING BUILDING

1/ McKean, John. *Leicester University Engineering Building: James Stirling and James Gowan*. London: Phaidon, 1994. **2/** McKean, John. *Pioneering British High-Tech: By Stirling & Gowan, Foster Associates and Richard Rogers Partnership*. London: Phaidon Press, 1999. **3/** Yukio Futagawa. *Leicester University Engineering Department, Leicester, Great Britain, 1959–63: Cambridge University History Faculty, Cambridge, Great Britain, 1964–66*. Tokyo: A.D.A. EDITA, 1974. **4/** Berman, Alan. *Jim Stirling and the Red Trilogy: Three Radical Buildings*. London: Frances Lincoln, 2010. **5/** Maxwell, Robert. *James Stirling/ Michel Wilford*. Basel: Birkhäuser, 1998. **6/** Arnell, Peter, and Ted Bickford, eds. *James Stirling: Buildings and Projects*. New York: Rizzoli, 1984. **7/** Vidler, Anthony. *James Frazer Stirling: Notes from the Archive*. New Haven: Yale University Press, 2010.

CASA DEL FASCIO

1/ Coppa, Alessandro. *Guiseppe Terragni*. Milan: 24 Ore Cultura, Pero, 2013. **2/** Terragni, Attilio Alberto; Daniel Libeskind, and Paolo Rosselli. *The Terragni Atlas: Built Architectures*. Milan: Skira, 2004. **3/** Eisenman, Peter, *Giuseppe Terragni, and Manfredo Tafuri. Giuseppe Terragni: Transformations, Decompositions, Critiques*. New York: Monacelli, 2003. **4/** Thiel-Siling, Sabine, and Wolfgang Bachmann. *Icons of Architecture: The 20th Century*. Munich: Prestel, 1998. **5/** Ching, Francis D. K.; Mark Jarzombek, and Vikramaditya Prakash. *A Global History of Architecture*. Hoboken, NJ: J. Wiley & Sons, 2007. **6/** Zevi, Bruno, *Ommagio a Terragni*. Milan: Etas/Kompass, 1968. **7/** Schumacher, Thomas L. *Surface & Symbol: Giuseppe Terragni and the Architecture of Italian Rationalism*. New York: Princeton Architectural Press, 1991.

L'UNITÉ D'HABITATION

1/ Corbusier, Le; Pierre Jeanneret, Willy Boesiger, Oscar Stonorov, and Max Bill. *Œuvre Complète*. Basel: Birkhäuser, 1999. **2/** Corbusier, Le. *Unité d'Habitation, Marseille-Michelet*. Paris: Fondation Le Corbusier, 1983. **3/** Curtis, William J. R. *Le Corbusier: Ideas and Forms*. Oxford: Phaidon, 1986. **4/** Jenkins, David. *Unite d'Habitation, Marseilles: Le Corbusier*. London: Phaidon Press, 1993.

HABITAT '67

1/ Kettle, John. *Beyond Habitat*. Cambridge, Massachusetts: The MIT Press, 1970. **2/** Safdie Moshe. *Habitat 67*. Montreal, Canada Queen's Printer, 1967. **3/** Safdie Moshe and John Gray. *Habitat; Moshe Safdie interviewed by John Gray*. Montreal: Canada Tundra Books, 1967. **4/** Murphy, Diana and Moshe Safdie. *Moshe Safdie*. Mulgrave, Vic: 2009. **5/** Safdie Moshe and John Gray. *Expo 67: Habitat*. Montreal: Canada Tundra Books, 1967.

KIMBELL ART MUSEUM

1/ Vandenberg, Maritz, and Michael Brawne. *Twentieth-Century Museums I: By Ludwig Mies van der Rohe, Louis Kahn and Richard Meier*. London: Phaidon, 1999. **2/** Kahn, Louis I. *Louis I. Kahn*. Tokyo: A+u Pub. Co., 1974. **3/** Kahn, Louis I.; David B. Brownlee, and David G. De Long. *Louis I. Kahn: In the Realm of Architecture*. New York, NY: Rizzoli, 2005. **4/** Lobell, John, and Louis I. Kahn. *Between Silence and Light: Spirit in the Architecture of Louis I. Kahn*. Boston: Shambhala, 2008.

SCHRÖDERHUIS (RIETVELD SCHRÖDER HOUSE)

1/ Overy, Paul. *The Rietveld Schroder House*. Cambridge: MIT Press, 1988. **2/** Frampton, Kenneth, and Yukio Futagawa. *Modern Architecture 1920–1945*. New York: Rizzoli, 1983. **3/** Küper, Marijke; W. Quist, and Hans Ibelings. *Gerrit Th. Rietveld: Casas Revista Internacional De Arquitectura (n° 39/40)*. Barcelona: Editorial Gustavo Gili, 2006. **4/** Mulder, Zijl, and Gerrit Thomas. *Rietveld Schroder House*. New York: Princeton Architectural Press, 1999.

NAKAGIN CAPSULE TOWER

1/ Weston, Richard. *Key Buildings of the 20th Century : Plans, Sections and Elevations*. New York: W.W. Norton & Co., 2010. **2/** Ross, Michael Franklin. *Beyond Metabolism: The New Japanese Architecture*. New York: Architectural Record Books, 1978. **3/** Koolhaas, Charlie. *Metaborizumu Torippu*. Tokyo: Heibonsha, 2012. **4/** Schmal, Peter Cachola; Ingeborg Flagge, and Jochen Visscher. *Kisho Kurokawa: Metabolism and Symbiosis*. Berlin: Jovis Verlag, 2005.

POSTSPARKASSE

1/ Hans, Hollein. *Global Architecture*. Japan: A.D.A. EDITA Tokyo Co. Ltd, 1978. **2/** Weston, Richard. *Key Buildings of the 20th Century: Plans, Sections and Elevations*. New York: W.W. Norton, 2010. **3/** Wagner, Otto. *Otto Wagners Postsparkasse*. Vienna: Zentralvereinigung der Architekten Österreichs, c.1975. **4/** Pile, John F. *A History of Interior Design*. United Kingdom: Laurence King, 2005. **5/** Geretsegger, Heinz, and Max Peintner. *Otto Wagner 1841–1918: The Expanding City and the Beginning of Modern Architecture*. New York: Rizzoli, 1979. **6/** Varnedoe, Kirk. *Vienna 1900: Art, Architecture, & Design*. New York: The Museum of Modern Art, 1986.

CASA MALAPARTE

1/ Davis, Colin. *Key Houses of the Twentieth Century*. New York: W.W. Norton, 2006. **2/** McDonough, Michael. *Malaparte: A House Like Me*. Clarkson Potter, 1999. **3/** Talamona, Marida. *Casa Malaparte*. New York: Princeton

Architectural Press, 1992. **4/** Garofalo, Francesco, and Luca Veresane. *Adalberto Libera*. New York: Princeton Architectural Press, 1992. **5/** Curtis, William J. R. *Modern Architecture Since 1900*. London: Phaidon Press Limited 1996. **6/** Quilici, Vieri. *Adalberto Libera: l'architettura come ideale*. Rome: Officina Edizioni, 1981.

SYDNEY OPERA HOUSE

1/ Norberg, Schulz, Christian. *Global Architecture*. Japan: A.D.A. EDITA Tokyo Co. Ltd, 1980. **2/** Watson, Anne. *Building a Masterpiece: The Sydney Opera House*. Sydney: Powerhouse, 2006. **3/** Drew, Philip. *Sydney Opera House: Jørn Utzon*. London: Phaidon, 1995. **4/** Weston, Richard. *Key Buildings of the 20th Century: Plans, Sections and Elevations*. New York: W.W. Norton & Co., 2010. **5/** Møller, Henrik Sten, and Vibe Udsen. *Jørn Utzon Houses*. Copenhagen: Living Architecture Publishing, 2006.

RUDOLPH HALL

1/ Monk, Tony. *The Art and Architecture of Paul Rudolph*. Chichester, West Sussex: Wiley-Academy, 1999. **2/** Rudolph, Paul, and Sibyl Moholy-Nagy. *The Architecture of Paul Rudolph*. New York: Praeger, 1970. **3/** Stoller, Ezra. *The Yale Art + Architecture Building*. New York: Princeton Architectural Press. 1999. **4/** Rudolph, Paul, and Yukio Futagawa. *Paul Rudolph, Architectural Drawings*. New York: Architectural Book Publishers, 1981. **5/** *Paul Rudolph: Drawings for the Art and Architecture Building at Yale 1959–1963*. New Haven: Yale University School of Architecture, 1988.

PHILLIPS EXETER ACADEMY LIBRARY

1/ Wiggins, Glenn E. *Louis I. Kahn: The Library at Phillips Exeter Academy*. New York: Wiley & Sons, Incorporated, 1997. **2/** Futagawa, Yukio. *Global Architecture 35: Kahn, Louis I. 1901–1974*. Tokyo: A.D.A. EDITA, 1975. **3/** Gast, Klaus-Peter. *Louis I Kahn: Complete Works*. Munich: DVA, 2002. **4/** McCarter, Robert. *Louis I Kahn*. London: Phaidon, 2005.

AEG TURBINE FACTORY

1/ Buddensieg, Tilmann. *Industriekultur: Peter Behrens and the AEG*. Cambridge: The MIT Press, 1984. **2/** Anderson, Stanford. *Peter Behrens and a New Architecture for the Twentieth Century*. Cambridge: The MIT Press, 2000. **3/** Sennott, R. Stephen. *Encyclopedia of 20th-Century Architecture*. New York: Fitzroy Dearborn, 2004. **4/** Anderson, Stanford. "Modern Architecture and Industry: Peter Behrens and the AEG Factories." In *Oppositions* 23, Winter 1981. Cambridge: The MIT Press, 1981.

FREDERICK C. ROBIE HOUSE

1/ Davis, Colin. *Key Houses of the Twentieth Century*. New York: W.W. Norton, 2006. **2/** Grehan, Farrell, and Frank Lloyd Wright. *Visions of Wright*. Boston: Bulfinch, 1997. **3/** Wright, Frank Lloyd. *The Robie House*. Palos Park, IL: Prairie School, 1968. **4/** Hoffmann, Donald, and Frank Lloyd Wright. *Frank Lloyd Wright's Robie House: The Illustrated Story of an Architectural Masterpiece*. New York: Dover Publishers, 1984.

SCHINDLER HOUSE

1/ Smith, Kathryn, and Grant Mudford. *Schindler House*. New York: Harry N. Abrams, 2001. **2/** Schindler, R. M.; Elizabeth A. T. Smith, and Michael Darling. *The Architecture of R.M. Schindler*. Los Angeles, CA: Museum of Contemporary Art, Los Angeles, 2001. **3/** Schindler, R. M., and Peter Noever. *MAK Center for Art and Architecture: R .M. Schindler*. Munich: Prestel, 1995. **4/** March, Lionel, and Judith Sheine. *RM Schindler: Composition and Construction*. London: Academy Editions, 1993. **5/** Gebhard, David. *Schindler*. Santa Barbara: Peregrine Smith, Inc., 1980. **6/** Sarnitz, August. *R.M. Schindler, Architect: 1887–1953*. New York: Rizzoli, 1988.

NATIONAL CONGRESS, BRAZIL

1/ Macedo, Danilo Matoso. *Congresso Nacional: Procedimentos projetuais e arquitetura brutalista*. Curitiba: X do.co.mo.mo brasil, 2013. **2/** Carranza, Luis E., and Fernando Luiz Lara. *Modern Architecture in Latin America: Art, Technology, and Utopia*. Austin: University of Texas Press, 2015. **3/** Galiano, Luis Fernandez. *Oscar Niemeyer: One Hundred Years*. Madrid: Arquitectura Viva, 2007. **4/** Mindlin, Henrique E. *Modern Architecture in Brazil*. Rio de Janeiro: Colibris Editora Ltda, 1956.

BAUHAUS DESSAU

1/ Irrgang, Christin. *The Bauhaus Building in Dessau*. Leipzig: Spector Books, 2014. **2/** Baumann, Kirsten. *Bauhaus Dessau: Architecture—Design—Concept*. Berlin: Jovis, 2007. **3/** Sharp, Dennis. *Bauhaus, Dessau: Walter Gropius*. New York: Phaidon, 2002. **4/** Colini, Laura, and Frank Eckardt, eds. *Bauhaus and the City: A Contest[ed] Heritage for a Challenging Future*. Würzburg: Königshausen & Neumann, 2011. **5/** Tafuri, Manfredo, and Francesco Dal Co. *Modern Architecture, Vol. 1*. Milan: Electa Editrice, 1976.

HONGKONG AND SHANGHAI BANK HEADQUARTERS

1/ Williams, Stephanie. *Hong Kong Bank: The Building of Norman Foster's Masterpiece*. London: Cape, 1989. **2/** Foster, Norman. *Norman Foster: Drawings 1958–2008*. London: Ivory Press, 2010. **3/** Hongkong and Shanghai Bank Headquarters. (n.d.). Retrieved from http://www.fosterandpartners.com/projects/hongkong-and-shanghai-bank-headquarters/. **4/** Sudjic, Deyan. *New Architecture: Foster, Rogers, Stirling*. London: Thames and Hudson Ltd., 1986.

GLASGOW SCHOOL OF ART

1/ Grigg, Jocelyn. *Charles Rennie Mackintosh*. Salt Lake City: Gibbs Smith, 1988. **2/** Plunkett, Drew; Peter Trowles, Paul Heyer, and Shashi Caan. *Four Studies on Charles Rennie Mackintosh*. New York: New York School of Interior Design, 1996. **3/** Young, Andrew McLaren. *Charles Rennie Mackintosh (1808–1928): Architecture, Design and Painting*. Edinburgh: Edinburgh Festival Society, 1968. **4/** Buchanan, William. *Mackintosh's Masterwork: Charles Rennie Mackintosh and the Glasgow School of Art*. San Francisco: Chronicle, 1989. **5/** Macaulay, James, and Mark Fiennes. *Charles Rennie Mackintosh*. New York: W.W. Norton, 2010.

VILLA MAIREA

1/ Aalto, Alvar. *Villa Mairea*. Helsinki: Alvar Aalto Foundation, 1998. **2/** Davis, Colin. *Key Houses of the Twentieth Century*. New York: W.W. Norton, 2006. **3/** Weston, Richard. *Villa Mairea (Architecture in Detail)*. London: Phaidon Press, 2002. **4/** Gullichsen, Kirsi, and Ulla Kinnunen, eds. *Inside the Villa Mairea: Art, Design, and Interior Architecture*. Jyväskylä: Alvar Aalto Museum/Mairea Foundation, 2010. **5/** Blomstedt, Aulis; Alvar Aalto, and Aino Aalto. *Villa Mairea*. Jyväskylä: Alvar Aalto Museum, 1981. **6/** Aalto, Alvar, and Karl Fleig, eds. *Alvar Aalto: Band I 1922–1962*. Zurich: Les Editions d'Architecture Artemis, 1963.

THE ASSEMBLY, CHANDIGARH

1/ Boesiger, W., ed. *Le Corbusier; Œuvre Complete 1957–1965*. New York: George Wittenborn, Inc., 1965. **2/** Corbusier, Le. *Creation Is a Patient Search*. New York: Praeger, 1960. **3/** Högner, Bärbel; Clemens Kroll, Arthur Rüegg, Arno Lederer, and Mahendra Narain Sharma. *Chandigarh: Living with Le Corbusier*. Berlin: Jovis Verlag, 2010. **4/** Corbusier, Le. *Chandigarh: City and Musée*. New York: Garland Publishers, 1983. **5/** Scheidegger, Ernst; Maristella Casciato, and Stanislaus von Moos. *Chandigarh 1956: Le Corbusier, Pierre Jeanneret, Jane B. Drew, E. Maxwell Fry*. Zürich: Scheidegger & Spiess, 2010.

STOCKHOLM PUBLIC LIBRARY

1/ Adams, Nicholas. *Gunnar Asplund*. Milan: Mondadori Electa, 2011. **2/** Frampton, Kenneth, and Yukio Futagawa. *Modern Architecture 1920–1945*. New York: Rizzoli, 1983. **3/** Holmdahl, Gustav; Sven Ivar Lind, and Kjell Ödeen. *Gunnar Asplund Architect, 1885–1940*. Stockholm: AB Tidskriften Byggmästaren, 1950. **4/** Wrede, Stuart. *The Architecture of Erik Gunnar Asplund*. Cambridge: The MIT Press, 1980. **5/** Jones, Peter Blundell. *Gunnar Asplund*. New York: Phaidon Press Inc., 2006.

NATIONAL OLYMPIC GYMNASIUM

1/ Boyd, Robin. *Kenzo Tange*. New York, G. Braziller, 1962. **2/** Tange, Kenzo, and Udo Kultermann. *Kenzo Tange, 1946–1969; Architecture and Urban Design*. New York: Praeger Publishers, 1970. **3/** Von der Muhll, H.R; Kenzo Tange and Udo Kultermann. *Kenzo Tange*. Zurich: Verlag fur Architekur Artemis, 1978. **4/** Kuan, Seng; Yukio Lippit and Harvard University, GSD. *Kenzo Tange: Architecture for the World*. Baden: Lars Muller; London: Springer [distributor], 2012.

SENDAI MEDIATHEQUE

1/ Gregory, Rob. *Key Contemporary Buildings: Plans, Sections, and Elevations*. New York: W.W. Norton & Company, 2008. **2/** Witte, Ron, ed. *Toyo Ito, Sendai Mediatheque (CASE series)*. Munich: Prestel, 2002. **3/** Ito, Toyo, and Mutsuro Sasaki. *Toyo Ito: Sendai Mediatheque. Miyagi, Japan; 1995–2000 (GA Detail 2)*. Tokyo: ADA EDITA, 2001. **4/** Ito, Toyo; Riken Yamamoto, Dana Buntrock, and Taro Igarashi. *Toyo Ito*. New York: Phaidon Press, 2009. **5/** Maffei, Andrea, ed. *Toyo Ito: Works, Projects, Writings*. Milan: Electa, 2001.

EINSTEIN TOWER

1/ Cobbers, Arnt. *Erich Mendelsohn, 1887–1953: The Analytical Visionary*. Los Angeles: Taschen, 2007. **2/** Hentschel, Klaus. *The Einstein Tower: An Intertexture of Dynamic Construction, Relativity Theory, and Astronomy*. Stanford: Stanford University Press, 1997. **3/** Zevi, Bruno. *Erich Mendelsohn: The Complete Works*. Basel: Birkhäuser Publishers, 1999. **4/** Mendelsohn, Erich. *Erich Mendelsohn: Architekt, 1887–1953: Gebaute Welten: Arbeiten für Europa, Palästina und Amerika*. Ostfildern-Ruit: Hatje, 1998. **5/** Morgenthaler, Hans Rudolf. *The Early Sketches of German Architect Erich Mendelsohn (1887–1953): No Compromise with Reality*. Lewiston, NY: E. Mellen Press, 1992. **6/** Von Eckardt, Wolf. *Eric Mendelsohn*. New York: George Braziller, Inc., 1960.

LEVER HOUSE

1/ Danz, Ernst-Joachim. *SOM: Architecture of Skidmore, Owings & Merrill, 1950–1962*. New York: Monacelli, 2009. **2/** Bussel, Abby. *SOM Evolutions: Recent Work of Skidmore, Owings & Merrill*. Boston: Birkhäuser, 2000. **3/** Weston, Richard. *Key Buildings of the 20th Century: Plans, Sections and Elevations*. New York: W.W. Norton, 2010.

DIAMOND RANCH HIGH SCHOOL

1/ Kipnis, Jeffrey, and Todd Gannon, ed. *Morphosis: Diamond Ranch High School, Diamond Bar, California; Thomas Blurock Architects, Executive Architects*. New York: Monacelli Press, 2001. **2/** Gregory, Rob. *Key Contemporary Buildings: Plans, Sections and Elevations*. New York: W.W. Norton & Company, 2008. **3/** Croft, Catherine. *Concrete Architecture*. London: Lauren King Publishing Ltd., 2004. **4/** Hille, R. Thomas. *Modern Schools: A Century of Design Education*. Hoboken, New Jersey: John Wiley & Sons, Inc., 2011.

5/ Futagawa, Yukio. *GA Document Extra 09: Morphosis*. Tokyo: A.D.A. EDITA, 1997.

GLASS HOUSE

1/ Johnson, Philip. *Johnson House, New Canaan, Connecticut, 1949*– edited by Yukio Futagawa, Tokyo: A.D.A. EDITA, 1972. 2/ Cassidy-Geiger, Maureen. *The Philip Johnson Glass House: An Architect in the Garden*. New York: Skira/ Rizzoli, 2016. 3/ Heyer, Paul. *American Architecture: Ideas and Ideologies in the Late Twentieth Century*. New York: Van Nostrand Reinhold, 1993. 4/ Saunders, William S. *Modern Architecture*. New York: Harry N. Abrams, Publishers, 1990. 5/ Sharp, Dennis. *Twentieth Century Architecture: A Visual History*. New York: Facts on File, 1990. 6/ Nakamura, Toshio, ed. *Glass House*. New York: The Monacelli Press, 2007.

FORD FOUNDATION HEADQUARTERS

1/ Futagawa, Yukio; Hiroshi Hara, Kevin Roche, John Dinkeloo and Associates. *The Ford Foundation Building, New York, 1967; The Oakland Museum, California, 1969*. Tokyo: A.D.A. EDITA, 1971. 2/ Huxtable, Ada Louise. "Bold Plan for Building Revealed." *The New York Times*. 1967. 3/ Roche, Kevin, and Francesco Dal Co. *Kevin Roche*. New York: Rizzoli, 1985. 4/ Weston, Richard. *Key Buildings of the Twentieth Century: Plans, Sections, and Elevations*. New York: W.W. Norton, 2004. 5/ Hozumi, Nobuo. *The Ford Foundation Headquarters, New York, N.Y., 1963–68*. Tokyo: A.D.A. EDITA, 1977.

OLYMPIC STADIUM, MUNICH

1/ Glaeser, Ludwig. *The Work of Frei Otto*. Connecticut: MoMA, New York Graphic Society, 1972. 2/ Songel, Juan María. *A Conversation with Frei Otto*. New York: Princeton Architectural Press, 2010. 3/ Otto, Frei; Bodo Rasch, Gerd Pfafferodt, Adelheid Grafin Schonborn, and Sabine Schanz. *Frei Otto, Bodo Rasch: Finding Form, Towards an Architecture of the Minimal*. Stuttgart: Axel Menges, 1995. 4/ Meissner, Irene, and Eberhard Möller. *Frei Otto: Forschen, Bauen, Inspirieren=Frei Otto-a Life of Research, Construction and Inspiration*. München: Detail-Institut Für Internationale Architektur-Dokumentation, 2015. 5/ "Die Verwirklichung einer Idee. Anlagen u. Bauten für die Olympischen Spiele 1972." *Bauen+Wohnen* (special issue), 1972.

GEHRY HOUSE

1/ Arnell, Peter; Ted Bickford, ed., and Mason Andrews. *Frank Gehry, Buildings and Projects*. New York: Rizzoli, 1985. 2/ Rappolt, Mark, and Robert Violette, ed. *Gehry Draws*. Cambridge: MIT Press, 2004. 3/ Gehry, Frank O.; Yukio Futagawa, Robert Violette. *Frank O. Gehry: Gehry Residence*. Tokyo: A.D.A. EDITA, 2015. 4/ Dal Co, Francesco, and Kurt W. Forester. *Frank O. Gehry: The Complete Works*. New York: The Monacelli Press, 1997.

IGUALADA CEMETERY

1/ Zabalbeascoa, Anatxu. *Igualada Cemetery: Enric Miralles and Carme Pinós*. London: Phaidon, 1996. 2/ Reed, Peter. *Groundswell: Constructing the Contemporary Landscape*. New York, NY: Museum of Modern Art, 2005. 3/ Berrizbeitia, Anita, and Linda Pollak. *Inside Outside: Between Architecture and Landscape*. Gloucester: Rockport Press, 1999. 4/ Betsky, Aaron. *Landscrapers: Building with the Land*. New York, NY: Thames & Hudson, 2002. 5/ Buchanan, Peter; Josep Maria Montaner, Dennis L. Dollens, and Lauren Kogod. *The Architecture of Enric Miralles and Carme Pinós*. New York: SITES/ Lumen Books, 1990.

CROWN HALL

1/ Mies van der Rohe, Ludwig. *The Mies van der Rohe Archive*. New York: Garland Pub, 1986. 2/ Blaser, Werner. *Mies Van Der Rohe — IIT Campus: Illinois Institute of Technology, Chicago*. Basel: Birkhäuser, 2002. 3/ Mies van der Rohe, Ludwig; Yukio Futagawa, and Ludwig Glaeser. *Crown Hall, IIT, Chicago, Illinois, U.S.A., 1952–56: New National Gallery, Berlin, West Germany, 1968*. Tokyo: A.D.A. EDITA, 1972. 4/ Blaser, Werner, and Ludwig Mies van der Rohe. *Mies Van Der Rohe: IIT Campus, Illinois Institute of Technology, Chicago*. Basel: Birkhäuser, 2002.

VANNA VENTURI HOUSE

1/ Venturi, Robert. *Complexity and Contradiction in Architecture*. New York: The Museum of Modern Art, 1966. 2/ Schwartz, Frederic; Vincent Scully, Jr., and Robert Venturi. *Mother's House: The Evolution of Vanna Venturi's House in Chestnut Hill*. New York: Rizzoli, 1992. 3/ Futagawa, Yukio; Paul Goldberger, Venturi and Rauch. *Venturi and Rauch: Vanna Venturi House, Chestnut Hill, Philadelphia, Pa., 1962; Peter Brant House, Greenwich, Conn., 1973; Carll Tucker III House, Westchester County, NY, 1975*. Tokyo: A.D.A. EDITA, 1976. 4/ Blackwood, Michael; Robert Venturi, Denise Scott Brown, Stephen Plumlee, Michael Blackwood Productions, Westdeutscher Rundfunk, British Broadcasting Corporation, Television Service. *Robert Venturi and Denise Scott Brown*. New York: Michael Blackwood Productions, 2006 Video. 5/ Carnicero, Iñaqui. *Louis Kahn y Robert Venturi: Coincidencias del Gianicolo a Chestnut Hill*. Madrid: Departamento de Proyectos Arquitectónicos, 2015.

LOVELL HEALTH HOUSE

1/ Hines, Thomas. *Richard Neutra and the Search for Modern Architecture*. New York: Rizzoli, 2006. 2/ Lavin, Sylvia. *Form Follows Libido: Architecture and Richard Neutra in a Psychoanalytic Culture*. Cambridge: The MIT Press, 2004. 3/ Weston, Richard. *Key Buildings of the 20th Century: Plans, Sections and Elevations*. New York: W.W. Norton & Co., 2010. 4/ Davies, Colin. *Key Houses of the Twentieth Century*. New York: W.W. Norton, 2006.

TUGENDHAT HOUSE

1/ Hammer-Tugendhat, Daniela; Ivo Hammer, and Wolf Tegethoff. *Tugendhat House: Ludwig Mies van der Rohe*. Vienna: Springer, 2015. **2/** Futagawa, Yoshio, and Yukio Futagawa. *Mies van der Rohe: Villa Tugendhat Brno, Czechoslovakia,1928–30*. Tokyo, Japan: A.D.A. EDITA, 2016. **3/** Mies van der Rohe, Ludwig; Beatriz Colomina, Moisés Puente, and Hans-Christian Schink. *Mies van der Rohe: Casas*. Barcelona: GG, 2009. **4/** Dunster, David. *Key Buildings of the Twentieth Century. Vol. 1*. London: Architectural Press, 1985.

BAKER HOUSE

1/ Anderson, Stanford; Gail Fenske, and David Fixler. *Aalto and America*. New Haven: Yale University Press, 2012. **2/** Menin, Sarah. *Baker House: Aalto at M.I.T.* Newcastle: Newcastle University, 1986. Dissertation. **3/** Ray, Nicholas. *Alvar Aalto*. New Haven: Yale University Press, 2005. **4/** Schildt, Göran, and Alvar Aalto. *Alvar Aalto in His Own Words*. New York: Rizzoli, 1998. **5/** Hästesko, Arne, and Alvar Aalto. *Alvar Aalto: What & When*. Helsinki: Rakennustieto Publishing, 2014. **6/** Fleig, Karl, and Alvar Aalto, eds. *Alvar Aalto; Band I 1922–1962*. Zurich: Les Editions d'Architecture Artemis, 1963.

BARRAGÁN HOUSE AND STUDIO

1/ Alfaro, Alfonso; Daniel Garza Usabiaga, and Juan Palomar. *Luis Barragán: His House*. Mexico City: RM, 2011. **2/** Barragán, Luis; Yukio Futagawa, and Emilio Ambasz. *House and Atelier for Luis Barragán, Tacubaya, Mexico City, 1947: Los Clubes, Suburb of Mexico City, 1963–69: San Cristobal, Suburb of Mexico City, 1967–68 (With the Collaboration of Arch. Andrés Casillas)*. Tokyo: A.D.A. EDITA, 1997. **3/** Futagawa, Yoshio, and Yukio Futagawa. *Luis Barragán: Barragán House: Mexico City, Mexico 1947–48*. Tokyo: A.D.A. EDITA Tokyo, 2009. **4/** Louis de Malave, Florita Z. *Luis Barragan, the Architect and His Work*. Monticello, Ill: Vance Bibliographies, 1983.

THE BEINECKE RARE BOOK & MANUSCRIPT LIBRARY

1/ Krinsky, Carol Herselle. *Gordon Bunshaft of SOM*. Cambridge: The MIT Press, 1988. **2/** Pavan, Vincenzo. *Scriptures in Stone: Tectonic Language and Decorative Language*. Milan: Skira, 2001. **3/** Perez, Adelyn. "AD Classics: Beinecke Rare Book and Manuscript Library/Gordon Bunshaft of Skidmore, Owings, & Merrill." *ArchDaily*. <http://www.archdaily.com/65987/ad-classics-beinecke-rare-book-and-manuscript-library-skidmore-owings-merrill>, 2010.

MUSEU DE ARTE DE SÃO PAULO

1/ Oliveira, Olivia de. *Lina Bo Bardi Built Work; 2G–Revista Internacional de Arquitectura (n° 23/ 24)*. Sao Paulo: Editora Gustavo Gilli, 2002. **2/** Frers, Lars, and Lars Meier. *Encountering Urban Places, Visual and Material Performances in the City*. Hampshire: Ashgate Publishing Ltd, 2007. **3/** Carranza, Luis E., and Fernando Luiz Lara. *Modern Architecture in Latin America: Art, Technology, and Utopia*. Austin: University of Texas Press, 2015.

BRION FAMILY TOMB

1/ McCarter, Robert. *Carlo Scarpa*. London: Phaidon Press, 2013. **2/** Dal Co, Francesco, and Giuseppe Mazzariol. *Carlo Scarpa: The Complete Works*. New York: Electa/Rizzoli, 1985. **3/** Beltramini, Guido, and Italo Zannier, eds. *Carlo Scarpa: Architecture and Design*. New York: Rizzoli, 2007. **4/** Saito, Yutaka, Hiroyuki Toyoda, and Nobuaki Furuya. *Carlo Scarpa*. Toyko: TOTO Shuppan, 1997.

NATIONAL ASSEMBLY BUILDING, BANGLADESH

1/ Kahn, Louis I.; Yukio Futagawa, and Kazi K. Ashraf. *Louis I. Kahn, National Capital of Bangladesh, Dhaka, Bangladesh, 1962–83*. Tokyo: A.D.A. EDITA Tokyo, 1994. **2/** Kahn, Louis I.; David B. Brownlee, Kate Norment, and David G. De Long. *Louis I. Kahn: In the Realm of Architecture*. New York: Rizzoli, 1991. **3/** Kries, Mateo; Jochen Eisenbrand, and Stanislaus von Moos. *Louis Kahn: The Power of Architecture*. Weil Am Rhein: Vitra Design Museum, 2012. **4/** Kahn, Nathaniel, dir.; Louis Kahn Project, Inc.; Mediaworks, Inc.; HBO/Cinemax Documentary Films; New Yorker Films. *My Architect: A Son's Journey*. DVD, 2003. **5/** McCarter, Robert. *Louis I. Kahn*. London: Phaidon, 2005.

NEUE STAATSGALERIE

1/ Rodiek, Thorsten. *James Stirling Die Neue Staatsgalerie Stuttgart*. Baden-Baden: Verlag Gerd Hatje, 1984. **2/** Baratelli, Alberto. *James Stirling: La Galleria di Stato di Stoccarda*. Florence: Alinea, 2002. **3/** Barthelmess, Stephan. *Das postmoderne Museum als Erscheinungsform von Architektur*. Munich: Tuduv, 1988. **4/** Maxwell, Robert. *James Stirling: Writings on Architecture*. London: Skira, 1998. **5/** Arnell, Peter; Ted Bickford, James Stirling, Michael Wilford and Associates. *James Stirling: Buildings and Projects; James Stirling, Michael Wilford, and Associates*. New York: Rizzoli, 1984.

NATIONAL MUSEUM OF ROMAN ART

1/ Weston, Richard. *Key Buildings of the 20th Century: Plans, Sections and Elevations*. New York: W.W. Norton & Co., 2010. **2/** Jodidio, Philip. *Architecture Now! Museums*. Cologne: Taschen, 2010. **3/** Cortes, Juan Antonio. *Rafael Moneo: International Portfolio 1985–2012*. Germany: Axel Menges, 2013. **4/** Gonzalez, Francisco, and Nicholas Ray. *Rafael Moneo: Building, Teaching, Writing*. Connecticut: Yale University Press, 2015. **5/** Casamonti, Marco. *Rafael Moneo (Minimum, Essential Architecture Library)*. Milan: Motta, 2009.

MAISON À BORDEAUX

1/ Koolhaas, Rem. *OMA Rem Koolhaas Living, Vivre, Leben*. Boston: Birkhäuser Verlag, 1998. **2/** Kara, Hanif; Andreas Georgoulias, and Jorge Silvetti. *Interdisciplinary Design: New Lessons from Architecture and Engineering*. Barcelona: Actar, 2012. **3/** Kolarevic, Branko, and Vera Parlac. *Building*

Dynamics: Exploring Architecture of Change. New York: Routledge, 2015. **4/** Böck, Ingrid, and Rem Koolhaas. *Six Canonical Projects by Rem Koolhaas: Essays on the History of Ideas*. Berlin: Jovis, 2015.

CASA MILÀ

1/ Güell, Xavier. *Antoni Gaudí*. Barcelona: Editorial Gustavo Gili, 1992. **2/** Zerbst, Rainer. *Gaudí, 1852–1926: Antoni Gaudí i Cornet: A Life Devoted to Architecture*. Cologne: Benedikt Taschen Verlag, 1988. **3/** Cuito, Aurora; Cristina Montes, and Antoni Gaudí. *Antoni Gaudí: Complete Works*. Cologne: Evergreen, 2009. **4/** Gaudí, Antoni; Michel Tapié, Joaquim Gomis, and Joan Prats Vallès. *Gaudi—La Pedrera*. Barcelona: Polígrafa, 1971. **5/** Collins, George R. *Antoni Gaudí*. New York: George Braziller, 1960.

SÄYNÄTSALO TOWN HALL

1/ Schildt, Göran, and Alvar Aalto. *Alvar Aalto: Masterworks*. New York: Universe Pub, 1998. **2/** Trencher, Michael. *The Alvar Aalto Guide*. New York: Princeton Architectural Press, 1996. **3/** Aalto, Alvar; Richard Weston, and Simo Rista. *Town Hall, Säynätsalo: Alvar Aalto*. London: Phaidon Press, 1994. **4/** Muto, Akira; Yukio Futagawa, and Alvar Aalto. *Alvar Aalto: Town Hall in Säynätsalo, Säynätsalo, Finland, 1950–52; Public Pensions Institute (Kansaneläkelaitos), Helsinki, Finland 1952–56*. Tokyo: A.D.A. EDITA, 1981.

LLOYD'S OF LONDON

1/ Rogers, Richard, & Architects. *Richard Rogers + Architects: From the House to the City*. London: Fiell, 2010. **2/** Cole, Barbie Campbell, and Ruth E. Rogers. *Richard Rogers + Architects*. New York: St. Martin's Press, 1985. **3/** Rogers, Richard, + Partners. *Lloyd's of London*. Milan: Edizioni Tecno, 1985. **4/** Powell, Ken, and Richard Partnership. *Lloyd's Building: Richard Rogers Partnership*. London: Phaidon Press, 1994. **5/** Gibbs, David. *Building Lloyd's*. London: Pentagram Design, 1986. **6/** Cook, Peter, and Richard Rogers. *Richard Rogers + Partners: An Architectural Monograph*. New York: St. Martin's Press, Inc., 1985.

INSTITUT DU MONDE ARABE

1/ Montaner, Josep Maria. *Neue Museen: Räume Für Kunst Und Kultur*. Stuttgart: Krämer, 1990. **2/** Lacroix, Hugo. *L'Institut Du Monde Arabe*. Paris: La Différence, 2007. **3/** Noever, Peter, and Regina Haslinger. *Architecture in Transition: Between Deconstruction and New Modernism*. Munich: Prestel, 1991. **4/** Nouvel, Jean. *Jean Nouvel, His Recent Works, 1987–1990*. Barcelona: Colegio De Arquitectos De Cataluña, 1989. **5/** Boissiere, Olivier. *Jean Nouvel: Jean Nouvel, Emmanuel Cattani and Associates*. Zurich: Artemis Velags-AG, 1992.

PARC DE LA VILLETTE

1/ Tschumi, Bernard; Jacques Derrida, and Anthony Vidler. *Tschumi Parc de la Villette*. London: Artifice, 2014. **2/** Tschumi, Bernard. *Cinégram Folie: Le Parc de La Villette*. Princeton: Princeton Architectural Press, 1987. **3/** de Bure, Gilles; Jasmine Benjamin, and Lisa Palmer. *Bernard Tschumi*. Boston: Birkhäuser Verlag, 2008. **4/** Tschumi, Bernard. *Architecture Concepts: Red Is Not a Color*. New York: Rizzoli, 2012.

JEWISH MUSEUM BERLIN

1/ Libeskind, Daniel. *Daniel Libeskind Jewish Museum Berlin*. Barcelona: Ediciones Poligrafa, 2011. **2/** Libeskind, Daniel; Connie Wolf, Mitchell Schwarzer, and James Edward Young. *Daniel Libeskind and the Contemporary Jewish Museum: New Jewish Architecture from Berlin to San Francisco*. New York: Rizzoli, 2008. **3/** Schneider, Bernhard. *Daniel Libeskind: Jewish Museum Berlin: Between the Lines*. New York: Prestel, 1999. **4/** Binet, Hélène, and Raoul Bunschoten. *A Passage Through Silence and Light*. London: Black Dog Publishing, 1997.

HILLSIDE TERRACE COMPLEX I–VI

1/ Maki, Fumihiko. *Fumihiko Maki*. London: Phaidon, 2009. **2/** Maki, Fumihiko, and Mark Mulligan. *Nurturing Dreams: Collected Essays on Architecture and the City*. Cambridge, MA: MIT, 2008. **3/** Taylor, Jennifer; Fumihiko Maki, and James Conner. *The Architecture of Fumihiko Maki: Space, City, Order, and Making*. Basel: Birkhäuser-Publishers for Architecture, 2003. **4/** Maki, Fumihiko, and Arata Isozaki. *New Public Architecture: Recent Projects by Fumihiko Maki and Arata Isozaki*. New York: Japan Society, 1985. **5/** a+t research group (Aurora Fernández Per, Javier Mozas, Alex S. Ollero). "Slow City," in *10 Stories of Collective Housing*, trans. Ken Mortimer, Vitoria-Gasteiz: a+t architecture publlishers, 2013.

SMITH HOUSE

1/ Meier, Richard. *Richard Meier: Smith House, Darien, Connecticut, 1967 / House in Old Westbury, Long Island, New York, 1971*. Tokyo: A.D.A. EDITA Tokyo, 1976. **2/** Clark, Roger H., and Michael Pause. *Precedents in Architecture, 2E*. New York: Van Nostrand Reinhold, 1996. **3/** Saunders, William S. *Modern Architecture*. New York: Harry N. Abrams Publishers, 1990. **4/** Eisenman, Peter; Michael Graves, Charles Gwathmey, John Hejduk, and Richard Meier. *Five Architects: Eisenman, Graves, Gwathmey, Hejduk, Meier*. London: Oxford University Press, 1975. **5/** Meier, Richard. *Richard Meier, Architect, 1964–1984*. New York: Rizzoli, 1984.

NEW NATIONAL GALLERY

1/ Mertins, Detlef, Ludwig Mies van der Rohe, and Phyllis Lambert. *Mies*. London: Phaidon, 2014. **2/** Vandenberg, Maritz, and Michael Brawne. *Twentieth-Century Museums I: Ludwig Mies van der Rohe, New National Gallery, Berlin:*

Louis Kahn, Kimbell Art Museum: Richard Meier, Museum für Kunsthandwerk. London: Phaidon, 1999. **3/** Vandenberg, Maritz, and Ludwig Mies van der Rohe. *New National Gallery, Berlin, Ludwig Mies van der Rohe*. London: Phaidon, 1998. **4/** Glaeser, Ludwig, and Yukio Futagawa. *Mies van der Rohe: Crown Hall, IIT, Chicago, Illinois, U.S.A. 1952–56. New National Gallery, Berlin, West Germany, 1968*. Tokyo: A.D.A. EDITA, 1974. **5/** Jarzombek, Mark. "Mies van der Rohe's New National Gallery and the Problem of Context," in *Assemblage*, No. 2. Cambridge: The MIT Press, 1987.

CASTELVECCHIO MUSEUM

1/ Murphy, Richard. *Carlo Scarpa & Castelvecchio*. Venice: Arsenale editrice, 1991. **2/** Marinelli, Sergio. *Castelvecchio a Verona*. Milan: Electa, 1991. **3/** Di Lieto, Alba. *I disegni di Carlo Scarpa per Castelvecchio*. Venice: Marsilio, 2006. **4/** Magnagnato, Licisco. *Carlo Scarpa a Castelvecchio*. Milan: Scotti, 1983.

PISCINA DE MARÉS

1/ Testa, Peter. *Álvaro Siza*. Boston: Birkhäuser Verlag, 1996. **2/** Moschini, Francesco. *Álvaro Siza: l'architetto che voleva essere scultore*. Galatina: Editrice Salentina, 2008. **3/** Siza, Álvaro, and Kenneth Frampton. *Alvaro Siza: Complete Works*. London: Phaidon, 2000. **4/** Jodidio, Philip; Alvaro Siza, Kristina Brigitta Köper, and Jacques Bosser. *Álvaro Siza: Complete Works 1952–2013*. Cologne: Taschen, 2013.

MICHAELERPLATZ HOUSE (LOOSHAUS)

1/ Gravagnuolo, Benedetto. *Adolf Loos*. New York: Rizzoli, 1982. **2/** Tournikiotis, Panayotis. *Adolf Loos*. New York, NY: Princeton Architectural Press, 2002. **3/** Münz, Ludwig, and Gustave Künstler. *Adolf Loos, Pioneer of Modern Architecture*. New York: Praeger, 1966. **4/** Stewart, Janet. *Fashioning Vienna: Adolf Loos's Cultural Criticism*. London: Routledge, 2000. **5/** Pogačnik, Marko. *Adolf Loos E Vienna: La Casa Sulla Michaelerplatz*. Macerata: Quodlibet, 2011.

RUSAKOV WORKERS' CLUB

1/ Fosso, Mario, and Maurizio Meriggi. *Konstantin S. Mel'nikov and the Construction of Moscow*. Milan: Skira, 2001. **2/** Thiel-Siling, Sabine, and Wolfgang Bachmann. *Icons of Architecture: The 20th Century*. New York: Prestel, 1998. **3/** Starr, S. Frederick. *Melnikov: Solo Architect in a Mass Society*. Princeton: Princeton University Press, 1978. **4/** Wortmann, Arthur, and Konstantin Stepanovich Mel'nikov. *Melnikov, The Muscles of Invention*. Rotterdam: Van Hezik-Fonds 90, 1990.

MILL OWNERS' ASSOCIATION BUILDING

1/ Boesiger, W., ed. *Le Corbusier et son atelier rue de Sèvres 35: Œuvre complete 1952–1957*. Zurich: Verlag für Architecktur, Artemis, 1957. **2/** Curtis, William J. R. *Le Corbusier: Ideas and Forms*. Oxford: Phaidon, 1986. **3/** Ching, Francis D. K.; Mark Jarzombek, and Vikramaditya Prakash. *A Global History of Architecture*. Hoboken: J. Wiley & Sons, 2011. **4/** Corbusier, Le; Yukio Futagawa, and Kenneth Frampton. *Millowners Association Building, Ahmedabad, India, 1954: Carpenter Center for Visual Arts, Harvard University, Cambridge, Massachusetts, U.S.A. 1961–64*. Tokyo, A.D.A. EDITA Tokyo, 1975.

STAHL HOUSE (CASE STUDY HOUSE NO. 22)

1/ Smith, Elizabeth A. T.; Julius Shulman, and Peter Gössel. *Case Study Houses: The Complete CSH Program 1945–1966*. Hong Kong: Taschen, 2009. **2/** Street-Porter, Tim. *L.A. Modern*. New York: Rizzoli, 2008. **3/** Jackson, N., and Peter Gössel. *Pierre Koenig, 1925–2004: Living with Steel*. Hong Kong: Taschen, 2007. **4/** Steele, James; Pierre Koenig, and David Jenkins. *Pierre Koenig*. London: Phaidon, 2002.

THE BREUER BUILDING (WHITNEY MUSEUM OF AMERICAN ART)

1/ McCarter, Robert, and Marcel Breuer. *Breuer*, 2016. **2/** Bergdoll, Barry, and Massey, Jonathan. *Marcel Breuer: Building Global Institutions*. Zurich, Switzerland: Lars Muller Publishers, 2016. **3/** Cobbers, Arnt. *Marcel Breuer: 1902–1981: Form Giver of the Twentieth Century*. Köln: Taschen, 2007. **4/** Remmele, Mathias; Alexandra Pioch, Alexander von Vegesack, and Marcel Breuer. *Marcel Breuer: Design and Architecture*. Weil am Rhein: Vitra Design Museum, 2003.

ROOFTOP REMODELING FALKESTRASSE

1/ Gössel, Peter, and Michael Mönninger. *Coop Himmelb(l)au: Complete Works 1968–2010*. Köln: Taschen, 2010. **2/** Offermann, Klaus. *Architekten, Coop Himmelblau*. Stuttgart: IRB Verlag, 1988. **3/** Prix, Wolf D.; Helmut Swiczinsky, Gudrun Hausegger, and Martina Kandeler-Fritsch. *Coop Himmelblau Austria: From Cloud to Cloud: Biennale di Venezia 1996*. Klagenfurt: Ritter, 1996. **4/** Vidler, Anthony. *Warped Space: Art, Architecture, and Anxiety in Modern Culture*. Cambridge: MIT, 2000. **5/** Moon, Karen. *Modeling Messages: The Architect and the Model*. New York: Monacelli, 2005.

LARKIN COMPANY ADMINISTRATION BUILDING

1/ Quinan, Jack. *Frank Lloyd Wright's Larkin Building: Myth and Fact*. Cambridge: The MIT Press, 1987. **2/** Sáenz de Oiza, F.J., et al. *AV Monografías 54: Frank Lloyd Wright*. Madrid: Arquitectura Viva, 1995. **3/** Lind, Carla. *Lost Wright: Frank Lloyd Wright's Vanished Masterpieces*. New York: Simon & Schuster, 1996. **4/** Cattermole, Paul. *Architectural Excellence: 500 Iconic Buildings*. Richmond Hill: Firefly Books, 2008. **5/** Banham, Reyner. "The Services of the Larkin 'A' Building," *The Journal of the Society of Architectural*

Historians, Vol. 37, No. 3 (Oct. 1978). Philadelphia: Society of Architectural Historians, 1978. Journal. **6/** Scully, Vincent Jr. *Frank Lloyd Wright*. New York: George Braziller, Inc., 1960.

FIAT WORKS

1/ Frampton, Kenneth. *Modern Architecture 1851–1945*. New York: Rizzoli International Publications, 1983. **2/** Sharp, Dennis. *Twentieth Century Architecture: a Visual History*. New York: Facts on File, 1990. **3/** Hofmann, Werner, and Udo Kultermann. *Modern Architecture in Color*. New York: The Viking Press, 1970. **4/** Kirk, Terry. *The Architecture of Modern Italy, Volume II: Visions of Utopia, 1900–Present*. New York: Princeton Architectural Press, 2005.

VILLA MÜLLER

1/ Loos, Adolf; Yehuda Safran, Wilfried Wang, and Mildred Budny. *The Architecture of Adolf Loos: An Arts Council Exhibition*. London: The Council, 1985. **2/** Colombian, Beatriz, "The Split Wall: Domestic Voyeurism," in *Sexuality and Space*. New York: Princeton University Press, 1992. **3/** Sarnitz, August. *Adolf Loos, 1870–1933: Architect, Cultural Critic, Dandy*. Cologne: Taschen, 2003. **4/** Tournikiotis, Panayotis. *Adolf Loos*. New York: Princeton Architectural Press, 2002. **5/** Loos, Adolf. *Adolf Loos*. Vienna: Graphische Sammlung Albertina, 1989. **6/** Risselada, Max, ed. *Raumplan versus Plan Libre: Adolf Loos and Le Corbusier 1919–1930*. New York: Rizzoli, 1988. **7/** Gravagnuolo, Benedetto. *Adolf Loos*. New York: Rizzoli, 1982.

VAN NELLE FACTORY

1/ Molenaar, Joris. *Brinkman et Van der Vlugt Architects: Rotterdam's City-Ideal in International Style*. Rotterdam: Nai010 Publ, 2012. **2/** Van der Oever, Martín. *Van Nelle Fabriek in Stereo*. Rotterdam: Uitgeverij 010 Publishers, 2002. **3/** J.A. Brinkman en L.C. Van der Vlugt (Firm); Jeroen Geurst, and Yukio Futagawa. *J.A. Brinkman and L.C. van der Vlugt: Van Nelle Factory, Rotterdam, the Netherlands, 1925–31*. Tokyo: A.D.A. EDITA Tokyo, 1994.

DYMAXION HOUSE

1/ Zung, Thomas T. K. *Buckminster Fuller: Anthology for the Millennium*. Carbondale: Southern Illinois University Press, 2014. **2/** Neder, Federico. *Fuller Houses: R. Buckminster Fuller's Dymaxion Dwellings and Other Domestic Adventures*. Baden, Switzerland: Lars Müller Publishers, 2008. **3/** Gorman, Michael John. *Buckminster Fuller : Designing for Mobility*. Milan: Skira, 2005. **4/** Hays, K. Michael, and Dana Miller. *Buckminster Fuller: Starting with the Universe*. New York: Whitney Museum of American Art, in association with Yale University Press, 2008. **5/** Sieden, Lloyd Steven. *Buckminster Fuller's Universe*. New York: Plenum Press, 1989.

QUERINI STAMPALIA RENOVATION

1/ McCarter, Robert. *Carlo Scarpa*. New York: Phaidon Press, 2013. **2/** Dal Co, Francesco. *Carlo Scarpa: Fondazione Querini Stampalia a Venezia*. Milan: Electa, 2006. **3/** Dal Co, Francesco, and Giuseppe Mazzariol. *Carlo Scarpa: The Complete Works*. New York: Electa/Rizzoli, 1985. **4/** Busetto, Giorgio. *Cronaca Veneziana: Feste E Vita Quotidiana Nella Venezia Del Settecento: Vedute Di Gabriel Bella E Incisioni Di Gaetano Zompini Dalle Raccolte Della Fondazione Scientifica Querini Stampalia Di Venezia*. Venice: Fondazione Scientifica Querini Stampalia, 1991.

HOUSE VI

1/ Eisenman, Peter and Antonini Saggio. *Universale Di Architettura: Trivellazioni nel futuro*. Torino: Testo & Immagine, 1996. **2/** Frank, Suzanne S., and Peter Eisenman. *Peter Eisenman's House VI: The Client's Response*. New York: Whitney Library of Design, 1994. **3/** Noever, Peter, and Peter Eisenman. *Peter Eisenman: Barefoot on White-hot Walls*. Ostfildern-Ruit: Hatje Cantz, 2005. **4/** Bradbury, Dominic, and Richard Powers. *The Iconic House: Architectural Masterworks Since 1900*. New York: Thames & Hudson, 2009. **5/** Luce, Kristina. "The Collision of Process and Form: Drawing's Imprint on Peter Eisenman's 'House VI.'" *The Getty Research Journal*, No. 2, 2010. **6/** Eisenman, Peter; Rosalind Krauss, and Manfredo Tafuri. *Houses of Cards: Critical Essays by Peter Eisenman, Rosalind Krauss, and Manfredo Tafuri*. New York: Oxford University Press, 1987.

BEURS VAN BERLAGE

1/ Berlage, Hendrik Petrus. *Hendrik Petrus Berlage: Disegni: IV Mostra Internazionale di Architettura*. Venice: La Biennale di Venezia, 1986. **2/** Polano, Sergio, Hendrik Petrus Berlage, Giovanni Fanelli, Jan de Heer, and Vincent van Rossem. *Hendrik Petrus Berlae*. Milan: Electa Architecture, 2002. **3/** Berlage, Hendrik Petrus, and Iain Boyd Whyte. *Hendrik Petrus Berlage. Thoughts on Style, 1886–1909*. Santa Monica: Getty Center for the History of Art and the Humanities, 1996. **4/** Bock, Manfred; Jet Collee, Hester Coucke, and Maarten Kloos. *Berlage in Amsterdam*. Amsterdam: Architectura & Natura Press, 1992. **5/** Haags Gemeentemuseum. *Berlage: Nederlandse Architectuur, 1856–1934*. The Hague: Haags Gemeentemuseum, 1975. **6/** Tafuri, Manfredo, and Francesco Dal Co. *Modern Architecture/1*. New York: Electa/Rizzoli, 1976. **7/** Zarzar, Karina Moraes. *Innovation, Identity, and Sustainability in H.P. Berlage's Stock Exchange*. Milan: XIII Generative Art Conference—Politecnico di Milano University, 2010.

GAMBLE HOUSE

1/ Bosley, Edward R. *Greene & Greene*. London: Phaidon, 2003. **2/** Bosley, Edward. *Gamble House: Greene & Greene*. New York: Phaidon, 2002. **3/** Mackintosh, Charles Rennie; Charles F. A. Voysey, and James Macaulay. *Arts & Crafts Houses 2, 2*. London: Phaidon, 1999. **4/** Smith, Bruce, and Alexander

Vertikoff. *Greene and Greene: Master Builders of the American Arts and Crafts Movement*. London: Thames and Hudson, 1998. **5/** Futagawa, Yukio, and Randell L. Makinson. *Greene & Greene: David B. Gamble House, Pasadena, California, 1908*. Tokyo: A.D.A. EDITA, 1984. **6/** Makinson, Randell L. *Greene & Greene*. Salt Lake City: Peregrine Smith, 1977.

LOVELL BEACH HOUSE

1/ Steele, James, and Peter Gössel. *R.M. Schindler 1887–1953: An Exploration of Space*. Köln: Taschen, 2005. **2/** Frampton, Kenneth, and Larkin, David. *American Masterworks: The Twentieth Century House*. New York: Rizzoli, 1995. **3/** Sarnitz, August, E. "Proportion and Beauty: The Lovell Beach House by Rudolph Michael Schindler, Newport Beach, 1922–1926". *Journal of the Society of Architectural Historians/Society of Architectural Historians*. 374–388.

TURIN EXHIBITION HALL

1/ Huxtable, Ada Louise. *Pier Luigi Nervi*. New York: George Braziller, Inc., 1960. **2/** Powell, Ken. *The Great Builders*. London: Thames & Hudson, 2011. **3/** Pace, Sergio. *Pier Luigi Nervi: Torino, La Committenza Industriale, Le Culture Architettoniche E Politecniche Italiane*. Cinisello Balsamo: Silvana, 2011. **4/** Nervi, Pier Luigi; Juergen Joedicke, and Ernst Priefert. *The Works of Pier Luigi Nervi*. London: Architectural Press, 1957. **5/** Sharp, Dennis. *The Illustrated Encyclopedia of Architects and Architecture*. New York: Whitney Library of Design, 1991.

MUNICIPAL ORPHANAGE, AMSTERDAM

1/ Strauven, Francis; Aldo van Eyck, and Herman Hertzberger. *Aldo Van Eyck's Orphanage: A Modern Monument*. Rotterdam: NAi, 1996. **2/** Hertzberger, Herman. *Space and the Architect: Lessons in Architecture 2*. Rotterdam: 010 Publishers, 2000. **3/** Ford, Edward R. *The Architectural Detail*. New York: Princeton Architectural Press, 2011. **4/** Simitch, Andrea, and Val Warke. *The Language of Architecture: 26 Principles Every Architect Should Know*. Beverly: Rockport Publishers, 2014. **5/** Ligtelijn, Vincent, ed. *Aldo van Eyck: Works*. Boston: Birkhäuser Publishers, 1999.

CARPENTER CENTER FOR THE VISUAL ARTS

1/ Boesiger, W., ed. *Le Corbusier et son atelier rue de Sèvres 35: Œuvre complete 1957–1965*. Zurich: Verlag für Architecktur, Artemis, 1965. **2/** Sekler, Eduard F., and William Curtis. *Le Corbusier Work*. Cambridge: Harvard University Press, 1978. **3/** Corbusier, Le; Yukio Futagawa, and Kenneth Frampton. *Millowners Association Building, Ahmedabad, India, 1954: Carpenter Center for Visual Arts, Harvard University, Cambridge, Massachusetts, U.S.A. 1961–64*. Tokyo: A.D.A. EDITA Tokyo, 1975. **4/** Corbusier, Le, and Richard Joseph Ingersoll. *Le Corbusier: A Marriage of Contours*. New York: Princeton Architectural Press, 1990. **5/** Brooks, Allen. *Le Corbusier: Carpenter Center, Unité d'Habitation, Firminy, and Other Buildings and Projects, 1961–1963*. New York: Garland Publication, 1984.

FREE UNIVERSITY OF BERLIN

1/ Feld, Gabriel, and Mohsen Mostafavi. *Free University, Berlin*. London: Architectural Association Publications, 1999. **2/** Avermaete, Tom. *Another Modern: The Post-War Architecture and Urbanism of Candilis-Josic-Woods*. Rotterdam: NAi Publishers, 2005. **3/** Krunic, Dina. *The Groundscraper: Candilis-Josic-Woods' Free University Building, Berlin 1963–1973*. Thesis. 2012. **4/** Smithson, Alison, ed. *Team 10 Primer*. Cambridge: The MIT Press, 1968.

BAGSVÆRD CHURCH

1/ Norberg-Schulz, Christian, and Yukio Futagawa. *Jörn Utzon, Church at Bagsværd, near Copenhagen, Denmark, 1973–76*. Tokyo: A.D.A. EDITA Tokyo, 1981. **2/** Utzon, Jørn; Kjeld Kjeldsen, Michael Juul Holm, and Mette Marcus. *Jørn Utzon: The Architect's Universe*. Humlebæk, Denmark: Louisiana Museum of Modern Art, 2008. **3/** Møller, Henrik Sten, and Vibe Udsen. *Jørn Utzon Houses*. Copenhagen: Living Architecture Publishing, 2006. **4/** Weston, Richard. *Key Buildings of the 20th Century: Plans, Sections and Elevations*. New York: W.W. Norton, 2010.

SESC POMPÉIA

1/ Oliveira, Olivia De. *The Architecture of Lina Bo Bardi: Subtle Substances*. Barcelona: Editorial Gustavo Gili, 2006. **2/** Oliveira, Olivia de. *Lina Bo Bardi Built Work; 2G – Revista Internacional de Arquitectura (n° 23/ 24)*. São Paulo: Editora Gustavo Gilli, 2002. **3/** Veikos, Cathrine. *Lina Bo Bardi: The Theory of Architectural Practice*. New York: Routledge, 2014.

CENTRE LE CORBUSIER (HEIDI WEBER HOUSE)

1/ Curtis, William J. R. *Le Corbusier: Ideas and Forms*. London: Phaidon, 2015. **2/** Dumont d'Ayot, Catherine, and Tim Benton. *Le Corbusier's Pavilion for Zurich: Model and Prototype of an Ideal Exhibition Space*. Zürich: Müller, 2013. **3/** *Heidi Weber: 50 Years Ambassador for Le Corbusier 1958–2008*. Zurich: Birkhäuser book, 2010. **4/** Žaknić, Ivan. *Le Corbusier Pavillion Suisse: The Biography of a Building*. Basel: Birkhauser, 2004.

GALLARATESE II APARTMENTS

1/ Frampton, Kenneth, and Vittorio Magnago Lampugnani. *World Architecture 1900–2000 a Critical Mosaic. Volume 4*. Wien: Springer, 1999. **2/** Nicolin, Pierluigi, and Y. Futagawa. *Carlo Aymonino/Aldo Rossi: Housing Complex at the Gallaratese Quarter, Milan, Italy. 1969–1974*. Tokyo: A.D.A. EDITA, 1981. **3/** Rossi, Aldo, and Peter Eisenman. *The Architecture of the City*. Cambridge, Mass: MIT Press, 1984.

CENTRAAL BEHEER BUILDING

1/ Frampton, Kenneth. *A Genealogy of Modern Architecture: Comparative Critical Analysis of Built Form*. Zürich: Lars Müller Publishers, 2015. **2/** Weston, Richard. *Key Buildings of the Twentieth Century: Plans, Sections and Elevations*. New York: W.W. Norton & Co., 2010. **3/** Hertzberger, Herman. *Architecture and Structuralism: The Ordering of Space*. Amsterdam: NAi010 Publishers, 2015. **4/** Hertzberger, Herman. *Cultuur onder dak*. Rotterdam: Uitgeverij 010 Publishers, 2004.

VITRA FIRE STATION

1/ Futagawa, Yukio. *GA Document Extra 03: Zaha Hadid*. Tokyo: A.D.A. EDITA, 1996. **2/** Hadid, Zaha; Alexandra Papadakis, and A. Papadakes. *Zaha Hadid: Testing the Boundaries*. London: Papadakis Publisher, 2005. **3/** Jodidio, Philip. *Hadid: Zaha Hadid Complete Works 1979–2013*. Cologne: Taschen, 2013. **4/** Sisson, Patrick. "21 First Drafts: Zaha Hadid's Vitra Fire Station." *Curbed*. <http://www.curbed.com/2015/8/5/9933580/21-first-drafts-zaha-hadids-vitra-fire-station> 05 Aug 2015.

YOKOHAMA INTERNATIONAL PORT TERMINAL

1/ Gregory, Rob. *Key Contemporary Buildings: Plans, Sections, and Elevations*. New York: W.W. Norton & Company, 2008. **2/** Ferre, Albert, Tomoko Sakamoto, Michael Kubo. *The Yokohama Project: Foreign Office Architects*. Barcelona: Actar, 2002. **3/** Carpo, Mario. *The Digital Turn in Architecture, 1992–2012*. Chichester: Wiley, 2013. **4/** Broto, Carles; Jacobo Krauel, Jay Noden, and William George. *Transportation Facilities*. Barcelona: LinksBooks, 2012.

PHOTO CREDITS

1/ Villa Savoye, Poissy, 1928 Paul Kozlowski ©2017 FLC/Artists Rights Society (ARS), New York. 2/ Chapelle Notre Dame du Haut, Ronchamp, 1950-1955 Photo : Paul Kozlowski ©2017 FLC/Artists Rights Society (ARS), New York. 3/ Barcelona Pavilion by Richard Moross (www.flickr.com/photos/richard-moross/4164341602/) CC BY 2.0. Modified. 4/ ©Katsuhisa Kida/ FOTOTECA. 5/ Jack E. Boucher/Courtesy Library of Congress Prints & Photographs Division, HABS IS,51-RACI,5—1. 6/ Jack E. Boucher/Courtesy Library of Congress Prints & Photographs Division, ILL,47-PLAN.V,1-9. 7/ Louis Kahn's Salk Institute by Jason Taellious (https://www.flickr.com/photos/dreamsjung/3040455466/) CC BY 2.0. Modified. 8/ ©Mark Lyon. 9/ Couvent Sainte-Marie de la Tourette, Eveux-sur-l'Arbresle, 1953 Photo: Olivier Martin-Gambier ©2017 FLC/Artists Rights Society (ARS), New York. 10/ TWA Flight Center by Jim.henderson (https://commons.wikimedia.org/wiki/File:AirTrain_JFK_passes_TWA_Flt_Ctr_jeh.JPG) CC BY-SA 4.0 International. Desaturated, Cropped. 11/ Philharmonie by Matthais Rosenkranz (https://www.flickr.com/photos/rosenkranz/294605986/) CC BY 3.0. Desaturated. 12/ Guggenheim 23 by Tony Hisgett (https://www.flickr.com/photos/hisgett/3798502025/) CC BY 2.0. Desaturated, cropped. 13/ Jack E. Boucher/Courtesy Library of Congress Prints & Photographs Division HABS PA,26-OHPY.V,1--3. 14/ Skogskyrkogården - Enskede – Stockholm by Esther Westerveld (https://www.flickr.com/photos/westher/14943642596/) CC BY 2.0 / Desaturated, Cropped. 15/ Seagram Building by Jules Antonio (https://www.flickr.com/photos/julesantonio/6268091900/) CC BY-SA 2.0. 16/ The Solomon R. Guggenheim Museum by Jules Antonio (https://www.flickr.com/photos/julesantonio/11990550696/) CC BY-SA 2.0. Desaturated. 17/ Eames House = Mecca by Lauren Manning (https://www.flickr.com/photos/laurenmanning/8008065034/) CC BY 2.0. Modified. 18/ Leicester University Engineering Building by NotFromUtrecht (https://upload.wikimedia.org/wikipedia/commons/a/ad/Leicester_University_Engineering_Building.jpg) CC BY-SA 3.0. Desaturated, Cropped. 19/ Casa del Fascio, Architect Guiseppe Terragni. Permission granted by Archivio Terragni. 20/ Unité d'Habitation, Marseille, 1945 Photo : Paul Kozlowski 1997 ©2017 FLC/ Artists Rights Society (ARS), New York. 21/ ©Timothy Hursley. 22/ Library of Congress, Prints & Photographs Division, photograph by Carol M. Highsmith LC-DIG-highsm-13209. 23/ Rietveld Schröderhuis winter 2014-15 02 by Luis Guillermo R. (https://commons.wikimedia.org/wiki/File%3ARietveld_Schr%C3%B6derhuis_winter_2014-15_02.JPG) CC BY 4.0 International. Desaturated, Cropped. 24/ Photo: Tomio Ohashi ©KISHO KUROKAWA architect & associates. 25/ Otto Wagner Postsparkasse Vienna - Dec 2014 - 2 by Andrew Nash (https://www.flickr.com/photos/andynash/16193628732/) CC BY-SA 3.0. Desaturated, Cropped. 26/ ©Eredi Curzio Malaparte. Image: Villa Malaparte by Francois Phillip (https://www.flickr.com/photos/frans16611/4729750386/) used under CC-BY 2.0. Modified. 27/ Public Domain. 28/ Yale Art and Architecture Building by Gunnar Klack (https://commons.wikimedia.org/wiki/File:Yale-Art-and-Architecture-Building-Rudolph-Hall-New-Haven-Connecticut-Apr-2014.jpg) CC 4.0 BY SA. Modified. 29/ Phillips Exeter Library, New Hampshire - Louis I. Kahn (1972) by Pablo Sanchez (https://www.flickr.com/photos/pablosanchez/3503858665/) CC BY 2.0. Modified. 30/ DSC06900 by IK's World Trip (https://www.flickr.com/photos/ikkoskinen/2618814478/) CC BY 2.0. Modified. 31/ Robie House, Hyde Park, by Frank Lloyd Wright by Naotake Murayama (https://www.flickr.com/photos/naotakem/9618352872/) CC BY 2.0. Modified. 32/ ©MAK Center/Joshua White. 33/ National Congress--Brasilia by Razvan Orendovici (https://www.flickr.com/photos/razvanorendovici/14630598183/) CC BY 2.0. Modified. 34/ Dessau-Bauhaus by Spyrosdrakopoulos (https://commons.wikimedia.org/wiki/File:6251_Dessau.JPG) CC BY-SA 4.0. Desaturated, Cropped. 35/ ©Ian Lambot / Arcaid. 36/ 080320101938 by IK's World Trip (https://www.flickr.com/photos/ikkoskinen/4418148288) CC BY 2.0. Modified. 37/ 4Y1A7841 by Ninara (https://www.flickr.com/photos/ninara/26710745140/) CC BY-SA 2.0. Modified. 38/ KIF_4646_Pano by duncid (https://www.flickr.com/photos/48013827@N00/275987220) CC BY-SA 2.0. Modified. 39/ 810_5725 by Bengt Nyman (https://www.flickr.com/photos/97469566@N00/16649751719) CC BY-SA 2.0. Modified. 40/ Yoyogi National Gymnasium by kanegen (https://www.flickr.com/photos/kanegen/3076874395) CC BY 2.0. Modified. 41/ Photo provided by Miyagi Prefecture Sightseeing Section. 42/ La tour Einstein (Potsdam, Allemagne) by Jean-Pierre Dalbéra (https://www.flickr.com/photos/dalbera/9616566364) CC BY 2.0. Modified. 43/ Photo: Ezra Stoller ©ESTO. 44/ ©Timothy Hursley. 45/ Library of Congress, Prints & Photographs Division, photograph by Carol M. Highsmith LC-DIG-highsm-04817. 46/ ©Richard Anderson 47/ Blick vom Olympiaberg auf das Olympiastadion by Amrei-Marie (https://commons.wikimedia.org/wiki/File:Blick_vom_Olympiaberg_auf_das_Olympiastadion.jpg) CC BY-SA 4.0 International. Desaturated, cropped. 48/ Gehry House, I by IK's World Trip (https://www.flickr.com/photos/ikkoskinen/350055881) CC BY 2.0. Modified. 49/ ©David Cabrera. 50/ S. R. Crown Hall by Arturo Duarte Jr. (https://commons.wikimedia.org/wiki/File:S.R._Crown_Hall.jpg) CC BY-SA 3.0. Desaturated. 51/ Photographer Unknown, Courtesy of Venturi, Scott Brown and Associates, Inc. 52/ Lovell House, Richard Neutra, Architect 1929 by MichaelJLocke (https://commons.wikimedia.org/wiki/File:Lovell_House,_Richard_Neutra,_Architect_1929.jpg) CC BY-SA 4.0. Desaturated, Cropped. 53/ Vila Tugendhat by Petr1987 (https://commons.wikimedia.org/wiki/File:Vila_Tugendhat_exterior_Dvorak2.JPG) CC BY-SA 4.0. Desaturated.

54/ Public Domain. **55/** Luis Barragán House and Studio Street view by Thomas Ledl (https://en.wikipedia.org/wiki/File:Luis_Barrag%C3%A1n_House_and_Studio_Street_view.JPG) CC BY-SA 4.0 Internation. Desaturated, cropped. **56/** Photo: Ezra Stoller ©ESTO. **57/** Museu de Arte de Sao Paulo by Dave Lonsdale (https://www.flickr.com/photos/davelonsdale/5819164997) CC BY 2.0. Modified. **58/** MAXXI Museo nazionale delle arti del XXI secolo, Roma. MAXXI Architettura Collection 59. Originali Arch. Scarpa [Tomba monumentale Brion], San Vito d'Altivole (TV). **59/** Panorama_of_National_Assembly_of_Bangladesh by Nahid Sultan (https://commons.wikimedia.org/wiki/File:Panorama_of_National_Assembly_of_Bangladesh.jpg) CC BY-SA 3.0. Desaturated, cropped. **60/** Die neue Staatsgalerie, Stuttgart - James Stirling, 1982 by Timothy Brown (https://www.flickr.com/photos/atelier_flir/2793727265/) CC BY 2.0. Modified. **61/** ©Michael Moran / OTTO. **62/** By Hans Werlemann / Copyright OMA. **63/** Casa Mila by Clarence (https://www.flickr.com/photos/bracketing_life/4104719680) CC BY 2.0. Modified. **64/** SaynatsaloTown Hall by Zache (https://commons.wikimedia.org/wiki/File:SaynatsaloTownHall4.jpg) CC BY SA 3.0. Desaturated, Cropped. **65/** ©Richard Bryant / Arcaid. **66/** ©2017 Artists Rights Society (ARS), New York / ADAGP, Paris. **67/** ©Bernard Tschumi Architects. **68/** ©Guenter Schneider. **69/** Hillside_Terrace_A_B by Wiiii (https://upload.wikimedia.org/wikipedia/commons/8/89/Hillside_Terrace_A_B_2010.jpg) CC 3.0 BY SA. Modified. **70/** ©Scott Frances/ OTTO. **71/** Neue Nationalgalerie by Rosmarie Voegtli (https://www.flickr.com/photos/rvoegtli/3353185093) CC BY 2.0. Modified. **72/** MAXXI Museo nazionale delle arti del XXI secolo, Roma. MAXXI Architettura Collection 98. [Museo di Castelvecchio], Verona. **73/** Swimming Pool Piscinas de Marés Leça da Palmeira by Christian Gänshirt (https://commons.wikimedia.org/wiki/File:Swimming_Pool_Piscinas_de_Mar%C3%A9s_Le%C3%A7a_da_Palmeira_by_%C3%81lvaro_Siza_foto_Christian_G%C3%A4nshirt.jpg) CC BY-SA 4.0. Desaturated, Cropped. **74/** P7099953_ShiftN by Paul Barker Hemings (https://www.flickr.com/photos/pollobarca/15276277612) CC BY-SA 2.0. Modified. **75/** Rusakov Club, Moscow by NVO (https://commons.wikimedia.org/wiki/File:Moscow,_Stromynka_6_July_2009_06.JPG) CC BY-SA 3.0. Desaturated, Cropped. **76/** Mill Owners' Association Building, Ahmedabad by Sanyam Bahga (https://commons.wikimedia.org/wiki/File:ATMA_House_187.jpg) CC BY-SA 3.0. Desaturated, Cropped. **77/** Julius Schulman ©J. Paul Getty Trust. Getty Research Institute, Los Angeles (2004.R.10). **78/** Whitney Museum of American Art by Jonathan Lin (https://www.flickr.com/photos/jonolist/14857063277/) CC BY-SA 2.0. Modified. **79/** ©Duccio Malagamba courtesy of COOP HIMMELB(L)AU. **80/** Courtesy of the Buffalo History Museum. **81/** Courtesy of Centro Storico Fiat. **82/** Villa Müller in Prag by Hpschaefer (https://commons.wikimedia.org/wiki/File:Villa-Mueller-Prag-2.) CC BY 3.0. Desaturated, Cropped. **83/** Van Nellefabriek by Hanno Lans (https://commons.wikimedia.org/wiki/File:Van_Nellefabriek_(20288847352).jpg) CC BY-SA 2.0. Modified. **84/** Courtesy, The Estate of R. Buckminster Fuller. **85/** MAXXI Museo nazionale delle arti del XXI secolo, Roma. MAXXI Architettura Collection 111. [Sede delle Fondazione Querini Stampalia], Venezia. **86/** Photo by Richard Frank, courtesy Eisenman Architects. **87/** Beurs van Berlage: Overzicht Damrakzijde by G.J. Dukker (https://commons.wikimedia.org/wiki/File:Overzicht_Damrakzijde_-_Amsterdam_-_20286196_-_RCE.jpg) CC BY-SA 4.0 International. Cropped. **88/** IMG_1238 Gamble House by Robert B. Moffatt (https://www.flickr.com/photos/55050575@N06/22392915088/) CC BY-SA 2.0. Modified. **89/** Lovell_Beach_House_photo_D_Ramey_Logan (https://commons.wikimedia.org/wiki/File:Lovell_Beach_House_photo_D_Ramey_Logan.jpg) CC BY-SA 3.0. Desaturated. **90/** Servizio fotografico (Torino, 1961) by Paolo Monti (https://commons.wikimedia.org/wiki/File:Paolo_Monti_-_Servizio_fotografico_(Torino,_1961)_-_BEIC_6337387.jpg) CC BY-SA 4.0 International. Courtesy Fondo Paolo Monti, owned by BEIC and located in the Civico Archivio Fotografico of Milan. **91/** Credit: Noelle Tay Li-Zhen. **92/** ©Scott Norsworthy. **93/** Freie Universitaet Berlin - Gebaeudekomplex Rost- und Silberlaube by torinberl (https://commons.wikimedia.org/wiki/File:Freie_Universitaet_Berlin_-_Gebaeudekomplex_Rost-_und_Silberlaube.jpg) CC BY-SA 3.0 Unported. Desaturated. **94/** jørn utzon, bagsværd kirke - bagsvaerd church, copenhagen 1967-1976 by seier+seier (https://www.flickr.com/photos/seier/5893565856) CC BY 2.0. Modified. **95/** ©Pedro Kok. **96/** Heidi Weber Pavilion by Le Corbusier by Fatlum Haliti (https://www.flickr.com/photos/lumlumi/439657731) CC BY 2.0. Modified. **97/** Burçin Yildirim ©Eredi Aldo Rossi / Fondazione Aldo Rossi. **98/** Hertzberger Centraal Beheer by Apdency (https://commons.wikimedia.org/wiki/File:Hertzberger_Centraal_Beheer1.jpg) CC BY-SA 3.0. Desaturated, Cropped. **99/** Feuerwehrhaus von Zaha Hadid bei Vitra in Weil am Rhein, links Schaudepot von Herzog & de Meuron by Andreas Schwarzkopf (https://commons.wikimedia.org/wiki/File:Feuerwehrhaus_von_Zaha_Hadid_bei_Vitra_in_Weil_am_Rhein,_links_Schaudepot_von_Herzog_%26_de_Meuron_1.jpg) CC BY-SA 3.0 Unported. Desaturated. **100/** Credit: Satoru Mishima, courtesy of FMA.

The best efforts of the authors and the publisher have been employed in obtaining permissions for, and determining proper attribution of, the photographs shown in this book. If, by regretful oversight, any credits are incomplete or missing, the publisher will take the necessary steps to ameliorate this condition in a reprint, upon being made aware of any such oversight.